DoggoNe ChicAgo

Sniffing Out the Best Places to Take Your Best Friend

Steve Dale, syndicated columnist, "My Pet World"

with **Janice Brown**

Contemporary Books

Chicago   New York   San Francisco   Lisbon   London   Madrid   Mexico City
Milan   New Delhi   San Juan   Seoul   Singapore   Sydney   Toronto

Library of Congress Cataloging-in-Publication Data

Dale, Steve, 1957–
    Doggone Chicago : sniffing out the best places to take your best friend / Steve Dale.—2nd ed.
        p.   cm.
    ISBN 0-8092-9481-8
    1. Travel with dogs—Illinois—Chicago Region—Guidebooks.   2. Chicago Region (Ill.)—Guidebooks.   I. Title.

SF427.4574. I3D35   2001
917.73′110433—dc21   00-65934

Contemporary Books

A Division of The McGraw·Hill Companies

Copyright © 2001 by Steve Dale. All rights reserved. Printed in the United States of America. Except as permitted under the United States Copyright Act of 1976, no part of this publication may be reproduced or distributed in any form or by any means, or stored in a database or retrieval system, without the prior written permission of the publisher.

1 2 3 4 5 6 7 8 9 0   AGM/AGM   0 9 8 7 6 5 4 3 2 1

ISBN 0-8092-9481-8

This book was set in Minion
Printed and bound by Quebecor Martinsburg

Cover design by Monica Baziuk
Cover photograph copyright © Jill Birschbach

McGraw-Hill books are available at special quantity discounts to use as premiums and sales promotions, or for use in corporate training programs. For more information, please write to the Director of Special Sales, Professional Publishing, McGraw-Hill, Two Penn Plaza, New York, NY 10121-2298. Or contact your local bookstore.

This book is printed on acid-free paper.

DEDICATION

To Chaser, very much a dog in every way, yet somehow more. Her gentle and soulful spirit has changed my life forever. If I could only tell Chaser how much she's taught me.

To Lucy, who makes people laugh and smile with her little tricks and her "yahoo" greeting whenever she walks into a room. Lucy has a gift. As a member of Chenny Troupe, she's able to use her nutty personality to help people.

To Sophie . . . still with us as I write this. But I fear that our regular house guest, who is ill, may not be a part of our lives when this book is released. Even though she's our neighbor Karen's dog, Sophie has been a member of our family from the day Karen moved here. As proof, she's featured prominently on my mother-in-law's refrigerator.

Here's a Sophie snapshot: For several days, whenever Sophie went out in our front yard, she'd run to a certain corner behind a bush and lie there. Karen finally figured out what Sophie was doing. Sophie, a German shepherd–mix, was caring the best she could for a baby bird that had fallen from its nest. Sophie's very being has always been to lavish unconditional love. She assumes that all dogs, all people, and all other living things love her, even if she sometimes greets them with the traditional herding-dog bop on the head with a paw.

And most of all, to the 14 abandoned dogs who have died in shelters just in the time it has taken you to read this page.

CONTENTS

 # FOREWORD

When Judith Pynn, a friend and editor, phoned me back in 1996 with the concept of a book about places to take dogs in the Chicago area, it seemed like a good idea. Coincidentally, I had just completed a feature for the *Chicago Tribune* on dog-friendly places around town, a small-scale version of the book she was describing.

Judith sounded surprised when I told her how many Chicago suburbs didn't allow dogs in parks at all. I explained that Cook County didn't even have a sanctioned dog park. While DuPage and Lake Counties did have dog parks, most were pretty new then, and people had no clue that they existed. What's more, the dog situation in Chicago city parks was a mess; rules about dogs were confusing, with people being ticketed left and right.

Judith said, "That will make your book, your clarifications, your information all the more valuable." She is a wise woman. The first volume of *Doggone Chicago: Sniffing Out the Best Places to Take Your Best Friend* was incredibly labor intensive, taking two years to complete. I never would have managed it without assistance from researchers—some of the canine persuasion, others just people.

When I started my research, Lucy was just over five months old, a nine-pound puppy. Robin and I credit this research required for *Doggone Chicago* for bringing about Lucy's early socialization. Before Lucy was even a year old, she had already visited a least a dozen bars, dined outdoors at more than a dozen restaurants, gone sight-seeing on a Lake Michigan cruise for dogs, and toured more than 50 parks and forest preserves. And that was just in her first six months.

Through the course of our fieldwork, local police and forest preserve officers threatened to ticket Robin and me on several occasions for either having the dogs off-leash or not having the correct parking sticker. We were nearly busted for speeding in one forest preserve (Robin was driving). Chaser was chased by savage bees. She also chased flocks of geese. Both Lucy and Chaser got stuck with burrs. Chaser rolled in dead fish. Both dogs threw up. We crashed an outdoor photo shoot for a wedding. And several of our research dogs, including Chaser, stepped in horse manure. Lucy's best friend, Sophie, got her "sea legs." Our car was demolished in an accident (I was driving). Both Lucy and Chaser were in the car with me, and while they suffered no physical effects, for months following the accident both dogs were afraid to continue their research—at least if it meant a car ride. The project proved so daunting the first time around that I nearly threw in the towel.

But it's readers like you who kept me going. On one occasion while at a DuPage County off-leash area, a woman pulled out a clipping from her purse. She said we just had to see this. It turned out to be the *Tribune* article I had written two years prior about places to take dogs. She had scribbled notes in ink all around the article. Of course, she had no idea I was the author.

"Look at this; these are wonderful places to go with your dogs," she said. "I just wish there more places for us to visit. Do you know any? If you can tell me a few, I'll share some with you."

As my editor Adam Miller knows, I persevered, finally cranking out the book, with one promise. I said, "This is it. Never again."

I appeared on each of the Chicago TV stations to promote the book. To this day, Lucy and Chaser are sometimes recognized when we take walks or visit dog-friendly areas. Usually these folks don't remember my name; they just assume I'm the guy who wrote the book—it's Lucy and Chaser they're thrilled about seeing in person.

Most important, this book helped to effect changes. For starters, those anti-quated No Dogs Allowed signs have been removed from city parks. The book also gave me the credibility needed to stand up and bark when the City of Chicago attempted to restrict dogs from eating with their people in outdoor restaurant patios. Moreover, many people have told me that *Doggone Chicago* helped moti-vate them to create dog parks.

And I'll admit it—I like to think I've been at least a little bit responsible for a few Sunday afternoons spent with the dog, as people explore dog parks or other places to cavort with the pooch. No question, even Robin and I have discovered new locales to take Lucy and Chaser as a result of the research. Still, I had no intention—no time—to update this book. In 1999, another publisher offered me the chance. I refused.

That very day, while out on a walk, Lucy and Chaser were recognized by the owners of an Australian shepherd. These people went on and on about how they used my book. The next day, a friend told me about someone she knows who purchased my book and loves it. Funny thing—he doesn't have a dog. But he says he now has a new insight into how dog owners feel about their dogs.

A few months later, I heard from Adam. He implored me to write an update of *Doggone Chicago*. I hesitated and really considered not doing this—I truly didn't have the time to finish by his deadline because of other projects to which I had committed, not to mention my regular columns and radio shows. Adam encouraged me to hire a researcher.

Finding a person interested in researching a book wasn't too hard, and many nearly qualified people applied. However, all these people missed one crucial ingredient—a love for dogs. That was until I met Janice Brown. She's involved with the Dog Advisory Work Group and has launched a new magazine for pet lovers called *Chicagoland Tails*. As soon as I spoke to Janice, I knew I'd found my researcher. She frenetically worked the phones to update facts and figures and, with Luna, tracked down new dog parks and dog-friendly places.

Aside from merely offering the chance to take your pooch somewhere new and different, this book can be a resource for developing a more socialized, happier, even less destructive dog. Here's how:

- As soon as your vet gives you the OK, introduce your puppy to as many upbeat and positive situations as possible. "The earlier your dog understands how to interact with other dogs and with people, the better off it will be in the long run," explains Karen Okura, behavior counselor and trainer at the Anti-Cruelty Society in Chicago. "Most dogs ultimately wind up at our doorstep because of behavior problems. Early socialization can prevent many of those problems."

- Choose to expose your pup to a wide variety of experiences. You won't find a wider variety than what's offered in these pages.

- Every dog deserves its day. Dogs aren't ornaments; they're intelligent beings, and they thrive on social and mental stimulation. In fact, many behavior disorders are created by plain old boredom combined with a lack of exercise. It's easy to stimulate your pet: merely check out one new park each week. Or take in one "Doggy Doing," visit one festival—pick anything from these pages and do it up with your dog. Your pup will understand that this is his or her time with you. Of course, that doesn't mean the entire family can't join in; you can even take Grandma. The idea is that your pooch is a member of the family too and should be treated as such.

Depending on where you go, the dog may get lots of exercise and will certainly enjoy the chance to get out of the house and explore new horizons. What's more, at some of the events listed here, your dog will be the focus. And of course, any dog understands that and will eat up the attention faster than a bowl of kibble.

- In addition, consider volunteering with your dog, either with an organized therapy group—such as Chenny Troupe—or individually. If you're the more energetic type, give a canine sport a whirl, such as freestyle, canine disc (Frisbee), agility, or flyball.

Tom Wehrli, president of the Windy City K-9 Disc Club, says confidently, "If one day a week, you exercise your dog by taking it to a place listed in the book—even if it's a local park—and on a second day, you volunteer or partake in a dog sport, you'll notice a dog with a whole new attitude about you and about life. Your previously bored dog is now an active member of the family, and the way your dog sees it, he or she even has a job."

- Any dog of any age, breed, or mix of breeds can take the American Kennel Club Canine Good Citizen Test (see p. 287). Keep in mind that a disobedient or aggressive dog will make it difficult, if not downright dangerous, to visit many of the places described in these chapters. The fact is that canines, being canines, will follow rules if they understand what they are; however, when there's no structure in their lives, some dogs will make up their own rules. Given the choice, all dogs prefer structure. Some idiots believe that obedience doesn't allow a dog to be a dog. The converse is true: it allows a dog to get out into the world. For example, don't even think about taking your dog to an off-leash place—where a dog has the ultimate experience in being a dog—unless your pet has an absolute understanding of the "come" command (see p. 338).

Aside from offering fun stuff to do—and there's plenty of it—I sincerely hope this book advances your family's relationship with your canine resident(s). In this very busy world we live in, it's a major feat to find free time to do much of anything, let alone research places to take your family dogs. We've done the research—believe me, that's the hard part. Now all you have to do is go out and have a tail-wagging good time.

PREFACE

The question I get asked most often is how I learn about canine events, festivals, and parties where dogs are welcome. Well, it's my job to know these things. Still, I can't credit two kinds of researchers enough. First, the researchers I hired to assist me on the first volume, along with Janice Brown, who researched this update.

But mostly, the best researchers have always been just plain folks. I learned about lots of places for the first edition by bark of mouth, talking with people at dog parks. Publicists representing restaurants heard about the project and wanted their clients' names to appear in the book. Representatives of park districts also helped.

But we are all only human—or canine, as the case may be. It was impossible to cover everything. We managed to visit a majority of the suburbs. If we missed your suburb, your favorite dog park or video store that allows dogs, or your neighborhood pet parade, please don't yank our collars too hard.

Note that, even though all the information from the first book has been updated, hours of operation, prices, and dog-friendly policies are subject to change. It's always a good idea to phone (or E-mail) first.

The following section explains how we did our research.

Parks and Beaches

It was the job of our canine researchers to rank parks and beaches on a scale from Worth a Sniff to Four Bones. Here's an explanation of those rankings. Remember, everything is rated from a dog's point of view: the more trees, the more fire hydrants, the better.

Worth a sniff Make it a quick one. These are very small parks, and in many cases they're surrounded by busy streets. These places have few, if any, mature trees—which also means few, if any, squirrels.

/ It's not worth howling to your buddies about—or driving, or even walking, out of your way for. These are small places with few amenities for a park-loving canine cruiser.

// This is an average park or beach, with enough room for at least a quick sprint or game of fetch. But there's no real redeeming quality.

/// Finally, a destination worth driving to. There are trees and probably a walking or running path, space for a sprint, and benches where worn-out people companions can sit and rest. The beaches offer space and places for serious canine swimming.

//// It's worth putting a leash on your person and leading him or her to this place. Actually, a leash may not be required, since off-leash places are considered special and generally garner higher ratings—typically either three or four bones, or halfway in between.

A Word About Off-Leash Places

After visits to hundreds of parks, here's how I see it. While off-leash forest preserves, parks, and beaches are generally rated higher, not all people or their dogs have earned the privilege to use these places.

Aggressive dogs are a real danger to people and other dogs, and we met too many of these angry and sometimes out-of-control canines.

Owners require total off-leash control, even if their dogs are extremely friendly. For one thing, you never know about the temperament of the dog that yours is approaching. If you need to recall your dog, it must listen. You both confront a host of potential dangers, ranging from cars to skunks. An instant recall may be required. If your dog isn't able to adhere to the "come" command, it's just not ready for an off-leash area. Don't feel bad. The truth is that most dogs who visit these places shouldn't be off-leash. In my view, their owners are taking a grave risk. I give a lot of credit to those owners who know that their dogs shouldn't be in these places, and they stay away.

Visiting off-leash places also means more serious work for you. There's no time for idle gossiping with friends; you must pay attention. Even if your dog always obeys, it won't necessarily come back if you don't call. Aside from the safety factor of allowing dogs to wander out of view, you don't know where the dog has made a deposit. Generally, the off-leash areas are riddled with feces. Aside from being a nuisance, this increases the potential for contracting several canine diseases.

When to Leash, When Not to Leash

Leashing is a sticky subject. In the vast majority of municipal parks and forest preserves, leashes are required by law.

However, in most of the municipal parks and forest preserves we visited, dogs were playing fetch off-leash all over. Whether to take a pooch off its leash is ultimately up to you. Because many people want to be active with their dogs, the listings in this book mention baseball and soccer fields and other places to play fetch or Frisbee. It's not easy to play those games when your dog is on a leash. Some communities are fine about dogs using tennis courts in the off-season, while others practically call in the National Guard for such an offense.

We tell you what the law is. In addition, we often provide further warnings in communities that are particularly rigid about adhering to the leash laws. But again, ultimately the decision to leash or not to leash is yours.

Some communities adhere strictly to leash laws; others do not. We admit that, through the course of researching hundreds of parks for this book, we were warned on more than one occasion to leash Lucy and Chaser. In other places, we wouldn't have thought about removing their leads. After a while, we garnered an instinct about this sort of thing. But for the record, there are reasons for laws, and we're not encouraging you to break the law.

Restaurants and Bars

My wife, Robin, and I sat outdoors at more than 50 restaurants and coffee shops, and about a half dozen bars, with Chaser and/or Lucy. We were rained on only once. That brings us to the one drawback to dining alfresco with canines. If the weather turns inclement, you can't simply grab a seat indoors. According to Illinois state law, dogs aren't allowed inside places with a food license.

At many restaurants, other dogs were also outside. We never once witnessed an unruly dog. Restaurateurs who have allowed canines to dine at their establishments confirm that they've rarely had any problems. You'll note that the vast majority of restaurants allowing doggy dining are in Chicago, as are all the bars that allow canine visitors.

Places to Stay

At many hotels, the policy on pets depends on with whom you happen to speak. On more than one occasion, a telephone researcher would be told that only dogs under 20 pounds are allowed. The very next day, I would call, and the weight limit would increase to 30 pounds. The good tidings are that some hotels do seem flexible (a pessimist would call their policies confused). If you happen to be convincing in your argument, you may be able to sway the management. Here's where having Canine Good Citizen Test certification (see p. 287) can help. In many phone calls, I was asked if the dog is well behaved, if the dog is a barker, or if the dog would eat the housekeeping staff.

I also learned that canine policy isn't the only flexible figure at hotels. Some places changed room rates with every inquiry. To help assure accuracy, we confirmed or fact-checked everything in this book. A second call to a hotel often meant a different room rate—sometimes higher, sometimes lower.

Festivals, Doggy Doings, and Places to Shop

Keep your dog's personality type in mind. It would be unfair, even inhumane, to take a dog that's sensitive to noise along to a Chicago city street festival. However, other dogs have grown up around this sort of commotion and seem to enjoy it.

Similarly, a dog that chews table legs or isn't housebroken shouldn't be walking the aisles of a furniture or carpet store. Know what you're getting into. If your dog turns into Cujo when other dogs are present, don't take him or her to a party crammed with other dogs.

Even with the aid of additional researchers, we couldn't possibly attend all the festivals or doggy doings, although we came pretty close. And with Robin's help, we did visit nearly each of the places to shop listed in the city and suburbs.

Naturally, rules change. Dates, times, and locations of events can also change. And of course, all prices listed in these pages are likewise subject to change. Call before visiting any store, festival, or canine special event.

ACKNOWLEDGMENTS

A pack of dog lovers helped me with my initial effort, and the same is true for this edition. Perhaps you were among them? If a little short guy with glasses (that's me) or one of our researchers approached you in a park or forest preserve, or at a festival, beach, or similar dog-friendly place, and asked about stuff to do with dogs—thanks for the tips. Also, thanks to the many park districts and county forest preserves for their cooperation and assistance.

Thanks as well to the many contributing veterinarians and to Patricia Montgomery at the Chicago Veterinary Medical Association. I'm likewise grateful to dog trainers for their advice and comments. I consider myself lucky—some of the best vets and trainers in the Chicago area participated in this project.

Without the toiling of initial researchers Carol Truesdell, Lisa Seeman, Gail Polzin, Steve Karmgard, and Marilynn Szarvas, I wouldn't have had enough material in the first place to mandate the current revision. Credit for this volume truly belongs to Janice Brown, who with her canine partner Luna not only updated existing listings but also introduced lots of new dog-friendly places. Not a surprise, they both know how to sniff out a good time. Janice's commitment to improving life for canines in Chicago is inspiring.

I thank John Nolan of Contemporary Books for throwing me a lifeline when I needed one.

I thank poor Adam Miller, my editor. I don't believe I've ever given another editor anywhere near the hard time I've given poor Adam. He should blame me, not my dogs.

I thank our original canine staff, as well as Luna.

I thank Karen Okura, behavior specialist at Anti-Cruelty in Chicago, for helping me learn about Chaser at a time when other professionals were suggesting that I give up. Karen's comments are also included in this book.

I thank the incredible Dr. Sheldon Rubin—this veterinarian wears his heart on his sleeve. His talents are exceeded only by his sincere compassion.

Most of all, I must thank Robin, my wife. Two dogs, a cat, and a lizard may make my life more fun, or more interesting, but Robin *is* my life. While working on the first installment of *Doggone*, she schlepped in 90-degree summers and below-zero winters. She's as devoted as any dog—and I do mean that as a compliment.

CAST OF CHARACTERS

Chaser: Chaser is a Brittany who can take credit for teaching her people a lot about dogs. Originally a country girl, Chaser, who is nine now, moved to Chicago when she was almost a year old. The adjustment wasn't easy. She was afraid of everything—other people, other dogs, and all forms of public transportation. Once, a Chicago cop actually stopped me because Chaser looked so pitiful that he thought she had been abused.

Today Chaser is the leader of the pack at home, a confident dog and a certified Canine Good Citizen. As her name implies, Chaser loves to chase. *Doggone Chicago* was a golden opportunity to terrify geese in parks.

She has a new habit; oddly, she indulges in it only from August through October. This is her season to terrify squirrels. She isn't interested in chasing them so much as she is in staring at them. Her record time is 25 minutes staring at a nervous squirrel four branches up before I got fed up and hauled her away. As much as Chaser craved visiting the parks for *Doggone*, she disdained the water at the beaches. Brittanys were, in fact, bred to retrieve waterfowl *in* the water, and according to breed books, she is supposed to enjoy swimming. But Chaser never read those books.

Lucy: She's quite the star with the swollen ego. As a result of the publicity we did for the first edition of *Doggone*, not to mention her appearances on various Animal Planet programs and "The Oprah Winfrey Show," Lucy now walks into TV studios alerting all to her presence, "Whao! Whao!"

Dog trainers are impressed with Lucy's sharp attention, but they also concede she has a mind of her own. One trainer simply says, "She's a nut!" Certainly, Lucy, a five-year-old North American shepherd (miniature Australian shepherd), was born to entertain. She'll play dead, roll over, crawl, sit, lie down, give paw, close and open a crate door, sing on command, jump into your arms, leap into or over pretty much anything, and finally take a bow for a fine performance. Lucy is on stage performing her little tricks each Wednesday for patients at the Rehabilitation Institute of Chicago when she "works" for Chenny Troupe.

Still, little Lucy doesn't excel at everything. She's one of those breeds that typically are great at Frisbee. But Lucy isn't typical. After three years of trying, she'll catch a Frisbee maybe one of every ten tosses. Well, that's about as efficient as some Cubs outfielders. Maybe it's not so shabby.

Lucy and Chaser have both passed the Canine Good Citizen Test. But sometimes with Lucy, you wonder how she ever did.

Bayla: Bayla, a keeshond-mix, is better off not remembering that she was found battered on the side of the road. Lisa scooped her up and took her for emergency care. There was even talk of putting her down, but Lisa said no. Despite her broken leg and other serious injuries, Bayla, who is now four years old, is as healthy as can be.

She had a blast researching this book for many reasons, most of them squirrel related. Bayla is obsessed with squirrels, spending hours looking out her front window, hoping that one will pass by.

Bonnie: Bonnie is a nine-year-old German shepherd dog and has slowed down some, battling hip dysplasia. However, just say the word "treat," and her pain is forgotten. Bonnie still gets a thrill from being with Lisa and going to parks. She had a high time researching this book. Her favorite toy is a plush hedgehog named "Hedgehog."

BootsMontgomery: Chaser and Lucy's neighbor across the hall, and one of their best friends. She's a nine-year-old Tibetan terrier, who didn't go to all that many parks with us. She was too busy doing her homework, learning the names of 40 individual toys.

Breathless: Another Tibetan terrier, Breathless seems embarrassed in the company of other dogs. She tolerated visiting the parks, but this research was no fun. For one thing, she got her paws dirty. Ten-year-old Breathless much prefers the Gold Coast.

Kalea: She saw squirrels, a groundhog, chipmunks, and even a raccoon while researching this book. However, Kalea was disappointed not to see any rabbits.

Nevertheless, Kalea, a seven-year-old Shetland sheepdog, had a marvelous time. She knows she's cute enough for people to offer her snacks. Unfortunately, no one offered her favorite food: frozen vegetables.

Luna: Janice and Barry rescued Luna from the Anti-Cruelty Society when she was only eight weeks old, and Luna is responsible for changing her parents' lives (for the better)! She's a white German shepherd/yellow Lab–mix who honors both breeds, with one ear up and one ear down. Luna is proud to have passed the Canine Good Citizen Test and is looking forward to passing the Chenny Troupe Test so she can join the canine-assisted-therapy group. Luna's day is complete if she gets to swim with her Kong, practice her agility-course skills, and return home to chase her two feline brothers, Jake and Obelix, around the house. We can all learn from Luna, who has no idea what stress is. Put Luna inside a small room, with Barry's table saw going at full blast, the doorbell ringing, and the cats playing a game of chase, and she'll simply snooze.

By the way, Luna thinks working on this book is the best job her mom has ever had.

Pork Chop: Pork Chop was Danny's dog and Snowball's best friend, and the three of them joined Carol in researching much of DuPage County. An eight-year-old beagle, Pork Chop couldn't handle the fame when the first book came out and moved to someplace in Michigan. He's living happily and anonymously without the autograph hounds.

Snowball: A four-year-old Maltese who is devoted to Animal Planet, from which he learns how to act tough at the parks. It works—this six-and-a-half-pound dynamo even impressed the big dogs while conducting his field research.

Sophie: Lucy's best friend in the whole world, who lives two floors down. I say, "Lucy, get your best friend," and she runs off to Sophie's door and barks, "I'm here—ready to play!" Sophie is always ready to play. A nine-year-old, 50-pound shepherd-mix, Sophie is gaga about playing with Lucy. But she doesn't discriminate; Sophie is ready and eager to play with any willing dog, cat, or person. She had a rollicking time traveling with her two stooges, Lucy and Chaser, to gather research—especially when the subject matter was a park.

Supporting Cast

Steve Dale: The person with whom Chaser, Lucy, and their agent, Ricky the cat, happen to live.

Robin Dale: This researcher was paid with love; she's my wife. She's also the person most responsible for spoiling Lucy and Chaser.

Janice Brown: Janice can never spend enough time with animals. Some of her first memories are of dressing up her childhood dog, Misty, who was rescued from Orphans of the Storm. Janice is the editor of *Chicagoland Tails* and promises never to have another job where she cannot take her dogs with her to work. Passionate about reducing the number of animals who are euthanatized each year, Janice is committed to creating a central lost-and-found system in Chicago, helping people to find their lost pets more efficiently. Janice knows there is nothing more wondrous than the unconditional love one receives from a pet. Janice is married to woodworker and general contractor Barry Gork, and they reside in East Ravenswood in Chicago. Janice's only regret is that Maple, their adopted pooch, joined the family too late to help out with this edition.

Steve Karmgard: Steve worked the phones, helping to learn about dog-friendly places. Steve has always had a special place in his heart for canines.

Gail Polzin: Gail is director of international communications at Evanston Northwestern Healthcare. I met Gail when she was the associate editor at *North Shore* magazine. Having had dogs all her life, she was an obvious choice to check out places near her home in Lake County. She also researched several outlying counties.

Lisa Seeman: Lisa was the office and Web manager at WUSN Radio and recently accepted a job as a project manager for Northern Trust Bank. Lisa's had dogs almost all her life. She says one of the biggest mistakes she ever made was to move into a place that didn't allow them: "I couldn't stand not having furry companions, so I got hamsters." She didn't live there long. Lisa helped to research the south suburbs.

Marilynn Szarvas: I chose her to make some phone calls, not because she's my mother and works cheap, but because she's great on the telephone.

Carol Truesdell: When I asked Carol to help research DuPage County, her first question was, "Do I need a passport?" This city gal mustered the courage to cross the county line. Carol is a self-employed reading specialist. She works with kids but has declined my challenge to teach her dogs to read.

Danny Engoren: A 15-year-old high school sophomore, Danny was only a 12-year-old when work on the first volume began. Danny, who helped Carol research DuPage County, has grown up with this book.

1 CHICAGO

In several ways Chicago rivals some of the dog-friendliest cities in the nation. In other ways the rules are confusing, hypocritical, and, of course, political.

Chicago is a city of neighborhoods. In each neighborhood, there are always places to meet for intellectual discourse. I'm referring here to the neighborhood bar. When it comes to the number of dog-friendly watering holes, Chicago takes the loving cup. In addition, many of the doggy doings are probably unique to this town. Certainly the Pug Crawl is an anomaly. Picture a platoon of 80 pugs lumbering from bar to bar.

In Chicago, the "Dog Days of Summer" is more than an expression; it's the annual canine get-together at Comiskey Park to watch the Chicago White Sox. Speaking of expression, some of the visiting-team players have a quizzical one as they look out to the throng of nearly four hundred barking dogs sitting on and under the right-field bleachers. But in Chicago, this all makes sense.

Pooches with business to conduct can host a group lunch at Fido's dog bakery or move and shake alfresco at one of the many restaurants that welcome canine clientele. Glance down Southport Avenue or Kinzie Street in June, and you might think you're in Paris. (That's stretching the point just a bit, but not much.)

"I think the Parisians have something there; seeing dogs in the sidewalk cafés is somehow very appealing," says Casey Eslick of Bistrot Zinc restaurant on Southport. "Chicago's outdoor dining scene is vastly different than it was only a few years ago. There are so many more cafés; they all have a certain feel, an atmosphere that the dogs play a role in. The scene has become very European."

Restaurants that gladly receive canine traffic range from hot-dog joints to fine-dining establishments. Bars with food licenses aren't permitted to allow dogs inside, but several welcome dogs to lounge on their patios.

Maurice Taniceau was visiting North Pier terminal, from Paris. Watching the boats go by while sitting outside at the Tavern on the Pier, he pointed to a woman at a nearby table sitting with her two Maltese.

In his distinctive French accent, he said, "This is wonderful!" He explained that he'd been to several American cities, and until he arrived in Chicago, he hadn't seen anything approaching the dog-friendly mentality of France.

Of course, this isn't Paris. Taniceau hasn't attempted to walk a dog off-leash, or even on-leash, at a city park or beach. The rules are confusing and sometimes contradicting. I'll dig into these later in the book.

As evidence that the situation is downright confounding, consider the "Taste" test. When I contacted both the City of Chicago Department of Special Events and the Park District, they assured me that dogs (on a leash) are allowed at the annual Taste of Chicago, although they strongly discourage dogs from attending when crowds begin to swell after 5 P.M. I understand and agree; it gets so crowded that even the most laid-back pooch can become stressed, and an anxious dog can be unpredictable.

Sure enough, I saw police escorting dog owners out of the festival area at midday, well before the really big crowds had amassed. The officers explained that they were under orders to remove all dogs. In a typically unnecessary, overzeal-ous attempt to remove the dogs, at least one certified service dog was tossed from the festival. By federal law, service dogs accompanying people with hear-ing or vision impairments are allowed absolutely anywhere people are allowed, including all festivals.

Of course, the police and the City aren't the only ones at fault; dog owners share the blame. Unruly and/or aggressive dogs create a nuisance—and even a danger—for people using the parks and beaches. These out-of-control canines are even a menace to other dogs. Ultimately, if more dog owners had well-trained and well-socialized companions, the City wouldn't receive the immense volume of complaints concerning dogs. Many of those complaints have nothing to do with the attitude of the dogs; the problem is the lazy attitudes of owners who refuse to pick up after their pets. In the line of research, I lost count of how many times I stepped in it in Chicago parks.

The good news is that, as frustrating as it may be for all parties, Chicago is still a fun place to be a dog.

Parks

Any Chicago neighborhood can now establish a dog park. The first edition of this book was released shortly after Wiggly Field (Grace-Noethling Park) opened. Back then, in 1998, this dog park in the Lincoln Park area was considered a daring experiment. With the exception of Wiggly, there wasn't a single safe place in this city of more than 750,000 dogs to legally play off a leash. Now there are seven dog-friendly areas, with more on the way, including beach spaces, that will soon sprout up along the lakefront (see the "Beaches" section).

Chicago's innovative formula for creating dog-friendly green places requires grassroots neighborhood support. Dog owners and non–dog owners work together creating solutions to problems where they live. Cities all over America are now looking at Chicago's example.

In what he called his first ever "dog interview," Mayor Richard M. Daley told me, "Most dog owners are responsible people. Like anything else, you have to give opportunities to those people who prove they are responsible. They deserve a place for their dogs to walk and swim. It's all a part of getting along with one another in a big city."

But these opportunities happened for dog owners in the Windy City only after a full-out war of the dogs was escalated to a shocking level in 1995, when a sicko planted hamburger meat laced with arsenic in Oz Park. In subsequent years, similar demented copycats did the same in the Rogers Park neighborhood and near the lake in Lincoln Park. This is, incidentally, a good reason not to allow dogs to wander too far off-leash; they can scarf down something pretty nasty.

When we did this book the first time around, Forrest Claypool, then superintendent of the Chicago Park District, noted that noisy, aggressive, and pooping dogs were at the top of the list of complaints by park users and neighbors living near parks. The police were told to strictly enforce leash laws.

They sure did.

In Oz Park, two officers made a habit of hiding behind trees. They'd holler, "Stop in the name of the law!" when they'd witness the horrendous crime of an owner allowing a dog off-leash for a game of fetch.

Surprised residents in lakefront high-rises looked on as one middle-aged woman was chased by police in their squad car near Osterman Beach on the North Side. The incident occurred after she let her two large mixed-breed dogs off-leash to romp on a cold day when no other beach users were in sight. According to eyewitnesses, this woman was not only screamed at but actually physically shaken by the police—treated as if she'd just robbed a bank.

I've witnessed similar radical actions by the police. I saw police ticket a little old lady with an obviously elderly dog. This poor woman, who could barely walk, had no idea what was going on; she didn't understand and/or couldn't hear the officer. Then there was the time in Lincoln Park when I was out with Lucy and Chaser—both on-leash—talking with another dog owner, whose dog also was leashed. We were at a place where people have historically allowed their dogs freedom to run. The police were circling in their car at a distance. It could be they thought a drug deal was about to go down. But somehow I doubt that. My guess is that they were just waiting for us to unclip the leashes from the dogs' collars.

Many dog owners who have been ticketed claim they were tagged only because the police believed they were likely to pay the fines, which typically range up to $200. Police officers who have worked in and around parks in ravaged South and West Side neighborhoods confirm that they were never told a thing about ticketing dog owners until they were transferred to relatively upscale Lincoln Park. Dogs romp off-leash in South and West Side parks too. However, tickets there for having dogs off-leash are nowhere as common as they are in more affluent neighborhoods. This furthers an argument that revenue may be at the source of some of the overzealous ticketing. Of course, the revenue department discounts this allegation. As one police officer told me, "The police don't write the laws—we enforce them. And dogs are supposed to be on a leash. What's more, we respond to what the community is concerned about—and on the North Side, dogs are an issue."

However, how do you obey the law when you don't know what the law is? Even the letter of the law itself is confusing. When I researched the first edition of *Doggone Chicago*, I encountered about a dozen parks around town that greeted owners with brown canine stop signs. They clearly read "No Dogs Allowed. Ordinance 30-7. Violators will be subjected to arrest and fine."

The rules were hypocritical and confusing because dogs are indeed allowed in parks as long as they're on a leash, according to city law and Park District rules. Still, those signs remained—and were enforced by some police.

An additional antiquated law actually mandated that dogs had to be muzzled in addition to being on-leash. Owners, who had no idea this hidden law existed, were sometimes ticketed with no other apparent rhyme or reason. After all, unless a dog is dangerously aggressive, who would even think of muzzling the pooch for a stroll through the park?

The first edition of this book was in part responsible for inspiring the Park District to remove those ugly brown "No Dogs Allowed" signs, which were typically in disrepair and laden with graffiti. However, it seemed there were more laws and interpretations of those laws than there are kinds of terriers at a dog show.

Concerning the law that all dogs should be on a leash, Claypool told me for the first edition, "Certainly, the Chicago police and our enforcement personnel have better things to do than arrest people who play Frisbee with their dog off a leash, or allow their dogs to run on the beaches in January. However, we do need this law in place should we need to apply it to irresponsible dog owners. I can assure you that if a dog is playing with its owner off a leash—and the dog isn't bothering anyone or in anyone's way—we will not harass you."

Good sentiment, and sometimes it matches reality—but not always. And dog owners were getting tired of erratic and often severe treatment. As a result of police actions against otherwise upstanding citizens, ordinary folks were pushed to belligerence. People began to flout leash laws with a vengeance while relationships with police disintegrated. Meanwhile, the mess was literally getting messier, with neighbors barking obscenities across rooms at local neighborhood meetings—and even depositing dog waste on the steps of owners who weren't picking up.

In other towns, before local skirmishes disintegrated this far, dogs were given their due: their own fenced-off places, called dog parks. This seemed like a logical step for Chicago. However, back in 1996, the Chicago Park District resisted, until Stacey Hawk came along.

Hawk, a Chicago-area German shepherd dog owner and supplier of music and video licensing to restaurants and bars, wanted one of these dog areas in her neighborhood. She persisted and ultimately headed a canine committee for her local neighborhood association. "I thought it was important to develop an alliance of support for dog areas," says Hawk. "Instead of the City's mandating a place for dogs, I felt the neighborhood should earn it, creating a sense of ownership and responsibility—like the difference between renting and owning."

Hawk and cofounder Diane Dorwart (who doesn't own a dog), with support from the neighborhood and the alderman and local veterinarians, transformed an overgrown lot used by gang members and street people into a dog park now known as Wiggly Field. Hawk went on to help create the Dog Advisory Work Group (D.A.W.G.), which includes people who live with canine companionship as well as those who live without.

Wiggly opened in 1997. While it was unquestionably successful, the Park District considered the Near North Side dog park an anomaly. Moreover, diminutive Wiggly Field, huddled under the noisy train tracks, was hardly enough to satisfy a city with about as many dogs as children. As a result, Wiggly was often overrun.

Sculptor Lauren Grey, who shares her life with a pair of Portuguese water dogs, called in to "Pet Central," my WGN Radio show, on a Saturday night in May of 1999.

Listeners had been phoning in that evening with horror stories about Chicago's finest at their worst, ambushing dog owners as they began innocent games of fetch. Lauren recounted her tale of woe. She talked about being chased by the cops up and down a hill near Foster Avenue Beach, and about her bum knees. Talk about victimless crimes. "It was a cold day," she said. "No one else was anywhere near my dogs." The officers hollered from the squad car, "Leash those dogs!"

"My patience with this nonsense was beyond its limits," she said.

I don't know for sure what it was, but I heard passion and intelligence in her voice. Off the air, after the show, I explained to Lauren that "the timing is right to strike." I knew that if she could create a coalition of the many loosely knit dog groups from neighborhoods all around the city, and then speak as one educated and reasonable voice for those groups, we might just get some dog parks. In a matter of days, Grey contacted a dozen such groups from around the city. She and longtime "Pet Central" listener Gayle Gavagan worked with me to create D.O.G./Chicago. In short time, I found myself speaking on behalf of dog owners—selling our position for dog areas—in front of commissioners at the Chicago Park District. In light of both the success of Wiggly Field and an overload of complaints from long-suffering dog owners, officials were at least open to the idea of creating dog-friendly areas throughout the park system.

As a result, we were able to set up a meeting with Drew Becher, who was then a high-level assistant to the mayor (Chicago's version of Michael J. Fox). Grey proceeded to do a way better job than Camryn Manheim from TV's "The Practice" at continuing to gather evidence, learning about how successful dog parks all over the country have succeeded and enlisting formidable expert veterinary assistance from Dr. Sheldon Rubin of Blum Animal Hospital and from the then executive director of Chicago's commission on animal care and control, Dr. Gene Mueller.

Becher, who is the owner of a soft-coated wheaten terrier named Disco, got it; he understood the message loud and clear. He will go down in canine history as the first person in Chicago city government ever to give a dog group legitimacy. He encouraged the Park District to work with D.O.G./Chicago, which it has done.

"When you ask a child to draw a crayon picture of the family, you get Mom, Dad, and the family pet," Becher says. "Pets are a part of the family."

As D.O.G./Chicago began to make estimable progress, D.A.W.G. was gaining momentum in Lincoln Park.

D.A.W.G. was a product of the Lincoln Central Association. Cynthia Bathurst, president of that association, is also the non–dog owning cochair of D.A.W.G. It became clear to Bathurst that in order to make peace in the war of the dogs, non–dog owners would also have to become involved. "When sharing urban spaces, everyone brings something to the table," she says.

D.O.G./Chicago, with assistance from Hawk, worked with the City and Park District to devise rules for dog parks, which would be called Dog Friendly Areas (DFAs). They also created a protocol for deciding where to put these DFAs, which includes proving formidable public sentiment for the dog area in the neighborhood, as well as support from the appropriate alderman and nearby park officials. Of course, the chosen site must make sense both for the safety of dogs and for the neighbors. Discussing issues openly at CAPS (Community Alternative Policing Strategy) meetings is also recommended. In some communities there are few dissenting views; in others many people snarl when park space is devoted to dogs. This contingent must be dealt with.

"The idea of involving both dog owners and non-owners at the neighborhood level is the secret to what I believe will be the long-term success of these areas," says Becher, who is now chief of staff at the Chicago Park District. "Sure, the Park District takes responsibility at some level, but ultimately it's people who make things work. For example, there's social pressure for community policing so that dogs are reasonably well behaved and the DFA is clean."

Research reveals that parks that previously didn't allow dogs become safer places when canines are welcomed. Grey, for instance, notes that her dogs have helped introduce her to neighbors she otherwise might not have met.

Even the mayor understands this. He told me, "Dogs take people out of their houses; they're out meeting people. They're talking to people in the morning and at night—it's wonderful."

In August of 1999 the hypocritical and confusing crapshoot of dog laws was consolidated into one easy-to-understand and reasonable law for both the City and the Park District. While dogs still are required to be on a leash no more than six feet long in parks, they may be taken off-leash in areas specifically designated for dogs. (Dogs are not allowed at all in fenced-off children's play lots, or inside Park District buildings or the botanic gardens.)

With this final agreement, in the summer of 2000 the war of the dogs ended.

Becher says that gripes about noisy, aggressive, and pooping dogs are no longer at the top of the list of public complaints at the Park District.

However, all problems aren't solved overnight, and in some pockets dogs remain a bone of contention.

While the overzealous ticketing has generally ended, individual police still apparently have it in for dog owners. New law or not, they don't care, or perhaps they just don't know the new rules. Nevertheless, Becher firmly maintains that no one should ever again be ticketed in a Chicago park for not having a dog muzzled (unless that dog has been deemed dangerous by the city's animal care and control department).

So, the good news is that most of the bizarre hunting down of people with dogs by the police has ended. In fact, the police have found that dog owners can help them to make CAPS more effective. At Margate Park, I spoke with a pair of police officers who drop in regularly to get information from dog owners about what's happening in the 'hood. They point out, "Dog owners are outdoors a lot, and they see what's going on." I've spoken to police who check in at Wiggly Field for the same reason.

A protocol and procedure is now in place for any community to create its own DFA. And D.A.W.G. has now expanded into a legit not-for-profit group, helping neighborhoods all around town jump through hoops so that they too can have DFAs. There's even an effort under way to get DFAs in the Cook County Forest Preserve, just like the wonderful spacious places for dogs to play in the DuPage and Lake County Forest Preserves. D.A.W.G. is also dealing with a variety of other canine-related issues, including dog fighting and legislation. A prime directive of D.A.W.G. is education.

This turn of events thrills Becher. "Clearly, dogs are being let off-leash in DFAs, rather than running on jogging paths. This is safer and smarter for all."

Bathurst adds, "Dogs are never a problem; it's advocating responsible ownership that needs to be addressed."

Mayor Daley notes that the most widespread complaint about dogs is those little gifts they leave behind. "I like when people carry extra plastic bags," he says. "If you see someone else (not picking up), you say, 'Do the right thing. Here's an extra plastic bag.' We all have responsibilities in life. You have to carry that out. Then we all enjoy a better city."

The mayor is correct, which is why D.A.W.G.'s current educational directive is a campaign called Scoop the Poop.

"This a real health issue; diseases may be transmitted to dogs and children by owners' not scooping," says Karen Okura, cochair of D.A.W.G.'s education committee. "It's also common courtesy; dog owners hate to scrape shoes too. And it's also the law."

Okura says it would be fun to have a citizen's poop patrol, hollering to dog owners who don't—as the mayor says—do the right thing, "Citizen's arrest! Citizen's arrest!"

Imagine: in 1998, Chicago barely had one dog park; today the city's protocol and insistence on involving communities in their own destinies is being used as a model for other cities. Still, Grey would like to see additional progress. "There are natural congregations where dogs and their people have been playing off-leash for years," she says. "And many of these places can't be fenced—mostly because a fence is considered unsightly. The neighbors do mind the fencing; they don't mind the dogs. One example is Nichols Park in Hyde Park. As long as the dogs are out of the way of others using park space, and they're unlikely to endanger themselves by running into a street, I can't see the harm. It would be nice to find a way to allow dogs at these places off-leash. Perhaps special permits can be granted for dogs who have earned the right to be in the special places."

Sound farfetched? Maybe not. After all, back in 1998, no one would have guessed that in only a few years ordinary citizens would sniff out dog parks by cooperating with non-owners, city government, and the Park District to create places for dogs to have a great time. Ultimately, dogs are the real winners.

This story is wonderful, despite wrangling and petty catfighting among selected members of assorted dog groups. We've learned from this too. Dogs have no ulterior motives, which proves they generally have superior ethics to people.

But there remains a lot of head scratching.

When I was researching the first edition, then superintendent Forrest Claypool told me that in the dead of winter—when there are obviously no tennis players around—the dogs can take over the tennis courts. This would seem like a no-brainer. Because they're enclosed, unused tennis courts are a great place to run dogs off-leash.

Becher echoes Claypool's good sentiments from several years back. But he also points out the fine print: "While the Park District technically has no problem with dogs playing in tennis courts in the winter, if the dogs are off-leash, it's still technically against the law. And the police could ticket."

However, Becher suggests that it's possible to engage the same community-driven process that creates dog-friendly areas in parks and dog-friendly beaches to create dog-friendly tennis courts. Again, approval from your alderman, support at CAPS meetings, and agreement from the neighborhood would be required. Obviously, if you're looking for Fido to use tennis courts in the spring, summer, or fall, it's not going to happen—but from let's say Thanksgiving through early March, why not? Becher says people would still have to promise to pick up (which is the law, regardless) and allow tennis players first dibs on courts should they be crazy enough to brave freezing temperatures.

Another hitch is that when city festivals, such as the Taste of Chicago or Blues Fest, are held in public parks, all laws seem to go down the tubes. I was greeted at the Jackson Avenue entrance to Taste of Chicago in 2000 with a hand-scribbled "No Dogs Allowed" sign. Entering farther north and to the east near Columbus Boulevard, not only was there no such sign, but also a police officer was holding a leash for a pet owner who had run off to grab a bite. I asked that officer if dogs were in fact allowed at the Taste. He shrugged and replied, "It's a park; why not?"

Technically, he's correct. Dogs are allowed in parks as long as they're on a leash and their people pick up.

Of course, not all dogs are "Taste" worthy. Attending any city festival is too much for most dogs to bear. These events may include live music and fireworks. In really crowded places, small dogs could be stepped on and injured. Then again, there are dogs, such as Luna, who love to party. The noise doesn't bother her—and she adores attention from strangers.

Becher says, "Dogs are still dogs, and you have to consider people who may be afraid of dogs, or potential unpredictability when something loud and surprising happens." He strongly discourages people from taking dogs to festivals, whether they're allowed or not. But he won't specifically offer the Park District's policy on this point. He refers me to the Mayor's Office of Special Events. Guess what? They skirt the issue too, telling me most festivals are too crowded for dogs, but dogs are allowed in parks. They proceed to refer me to officials at the Park District.

While the vast majority of canines aren't suited for attending the big festivals, many have the temperament to attend smaller, somewhat quieter neighborhood festivals—at which the canine policy is equally unclear.

In summary, take your pooch along if you're certain your dog has the appropriate disposition to handle commotion. But don't be surprised if a police officer, for no apparent reason, tells you to return to your doghouse.

For more information on how to develop a dog-friendly area in your community—which is the best way to go—call the Park District's Dog Hot Line, (312) 744-DOGS (3647). The Dog Advisory Work Group's mission includes assisting neighborhood groups through the process; call (312) 409-2169.

Chicago's Dog Friendly Areas

A DFA is a designated space specifically designed for use by dogs and their owners for off-leash recreation, socialization, exercise, and training. Currently there are seven Dog Friendly Areas in Chicago. Several groups are working within their neighborhoods and with the Park District to create new DFAs. Thus, it's probable that by the time you read this, there will be additional DFAs. (For further information on DFAs, see p. 7.) DFAs are for well-socialized dogs and their people. But you must abide by the rules:

1. Owners are legally responsible for their dogs and any injuries caused by their dogs.
2. Owners must stay with their dogs within the fenced area.
3. Dogs must be leashed prior to entering and upon leaving the park. Gates to the park must remain closed when not in use.
4. Owners must immediately clean up after their dogs. Failure to do so can result in a fine of up to $500 (City of Chicago Ordinance 7-12-420).
5. Dogs with a known history of or who exhibit dangerous behavior are prohibited in the area.
6. Dogs must be healthy, fully immunized, dewormed, licensed, and wearing ID tags.
7. Children under 12 must be accompanied by an adult; young children must be closely supervised.
8. Only three dogs per person are allowed.
9. Puppies under four months old and female dogs in heat are prohibited.
10. Dogs must be watched at all times.
11. Cooperation among dog owners is essential.

ARRIGO PARK (LITTLE ITALY) // This lovely park is surrounded by a black iron gate, so dogs can't run out. And it's filled with begonias. The park is about three blocks long and a block wide, with an asphalt running track that extends for about a mile around the perimeter.

Nearby parking is restricted to residents only. Arrigo Park is across the street from Cabrini Hospital, at Lexington, Cabrini, and Lytle Streets. (312) 742-PLAY (7529).

CALIFORNIA PARK (NORTH CENTRAL/IRVING PARK) ✓   Lucy and Chaser's canine friend BootsMontgomery thinks the girls have a great job visiting parks. So, they invited BootsM. along for this excursion, but poor Boots was bored. There was nothing to do. There's a tennis court where dogs could play while tennis isn't in season, but the gate was locked. Dogs aren't allowed inside the nearby McFetridge Sports Complex. On top of this, there's very little grass. You're much better off crossing Irving Park Road for a run around Horner Park.

California Park is bounded by Irving Park Road, Grace Street, California Avenue, and the Chicago River. (312) 742-PLAY (7529).

CHURCHILL FIELD (BUCKTOWN) ✓ ½   This tiny park is little more than a baseball field. It's become a popular spot for the dogs to come out to play. The stumbling point is that they are off-leash, and this park is not a designated DFA. These dog owners risk being ticketed. Churchill will most likely have a dog-friendly area in the future, but for now controversy simmers. Most members of the community agree that a DFA is necessary, but surfacing options are a subject of debate. Hopefully by the time you read this, the details will have been worked out, and Rover can go to Churchill to play off-leash legally.

In the meantime, alternative measures have been taken. The energetic dogs ripped up the sod on the athletic field, and the Park District had to put new grass down. To prevent the dogs from destroying it again, the Park District has installed temporary snow fencing to keep the canines corralled within a specific area.

Churchill Field is bounded by Damen, Winchester, and Bloomingdale Avenues. (312) 742-PLAY (7529).

COLISEUM PARK (DFA) ✓✓ ½   A green park space (known as Coliseum Park) surrounds the fenced-in dog-friendly area (known as Coliseum Park DFA). There's a lot of grass in the park space, which was freshly mowed on the day Janice and Luna visited. Right in the center is a rubber-matted playground with brightly colored equipment. The real rub is that you and your off-leash dog can only admire this beautiful park from the other side of the fence, while trapped in the nothing-to-write-home-about dog-friendly area.

Janice calls this DFA an oversize dog run. If it were five feet to the west, it would be directly under the train tracks. The trains go by so often that some sensitive dogs may not be able to handle the ruckus.

Double gates open up to a long and narrow asphalt area with small patches of grass mixed in. A few large flat rocks sit side by side, eight bright red metal poles stick up from the ground, creating an overgrown canine obstacle course, and other unusual rock formations are scattered about. It's unclear if these trappings were for the dogs' enjoyment or if they were added as art for humans to admire. They do make this DFA unique. The doggy play area encompasses a giant electrical transmitter. The equipment is blocked off so that dogs can't get too close, but it's conspicuous. A small tree and a patch of grass were planted on the south end to disguise the transmitter; it doesn't work. Maybe by the time we do our 10th edition, the landscaping will have grown in. Or could this be why they added the "art"—to detract from that metal monstrosity in the corner?

After a few locals arrived, Janice got the inside scoop on Coliseum Park. She found out that not many neighborhood kids play beyond the DFA, in the park space itself. Here—in the area *not* officially designated as the DFA—the canine contingency runs free. This is quite safe for the dogs, since the entire park is fenced in. However, the rules state that dogs must be leashed outside the DFA.

While Janice received some history of the DFA, Luna got to play with an adorable standard poodle named Thunder and her brother Cocoa, a miniature poodle. They were all on the playground side, in the large grassy area. Janice understood that this was against the rules and that she risked getting a ticket, but she figured, When in Rome . . . . Within 15 minutes, at least six dogs were running around the park, with not one small child on the horizon. Janice gleaned that at 10 A.M. on weekdays a day-care group comes to use the park, and that's about it.

A cop drove by on a scooter, and nobody flinched. The dog owners seemed confident that the officer was more interested in illegally parked cars than he was in frolicking dogs; and they were right. He scooted by without so much as a nod in their direction.

More good news is that the large park area outside of the DFA is impeccable: not a pile anywhere. Dog owners police themselves carefully, not wanting to leave any evidence behind. The system of letting the dogs run off-leash in the park when it's empty appears to be working so far, but this is not a long-term solution for park users. The community needs to join with the Park District to come up with a plan that works for everybody.

Coliseum Park is at 14th Place and Wabash Avenue. (312) 742-DOGS (3647).

DOG LOT (DFA–RIVER NORTH) //½   This is, paws down, the most urban of all the dog-friendly areas. In fact, Janice and Barry drove right by it at least 10 times, thinking, "This can't be it." Behind the giant Office Max, on the southwest corner of Orleans and Ohio, right next to the exit of I-90/94, sits a long, narrow strip of concrete, lined with bushes. This dog park might be better described as a dog run, of best use to a greyhound practicing for an Olympic sprint. Posted on the outside of a wrought-iron gate is a tiny sign citing the "pet owner" ordinance, reminding people that it is the law to pick up after your dog. On the other side of the gate, there are plastic bags hanging, making it as easy as pie to follow the rules. With these two clues, Janice and Barry discerned they were in the right place.

The night Janice and Barry were there, the gate was open. Janice thought it was due to the electrical work that was going on. But the Commonwealth Edison workers said they've never seen the gate closed. This is a concern if you have a dog that likes to escape. Being so close to major streets, not to mention the expressway, they never took Luna off the leash.

In the midst of wrecking balls, scaffolding, and cements trucks, this park does offer city dogs a place to play.

Dog Lot is at Orleans and Ohio Streets, on the southwest corner. (312) 742-DOGS (3647).

DOUGLAS PARK (NORTH LAWNDALE) // They dog paddle to their hearts' content off one of the few man-made beaches in the city. The little lake in Douglas Park is shallow, great for pups who are insecure about water.

Several cross-country skiers visit this park with dogs, and there's lots of space for playing fetch.

Douglas Park is bounded by Roosevelt Road, 19th Street, and California and Albany Avenues, and Sacramento Avenue cuts right through it. (312) 742-PLAY (7529).

GARFIELD PARK (GARFIELD PARK) // ½ Once a showcase among city parks, Garfield no longer has center stage because of the failing neighborhood around it. However, given a chance, Garfield still ranks as a park of stature. Its tree-lined pathways are particularly inspiring from Homan Avenue to Hamlin Boulevard. What inspires the dogs is all the squirrels that these trees attract. Dogs are allowed to sit on benches and enjoy the flower gardens, but they aren't allowed inside the Garfield Park Conservatory.

At the south end of the park is the recently renovated gazebo, which is sometimes used for weddings. It can accommodate 50 people and several dogs. When not reserved for weddings, it's a popular place for guys or gals to pop the question.

Live concerts are sometimes held at the band shell. There are several baseball diamonds and 14 tennis courts.

Garfield Park is bounded by Hamlin Boulevard, Fifth and Central Park Avenues, and Lake Street. (312) 742-PLAY (7529).

GOMPERS PARK (ALBANY PARK/NORTH PARK) //   The view of nearby Saint Lucas and Bohemian National Cemeteries isn't too upbeat. On the whole, Gompers is a quiet park. With the possible exceptions of Halloween and Friday the 13th, those neighbors don't make much noise. Here along the banks of the Chicago River, the scenery is picturesque. A fence prevents dogs from entering the river. Indeed, the Chicago River is better to look at from a distance than to actually allow your dog to swim in. Dogs are discouraged from being in the children's play area, but they're welcome to score on the football field or baseball diamonds, as long as no games are in progress.

Gompers Park is bounded by Pulaski Road, Foster Avenue, and Keeler and Winnemac Streets. (312) 742-PLAY (7529).

GRANT PARK (DOWNTOWN) // ½   This flower-filled park across from Lake Michigan is very pretty. You can enjoy a tulip display in the spring, a wide assortment of flowers throughout the summer, and mums in the fall. The well-manicured green space makes for some quality sniffing, but there isn't much else to occupy a dog.

Over the summer months, the city music festivals attract more people to this park than fleas to a dirty dog. For pups who can attune themselves to the crush of humanity, this is a perfect place for making new friends. Dogs are allowed at the Petrillo Music Shell, at Jackson Boulevard and Columbus Drive. However, most hounds don't cotton to the mob scene or the live music; it's too noisy (for a listing of festivals, see p. 59).

Lake Michigan is just on the other side of Lake Shore Drive, which borders the east side of the park. But there's nowhere for dogs to take a dip, and swimming is absolutely not allowed in Buckingham Fountain. Still, the fountain's display of dancing lights and water is beautiful, and it continues throughout spring and summer evenings.

Tourists are attracted to the park to shoot photos of the flowers, Buckingham Fountain, the view of Lake Michigan . . . and of course, the dogs. Actually, this does happen. Walking Lucy through the park, I was stopped by a contingent of tourists who were snapping photos of skyscrapers, pigeons, and virtually everything else. One of them asked, "Can we take a picture of your dog?" I said, "Sure," and proceeded to tell Lucy to sit so we could pose. The tourist got angry and pointed his finger at me. "Not you," he said. "I just want the dog in the picture." After he got his shot of Lucy, he went on to take pictures of trees.

Grant Park is bounded by Lake Shore Drive, Michigan Avenue, and Monroe and 11th Streets. (312) 742-PLAY (7529).

HAMLIN PARK (DFA) */// *   On the southwest side of Hamlin Park sits an L-shape fenced-in area where dogs can play together and owners socialize with their neighbors. The way that this park is configured makes it a bit awkward for dogs to get a good run in. However, the vertical stretch does allow for healthy throws of the tennis ball.

According to current plans, all of Chicago's DFAs will eventually be asphalt. Right now this surface is still muddy and dusty. Surfacing plans have been delayed due to the extensive tree canopies that cover the park. When asphalt is laid, it cuts off a majority of the oxygen and water supply to the trees. The Hamlin Park DFA will require a unique solution, and alternative surfaces are being investigated. There also are no benches at this park, which isn't all bad— it forces dog owners to be more involved with their dogs. The atmosphere is friendly, and locals know all the neighborhood dogs.

Hamlin Park is at 3035 N. Hoyne Avenue, at the corner of Wellington and Hoyne Avenues; the DFA is at the southwest corner of the park. (773) 525-8592.

HORNER PARK (NORTH CENTER/ALBANY PARK) */// *   With all the trees, squirrels, and chipmunks, it's no wonder that dogs love Horner Park so much. Owners love it too, particularly throughout the winter. Baseball and soccer fields are empty then, making for great fetch space.

On sunny summer weekends, picnickers take over the grass, and bicyclists and skaters force dogs off the paved paths. When softball and baseball games are in progress, players get pretty aggressive about chasing the hounds away. I won't repeat the language used to persuade Lucy to go elsewhere when she accidentally wandered onto a soccer field. If Lucy didn't understand the graphic language, she must have understood the tone, as she ran back whining to Chaser.

Lucy and Chaser always meet other dogs at Horner Park. During one visit, they met a gang of yellow and black Labrador retrievers out for a training session. The dogs were holding a perfect sit/stay, until troublemaker Lucy arrived with her butt up in the air, ready to play. Once Lucy wore out the Labs, she happened upon a Shetland sheepdog whose owner promised, "My dog never gets tired; she'll wear your dog out." Indeed, it looked promising at first, as the sheltie barked out "Chase me, chase me." But alas, 20 minutes later the sheltie just stopped running and looked up at her owner as if to say, "Let's get out of here!" Lucy looked truly disappointed.

Dogs are not welcome in the children's play lot. And passage to the Chicago River, which borders the park to the east, is fenced off. No one complains, since the river is pretty mucky here. When fall colors are on display, the river and the nearby foliage provide an appealing backdrop for photos.

Horner Park is bounded by the Chicago River, California and Montrose Avenues, and Irving Park Road. (312) 742-PLAY (7529).

INDIAN BOUNDARY PARK (WEST RIDGE/ROGERS PARK) // ½   For bird dogs, this park is better than watching wildlife shows on TV—it's the real thing. Ducks and geese are found at the bird sanctuary behind a chain-link fence. They seem to have got used to the dogs pointing in their direction. In fact, one audacious goose walked right up to the fence and reprimanded Chaser with a blaring "Honk! Honk!" Dogs are also not allowed behind the fence at the minizoo on the north side of the park. Chaser and Lucy walked around the perimeter of the zoo with their noses straight up in the air. They clearly enjoyed the fragrant aroma of the camel, bison, and goats.

Because of the zoo and a great kids' play lot, Indian Boundary is a magnet for children. In fact, so many children surrounded Chaser and Lucy that our nieces got jealous. "Let's not allow anyone to pet the dogs," demanded then six-year-old Mallory.

One little boy—apparently a future real estate tycoon—lugged a huge For Sale sign around the park, the kind that usually sits on lawns in front of homes. He walked up to Chaser and said, "Hey, dog, would you like to buy a doghouse?"

When the fountain isn't operating, the concrete pool surrounding it becomes an in-line skating rink where dogs sometimes join their owners goin' 'round and 'round.

Indian Boundary Park is bounded by Estes and Lunt Avenues and Rockwell Street. (312) 742-PLAY (7529).

JACKSON PARK (BRONZEVILLE/DOUGLAS-GRAND BOULEVARD) // ½   At the center of the park lies Wooded Island. As its name implies, this area is filled with trees and is accessible only by bridges. One lazy afternoon, the only sound we heard was a momentary bark from a miniature schnauzer who caught a glimpse of a passing squirrel. At Wooded Island, rushing traffic from nearby Lake Shore Drive is out of sight and out of mind. The east side of the park is near the water and adjoining Jackson Park Beach (see p. 35). Parking can be at a premium on the weekends, so you might be better off biking or walking.

Jackson Park is bounded by Lake Michigan, Stony Island, and 56th and 67th Places. (312) 742-PLAY (7529).

JONQUIL PARK (LINCOLN PARK/DEPAUL) ✔   Location, location, location. Ordinarily, such a puny park wouldn't attract much notice. However, Jonquil Park's locale in the heart of the Lincoln Park neighborhood makes it an ideal meeting spot. At one time, the midday regulars gathered daily at about noon; they included dog walkers and nannies with their respective charges. The after-work clique started to arrive at 4:30 P.M. and kept coming until around 6:30.

That was until a band of anti-dog antagonists campaigned to outlaw dogs from this park—and until a better alternative, Grace-Noethling Park (Wiggly Field), opened down the road.

As a result, this park is no longer as heavily used, and no wonder. Neighbors have been known to storm out of their homes to shoo dog owners from the grounds. Because of the griping, this is one of those parks visited by police officers to cite owners for taking their companions off-leash.

Jonquil Park is bounded by Lincoln, Seminary, and Wrightwood Avenues and Drummond Street. (312) 742-PLAY (7529).

LAKESHORE PARK (STREETERVILLE) ✔ ½   For those who enjoy running in circles, one of Chicago's finest running tracks is located here. Add to that a couple of baseball fields. This modest park is across the street from Northwestern University's downtown campus. It's also a regular stop for the concierge staff who walk the canine guests at the Ritz-Carlton Hotel (see "Places to Stay," p. 121).

Lakeshore Park is bounded by Chicago Avenue, Chestnut Street, Inner Lake Shore Drive, and the Museum of Contemporary Art. (312) 742-PLAY (7529).

LEGION PARK (NORTH PARK) ✔✔ ½   Sitting on a bench, watching the ducks in the Chicago River, I'm thinking about the peaceful setting. Chaser, staring intently at the waterfowl, is kept in place by a fence and a couple of years of obedience training. I don't have to wonder what she's thinking: a duckling dinner complete with feathers.

Legion Park is like a miniature forest, thick with all kinds of trees. I think Chaser sniffed each one. One owner made an even more impressive claim—that his Doberman, Max, marked each trunk.

Legion Park is bounded by Virginia, Foster, and Peterson Avenues, the Chicago River, and Troy Street. (312) 742-PLAY (7529).

LINCOLN PARK (LINCOLN PARK/LAKEVIEW/UPTOWN/EDGEWATER) ✔✔✔ ½   At 1,208 acres, this is one of the longest stretches of urban park in the nation, running along Lake Michigan from the Chicago Historical Society at North Avenue to Kathy Osterman Beach (see "Beaches," p. 44) at Ardmore Avenue in Edgewater. The park is set alongside some of the most populated areas of the city, most notably its namesake Lincoln Park neighborhood.

The park is always busy. At any given moment hundreds of dogs are working out, and many of them are off-leash. Although most responsible owners have nothing to worry about, cops periodically give out tickets for letting dogs off-leash to play fetch. Given the enormous hound population in the park, you run a greater chance of getting caught in a speed trap en route. Then again, that rationalization doesn't help when it's you and your dog who are tagged.

This park is a point of assembly for people with all sorts of interests. Social groups consisting of yuppie-aged singles meet after work at North Avenue to play football, softball, or beach volleyball. Jogging clubs start their runs at the Totem Pole north of Addison Street at Recreation Drive. Soccer leagues with young children kick the ball at Montrose Avenue. Lesbian softball leagues compete in the fields just south of Irving Park Road. This park is a living illustration of Jesse Jackson's Rainbow Coalition.

Lincoln Park's bicycle paths are as busy as the Dan Ryan Expressway, with in-line skaters in the summer and cross-country skiers in the winter. If it's trendy, you'll find followers participating with their dogs in Lincoln Park. One craze with "legs" is a Norwegian alpine sport called skijoring in which canine power is harnessed to pull cross-country skiers across the snow.

Dogs are a common thread through all the assorted interests and groups that hang out at the park. Canines are always in attendance.

One place that most certainly has gone to the dogs is affectionately called "Bark Park." This is a patch of grass within Lincoln Park, south of Addison Street and east of Dog Beach. Regulars from the Lincoln Park and Wrigleyville neighborhoods meet here daily. The location appeals to dog owners because it's bounded by a fence on the west and the lake on the east, helping to keep wandering pups from running off. It's near here, along the rocks at the lake, where Newfoundlands and Labradors spend entire afternoons diving.

Mildred Hopkins lives in a nearby high-rise. She doesn't own a dog, but she comes here to watch the show. She even carries biscuits in her purse to distribute. Several canines have unsuccessfully attempted to snatch her handbag.

Of course, some dogs prefer a more relaxed lifestyle, as evidenced by the familiar line of canine sun worshippers sprawled along the rocks at the lake— anywhere from Montrose Avenue south to Addison Street. Dogs may also offer strategic advice to the players at the Chess Pavilion (just south of LaSalle Drive).

Lincoln Park isn't just a sunny-weather haven. In fact, snow is essential for the toboggan hill at Wilson Avenue at Simonds Drive. While many pooches slide down on toboggans, some not-so-conventional modes of transport have been used as well, such as skillets and garbage pail lids. Some owners have been spied skiing down the hill while cradling toy breeds in their arms.

Dogs are not allowed in the children's play areas, the archery range, the Waveland Golf Course, the Lincoln Park Zoo, or the Lincoln Park Conservatory. That still leaves them able to sniff the incredible flowerbeds outside the conservatory and at Peace Garden near Wilson Avenue.

Lincoln Park is bounded by North and Ardmore Avenues, Clark Street, and Marine Drive. Access to the park is through various underground walkways and at all Lake Shore Drive exits, from LaSalle Drive/North Avenue on the south to Bryn Mawr Avenue on the north. Metered parking is available in the park, but at many places the spots fill up fast. (312) 742-PLAY (7529).

MARQUETTE PARK (CHICAGO LAWN) // ½   The park's perimeter surrounds a lagoon. At its center is an island with a golf course (dogs are not welcome) and a baseball diamond. When there's no game in progress, the ball field is a safe place to play catch, since there's no way a dog can run off without crossing a body of water.

There are actually seven baseball fields here. To escape the outfielders and the dogs chasing after balls, stroll down the secluded tree-lined walkways throughout the park. Don't miss the flower garden on the park's west side. At the outdoor track, test your pup's legs against those of any challenger by conducting your own dog race.

Marquette Park is bounded by Marquette Road, 71st Street, and Central Park and California Avenues. (312) 742-PLAY (7529).

MATHER PARK (WEST RIDGE/WEST ROGERS PARK) //   The good news is that Mather High School borders the park, so there is lots of grass for play space. It's a tailor-made spot for tossing a Frisbee. The bad news is that there's no parking on nearby streets from 8 A.M. to 4 P.M. There are also tennis and basketball courts and a baseball diamond.

Mather Park is bounded by Peterson, California, and Thorndale Avenues and Richmond Street. (312) 742-PLAY (7529).

McKINLEY PARK (SOUTH LAWNDALE) //   The aroma of a good barbecue is hard to resist for dogs or their people. Paws down, McKinley Park is a favorite for dogs to sample barbecued chicken and ribs as well as toasted marshmallows.

Dogs are discouraged from Park District lagoons, frozen or otherwise. One year, a young boy died by falling through the thin ice here. In an attempt to rescue the child, a passerby and his dog followed on the ice. The ice cracked under the dog, which also became a casualty. In summer months, the lagoons are sometimes used as swimming pools for dogs, but the Park District frowns on the activity.

McKinley Park is bounded by Damen and Western Avenues, Pershing Road, and 37th Street. (312) 742-PLAY (7529).

MERRIMAC PARK (DUNNING) ✓   A friendly sort of place where every pup knows your smell. However, this small park offers no distinguishing feature. Merrimac Park is at the western edge of Chicago, near Harwood Heights to the northwest and Norridge to the west. The park is bounded by Irving Park Road, Narragansett and Mobile Avenues, and Byron Street. (312) 742-PLAY (7529).

MOUNT GREENWOOD PARK (MOUNT GREENWOOD) ✓ ½   This was once the last parcel of farmland within Chicago city limits. Today the park is barely within those limits, located at the southwest corner of Chicago, near Alsip. Its only attribute is significant space for all-out running. Combine the green area of the park with the grassy grounds of the nearby Chicago High School for Agricultural Sciences, and dogs have more room to score touchdowns than the Chicago Bears.

Mount Greenwood Park is bounded by 111th and 112th Streets, and Central Park and Hamlin Avenues. (312) 742-PLAY (7529).

NICHOLS PARK (HYDE PARK) ✓✓ ½   Intellectual students and their Pulitzer Prize–winning professors from the nearby University of Chicago meet at this park with their dogs. The disappointing news is that dogs here are no brainier than they are anywhere else.

Chaser was coasting down what the locals call "the dog hill" with a black Labrador. The Lab's owner, a psychology professor, called in vain, "Butch, Butch . . . oh, Butch!" As the owner advanced toward the dog, the dog continued to run farther away. (The professor was smoking a pipe and wearing a tweed jacket with well-worn patches at the elbows.) He then uttered the most ridiculous command I've ever heard. He hollered, "Cease, you loquacious canine!" Do you think I took advantage of this situation to show off to this professor? Darn right, I did.

It was time to show this smug guy how a well-trained dog acts. Nonchalantly, I call out, "Chaser, come." Chaser does an about-face and runs full-speed toward us. She plops herself down in a perfect sit, right at the feet of the professor. She came—to the wrong person, I admit—but at least she did obey the command.

Butch eventually returned when he was good and ready.

"Dog hill" is definitely the highlight. Dog owners meet here after school and after work to socialize.

Nichols Park is bounded by 55th Place, 54th Street, Ridgewood Court, and Kimbark Avenue. (312) 742-PLAY (7529).

OZ PARK (LINCOLN PARK) // A statue of the Tin Man at the northeast corner of the park greets all visitors. However, Toto isn't here, so dogs head off to the dog hill on the southwest side of the park. Yupsters can pick up more than their canines' waste here. Bill Adams makes the five-mile trip to the park on bicycle with his Australian shepherd. He says with pride, "I have the kind of dog that picks up the babes." His dog's name? Magnet.

It seems Magnet is trained for the job. Magnet politely introduces herself by dropping a tennis ball at the feet of a prospective date. "She's responsible for my social life," Adams says.

While Magnet is busy making the rounds, most dogs frolic up and down the hill without their leashes. The hill is just as much fun with a couple of inches of snow on the ground—dogs and people slide down together. However, when school is in session, staff members will chase dog owners away. (The hill is just west of Lincoln Park High School.)

Don't even think about letting your hound step onto the tennis courts, through the gates of the lush garden, or onto the children's playground. That's because some neighbors enjoy hounding dog owners, calling the police the moment a dog wanders into a forbidden zone or does number two without the owner's picking up.

A group of dog owners is fighting for specified off-leash hours in a restricted area at Oz Park where dogs could legally run off-leash, just as they've been illegally running with leashes off for years. Some contentious non–dog owners feel threatened by dogs off-leash, and they're totally against this idea, even militantly against this idea. Many local dog owners argue that they're courteous of other park users and let their dogs off-leash away from the crowds so they don't cause any problems. They're determined to let their dogs run free as they have for many years, despite continued ticketing by the police.

The Park District agrees that the dog situation at Oz needs to be addressed. So far, decision makers are not convinced that off-leash hours are the best solution. Allowing dogs to run around off-leash without being contained by a fence has never been done in the city. The number one concern is the safety of the dogs. Even the most well-behaved, well-trained dog may see a squirrel or another dog and run off to investigate. Also, without a fence, there is no way to guarantee that dogs will stay in the specified area. Oz Park gets a lot of use, and—let's face it— not everybody likes dogs. The Park District's goal is to have parks and public spaces that are safe for all community members.

The dog issue remains a point of contention in the neighborhood. However, a plan to breach the impasse has been initiated, and hopefully as you read this, the conflicts have been resolved.

Oz Park is bounded by Dickens, Lincoln, and Webster Avenues and Larrabee Street. (312) 742-PLAY (7529).

PLAYLOT 480 (DEARBORN PARK) ⁄ ½   This park doesn't boast a fancy name or, for that matter, anything else. But it is the commuter dog station where residents of the Dearborn Park neighborhood meet daily before and after work. Playlot 480 is filled with dog lovers, but watch out: nearby play lots fall into that other category. (These other nearby parks and play lots aren't listed here. Their small size, concrete structures, and anti-dog sentiment don't merit a visit. Besides, most prohibit dogs.)

Playlot 480 is bounded by Michigan Avenue, Plymouth Court, 14th Street, and the railroad tracks. (312) 742-PLAY (7529).

PORTAGE PARK (PORTAGE PARK) ⁄⁄   Chicago 16-inch softball is the game of choice on weekends. Locals might swing baseball bats aimed at your head at the mere mention of a 12-inch softball. Playing with the oversize softball is a Chicago tradition.

This park features paved walkways. Chaser found the paths ideal for pulling her pal Stan Paziora's wheelchair. Stan held on to the leash and hollered "Mush" as he laughed, "Ho, ho, ho." It's as if he were Santa, and Chaser were all those reindeer rolled into one pooch. As for Chaser, she loved the exercise and really, really loved the treats Stan offered along the way. Stan has since passed away, and Chaser misses him.

Dogs are not allowed in the swimming pool area. Portage Park is bounded by Irving Park Road and Berteau, Long, and Central Avenues. (312) 742- PLAY (7529).

"PUPTOWN" (MARGATE PARK) (DFA) ⁄⁄⁄ ½   This official dog-friendly area came about in the winter of 1999. Its inception was greatly supported by Alderman Mary Ann Smith, and it's been a big hit in the neighborhood. Only minutes from Janice and Barry's workshop, this is Luna's home away from home. She knows if she's getting a play session or not the second they pull out of their parking lot, based on which way they turn! At printing time, this park was soil, with only spots of grass, although at one time the entire area sported a healthy green lawn. With so much canine traffic, and all of those adorable paws running around, it's hard for the grass to grow. Plans are in the works to hard-surface this DFA. Painted asphalt will be put in, and a few trees will be added for extra shade. A doggy drinking fountain is also scheduled to be installed, as well as a couple of benches.

In the spring and early summer of 2000, several dogs who played primarily at Puptown contracted whipworm, a parasite that is transmitted through feces and lives in the soil. The Dog Advisory Work Group has researched the surfacing issue, and unfortunately there is no perfect solution. D.A.W.G. advisers Dr. Sue Ferraro, president of the Chicago Veterinary Medical Association, and Dr. Rae Ann Van Pelt agree that hard-surfacing (asphalt or concrete) is the most desirable option for Chicago DFAs. D.A.W.G. concludes that surfacing considerations need to be addressed as "what's best for the greater good of the majority of park users, and what's reasonably the best for most animals." Some opponents argue that dogs have an increased risk of getting osteoarthritis on hard surfaces, but research shows that surfacing is not a primary contributing factor for this disease.

Dogs should not run for hours at a time on any hard-surfaced area, including DFAs. People need to cross-train to attain the best workout; so do dogs. Living in a big city presents some unique challenges to dog owners. If you don't drive, you could find a friend with a car and go to one of the off-leash areas outside of the city. Or, with changes in the beach ordinance, playing on the sand with your dog looms as another alternative.

This park is the largest of all the DFAs, and it's not all that big, so it is definitely overcrowded in peak hours. Its rectangular shape allows for a satisfying game of catch, fetch, or Frisbee. Luna looks forward to running with four-legged regulars Lucy, Coby, and Sam. The spot has lots of repeat customers, making it a nice place to meet neighbors and keep up with community news. In winter the dogs love to arrive early in the morning and tramp through the freshly fallen snow. Dog owners have been known to get into a few rousing snowball fights. Keeper, a tiny but mighty Jack Russell terrier, loves these fights; she eats the ammunition.

My own little Lucy and Chaser are regulars here too. On one visit, Chaser lived up to her name—which is pretty rare these days—and joined in a memorable game of chase. Along with Chaser, a 50- or 60-pound mixed-breed pooch, two boxers, a chocolate Lab, a Rhodesian Ridgeback, and a standard poodle were being pursued—actually, they were being herded—by one dog. Pushing all the big dogs around was a 20-pound French bulldog. This dog's ears might have been larger than its head. As usual, Lucy wanted nothing to do with canine games. At one point as the pack ran by, nearly knocking Robin over, she turned to ask, "Where's Lucy?"

Lucy was cuddled up with a police officer. "You poor thing. All these tough guys—it's too much for a little princess like you," she cooed. The officer didn't know how right she was. She explained, "I come here to get my doggy fix, and free entertainment. And being with their dogs, people feel really loose. It's a good time for me to do some real sniffing around myself, to find out what's going on in the neighborhood."

Puptown/Margate Park is located at 4921 N. Marine Drive, just north of Lawrence Avenue, just west of Lake Shore Drive. (773) 275-8448.

REVERE PARK (NORTH CENTER) ✔ ½   This lovely park is dotted with trees—perfect for any canine. To keep canines in line, locals take dog training classes at this park. However, for a real workout, Horner Park (see p. 16), located across Irving Park Road, is a better choice.

Revere Park is bounded by Irving Park Road, Rockwell and Byron Streets, and Campbell Avenue. (312) 742-PLAY (7529).

RIDGE PARK (BEVERLY) ✔✔   With Ridge Park located near the Rock Island commuter train stop, a summer ritual is meeting the family and the dog in the park after work. This is the definitive meeting place for dog owners in the Beverly area, in part because of its proximity to the tracks. The park features six softball fields, so there's plenty of space for stretching canine legs.

Ridge Park is bounded by 96th Street, 97th Place, Longwood Drive, and the railroad tracks. (312) 742-PLAY (7529).

RIVER PARK (LINCOLN SQUARE/NORTH PARK) ✔✔   This tree-filled park is a smaller version of nearby Legion Park. River Park is divided into two parts: East and West. Dog training classes frequently meet in East River Park, which is used more often by dog owners than West River Park. Perhaps the smells are better.

There are baseball fields on both sides of the park. As its name implies, the north branch of the Chicago River splits the park into halves. Access to the river is cut off to dogs and people.

East River Park is bounded by Francisco and Foster Avenues, Argyle Street, and the river. West River Park is bounded by Francisco and Foster Avenues, Albany Street, and the river. (312) 742-PLAY (7529).

ROGERS PARK (WEST RIDGE/ROGERS PARK) ✔✔   Found in its namesake neighborhood, this decent-size park is fine for a fast run with the pooch. There are three baseball diamonds and several tennis courts. Parking is provided. Here is another hangout where nearby residents mingle after work with their dogs. The owners talk while the dogs romp.

Rogers Park is bounded by Jarlath Street and Campbell, Sherwin, and Washtenaw Avenues. (312) 742-PLAY (7529).

SHERMAN PARK (NEW CITY) //   Here's a favorite neighborhood place for dogs to hang out. The park's 60 acres include five baseball diamonds and three soccer/football fields. A bicycle path follows the twisting shape of the lagoon. Dogs are discouraged from diving into the water. However, they are allowed to race against their owners on the outdoor track.

Sherman Park is bounded by Garfield Boulevard, Racine Avenue, and Loomis and 52nd Streets. (312) 742-PLAY (7529).

WALSH PARK (DFA) /// ½   Renovations were completed in the summer of 2000 at this 4,500-square-foot park. Walsh Park Advisory Council/Dog Owner Guideline Society (D.O.G.S.) fought hard for this park and is committed to its success. "This park has gone through major changes," D.O.G.S. chairperson Ananda Breslof says.

Four years ago this space was just an area that Felix the dog walker enclosed with snow fencing. Today it is an official dog-friendly area, offering recreation for neighborhood dogs. There's a wide play area next to a Boston ivy–covered wall, with a large pea gravel area toward the back, complemented by large shade trees. In deference to the hot and humid summers in Chicago, the asphalt is painted a light sand color to reflect the heat. The space is right next to a playground, and lots of families use the park, so be sure your dog is on-leash when walking to and from the fenced-in section. D.O.G.S. is currently raising funds for a doggy drinking fountain.

The entrance to Walsh Park is on Marshfield Avenue between Wabansia and Bloomingdale Avenues. 1722 N. Ashland Avenue. (312) 742-DOGS (3647) or you can contact D.O.G.S. via E-mail at walshparkdogs@aol.com.

WARREN PARK (ROGERS PARK) ///   When snow covers the ground, this is one of the top parks in the city for dogs. Fun-lovers make tracks for the toboggan and sledding hill. No one seems to mind if Fido (on a leash, please) shares the slope. Lazy pooches prefer hitching a ride on a sled rather than racing along beside them. At the same time, some muscular dogs are put to work hauling the kids and then the conveyance back up the hill.

The hill, which overlooks a golf course, is also an ideal place to run the dog and the kids ragged in the summer. The standard operating procedure here is to dash up and down nonstop until exhausted. Lucy, Chaser, and nieces Mallory and Jamie spent the better part of a summer afternoon doing just that. Chaser pooped out and barely crawled out of the park. The kids fell asleep in the car. Lucy wasn't fazed.

Seniors and their lapdogs meet at the benches in the center of the park. This is where 84-year-old Ida Walters and her 10-year-old Pekingese named Sam enjoy a weekly rendezvous with 83-year-old William T. Tyler and his 9-year-old miniature schnauzer, Calvin (named for President Coolidge). Walters and Tyler have a thing going on—they've been playing chess at the park's chess pavilion for five years. Tyler said that he usually wins. Walters winked and admonished, "Don't believe that old crow; I win."

Dogs are not welcome at the children's playground. However, when the baseball diamonds and soccer fields aren't being used, canines can chase to their hearts' content.

There's ample parking in the off-hours, but you'll have to find a street space when it gets crowded. Warren Park is bounded by Pratt Boulevard and Western, Seeley, and Arthur Avenues. (312) 742-PLAY (7529).

WASHINGTON PARK (WASHINGTON PARK) // ½   Snyder, a Labrador retriever–mix, stared intently, as if waiting for a snag on the fishing pole. The old-timer beside him recast his line into the lagoon at 57th Street and Payne Drive and commented, "My dog would rather eat the bait than the fish." Indeed, when he pulled the line from the water, Snyder made a dive to snatch the worm. "One time, Snyder even got the hook caught in his mouth," added Nate, the fisherman. "I wonder how much this dog has working upstairs. He's fun, but he isn't very bright."

A nearby wetland features native plants and passing waterfowl. The Park District discourages dogs from terrifying the ducks. But the dogs haven't been listening.

A bridle path, which is perfect for joggers and their dogs, meanders its way through the park's more than 300 acres.

Dogs aren't allowed at the park's Aquatic Center or the nearby DuSable Museum.

Roads wind through the grounds, and there's usually plenty of available parking. Washington Park is bounded by 51st and 60th Streets, Martin Luther King Drive, and Cottage Grove Avenue. (312) 742-PLAY (7529).

WELLES PARK (LINCOLN SQUARE) //   This small park bustles. Its central North Side location, off several major thoroughfares, offers easy access. There's a paved walking path for on-leash strolls. Other highlights include tennis courts and three baseball diamonds. Dogs aren't allowed inside the horseshoe ring, but you may tie Fido to the fence.

Welles Park is bounded by Montrose, Western, and Lincoln Avenues and Sunnyside Street. (312) 742- PLAY (7529).

WICKER PARK (DFA) /// This small, gated Dog Friendly Area attracts lots of neighborhood dogs. Dog walkers were among the strongest supporters of this park, which today presents some problems. The rules state that only three dogs are allowed per person—but dog walkers are often seen entering with anywhere from four to eight dogs apiece. You need two eyes to watch two dogs, three eyes for three dogs—so watching eight dogs is pretty tough, unless you happen to be a Martian with eight eyes. Community members contend that people can't pick up when they can't keep an eye on the dogs. Indeed, there is too much poo in these parks. A hard surface is in this park's future, but currently wood chips cover the ground. The chips retain urine, and the smell is offensive in hot or humid weather.

Dogs who like to chew have a field day here. We watched one puppy conducting his own wood-chip taste test. The dog's owner ended up with her hand in its mouth every few minutes, pulling out pieces of wood.

The benches at Wicker Park allow for owners to read, relax, and chat with friends. As a result, too many dogs run around without direct supervision. According to Janice, the atmosphere at Wicker Park didn't seem as welcoming as that of other DFAs; perhaps this is due to acrimony among some in the community.

Wicker Park is located at 1425 N. Damen Avenue. (312) 742-DOGS (3647).

"WIGGLY FIELD"/GRACE-NOETHLING PARK (DFA) /// ½ Established as a "pilot" park in 1997, Wiggly Field is now in many ways a model for how other DFAs in the city should be maintained and operated. The park came about because of an anti-dog campaign launched at several nearby parks, including Oz and Jonquil Parks. If those anti-dog terrorists were to get their way, where would the dogs go? After several years of hard work, a committed legion of dog lovers teamed up with the Wrightwood Neighborhood Association and finally persuaded the Park District to devote a park for the dogs. However, back then, all of the funds for the project had to be raised by the Neighborhood Association.

The proven success of this park has been instrumental in creating the Park District's policy and blueprint for groups wishing to establish DFAs. Stacey Hawk, cochair for the Wrightwood Neighbors/Wiggly Field Committee, says, "I am committed to helping people understand the importance of DFAs and continue to offer support and guidance in attaining one in other neighborhoods."

The pint-size park snuggled under the elevated train tracks draws dogs and their humans from miles away. The territory used to have grass, but because of the intense canine traffic, combined with the risk of parasite transmission in soil, Wiggly has been hard-surfaced. A black top would be too hot for the dogs' paws in summertime, so the asphalt is painted green to reflect the heat. The doggy drinking fountain also helps to keep the canines cool.

This is the only DFA with a special "time-out" area that is fenced off, for dogs that need time and space to chill out. There is also a special area planned for agility equipment to be set up. This is designed to be a members-only activity, providing something for the dogs do to besides chase tennis balls.

Screeching trains do scare some sound-sensitive pups. If you're concerned, come early Sunday morning or Sunday evening, when the fewest trains run. One of the chief benefits of this park relates not solely to the dogs but also to their people: Wiggly Field is known to be a choice place for singles to talk and get to know each other—as well as their dogs. The kiosk at the park provides information on upcoming events, public service announcements concerning canines, and a place for pet news to be spread quickly.

Having a couple of comfortable benches here is both good and bad. On the upside, they provide a place for people to sit and read the newspaper, or settle in with a good book and some coffee. On the downside, your attention to duty may wander. Given the confined space of the DFA, some dogs get testy. Owners need to stay close to their dogs; if you're relaxing on a bench or chatting with friends, you're not paying attention to your dog. These habits also contribute to the problem Wiggly has with owners not picking up. Still, this park is quite tidy. That's thanks in part to the volunteer cleanup crew. There is pride in ownership among those involved in Wiggly.

Wiggly Field/Grace-Noethling Park is at 2645 N. Sheffield Avenue. (773) 348-2832.

WINNEMAC PARK (LINCOLN SQUARE) // ½   The shabby, broken-up tennis court isn't of much use for people, but it easily lends itself to playing fetch: a pup can't run off within the confines of a fence. In general, the Chicago Park District allows dogs on the courts over the winter months, as long as owners pick up. However, on our visit these crude courts were locked up tight.

Lucy and Chaser ran across a large grassy area, past a rugby game, past two kids launching rocket ships, and past a grandpa on a leisurely stroll. Grandpa apparently can't see very well—about Lucy, he asked, "What kind of rabbit is that?" . . . Or was he being a sly fox?

Adding to the space is the adjacent Amundsen High School football field. We tossed Lucy a Frisbee at the 40-yard line, and she took off to score a touchdown. You can drive through the center of the park on Winnemac Avenue

Ticked Off

Lyme disease is carried by the deer tick, one of several tick species that make themselves at home in forest preserves around Chicago. And as the deer population continues to rise, so do the number of ticks. The parasites also hitch rides on numerous other critters, such as raccoon and rats.

Some vets think the entire scare about Lyme disease in dogs is just that—a scare, an overrated, unlikely occurrence. However, other vets urge their woodsy clients to vaccinate.

Opinions concerning that course also vary. There are vets who question the effectiveness of the Lyme disease vaccine. Dr. Steven A. Levy of Durham, Connecticut, authored the veterinary reports about the vaccine, and he has no such doubts. His research indicates the vaccine is somewhere between 80 and 100 percent effective, and he suspects that number is closer to 100 percent.

If you visit the woods or forest preserves regularly, Levy recommends the Preventick collar, Frontline spray, or Frontline Top Spot as an adjunct to the vaccine. Chicago veterinarian Dr. Rae Ann Van Pelt prefers ProTICall. However, recent studies indicate potential long-range problems with permethrin, the active chemical ingredient in ProTICall. And Preventick collars applied too tightly may cause skin irritation; applied too loosely, they don't always work. Also, the active ingredient in Preventick is amitraz, which may be toxic if swallowed. Levy warns that the vast majority of over-the-counter products are undependable. The bottom line is that your pet needs something, but check with your vet to determine which product is best.

Symptoms of Lyme disease in dogs include lameness, swollen joints, fever, breathing problems, and, most seriously, kidney failure.

Following a hike in the woods or a run in a forest preserve off-leash area, carefully check your dog for bloodsuckers. Deer ticks are most prevalent in the spring and fall. Other tick species can infect canines with different diseases (including canine ehrlichiosis and Rocky Mountain spotted fever). Levy says northern Illinois, southern Wisconsin, and northwest Indiana are considered reasonably high contact areas for ticks. The threat is even greater should you take Fido camping in the Upper Peninsula of Michigan, central or northern Wisconsin, or Minnesota.

To pull out a tick, don't burn it off, as some books suggest. The mouthparts are likely to remain attached. You may also singe your dog, and dogs don't carry fire insurance.

Use gloves, so you don't chance touching the tick with your bare hands. Simply pluck the bloodsucker out with tweezers, grasping the tick by the head. Then clean the area. If the mouthparts remain attached, there isn't much you can do—they'll eventually fall out.

Be sure to save the tick. In case your dog does have a reaction, your vet can match the tick species with the symptoms.

(which dead-ends at Damen Avenue). There's no legal parking on Winnemac inside the park, but the warning signs don't seem to deter anyone. The park is bounded by the Branch of the Chicago Junior College and its large grassy area where dogs are allowed. Other park borders are Foster and Damen Avenues, and Argyle and Leavitt Streets. (312) 742-PLAY (7529).

WRIGHTWOOD PARK (ROSCOE VILLAGE) // Lucy was a student at a dog training class held inside the field house near the center of the park. Before and after class, dogs dashed around the baseball field. During one mad run for a tennis ball, little 18-pound Lucy was knocked down by two Labradors and a golden retriever. After sliding into third base, she returned very proudly with a ball in her mouth—a wet mass of mud. It had rained the night before, and Lucy paid the price. So did the backseat of our car.

After complying with sit/stays for an hour, the dogs seem to have more energy than usual. Sometimes the canines are cheered on by spectators watching from their balconies. Even dogs who haven't taken the course can be allowed to run free, since most of the park is fenced in. The dogs romp day or night, because the facility is particularly well lit.

Lazier pups can sit with their owners at the cluster of benches found on the northeast side of the park.

Dogs aren't allowed in the swimming pool area and are discouraged from visiting the kids' play lot.

Wrightwood Park is bounded by Wrightwood, Lill, Greenview, and Bosworth Avenues. (312) 742-PLAY (7529).

Cook County
Forest Preserve District

The Cook County Forest Preserve District welcomes dogs, as long as they're on a leash and as long as human companions pick up. Most of the Cook County Forest Preserve land is outside of the Chicago city borders, but two prominent parks are located in the city. The Cook County Forest Preserve parks are open from sunrise to sunset. A free map and further information are available; call (773) 261-8400.

DAN RYAN WOODS (BEVERLY) **//** ½ This is an open area, well suited for canine running games. The 16 picnic groves make it a popular destination. What's more, the setting is romantic—while Bowser nibbles on a piece of chicken, you can gaze at the spectacular Chicago skyline. The view is best just east of Western Avenue and north of 87th Street. For another perspective, try just north of the parking area. Or get away from it all in the secluded wooded area from 83rd Street to 90th Street.

Dan Ryan Woods is bounded by 83rd and 90th Streets, Western Avenue, railroad tracks, and 92nd Place. (773) 261-8400.

WOLF LAKE AND EGGERS GROVE (HEGEWISCH) **///** Dogs aren't allowed in the lake itself, but it's a peaceful place to picnic—rich in nature and vegetation. It's one of the only places to easily sight shore and migrating birds, as long as the dog doesn't scare them off. It's also one of the only places in the county to see the rare sassafras tree, if you know what to look for. Unfortunately, we couldn't find anyone at the Forest Preserve office capable of describing it— that's how rare it is.

Wolf Lake and Eggers Grove are west of the Indiana Toll Road. Exit at South Avenue, and head north to the Wolf Lake access road near the railroad tracks, or continue north to 112th Street, where there's additional parking. The park is bounded by the Pennsylvania Railroad tracks, South Avenue, Wolf Lake Boulevard, and 112th and 130th Streets. (773) 261-8400.

Beaches

Just as any neighborhood can establish a dog-friendly area, the same is now true for beaches. However, unlike the fenced-off dog areas, it's unlikely many beaches will be created solely for dogs. Instead, specific hours of operation will be designated for their enjoyment.

The Chicago Park District and the City made dog-friendly beaches a legal possibility in the summer of 2000. So, there likely will be at least one or two "official" dog-friendly stretches by the time you read this.

The process of creating dog-friendly beaches is pretty much the same as creating a dog-friendly area in a park. A group of interested parties must establish an undercurrent of community support and then work out sensible logistics with the Park District. Obviously, we can't have dogs running around Oak Street Beach at noon during the middle of summer," says Drew Becher, chief of staff at the Park District.

The process includes setting specific hours during which canine users are allowed to romp. Those hours will be decided based on a user survey and what the neighborhood wants. Because of this, community organizations associated with Lincoln Park must be involved in the process. The subject must also be brought up at local neighborhood forums and/or CAPS (Community Alternative Policing Strategy) meetings to allow any objectors to voice opinions. And their objections must be dealt with. Approval from the alderman is more than helpful (hey, this is still Chicago).

It's likely that the hours during which a beach will transform into a dog-friendly place will vary depending on the season. For example, a beach might allow dogs during the beach season only from 6 to 7 A.M. but allow four-legged users from 6 A.M. to 6 P.M. through the fall and winter months.

While I personally express anger when police slap fines on dog owners for daring to take their dogs off-leash for fetch in secluded park spaces, I feel the police ought to be strict about fining people who are silly enough to tote their pups to the beach during the season.

An estimated 10 to 12 million people utilize 15 miles of lakefront in the beach season. Chicago has more beachgoers over four months than balmier cities have over the course of a year. When the sun worshippers are packed tighter than sardines, and the family decides to bring Fido, tempers can flare. Exposing dogs to these crowds is not only against the law but also dangerous to both dogs and people.

Still, savvy owners know that even when there isn't an officially proclaimed dog-friendly beach, it's possible to use the beaches—even in the height of the season—before they open at 9 A.M. and/or after they close at 9:30 P.M. Beach season is from Memorial Day through Labor Day.

When beaches are not considered in season—particularly as snow is falling or the wind off the lake makes Chicagoans feel as if they're living in the Arctic Circle—it seems reasonable to let the big dogs run. But then, owners are technically in violation of the leash law. While the majority of police couldn't care less if a dog is off its leash and running along a beach in November or February, others do ticket.

In theory, there should be no penalty for taking your pooch to these places when the beaches are closed for the season. But this is only a theory—and the law doesn't allow for theory. Also keep in mind the potential danger. A dog could become confused and run the wrong way on Lake Michigan ice and head toward Indiana. A dog could also tumble, crack through the ice, and fall into the freezing water. Worse yet, an owner may follow the dog on the journey. These perils are real and should be soberly considered.

All beaches are free (visiting after 11 P.M. and before 5 A.M. is prohibited). For more information about beaches in Chicago, call (312) 747-0832. For more information on how to develop a dog-friendly beach in your community—which is the best way to go—call the Park District's Dog Hot Line, (312) 744-DOGS (3647). The Dog Advisory Work Group assists neighborhood groups through the process; call (312) 409-2169.

What follows is a description of Chicago beaches—with one exception, they're all beaches for people—listed geographically, from south to north.

CALUMET BEACH/PARK // A formidable stretch of beach used by border-crossing canines from Indiana. A Coast Guard station divides the beach into two. Dogs prefer the smaller stretch, located east of the station, because it's less deep and not so crowded.

This is a popular spot for picnickers. Softball fields are located near the picnic grounds. On the northeast edge of the park is a nearly hidden forested area for dogs and people seeking a retreat. Metered parking spots seem to go on forever on an early Sunday morning in January, but finding a space on a Sunday afternoon in June is another matter.

Take South Shore Drive to the 95th Street exit; the beach continues to 103rd Street. Parking is found directly off the exit at 95th to Foreman Drive. (312) 747-0832.

RAINBOW BEACH/PARK // ½   Basset hounds, beware: the slope drops fast into deep water. Unless your dog is an expert swimmer, exercise caution. Rainbow Park is a haven for picnickers, with facilities conveniently located behind the beach.

The real find is a very shallow beach just south of the water filtration plant at 79th Street. This beach is totally separate from Rainbow. For dog owners, the unnamed location is a hidden gem. This isn't an officially designated Park District location for people and therefore would be a swell place to designate for dogs at specific times.

Take South Shore Drive to the 79th Street exit. The beach runs from 76th to 79th Streets; metered parking is available at 79th Street. (312) 747-0832.

SOUTH SHORE BEACH /   Generally, this beach is too packed and too small for dogs to squeeze into. Parking off 71st Street is limited. Take South Shore Drive, and exit at 71st Street. (312) 747-0832.

JACKSON PARK BEACH //   Here's the perfect puppy beach; you can stroll into the surf about 100 yards and find that the water level remains around your knees and still at canine wading level. The wave action is gentle, too.

It's worth seeing the renovated beach house, which was originally created for the 1893 Columbian Exposition. Chaser has "christened" its wall. And don't miss the adjacent park space (see page 17).

Take Lake Shore Drive to the 63rd Street exit. Limited metered parking is off 63rd Street. (312) 747-0832.

57TH STREET BEACH // ½   The actual 57th Street Beach tucked behind the Museum of Science and Industry is nothing to speak of for dog owners. However, just north of the beach, daredevil dogs dive from a rock ledge. The ledge is near a breakwater called Promontory Point, a traditional place where Chicago canines have come to swim for years. The fact that triathletes train here should tell you that this place isn't for chubby puppies or toy dogs, but it is a great spot for the big dogs to dive in and do their thing. The Park District would be sympathetic to naming Promontory Point an official dog-friendly beach—because of its location away from where people swim and because it's always been used by dogs—but as of this writing, no community leader has officially pursued the effort.

Take Lake Shore Drive to the 57th Street exit. Parking is in the museum lots, and it fills up fast, especially on weekends. (312) 747-0832.

31ST STREET BEACH / ½   With the growth of the nearby Dearborn Park and Printer's Row neighborhoods, this beach is increasingly popular with people, their dogs, and the police who ticket when people come with their dogs. Of course, the neighborhood could do it all legally and create a dog-friendly beach here.

On the south side of the beach, dogs dive off the rocks into the water. Because this area is clearly away from the beach, it's astounding that police waste their time and our tax dollars bothering. George Pimeros lets his Lab dive off these rocks, but he always takes a friend to act as a sentry in case the police rear their heads. "There are gang members in this park, and people throwing beer bottles on the beach—and all the police worry about is dogs," he says. "Does this make sense?"

Take Lake Shore Drive to the 31st Street exit. Metered parking is at 31st Street. (312) 747-0832.

12TH STREET BEACH /   The good news is that this beach is hardly ever crowded. The bad news is that it's mighty hard to find, located east of the museum campus, behind the Adler Planetarium and south of the John G. Shedd Aquarium. If you arrive early enough to beat the museum traffic, you can enjoy a spectacular sunrise and view of the Chicago skyline. Because the drop-off in the water is sharp, this place is best for dogs who truly know the doggy paddle. (312) 747-0832.

OLIVE PARK BEACH / ½   A great destination following a jog from either Hyde Park from the south or Lincoln Park from the north. Olive Park Beach is near dog-friendly activities at Navy Pier (see p. 66). Dogs aren't allowed in the children's play lot.

Located just north of Navy Pier; take Lake Shore Drive to Randolph Street (when coming from the south) or Grand Avenue (coming from the north). Parking at the Pier fills up fast; nearby city lots and limited metered street parking can be found along Grand Avenue and Illinois Street. (312) 747-0832.

OAK STREET BEACH //   Paws down, the city's most popular beach, where natives and tourists flock.

Throughout the summer, dogs are among the predawn visitors, appearing well before the beaches officially open to biped users. The hounds arrive from

Puppy Preschool

Educators don't agree on much. However, there is a growing consensus from dog trainers that preschool is a good idea for puppies. That means starting training classes virtually the moment you get the pup home.

"It's a matter of playing the odds," says Chicago vet Dr. Rae Ann Van Pelt. "I believe the benefits of early socialization and training outweigh the risks of potential exposure [to dangerous viruses]."

Way back in time, in the 1960s and early '70s, pups didn't begin training until they were nearly a year old.

"We now realize that was a mistake," says Dr. Sanford Blum, a well-respected (and now retired) Chicago vet who practiced for 48 years.

Margaret Gibbs, who offers training classes in Riverwoods, was one of the first to change the criterion. She pushed for dogs to begin training much earlier. Still, until the past couple of years, most puppies didn't start their training until they completed their full series of vaccinations. That's usually at about four months of age. Then you may have to wait at least a week or two to actually start the local class. It isn't unusual for dogs to begin training at six months.

Preschool means starting way earlier, certainly by the time the puppy is four months old.

The push to begin earlier is based on the work of legendary canine researcher John Paul Scott more than 30 years ago. He discovered that puppies learn a lot very easily during a fleeting window of opportunity between their 3rd and 14th weeks. He called this the critical period of socialization.

One problem is that dogs aren't usually placed in homes until they're 11 to 13 weeks old. Because of this, Scott felt that it was imperative for breeders to socialize dogs. But, if need be, starting at week 16 is far better than starting at six to eight months. "Remember, the earlier the better," he told me shortly before his death.

"There's no question, puppies enjoy a particularly accelerated rate of learning during that critical stage," says Dr. Nicholas Dodman, director of the behavior clinic at Tufts University School of Veterinary Medicine, in North Grafton, Massachusetts.

continued

Puppy guru and behaviorist Dr. Ian Dunbar of Berkeley, California, suggests that owners invite a hundred people to meet the puppy before its fourth month. Dodman agrees: "Expose your pups to all kinds of extreme extraneous conditions—rabbis on roller skates, cross-eyed Martians, elderly women wearing hats, whatever."

Dodman cautions that owners are taking a risk with a puppy preschool. "The puppies are so amazingly impressionable. Positive experiences are wonderful, developing a well-socialized, confident, and friendly dog. But a negative experience can affect a dog for life. And it can happen even in a puppy class with the best of intentions."

Dodman stages this scenario: You walk into the puppy preschool, and one boisterous pup bolts from a corner, startling your younger pup, maybe giving her a nip. Your pup runs to you for protection, and—oops—you step on her tail. Then, in attempting to scoop her up, you fumble and drop her. In less than a minute, you've created a fearful dog." On the plus side, Chicago trainer Cis Frankel notes that those sorts of experiences don't happen often. Besides, bad experiences can be "undone" easily using treats and praise.

Frankel adds, "Leaving the dog at home under its owners' guidance is the cause of many behavior problems which later become reasons for a dog's being dropped off at a shelter. I'm sure more concerned about the countless number of dogs being euthanized for behavior disorders than a few who may get parvo or some other virus, or get stepped on."

According to the American Humane Association, 10.4 million dogs arrive at shelters annually, and 6.3 million are euthanatized. About 50,000 dogs and cats are euthanatized annually in the Chicago area alone. There are no figures on how many of the dogs suffered behavior disorders.

"There's no question, most dogs being brought into shelters, and ultimately being put down, have behavior problems, or at least their owners think they have behavior problems," says Karen Okura, director of training at the Anti-Cruelty Society in Chicago.

Frankel also points out, "Even a trip to the veterinary office is a risk for exposure or disease. Children who attend preschool frequently catch colds; you can't live in a shell."

However, vets who discourage very early training counter that unlike the potentially deadly parvovirus, children rarely die of the common cold. In puppies, corona may also be deadly. Happily, distemper is now rare.

New York City vet Dr. Jim DeBitteto adds that the expense of treating a pup with parvo or corona might deplete a budget that otherwise might have been spent on training. "Starting puppies too early isn't worth the risk," he believes.

Van Pelt states that trainers in the preschool classes should take responsibility for sending home any dogs that appear ill. Trainers should also require proof that the dogs in the class are in the process of being vaccinated.

Choosing the right class is important. "Absolutely avoid dictatorial trainers who manhandle dogs," Dodman says.

Frankel adds, "Trainers should understand that these puppies have a great capacity to learn, but limited attention spans—after all, they're babies."

Dunbar says, "If the class isn't fun for you and fun for your dog, it's not the right class."

According to Dodman, ideally, trainers shouldn't be mixing eight-week-old pups with eight-month-old toddler dogs. However, the reality is that trainers rarely have classes meant solely for young pups. "Mixing the ages of these puppies, from the very young to almost adult, is how bad experiences can occur," he says.

DeBitteto offers a compromise. His advice is to enroll your pup in a class at about its 12th week. "At least at that age the pup will be stronger," he says. With two of the three vaccinations complete, the odds of getting the parvovirus or corona virus lessen dramatically. The truth is that because of new strains, even a fully inoculated dog of any age stands a chance of getting the viruses.

Despite his reluctance to begin puppies in preschools, DeBitteto is the first to sing the praises of early socialization. He doesn't endorse restrictions on socializing the puppy around people.

As for socializing with other dogs, he says, "Take your dog to a friend's house with a dog that you're reasonably sure is healthy and that you can trust with your pup. Let them play in an enclosed yard." He explains, "The idea isn't to avoid exposure; the idea is to control exposure."

He advises, "Meanwhile, pick up a book on puppy training or a video, and start the process until the series of vaccines has been fully completed."

Chicago vet Dr. Shelly Rubin adds, "Listen, I tell my clients to pick up a book even before the puppy gets home. But most people don't follow up."

Blum concludes, "You didn't begin your schooling when you were 18 years old. A long time ago, we learned that children do best when they begin going to school very early on. The same is true for dogs."

the nearby Gold Coast neighborhood. You know you're in a ritzy area when you can count the dogs with painted nails or jewelry. For example, Chaser was given a proper introduction to Pearl, a bichon frise sporting a string of what I can only assume were fake pearls. But around here, you never know. "My dear sweet dog," said the bichon's owner to Chaser. "This is Pearl. She adores the beach, but please don't kick sand on her. My maid will not arrive today to clean her up."

Police, however, will arrive, and they write a flurry of tickets to the well-heeled dog owners. To avoid this, Oak Street Beach could set aside specific hours for dogs, if and when the community wants it badly enough.

The beach is U-shape, with the bottom side of the U surrounded by water; this design is particularly desirable for off-leash work because there is no place for a dog to run off.

For a relatively tranquil setting, check out the tiny gazebo and bounty of fresh flowers just south of the beach.

You can rent in-line skates or bicycles in the summer months. You can also practice your language skills: tourists from all over the world come here. And friendly encounters with tourists aren't the only possibilities. One owner explains why he comes down from Rogers Park with his black Labrador named Hank. "This beach is a chick palace, and with Hank here, it's like a singles bar on sand."

Take Lake Shore Drive to LaSalle Drive (from the south or north) or to Michigan Avenue (from the north). Look for a metered space west of Michigan Avenue, and then walk back to the beach. Or park in a city lot. Don't bother looking in the Gold Coast north of Oak Street; the parking on the side streets there is zoned for residents only. Access the beach from the Inner Lake Shore Drive underpass or at Oak Street at Michigan Avenue. (312) 787-0832.

NORTH AVENUE BEACH // ½ Navigating the concourse along this beach is a challenge. Street-smart dogs learn to dodge in-line skaters, joggers with baby carriages, bicyclists, police motor scooters, and police on horseback. This is without a doubt Chicago's busiest beach and tough going for dogs not socialized to city life.

Folks are packed tighter than dogs at the Westminster dog show. Beyond the hordes of sun worshipers, beach volleyball games are held here, and there's an outdoor health club as well as a rink for roller hockey. That leaves little space for dogs to even walk by.

Don't despair. On the west side of the Lake Shore Drive overpass, there's a large green space where several baseball diamonds converge. On weekdays, before the social clubs and organized leagues take the field, you can get in a few innings of doggy "fetchball."

There's also a secret dog lovers' hangout on the cluster of rocks that jut out into the water just north of the beach at Fullerton Parkway. The majority of nearby police marvel at canine diving skills. Regardless, diving in off-leash—even though the dogs are away from the beach itself—is still against leash laws. Therefore, my hope is that nearby users of this place will make it all legal rather than continuing their battles with the badge.

Take Lake Shore Drive to North Avenue (where there is very little metered parking) or Fullerton Parkway (where there's even less metered parking). Pedestrians can cross over from Lincoln Park or on the walkway over Lake Shore Drive, located near LaSalle Drive. (312) 787-0832.

**DOG BEACH /// **   What a hypocritical mess!

The Chicago Park District never intended for this place to exist. No one predicted that the natural wave action would create this small parcel of beach at the north corner of Belmont Harbor.

A chain-link fence, which was erected years earlier, extends to the harbor's entrance. The fence happens to open where the beach was formed, so dogs can't possibly run out from the beach and bolt into the park. Several neighborhood dog owners realized this and invited themselves in.

It took all of about two minutes for the place to grow in popularity in dog-dense Lakeview.

The Park District brass weren't particularly enthused about Dog Beach, and they still aren't.

On the upside, to date, this is the closest thing dogs have to their own beach space in Chicago. The fact that it became so incredibly popular so quickly should speak to the need for such a place.

This beach is free, unlike some suburban dog beaches.

Doug Fisher of Park Ridge has come here to let his Afghan hound run with abandon. "Where I live, I can barely walk Sinbad because of all the restrictions," he says. "Here, I can run my dog." Finding a fenced-in beach for a sight hound to all-out sprint isn't easy. However, Fisher and others—especially suburbanites—are sometimes welcomed to the city with a ticket. After all, the police point out, this isn't an official dog park.

Television segments on dogs are often taped here. I personally taped two spots at Dog Beach to promote the first edition of this book, as well as one for "The Oprah Winfrey Show." In fact, I've even seen Park District officials talk about Dog Beach on TV with the implication that this is a good place to take dogs.

Chief of staff Drew Becher points out that Dog Beach hasn't gone through the community process that dog-friendly beaches must now follow.

However, this place has been used for years and could somehow be "grand-fathered in" if the Park District really wanted that to happen. What's more, because it's nowhere near a beach used for people, an argument concerning competing usage can't be made. This beach is strictly for dogs, and everyone knows it.

As for the community's using this place, all you have to do is drive by on a sunny Saturday or Sunday in the spring or summer. In fact, you might find upwards of 35 big dogs on this toy-dog-size beach. Generally, even in these close confines, the well-socialized city dogs get along fine—but there are always a few beach bullies.

Becher also points to real concerns that this beach isn't a healthy place for dogs. To some extent, he's absolutely correct. Local veterinarians, including Dr. Sheldon Rubin at nearby Blum Animal Hospital, confirm that dogs who swim here regularly are often treated for an assortment of problems, including skin, eye, and ear irritations. There's a lot of gasoline in the water, and who knows what other garbage is thrown overboard from boats.

"For an occasional swim, I see no problem," says Chicago vet Dr. Donna Solomon, who also treats dogs suffering from the effects of too much of a good thing. She adds, "Owners should consider that Dog Beach is not the cleanest part of the lake. I recommend that dogs be bathed after spending any length of time in the water."

Dead fish sometimes wash up on the shore following storms. This is when Chaser will attempt to pull me from blocks away to visit. Dead fish are the ulti-mate delicacy.

On one visit, a school of dead fish with a sizable graduating class lay hidden in a corner, beyond our sight—but not beyond the reach of Chaser. One whiff and she bolted, joyously rolling in the stinking collection of rotting fish.

The walk home from Dog Beach was interesting. Robin noticed that after a while, there wasn't a single fellow pedestrian on our side of the street. Even other dogs just passed by Chaser, turning up their noses. Whenever we arrived at a street corner, everyone crossed—even against the light.

Dog Beach is at the end of a working harbor, and a few boat owners have complained about the dogs, mostly based on the fear that a pooch will swim out too far and be struck by a boat.

Because of the debris in the water, the boat traffic, and the limited space, this isn't the best possible location for a dog beach. But it's here, and it's used a lot. So, why ticket people, most of whom have no idea that this isn't a sanctioned dog beach? Because the fence surrounds the beach, these dogs don't present a nuisance to other park users.

Stacey Hawk, cofounder of the Dog Advisory Work Group, has the best solution. She says that if a Dog Beach user organizes other dog owners, the process of sanctioning the space as a dog-friendly beach shouldn't be too difficult. But to date no one has been willing to lead the pack.

Take Lake Shore Drive to Recreation Drive (from the south) or to Irving Park Road (from the north or south). Parking is available at metered spaces in Lincoln Park, near the Totem Pole; then walk south. (312) 747-0832.

**MONTROSE/WILSON AVENUE BEACH /// ** "Amateurs play at Dog Beach, but the pros work out here," says Bill Williams, who visits daily with Dude, his rottweiler. The water is cleaner than at Dog Beach, and there's plenty of adjacent parkland (see Lincoln Park, p. 18).

This beach offers a spacious and easy slope into the water. When the lake level is low, little lagoons form. This is where Lucy learned to do the doggy paddle.

During the beach season, dog owners must avoid the beach (except for off-hours, as described). However, the breakwaters farther from the beach serve as Olympic canine diving boards.

Because of its shallow incline, Montrose/Wilson Avenue is often one of the first beaches to freeze over. Make certain the ice is solid before allowing your dog to run out. Even in mid-January, the ice will be solid only to a point. Lake Michigan never totally freezes over. Exercise caution at all beaches—but at this location especially, which is noted as one where dogs have required rescuing on thin ice and even have perished.

Given all of its attributes, it would be fitting for this beach to set aside some time and space for dogs. However, the neighborhood would have to prove a need and desire, as described earlier, to develop a dog-friendly beach.

Take Lake Shore Drive to either the Montrose or Wilson Avenue exit. Metered parking is available in Lincoln Park. (312) 747-0832.

FOSTER AVENUE BEACH // ½ As the axiom goes, if you don't like the weather in Chicago, wait a minute and it will change. Lucy and I were enjoying a pleasant November evening on the beach. At this time of year, the sun is long gone by 5:30 P.M., but the temperature was still about 50 degrees. By 5:45, the wind had shifted and the waves were pulsating, rocking the sandy shore and blowing lake spray into our faces. And the mercury dropped at least 20 degrees. Even little Lucy, who usually doesn't much mind the cold, let out a howl. With that, we bolted.

Foster Avenue Beach faces northeast, and it's especially susceptible to getting the worst of the northerly winds. Otherwise, it's a nice expanse of beach and a very popular destination. In fact, it might be best described as a smaller version of the Montrose/Wilson Avenue Beach. It's another ideal location for canine owners to develop a dog-friendly beach with designated dog hours.

Take Lake Shore Drive to the Foster Avenue exit. Metered parking is available in the park but fills up fast in peak hours. The beach itself extends from Foster Avenue to Berwyn Avenue. (312) 747-0832.

KATHY OSTERMAN BEACH // This beach is used extensively by residents of the nearby high-rises along the stretch of Sheridan Road that looks a lot like Miami Beach. The density of dogs here is formidable, and this would be yet another great location for dogs to play during designated hours. As of this writing, an effort is underway to sanction that very activity.

Take Lake Shore Drive to the Bryn Mawr Avenue exit; park here, and walk north for several blocks. Or take Lake Shore Drive into Sheridan Road and do your best to find street parking, from Hollywood to Ardmore Avenues. (312) 747-0832.

BERGER BEACH AND PARK *(worth a sniff)* Although officially designated a beach, "rocky outcrop" is a more accurate description. Swimming is dangerous for people and also for their pets. The only canine accessories here are a single bush and a fleeting paved walkway.

Take Sheridan Road to Granville Avenue, and head one block east. There's little nearby parking. (312) 747-0832.

HARDIGAN BEACH // ½ Since dogs use this beach with some regularity anyhow, it would seem a perfect locale for nearby residents to create a dog-friendly beach, so that dogs would legally be allowed at specific times. The local zoned parking could operate in favor of this neighborhood's getting dog beach times, underscoring that the beach is truly for nearby residents only, since outsiders would be dissuaded from driving in.

There's plenty of privacy at this secluded street-end tract, used by locals from east Rogers Park. The beach isn't packed, and dogs actually deter some visitors whom neighbors don't exactly want.

On one crisp sunny October Saturday morning, a snoozing street person clutching his bottle was the only company Lucy and I had. That's until a wide-awake street person entered the scene, seeking to bum a cigarette. We explained that neither Lucy nor I smoke. This place isn't necessarily any more of a hangout for derelicts than any other beach; it just happened to be our luck on this morning.

Cabin Fever

Rain, sleet, or snow, Fido can't always be on the go, sniffing out the best place. What if it's raining cats and dogs? Or if it's just too darn cold? Or what if you have a cold, the sneezin' and wheezin' kind?

"Dogs get cabin fever too," says lecturer and trainer Suzanne Clothier of Johnsville, New York. "When the dog stays in for more than a couple of days, you're pushing it; that energy has to go someplace." Much better to focus on a game rather than the consequences of not having an energy release, including nonstop barking, or taking out frustrations on other household pets or the children. If you have two or three dogs, ever notice how they begin to get on one another's nerves when they don't spend enough time outdoors? According to Clothier, the answer for occupying dogs is the same as it is for kids: indoor games.

"The best games involve a dog's natural abilities, especially using the sense of smell; dogs love games that involve food," adds Berkeley-based veterinarian Dr. Ian Dunbar, founder of the Association of Pet Dog Trainers and author of *How to Teach a New Dog Old Tricks*.

"A side benefit of games is that they also build on obedience and concentration," Clothier points out. "Most important, the dogs really are having a good time." It's also a way to entertain the kids, sort of killing two birds with one biscuit. Thinking tires dogs nearly as much as a run around the block. Dunbar is noted for saying, "A tired dog is a good dog." No doubt most parents would also agree that a tired kid is a good kid.

Very basic obedience is necessary for these games. When children under seven years are participating, adult supervision is suggested. These games should never be played with dogs who have a history of displaying aggression to children or other household dogs. Otherwise, any breed or mixed breed can play any of these games.

Shell Game

Required stuff: One child to hide, and three preferably old and large blankets or sheets.

The rules: Bundle up each of the king-size blankets or sheets and place them in a row, allowing two to three feet of space between bundles. Fluffy sit/stays in another room (an adult can be there to enforce this) while the child hides

continued

under one of the bundles. Think of the old shell game. To release the dog, the supervising adult says, "Find Susie!" Or, if the dog can do a sit/stay on its own, Susie calls out, "Fluffy, come!" When Fluffy sniffs out Susie, she can reward the dog with a cookie and praise.

Hide-and-Seek

Required stuff: One person to hide, and kibble or dog biscuits broken into small pieces.

The rules: Tell Fido to "sit/stay" (an adult can enforce the command if necessary), while someone (you or another person) with a dog treat "hides" no more than 10 feet away so that the pooch can see what's happening. The "hiding" person calls out, "Fido, come!" Naturally, since the quarry is holding a treat, Fido will dash over in record time. When he does, say, "Good boy!" and give him the goodie.

Now do the same thing, but this time hide by turning a corner into the next room. While Fido is on his "sit/stay," let him see you turn in to that room. Stand in the center of the room and call, "Fido, come!" Again, knowing a treat awaits, Fido will be there in an instant. Next time around, return to that same room and now do a better job of concealment, really trying not to be found, by hiding behind or under a piece of furniture. Call, "Fido, come!" When he finds you, make a big deal, praising him lavishly, and give him a cookie. (It's always a good idea to have the pooch sit before you give up the cookie.)

Now the fun really starts. Begin hiding throughout the house, upstairs or downstairs. Eventually, you'll be hiding in closets, in shower stalls, under the covers in bed, and in all sorts of creative places. Once Fido gets the idea, cut down on the treats, offering a cookie only every two or three times he sniffs you out. If a hiding place has the dog baffled, clear your throat or cough for a hint.

If you want to make the game harder, play at night with all the lights off. Or add a player, each hiding in a different place, and Fido must round up both of you.

If you want to play major-league scent-discrimination hide-and-seek, two people hide, and someone else—such as Mom—tells Fido which person he must find. He gets a cookie only if he finds the right person. Elevate to graduate-level search-and-rescue by teaching him to find inanimate objects. Show Fido your keys, his favorite squeaky toy, or your slippers. Begin just as you did when you hid right in front of Fido, and slowly advance the objects to harder-to-find places.

If your dog succeeds at this level, the pooch has the potential of turning "pro," becoming a real search-and-rescue dog, finding people lost in the woods or in crumbled buildings.

Dunbar's Dinner Diversion

Required stuff: The dog's usual kibble or cookies.

The rules: This is a sort of hide-and-seek using the dog's food, or biscuits broken into halves or quarters. Begin by placing Fluffy in a sit/stay, and then scatter the food down the hall along the baseboard, in a place where Fluffy can actually watch you "hide" it. An adult may have to enforce the sit/stay. When you're ready to release Fluffy, walk back to her and say, "Sniff dinner!" or "Seek." Again, Fluffy will be at it in a flash, having seen you hiding the kibble. However, next time around, walk into another room, and "hide" the kibble in there. Fluffy will understand that this is where the kibble is because she saw you walk into that room. At first, make the hiding places easy, but soon, you'll be able to hide the kibble all over the house.

By the way, many real pros use the command "Seek it" for finding favorite objects such as dog toys or dog food. "Find it" is a command specifically used to find a person, or objects with a human scent.

The street person wasn't too intimidated by Lucy, but when a Labrador retriever showed up, he hightailed it out of there. The Lab was hardly a threat, but the dog's mere size was enough to send the man packing.

The beach itself is small and generally kept clean. The layout makes it difficult for a dog to run off. There's also an adjoining children's play lot.

From Sheridan Road, turn east at Albion Avenue. Parking is limited to nearby residents only. (312) 747-0832.

NORTH SHORE BEACH / ½   Solitude is a wonderful attribute. If you show up in off hours, you and your pooch may have the beach all to yourselves.

Take Sheridan Road to either North Shore Avenue or Columbia Avenue, and turn east for beach access. Parking is limited to nearby residents only. (312) 747-0832.

LOYOLA BEACH/PARK / / /   This is the best expanse of dog beach in town, and it was the least discovered, until I wrote just that in the first edition of *Doggone Chicago*. This turn of events has not endeared me to nearby residents, who were inundated with "foreign" dogs from Lincoln Park and Wrigleyville in the city, and from Evanston.

Even during beach season, dogs have periodically enjoyed a stretch of unused space near Farwell Avenue. Certainly, this stands out as a place to make it all legal and create a dog-friendly beach. As usage has increased, so has the number of tickets issued for violations of the leash law.

At the nearby breakwaters, champion canine swimmers do more than the mere dog paddle. Of course, Lucy and Chaser are spectators at the sport of diving. They prefer activities that don't involve water, such as running along the jogging path (on-leash), which leads to a large park space north of the beach. Here there are baseball diamonds, including one that is completely fenced in. When there's no game, your pooch can go deep to chase imaginary fly balls, or just plain flies.

At Lunt Avenue, an informal congregation of dog owners has been meeting for years, letting their dogs off-leash. However, in recent years, they've been watching over their shoulders increasingly for police. They can do better: as explained in the introduction to the "Parks" section, local residents now have a means to create a dog-friendly area.

Take Sheridan Road to the parking and beach access at Touhy and Greenleaf Avenues. Parking in the lots is limited and fills up quickly in peak hours. Due to resident-only zoned parking restrictions, side-street spaces are hard to come by. The beach area extends from Touhy Avenue to Pratt Avenue. (312) 747-0832.

HOWARD STREET BEACH/PARK ✓   Because of limited parking, Howard Street Beach is used mostly by people who live within walking distance. This small, quiet outpost is a great choice for seekers of solitude in the big city. Dogs are not allowed at the adjoining children's play lot.

Take Sheridan Road to Howard Street, and head east. Parking is limited to nearby residents only. (312) 747-0832.

ROGERS AVENUE BEACH/PARK *(worth a sniff)*   This compact beach is encrusted with small stones, which is mighty tough on dog paws.

Take Sheridan Road to Rogers Avenue, and go east to Eastlake Terrace. Parking is limited to nearby residents only. (312) 747-0832.

JUNEWAY TERRACE BEACH ½✓   Some dogs dive off the boulders near this petite beach kissing the Evanston border. Leash laws aside, the small plot of grass is too close to the main drag for dogs to be trusted off-leash.

Take Sheridan Road to where it intersects with Juneway Terrace. Parking is limited to nearby residents only. (312) 747-0832.

Doggy Doings

Being in the Chicago area, your pooch can have quite the social life attending a fancy soiree, a baseball game, playing dog sports, or walking for a cause along the lakefront. Have fun, but remember to call in advance to confirm dates and times.

AIDS Walk Chicago Dogs are welcome to join their people in this walk that benefits various local AIDS organizations. In fact, Barbara Kerant of Greyhounds Only, Inc., organizes "Team Greyhound," and more than a hundred dogs have participated in the walk over three years. The benefits, she says, are twofold: providing exposure to the friendly rescued dogs, and raising money for a good cause. Kerant adds that when her canines are fund-raising, they raise more money than she does. Brian Wiley, executive director of the AIDS Walk, happily registers dogs, even providing them an individual "walker number," just like ones that human participants receive. Wellness stations along the 5K lakefront stroll serve both two-legged and four-legged walkers. The walk begins at Roosevelt and Columbus Streets, travels north to the Chicago Yacht Club, and backtracks to the starting point. People and dogs are sponsored for each mile they complete. The walk is always the fourth Sunday in September. (312) 422-8200; or check the website at aidswalkchicago.org.

All For Doggies This boarding and training facility offers several special programs including "Out of the Snow with Fido." On Saturdays and Sundays, November through early March, All For Doggies opens their facility as an indoor park for dogs. The dogs get out of the cold (and so do their people) and play games of chase while pop music plays in the background. Free biscuits are provided for the pups, and free coffee for their people. Dog publications, *Chipawgo* and *Chicagoland Tails*, are available for information and news.

"On some days it's just too cold to visit the dog parks," says owner Daniel Rubenstein.

There's also agility equipment available to work on. And for dogs who still feel the urge, they have the option to go outdoors to romp in a safely enclosed area.

"Out of the Snow with Fido" is from 10 A.M. to noon on Saturdays and from 2 to 4 P.M. on Sundays. The first visit is free, and all subsequent visits are $10.

As a boarding facility, All for Doggies offers "doggy daycare," and the price includes pick-up and delivery service in their DoggyMobile. Daily boarding includes socialization with "classmates," two meals, and games of fetch for $20. Overnight boarding is $35. 1760 North Kilbourn Avenue (off Grand Avenue). Call (773) 395-0900.

Anti-Cruelty Society Dog Wash   Back in 1994, I had the distinct honor of scrubbing up as a celebrity dog washer for the annual Anti-Cruelty Society Dog Wash. The job isn't all that it's cracked up to be. It's clear that some people wait for this annual event to give their hounds an annual bath.

Volunteers deserve an award for scrubbing, hosing down, and bathing the filthy pooches from 10 A.M. to 2 P.M. on either the second or third Saturday in July at the shelter, 157 W. Grand Avenue. The fee is $10 or $20, depending on the size of your dog, and benefits the Anti-Cruelty Society. Call (312) 644-8338, ext. 301.

Bark in the Park   If you jog with your dog, you might as well do it for a good cause. For several years the Anti-Cruelty Society has held a successful and fun fundraiser—a 5K run/walk along the lakefront. Aside from the event happening on unusually cold days in May, there was no real glitch—until the Bark in the Park, 2000. That year, May was especially hot and humid, and some dogs were fatally struck by heat stroke.

Having veterinarians along the route, everything possible was done for these fallen dogs. Dr. Gene Mueller, director of the Anti-Cruelty Society, was dumbfounded. He attributes the problems to owners who don't typically run with their dogs expecting too much too soon. Obviously, this is not how the humane organization expected their event to turn out. From this point forward, it is unlikely that there will be a 5K run at Bark in the Park. The fundraiser will continue as a walk, and will probably feature some canine games and special appearances by local Chicago celebrities.

The revamped Bark in the Park is still scheduled on the first Saturday in May in Lincoln Park near Montrose Avenue Beach. Call (312) 644-8338, ext. 311.

Dog Days of Summer   The Chicago White Sox invited dogs to the ballpark, and 350 canines showed up at their first annual Dog Days of Summer promotion in 1996. Even more showed up in '97. When I checked in 2000, they told me they had hit their limit at 500 dogs.

Lucy and I had the privilege of judging the contests for "Best Costume" and "Most Talented Dog" in '96. The winners were a dachshund wearing cool sunglasses, who sat behind the wheel of a battery-operated car, and a basset hound who could roll over and play dead on command—for a basset, this is a Mensa-class skill. The top dogs strutted their stuff out on the field before the game. But the dog who garnered the most attention was our own little Lucy. As all the dogs departed the field, Lucy stopped just inside fair territory at third base. She proceeded to do what dogs do on grass. The crowd cheered. But one member of the grounds crew didn't share the enthusiasm. He hollered, "I don't get paid to pick up – – – –!"

Frisbee-catching dogs leaped into the sky to snare discs before the game. During the game, the canine throng took their seats in the right-field bleachers. The team laid out the red carpet for the canine guests—well, actually it was more like green sod with two fire hydrants. Dogs had their own showers for cooling off, hot-dog vendors carried biscuits, Hills Pet Nutrition gave away treats, the Chicago Veterinary Medical Association had vets on hand to answer questions, and several breed rescue groups set up booths, as did the Anti-Cruelty Society. Game tickets are $14 for the bleacher seats where dogs can sit, and there's no charge for dogs. However, canine reservations are required. 333 W. 35th Street; call (321) 674-1000.

Dogs Night Out This canine soiree benefits the Lake Shore Animal Shelter, a no-kill facility on the Near Northwest Side. The event features an elegant buffet for four-legged guests and a separate spread for their people. Raffle prizes include overnight stays at dog-friendly hotels, cases of wine, and a sumptuous supply of dog treats.

Chicago celebrities wouldn't miss the affair. Legendary radio jock John Records Landecker of WJMK Radio is a regular judge for the canine contests, and so is astrologer Lauren Brady. The canine contests are always entertaining. Categories include Best Dressed, Dog/Owner Look-Alike, and Best Dog Trick.

On one 90-degree-plus evening, the usually reticent Chaser caught TV personality Norman Mark, who was serving as emcee, as he reached into the doggy dish to snatch some ice to wipe over his forehead. Chaser went "Woof" in her own not-so-self-confident way. At least 20 people turned around and chuckled at poor Norman. He never did figure out which dog "woofed" on him for stealing ice from the doggy bowl. I never did confess to Norman either, so I hope he considers this disclosure our apology.

Now that Norman has departed for the West Coast, emcee duties have been taken over by comedian Sonya White and broadcaster Jack Curran.

The event is typically held at the elegant Dewes Mansion, 503 W. Wrightwood Avenue. Owner Jim Graca and his English springer spaniel, Bingo, generously donate the venue for the evening. The mansion, which was built in 1896 for brewery owner Frances Dewes, features a cupid-decorated fountain in the first-floor foyer. Chaser isn't the only pooch who sneaked a sip of water from it. To her, this is the greatest doggy water bowl she's ever seen, and it's just the right height. Dogs are allowed throughout the mansion to sniff antique furniture, take the measure of marble floors, and peer out the stained-glass windows. Graca says he doesn't worry: "I have yet to see a dog drop a lit cigarette on a rug, or leave a glass ring on the furniture." He adds that people, not their dogs, have been responsible for all broken plate incidents that have occurred since he began to host Dogs Night Out in 1999.

If it's really hot, dishes of ice water are set out for the dogs, or for hot emcees. Tickets are $65 in advance, $70 at the door. Call (312) 733-6073.

Pet Check at Comiskey Park Comiskey was the first major-league ballpark to welcome dogs. Outside at Gate 6, dogs pay $3 to enter the stadium (admission benefits Canine Companions for Independence, a nonprofit group that breeds, raises, and trains dogs to assist people with disabilities). However, they're stuck in the Bob Uecker seats; the kennels are located down below the bleachers at Gate 7, where hot-dog vendors never tread. During the seventh-inning stretch—or anytime you like—you can check in with your pet.

Pet Check came about to prevent dogs from being held prisoner in hot cars during games.

Be aware: Dog owners are warned against taking pups out to the ball game on Saturday nights because of the fireworks displays. Then again, the scoreboard fireworks boom after each Sox home run. The commotion and crowds are just too over the top for some canines. Reservations are required. 333 W. 35th Street; call the Pet Check hot line at (312) 674-5503 or (312) 674-1000.

Pug Crawl Imagine 80 pugs marching down North Halsted Street. The pugs assemble at the Local Option (1102 W. Webster Street) for the twice-annual event. After about an hour sniffing around at that watering hole, the army of dog soldiers marches to two other nearby bars.

The Pug Crawl is held from 1 P.M. to 5:30 P.M. on two Saturday afternoons a year, in early May and in early September.

It all started when Ben Friedman, manager at the Local Option, held a birthday party for his pug named Knuckles in 1994. "Between the pugs belonging to ex-girlfriends, and other friends, we had about six pugs. I thought it was a great scene—so we simply put out the word to pug people."

Subsequent Pug Crawls have been dubbed "The Million Pug March" and "Running of the Pugs." One couple and their pug rode in from northwest Indiana on a Harley. Each wore a leather biker outfit, including the pug.

While the pug brigade was hiking down the street, an onlooker commented to Friedman, "It's an amazing coincidence—all those people have the same kind of dog."

Recent Pug Crawls have been taped, with the intent to produce a video; perhaps you'll see it soon at Blockbuster.

In addition to the Pug Crawl, there's an annual Christmas party. Friedman calls that event "Pugs Against Hunger." Pugs meet on a Saturday afternoon in early or mid-December at the Local Option. Those who attend must take canned (people) food, which is donated to an organization that feeds the hungry.

There's no charge to participate in any of the pug events. Call (773) 348-2008.

Scrub Your Pup For dogs who look and smell more like Pigpen than Snoopy, check out this do-it-yourself dog wash. All washes at Scrub Your Pup are $15 (shampoos, towels, and brushes are included). You can also drop your dirty dog off for professional grooming. Prices range from $27 to $60, depending on your dog's size and coat. There's free parking in back. 2935 N. Clark Street; call (773) 348-6218.

Shoreline Marine Boat Rides Dogs are welcome guests on the 30-minute sightseeing excursions and shuttle-service rides offered by Shoreline Marine. Dorothy Wiespt, who resides in a lakefront high-rise, takes her standard poodle for a weekly ride. "I like for Beau to get out, and the truth is that I'm too lazy to walk her as often as I should; so, we let the captain do the driving."

The rides depart from Navy Pier (Illinois Street at the lakefront) every half hour from 10 A.M. to 11 P.M. daily (additional late-night rides may be available on Fridays and Saturdays). Fees: $7 for adults, $3 for children under 12 years.

The John G. Shedd Aquarium (1200 S. Lake Shore Drive) is another point of embarkment, every half-hour from 11:15 A.M. to 5:45 P.M. daily. Fees: $6 for adults, $3 for children under 12 years.

Cruises leave from Buckingham Fountain (Congress Parkway at the lakefront) June 1 through August 31, every half hour, from 7:15 P.M. to 11:15 P.M. Fees: $6 for adults, $3 for children under 12 years.

Shuttle service from Navy Pier to the Shedd Aquarium begins June 1 and continues throughout the summer from 10 A.M. to 6 P.M. daily. The 12-minute rides are $5 for adults, $2 for children under 12 years, and are available about every 30 minutes during the week and more often on the weekends. For further information call (312) 222-9328.

Windy City K-9 Club   This upscale kennel is like an East Bank Club for dogs.

Yes, you can board your dogs in this temperature- and air-controlled facility. In addition to providing comfort, this feature somewhat limits the chances of dogs' getting kennel cough or other illnesses from one another. Boarding is $25 per night ($40 for double occupancy) and includes a biscuit before bedtime. But while a trusted and clean boarding facility is always hard to find, it's all the other stuff that goes on here that merits the listing.

- Doggy day care is available Monday through Friday for pups who don't want to stay home alone. There are scheduled morning drop-off and afternoon pickup times. Windy City will even pick up and deliver dogs who don't drive; the cost is $20 for a one-way ticket and $35 for round trip.

- Your best friend can take a flier at flyball—a structured relay race for dogs. Classes are offered in the evening, taught by the Black Sheep Squadron WCK-9 Club. Eight-week sessions take place on Mondays at 7 P.M. and 8:45 P.M. and cost $120 to $160.

- Here dogs can learn how to negotiate anything—on the doggy obstacle course. Agility lessons are held on Wednesdays at 6:30 P.M., 7:30 P.M., and 8:30 P.M. or on Thursdays at 7 P.M., 8 P.M., and 9 P.M. in eight-week sessions, $125 to $175. Call in advance.

- In addition, there's a self-service dog wash, $15 per dog for one hour. Grooming is also available starting at $25 for a basic bath.

- There's also a small upscale gift shop where toys, leashes, and other essentials are sold. You'll find a good selection of small bags that attach to your dog's leash to carry money, keys, and, of course, a supply of plastic bags.

The Windy City K-9 Club facility is a popular spot for private parties. Your dog can celebrate a birthday, a bar mitzvah, or even a wedding in style.

Ring rental is available for open training, agility, or playtime. Call for information. 1629 N. Elston Avenue; (773) 384-K9K9 (5959).

Farmer's Markets

Farmer's markets are a throwback to the days when neighbors met outdoors to purchase fresh items for dinner. Today's markets offer everything from flowers, fruit, and jam to unique sauces, hearty breads, and organic cheeses. Even if you don't buy anything, you can fill up on tasters! From springtime through fall, Janice, Barry, and Luna often visit their local market, on Tuesdays. It's a nice lunch break, and it always inspires Janice to eat more vegetables because they look so pretty sitting next to each other with their bright colors.

While Janice and Barry may tend to window-shop, Luna is constantly busy, walking from booth to booth with a purpose. At least in Janice's neighborhood market, very few scraps go to waste, thanks to Luna. Janice's four-legged vacuum cleaner snacks on crackers, squashed fruit, soy nuts, and bread crumbs. She has also been spotted licking the sign that hangs from the pasta sauce vendor. The woman nicely thanked Luna for cleaning the sign, tossing her a cracker as a gratuity.

If the market falls on a holiday (such as the Fourth of July), it generally is rescheduled or skipped for that week. Farmer's markets don't shut down in the rain—unless it's really bad outside; call for specific information. (312) 744-9187 or visit the website at ci.chi.il.us/consumerservices.

Tuesdays

Federal Plaza Adams and Dearborn Streets; Federal Building Plaza, east of the Post Office; weekly, June through October. Open 7 A.M. to 3 P.M. (312) 744-9187.

Gately 103rd Street and Cottage Grove Avenue; Smith School parking lot; weekly, June through October. Open 7 A.M. to 2 P.M. (312) 744-9187.

Lincoln Square Lincoln, Leland, and Western Avenues; city parking lot; weekly, June through October. Open 7 A.M. to 2 P.M. (312) 744-9187.

Logan Square Logan Boulevard and Kedzie Avenue; parking lot on the southeast corner; monthly, June through October. Open noon to 7 P.M. (312) 744-9187.

Museum of Contemporary Art/Streeterville Chicago Avenue and Mies van der Rohe Street; on the sidewalk along Chicago Avenue; Natural Market and Regular Market on alternate weeks, June through October. Open 11 A.M. to 7 P.M. (312) 744-9187.

Wednesdays

Ashburn 82nd Street and Kedzie Avenue; Brown's Chicken parking lot; monthly, July through October. Open 7 A.M. to 2 P.M. (312) 744-9187.

Chicago's Green City Market Clark and LaSalle Streets; Chicago Historical Society new parking lot, one block north of building off Stockton Drive; organic local products and cooking demonstrations; weekly, June through September. Open 11 A.M. to 6 P.M. (312) 744-9187.

Lawndale Grenshaw Street and Homan Avenue; Community Bank of Lawndale parking lot; weekly, June through October. Open 7 A.M. to 2 P.M. (312) 744-9187.

South Shore 70th Street and Jeffrey Avenue; South Shore Bank parking lot; weekly, June through October. Open 7 A.M. to 2 P.M. (312) 744-9187.

Thursdays

Daley Plaza Washington and Clark Streets; Richard J. Daley Center Plaza; biweekly, June through September. Open 7 A.M. to 3 P.M. (312) 744-9187.

Eli's/Dunning Montrose and Forest Preserve Avenues; Eli's Cheesecake Company parking lot; biweekly, June through October. Open 7 A.M. to 2 P.M. (312) 744-9187.

Gresham 78th Street and Racine Avenue; 17th Ward Office parking lot; weekly, June through October. Open 7 A.M. to 2 P.M. (312) 744-9187.

Hyde Park 52nd Place and Harper Court; cul-de-sac at Harper Court; weekly, June through October. Open 7 A.M. to 2 P.M. (312) 744-9187.

Prudential Plaza Lake Street and Beaubien Court; Prudential Building Plaza; biweekly, June through October. Open 7 A.M. to 3 P.M. (312) 744-9187.

Riverside Plaza Washington and Canal Streets; at 2 N. Riverside Plaza; biweekly, June through October. Open 7 A.M. to 3 P.M. (312) 744-9187.

Saturdays

Austin Madison Street and Central Avenue; Emmet Academy parking lot; weekly, June through October. Open 7 A.M. to 2 P.M. (312) 744-9187.

Edgewater Broadway and Thorndale Avenues; Broadway Armory parking lot; weekly, June through October. Open 7 A.M. to 2 P.M. (312) 744-9187.

Englewood 63rd and Halsted Streets; Plaza at the northeast corner; weekly, June through October. Open 7 A.M. to 2 P.M. (312) 744-9187.

Lincoln Park Armitage Avenue and Orchard Street; Lincoln Park High School parking lot; weekly, June through October. Open 7 A.M. to 2 P.M. (312) 744-9187.

Morgan Park 95th and Winston Streets; on Winston just south of 95th Street; weekly, June through October. Open 7 A.M. to 2 P.M. (312) 744-9187.

Near North Dearborn and Division Streets; on Division between Clark and State Streets; weekly, June through October. Open 7 A.M. to 2 P.M. (312) 744-9187.

Near South 29th Street and Martin Luther King Drive; Dunbar Vocational Career Academy parking lot; weekly, June through October. Open 7 A.M. to 2 P.M. (312) 744-9187.

North Center Belle Plaine, Lincoln, and Damen Avenues; North Center Town Square; weekly, June through October. Open 7 A.M. to 2 P.M. (312) 744-9187.

North Halsted Grace Avenue, Broadway, and Halsted Street; Faith Tabernacle Church parking lot; weekly, June through October. Open 7 A.M. to 2 P.M. (312) 744-9187.

Printer's Row Polk and Dearborn Streets; on the sidewalk between Dearborn and Federal; weekly, June through October. Open 7 A.M. to 2 P.M. (312) 744-9187.

Sundays

Beverly 95th Street and Longwood Avenue; city parking lot on the southeast corner; biweekly, June through October. Open 7 A.M. to 2 P.M. (312) 744-9187.

Bucktown Belden and Western Avenues; Mid-America Bank parking lot; biweekly, June through October. Open 7 A.M. to 2 P.M. (312) 744-9187.

East Side 106th Street and Ewing Avenue; Royal Savings Bank parking lot; monthly, June through September. Open 7 A.M. to 2 P.M. (312) 744-9187.

Lincoln Park Zoo Stockton Drive and Lincoln Park Zoo; on the grounds of the Farm-in-the-Zoo; monthly, June through September. Open 9 A.M. to 4:30 P.M. (312) 744-9187.

Loyola/Rogers Park Arthur Drive and Sheridan Road; Loyola University parking lot on the southwest corner; biweekly, July through October. Open 7 A.M. to 2 P.M. (312) 744-9187.

Norwood Park Raven Street and Northwest Highway; Pullman Bank parking lot; monthly, July through October. Open 7 A.M. to 2 P.M. (312) 744-9187.

Festivals

Chicago city festivals attract many millions of people. No one has kept count of canine attendance, but dogs are welcome at the events as long as they're leashed and their owners pick up.

However, Jim Law, executive director of the City of Chicago Department of Special Events, warns, "We discourage dogs from going to the music festivals in Grant Park, the Taste of Chicago, and the Air and Water Show because the crowds are so overwhelming. Our concern is for the safety and welfare of the dogs."

At the congested Grant Park music festivals and Taste of Chicago, only a couple of inches of grass space act as a buffer zone between picnickers. When fried chicken or barbecued ribs are the main course for your picnicking neighbors, Fido isn't likely to obey the border-crossing regulations. After waiting in line for 20 minutes to purchase a meal, these neighbors are unlikely to have a sense of humor about a food-snatching incident. On top of that, people come to hear artists ranging from Aretha Franklin to Herb Alpert, and they consider the music festivals to be "no bark zones."

Of course, there's also the problem of getting the pooch to the party in the first place. Parking is limited, and spaces often fill up hours before an event begins. Pets are forbidden on public transportation and commuter train lines.

Most people who arrive with dogs either skate or walk in, and they wisely stay on the periphery so they don't get trampled. The smaller neighborhood festivals are more in line with canine tastes. Still, even these are suitable only for city-smart dogs who won't be intimidated by the crush of bodies, the close proximity to other canines, and the general cacophony. If you do take your best friend to a festival, don't forget to take along water for the pooch. In years past, many dogs attending festivals have suffered from overheating.

Note: Special parking arrangements are frequently available for people with disabilities who tote their dogs—either certified assistance dogs or mere pets; call (312) 744-9854.

So, with these caveats, here's a guide to Fido-friendly festivals.

Andersonville MidsommarFest Leave the Swedish meatballs at home; you'll find plenty at this celebration of the Andersonville neighborhood and its Scandinavian roots.

At the door of Swedish Bakery, 5348 N. Clark Street, there's a canine cooling center. Dogs can dive into the refreshing kiddy swimming pool. At noon on Saturday, there's a pet parade with special awards for the "Ugliest," "Prettiest," "Largest," and "Smallest" dogs. Tricky dogs can enter the talent contest or go out for "Best Costume." This festival is on Clark Street between Balmoral and Foster Avenues on a weekend in early June. The suggested donation is $5 (free for children under 12 years and seniors). (773) 728-2995.

Around the Coyote Here's an avant-garde celebration of the arts in the Bucktown/Wicker Park neighborhoods. Many of the 60 galleries in the area open their doors to all guests, including canines.

But not all do. Even demure Chaser was occasionally turned away by snooty virtuosos who refuse four-legged art lovers. Such unpleasantries aside, the majority of the storefront galleries welcome any guest who won't growl at their works. Walking into one gallery, Chaser decided to lick up some of the artwork, a ceramic water bowl made for dogs. A country girl at heart, Chaser noted the practical value.

There are two live music stages—one at the Pontiac Cafe, 1531 N. Damen Avenue, and one at Mad Bar, 1640 N. Damen Avenue. There are also vendors at Wicker Park, 1425 N. Damen Avenue. Your dog will probably beg you to stop at the official dog-friendly area in the park. The festival is always on the second weekend in September, and there is a suggested donation of $5. (773) 342-6777. For more information go to the website at aroundthecoyote.org.

Belmont/Sheffield Street Fair Beware: the hot asphalt takes its toll on both dogs and their people. One year, it was about 100 degrees in Chicago, but the asphalt and the heat from the cooking food warmed the temperature to at least 120 degrees on Sheffield Avenue. Happily, vendors offered dogs ice.

The crush of partygoers can get pretty intense. There's live rock and pop music as well as food booths. This event is typically held on the first weekend in June on Sheffield Avenue from Belmont Avenue to Fletcher Avenue. Admission is $5 (children under 12 years and seniors are free). (773) 868-3010.

Chicago Air and Water Show Chicago's oldest city festival now attracts about two million spectators along the lakefront, from Fullerton Parkway to Navy Pier. Center stage is usually at North Avenue. Midair acrobatics are performed by either the United States Air Force Thunderbirds or Blue Angels (they appear in alternating years). The event also includes powerboat stunts and search-and-rescue demonstrations on the lake. The absolute thrill arrives as jet pilots maneuver at up to seven hundred miles per hour through the gauntlet of high-rises along the lakefront. Some sensitive pooches who live in these high-rises require tranquilizers because of the noise. While dogs are welcome, owners won't be doing their pets' sensitive ears any favors. The show is typically held on an August weekend. Admission is free. (312) 744-3370.

Chicago Blues Festival The city synonymous with the blues is host to one of the most respected and well-attended blues fests in the nation. More than half a million people typically turn out for the three-day event, which is always held over the first weekend in June in Grant Park at the Petrillo Music Shell, Jackson Boulevard at Columbus Drive. Legendary performers such as Muddy Waters, Willie Dixon, Buddy Guy, and Koko Taylor have wowed the crowds. Admission is free. (312) 744-3370.

Chicago Gospel Festival This event is billed as the world's largest outdoor free gospel festival, and about 350,000 people rush over to the Petrillo Music Shell in Grant Park, Jackson Boulevard at Columbus Drive. It always takes place on a mid-June weekend. Entertainment includes traditional artists such as Albertina Walker, and contemporary performers such as Nicholas Ashford and Valerie Simpson. (312) 744-3370.

Chicago Jazz Festival A quieter event than the rollicking Blues Fest but nearly as popular, the four-day Jazz Festival is always held over Labor Day weekend at the Petrillo Music Shell in Grant Park, Jackson Boulevard at Columbus Drive. This annual tradition is the grand finale to Chicago's Jazz Week and Jazz Awareness Month. Performers have included Milt Jackson, Sonny Seals, and the late Count Basie. Admission is free. (312) 744-3370.

Goose Island Fest Live music, chili prepared at the Windy City Chili Cook-Off, and beverages from the Goose Island Brewing Company are on tap. It may be a farewell to summer, but dogs are too busy scavenging for dropped morsels of bratwurst to care what this celebration is for. And most people are too busy partying to care much more. The festival takes place in mid- to late August and is held on Marcey Street from Willow to Wisconsin, just south of Clybourn Avenue. Admission is $5 during the day and $10 at night (free for children under 12 years and seniors). (773) 348-6784.

Lincoln Park Jazz Fest Vendors sell everything from African art to theater posters to outrageous T-shirts. Live music stages are erected on Lincoln Park West from Armitage Avenue to Dickens and at the Chicago Cultural Center. The fest is held on the third weekend in June. Admission is $5 during the day and $10 at night (free for children under 12 years and seniors). (773) 348-6784.

Moon Festival The highlight is a parade that features costumes representing characters from Chinese mythology. Be warned: this is said to be the time for women to ask the Queen of Heaven for a future husband. Chinese culture notwithstanding, the very best way to meet a sweetie is to tote a puppy. Lots of food booths sell cuisine from various regions in China, with the specialty on this day being moon cakes made of rice flour and filled with sweet mashed lotus seeds or red beans. Even if you don't care for this delicacy, your dog will likely appreciate its distinctive flavor. More action revolves around the sidewalk sale and the treasure hunt. Unfortunately, they don't hide dog treats. This event always takes place on one day in late September at the Chinatown Square Mall, at Cermak Road and Archer Avenue at Wentworth and Princeton Avenues. Admission is free. (312) 326-5320.

North Halsted Market Days It can be hard to tell the people from their dogs. We saw one guy wearing a choke collar adorned with dog tags. He was being steered by his partner with a leather leash. Then, there's the standard poodle who wore what appeared to be a long white evening gown with a sign around her backside that read "Don't cry for me Argentina."

Free condoms are passed out by the dancing transvestites. In this arena, recorded music ranges from old Ethel Merman show tunes to "YMCA" by the Village People. Live bands also play at the festival. Vendors sell T-shirts, collectibles, and vintage clothing. Food from an array of mostly local restaurants is offered.

North Halsted Market Days is a favorite festival for canines. But you can't assume that all dogs are friendly. Lucy was nailed by a Great Dane; her screams following the attack were so terrifying that dozens of concerned spectators immediately surrounded her. Lucky Lucy got away with only a scratch. Robin and I later learned that this particular Great Dane attends festivals all over the city and has bitten other dogs. It's unfortunate that this beautiful Dane is so aggressive. It's even more unfortunate that its owner endangers other dogs. North Halsted Market Days is on Halsted Street between Belmont Avenue and Addison and is held on an early August weekend. Admission is $3. (773) 868-3010.

Oz Festival This festival began in Oz Park but has since grown too big for that locale. This is good because many of the residents around Oz Park aren't so crazy about dogs. The event has become more dog friendly at its new location in Lincoln Park, south of the Lincoln Park Zoo between Cannon Drive and the Lincoln Park Lagoon, north of LaSalle Drive.

A few years back, about 50 canines participated in a unique kind of dog show. Judges awarded prizes for the smallest and the largest dogs, the dog that looked the most like Toto from *The Wizard of Oz*, and the dog that looked the most like beloved sportscaster, the late Harry Caray. Each year, the dog show gets bigger.

Many craft and food vendors supply water and/or ice for dogs. At a recent fest, one happy dog was having a fine old time allowing the Tin Man, Scarecrow, and Dorothy characters to pet him. However, when the Cowardly Lion reached down to give him a pat, the dog growled and nipped at the man's feet. "That dog forces me to stay in character," the Cowardly Lion said.

Later a little boy walked up to Lucy and asked, "Do you do tricks?" Lucy never met an audience she didn't like—even if it's only a six-year-old and his mom. I instructed Lucy to sing, roll over, jump over the boy, take a bow, and then jump into my arms. Lucy actually attracted a crowd. An older gentleman approached Lucy and cheerfully said, "You're good enough for that Ed Sullivan Show." Guess he hasn't watched TV in a while.

The Oz Festival features lots of activities and entertainment geared toward children. It's held on the first weekend in August; admission is $5 (children under 12 years and seniors are free). (312) 409-5466.

Printer's Row Book Fair Each year on the first weekend in June, 175 vendors offer thousands of books for sale. Trashy used paperback novels might sell for $1, while antiquarian volumes can cost several hundred. The fair is on South Dearborn Street between Congress Parkway and Polk Street. Admission is free. (312) 987-1980.

Retro on Roscoe Where are Dick Clark and Lassie when you need them? This fest is a blast from the past, featuring music from the '50s, '60s, and '70s. People arrive wearing their now skintight bell-bottoms. One greyhound was spotted modeling a psychedelic vest. Another pooch was doing its version of "The Twist." This event features an antique car show, handmade crafts, and children's activities, in addition to three music stages. Retro weekend is in mid-August on Roscoe Avenue from Damen to Hamilton Avenues. Admission is $5 (free for children under 12 years and seniors). (773) 665-4682.

Rock-Around-the-Block Festival Groove to Chicago's hottest music acts, booked by the Vic, Wild Hare, and Cubby Bear clubs. While live music is featured at most other Chicago neighborhood festivals, the decibel level at this one is too high for most pups. The bands play on a weekend in mid-July at the intersection of Lincoln, Belmont, and Ashland Avenues. Any dogs who dream of doing "Baywatch" duty can have their pictures taken posing as surfer dogs. Admission is $5 (free for children under 12 years and seniors). (773) 348-6784.

Taste of Chicago   It all began in 1980, the grandfather of gastronomic extravaganzas. About 70 restaurants provide tastings of items ranging from turtle soup to kofta (Indian meatballs with yogurt sauce). The 10- or 11-day food frenzy is held in Grant Park and on Columbus Drive from Adams Street to Van Buren Street, just east of Michigan Avenue. The Taste always culminates with a concert and fireworks on July 3.

Musical events include free evening concerts (acts such as Hank Williams Jr., Patti LaBelle, and Al Green have appeared at the Petrillo Music Shell) and a Taste Stage showcasing local bands; as of 2001, such acts will be scheduled to appear at the new Millennium Park. There is a Children's Fun Time Stage and a Family Village for visiting kids and families. Destinations for those who love to cook include the Chef's Demonstration Tent and the Gourmet Dining Pavilion. Also, various radio stations conduct live remote broadcasts.

Yes, all dogs go to sniff heaven when they attend the Taste. Just be aware that 150,000 to 200,000 people per day also attend. If that's not busy enough, on July 3, the Chicago Police Department estimates that about a million people swarm Grant Park. Many dogs don't react well to fireworks or crowds. So, be kind to your best friend, and if you must take Fido, quit the scene early, before the rockets' red glare. Doing so also helps you beat the traffic.

The City has always insisted that dogs are allowed at the Taste. In the past, though, there have been incidents in which people with well-behaved dogs on leashes were asked to leave the premises. At the 2000 Taste, some police didn't seem to mind four-legged festivalgoers. Luna walked around licking up barbecue sauce and melted ice cream with no objection from the men and women in blue. Still, signs at some entrances to the Taste specified "only muzzled dogs allowed."

When I asked a police commander about the ridiculous muzzle signs, he said, "It's the law." I replied, "No, it isn't." Lucy and Chaser were snoozing at home at the time. I didn't have a dog near me, which I'm sure confused the officer.

He said, "Why do you care so much? What are you, the leader of the dog union?"

Some police even threatened to issue tickets to festivalgoers with dogs. One person with a seemingly well-behaved dog on a leash told me, "I have to go. See that cop there? He's following me, and he's given me one minute to get my dog out of here." At the end of her leash was an American bulldog.

Less than five minutes later, I met Chad, a golden retriever. His owner told me that the police crowded around the pair twice, asking if they could pet the dog. She was wearing a bikini, and Chad was wearing a great big golden smile. When I told her that some people with dogs had been asked to leave the Taste, she seemed surprised. "How could anyone not love Chad? Who would have the heart to throw this beautiful dog out?"

The Taste of Chicago gives you one of the best spots in the city to relax on a blanket and people-watch. (312) 744-3370.

Taste of Lincoln Avenue This is the most well-attended of the city's street and/or neighborhood festivals, drawing more than 70,000 people and hundreds of dogs. The block-long Kid's Karnival bustles with face painters, children's games, and arts and crafts activities. Barney has also appeared at this festival, leaving one organizer grumbling, "I wish we could call this a Taste of Barney, but the dogs don't find him tasty—too bad."

Only the sprawling Taste of Chicago offers more restaurant booths. This festival is on Lincoln Avenue from Fullerton to Wrightwood Avenues on the last weekend in July. Admission is $4 (free for children under 12 years and seniors). (773) 348-6784.

Venetian Night Chicago's oldest lakefront festival features a themed boat parade and an elaborate fireworks extravaganza synchronized to music. This free event takes place along the lakefront between the Shedd Aquarium and Monroe Harbor. On a Saturday evening in late July, the activities kick off at 7 P.M. with the Grant Park Symphony Orchestra at the Petrillo Band Shell. The lighted boat parade begins at 8:30 P.M., with fireworks at 9:30. Preceding the parade, the U.S. Coast Guard and Chicago Park District Rainbow fleet demonstrate air and sea rescues.

Here's our canine tip: Arrive several hours before the floating parade lifts anchor, and claim a picnic space on the grass near the Planetarium. The view of the city is inspiring. While this place is hardly a secret, for some reason it doesn't get packed with people until later. For the sake of the dog's ears, split before the fireworks begin. This way you also get a jump on the traffic. Admission is free. (312) 744-3370.

Viva! Chicago The Latin music festival is always held over a summer weekend in Grant Park at the Petrillo Music Shell, Jackson Boulevard at Columbus Drive. Latin artists from all over the world perform. The types of music include salsa, Latin pop, rumba, merengue, cha-cha, and Latin alternative rock. Admission is free. (312) 744-3370.

Recreation Areas

Navy Pier When the City of Chicago and State of Illinois decided to spend more than $150 million to renovate Navy Pier, the plan included creating a place for families to enjoy. Happily, canine members of the family aren't excluded.

Dogs are welcome to accompany their people throughout the outdoor promenade, where the view of the Chicago skyline is awesome. Dogs can also be taken in the open-air walkway where the kiosks stand. One vendor even specializes in pet-related items. Dogs likewise are invited to catch the rays at the beer garden on the east edge of the pier.

Navy Pier was constructed in 1916 as a shipping and recreational facility. Throughout both World Wars, it was used as a principal training ground for Navy personnel. In the 1960s, it was transformed into a temporary facility for the University of Illinois at Chicago. Later, it fell into disuse and became run-down. Among the attractions on the mile-long pier are various restaurants, including dog-friendly Bubba Gump Shrimp Company (see p. 93) and Charlie's Ale House (see p. 93). To work off the calories, rent in-line skates or bicycles on the west side of the pier at Bike Chicago, (312) 944-2337. Children and dogs can cool off by running through the fountain at Gateway Park at the entrance to Navy Pier.

Dogs are not allowed indoors at Festival Hall, at the indoor food court, or in the Botanic Garden. And while dogs are welcome in the amusement area, they aren't supposed to ride the Ferris wheel. But we're told no one has yet made that request.

Parking at the pier itself is limited and fills up fast. More parking is available in nearby lots on Grand Avenue and Illinois Street. However, dogs are forbidden on the free shuttle buses from the parking lots. Most parking is within a six-block radius, and the walk is pleasant in summer months. Throughout the winter, parking is easier to come by. Admission to Navy Pier is free, at Illinois Street at the lakefront. (312) 595-5100.

Midway Plaisance Bordering the southern end of the University of Chicago campus in the historic Hyde Park neighborhood is a 12-block stretch that is perfect for practicing the Frisbee toss. This boulevard lane along 59th Street and Midway Plaisance features lots of green space between the major streets that stretch from Stony Island Avenue on the east to Cottage Grove Avenue on the west. Definitely keep the leash on out-of-control pups who may bolt into the streets.

University of Illinois There's a gated-in grassy space at the southwest corner of the main campus where locals in the Little Italy area take their hounds. You'll even find special bag-disposal receptacles. This dog play area is at the corner of Morgan and Taylor Streets.

Bars

Dogs have something to learn from visiting a bar, according to Chicago dog trainer Cis Frankel: "For puppies, experiencing all the madness that goes on in a bar is great socialization, just so it's all a positive experience."

Lakeview resident Gary Katauskas says he frequently totes his 12-week-old Labrador retriever puppy with him on guys' night out. He doesn't waste time babbling about puppy socialization. He cuts right to the chase. "Let's face it: dogs are a chick magnet."

While that may be true, others merely want to bond with their pets. Mary Wagstaff sat at her regular bar stool at the Marquee Lounge in DePaul with her five-and-a-half-year-old black Labrador retriever named Opal. "Just call us drinking buddies," she said and laughed. "I work full time, so I treasure the time I have with my dog."

Opal stood on her hind legs, reached up, and unsuccessfully attempted to swipe a pretzel. "You should know I watch her salt intake," Wagstaff said, as she removed the tempting snack food.

Another Marquee Lounge regular is a yellow Labrador retriever named Ernie. The poor guy has to drown his sorrows—and for good reason. Several years ago he was in an accident, and a part of his tail was cut off. It's the same routine every visit: Ernie sits near the bar, sips on a cold one, and listens to Sinatra music.

Dr. Ed McGinniss of Lake Villa, past president of the Chicago Veterinary Medical Association, says, "I don't officially endorse dogs drinking beer; still, a sip every now and then can't hurt."

The vet also points out the risks of hanging out in smoky bars. Recent studies have proved that dogs are as susceptible to secondhand cigarette smoke as people are.

Still, people aren't deterred. Taking dogs to the neighborhood pub is a trend. Some tavern owners are worried about the City's bearing down. One owner said,

"The City makes it tough enough on small businesses. Zoned parking and obsessive parking enforcement discourage people from driving here; the higher taxes, the liquor licensing, the politics, the crime—it's ridiculous. But if they don't allow dogs inside my bar, I'm gone."

There's no ordinance that specifically bans dogs from neighborhood taverns. Bars with kitchens, however, are subject to city and state health ordinances and can't allow canines indoors. They can, however, allow dogs on outdoor patios that have their own entrances.

One highly placed official at the Chicago Department of Revenue says that the City looks the other way because there has never been a complaint. He even jokes, "That's as long as the dogs aren't served underage." Of course, if the City begins to get complaints, it will crack down.

The greatest concern is irresponsible owners whose visiting pooches behave badly. Scott Johnson, the owner of Jake's in Lincoln Park, says, "One particular dog was using our bar floor as a toilet. After the second incident, I asked him to leave. We're not a preschool for dogs. And my job isn't local dog trainer. I expect well-trained dogs who sit beside their owners. If your dog can't tolerate other dogs, leave him home."

Proving that well-socialized dogs still know how to party, Eugene Frankowski, owner of Cody's Public House in Roscoe Village, hosts an annual birthday bash on November 7. The bar is named for Frankowski's American foxhound/Rhodesian Ridgeback–mix. The occasion is actually a party for CJ, Cody's son.

Here they are, the places where your pooch may grab a cold one. To make sure the welcome mat has been dusted off, it's always a good idea to phone first.

First, here are bars where dogs are allowed inside:

Bucktown/Wicker Park

Danny's Tavern A relaxed, dog-friendly place to hang out with your pooch. Dogs must behave and be able to socialize with the locals. After 10 P.M. Danny's gets crowded, so the canine contingent must disperse. 1951 W. Dickens Avenue; (773) 489-6457.

Quencher's Saloon You can help yourself and your dog to free popcorn. Sadly, two fixtures dogs dug most about this bar—the giant sign promoting Red Dog beer and the moose head mounted on the wall—have both been stolen. Thus far, even with bloodhounds on the trail, the culprit has not been apprehended. There are cozy couches for people—not dogs—to lounge on. Live music is offered many nights, and there is no cover charge for people or their dogs. However, the music may be too loud for most canine eardrums. 2401 N. Western Avenue; (773) 276-9730.

Rainbo Club "We're extremely dog friendly," says manager Ken Ellis. "To tell you the truth, some dogs are more pleasant than our customers. So far, we've never turned down a dog."

The Rainbo looks like the set of "Happy Days." It's a throwback to an era when the music was simpler, the beer was cheaper, and a guy could walk into a bar with his dog. That's the way it remains here—except for the price of the beer. 1150 N. Damen Avenue; (773) 489-5999.

DePaul

Local Option A longtime haven for dog lovers. On any given late afternoon or weeknight, you may be greeted at the door by two or three canine bouncers. However, you'll want to rule out toting the dog on Friday or Saturday nights, when the bar gets packed. This is where the twice-annual Pug Crawl embarks. Imagine 80 pugs marching around the DePaul neighborhood, going from bar to bar to bar. Recent marches have been the "Million Pug March" and "Running of the Pugs." While Labrador retrievers are the most popular breed in America, according to the American Kennel Club, pugs are the dog of choice at this bar. 1102 W. Webster Avenue; (773) 988-7427.

Marquee Lounge The bartender has been known to whip out a tennis ball for a game of fetch. Dogs can snack on the complimentary pretzels, and lucky for them, water is also provided. This is a champion among doggy taverns. As one patron who hails from a small town said, "Whoa! I love this city! I love to walk up to people and say, 'Can I pet your dog?' It's been a great icebreaker. I've met a few new friends that way." When it gets crowded, Nick, the owner, worries about the dogs' getting hurt and relies on people to use their judgment and know when it's time to take their best friend home. 1973 N. Halsted Street; (312) 988-7427.

Lincoln Park

Glasgott's Groggery Relax and take in the weekend games with your pup. The two of you can choose from more than 20 beers on tap and watch sports on any or all of the eight TVs. Wally, an Irish wolfhound, feels right at home at this local Irish bar and has been bringing his human with him for years. 2158 N. Halsted Street; (773) 281-1205.

Jake's The wait staff dotes on canine customers, offering free hugs and—even better—free treats. 2932 N. Clark Street; (773) 248-3318.

Parkway Tavern Ignoring the yuppification of the neighborhood around it, this tavern solidly remains an old-time hangout, and a place where dogs are part of the fabric. Just make sure your pooch doesn't get addicted to the free popcorn, or the jukebox—or you'll be spending all your quarters listening to "Ain't Nothing but a Hound Dog." Even if it is your pup's favorite song, beware; the music can get loud. 748 W. Fullerton Parkway; (773) 327-8164.

Vaughan's Formerly Redmond's, this is now an Irish bar, offering Irish and English beers. Bartender Lorraine O'Shea says, "Dogs are welcome. We've had every kind of dog imaginable, and I mean the kind with two legs—you know how these guys are around here." When asked if any Irish wolfhounds have visited, she says, "Hey, got me there. But I know we'd love to have one."

When this place was still Redmond's, Lucy and Chaser joined Robin and me to watch the U.S. Open tennis tournament. The place seemed quiet on this Sunday afternoon. However, it soon began to fill up with canines and their people. A collie and a rottweiler started to play, and dog treats were passed around faster than Monica Seles serves. Much to the chagrin of Robin, who is a tennis fan, the subject changed from the match to finding a good dog trainer.

Dogs are discouraged from entering when it gets extremely crowded, particularly on Friday and Saturday evenings.

By the way, Redmond's, which moved up the street, now has a kitchen and no longer allows canine traffic. 2917 N. Sheffield Avenue; (773) 281-8188.

Wrightwood Tap This neighborhood bar welcomes dogs of any kind—just be sure Fido makes a "pit stop" *before* he enters. There's a bowl of water outside the front door. They don't have a kitchen, but you and your canine companion can order food from participating restaurants (there's free delivery). And while you're waiting, your dog will get a complimentary appetizer (a dog biscuit). Just don't get swept away. At times it gets so crowded that, if you have four paws, one or more of them likely will be stepped on. Leo, the manager, worries about the safety of the dogs and discourages people from keeping their dogs out too late. After all, they need their beauty rest. 1059 W. Wrightwood; (773) 549-4949.

North Central

Foley's Bar & Grill Dogs stop in with their people to watch the Chicago Bears. However, owner Wanda Foley reports that few dogs can make it through an entire game. During commercial breaks, she offers dog treats. This bar features several Irish beers. 1841 W. Irving Park Road; (773) 929-1210.

Roscoe Village

Cody's Public House This Roscoe Village bar in the 'hood has always welcomed dogs. Still, owner Eugene Frankowski is reluctant to bark that fact out loud. "My biggest fear is being invaded by crazy suburbanites and their rowdy dogs," he says. "We're laid back and generally pretty quiet—and we like it that way." If you take your dog here, tell her not to spread the word later when she goes to the dog park. 1658 W. Barry Avenue; (773) 528-4050.

Finley Dunne's Tavern Regulars include co-owner Joe Kenny's Labrador/shepherd–mix, Jagermeister, and Ashton, co-owner D. J. Cheatham's Labrador/Doberman–mix. Both of these dogs love people and other dogs, and one requirement is that your dog is equally as social. The bar is named for Finley Dunne, a columnist with the *Chicago Evening Post* in the 1890s. "He was the Mike Royko of his day," Kenny says, "the kind of guy that probably appreciated a good loyal dog." 3458 N. Lincoln Avenue; (773) 477-7311.

Hungry Brain This bar is named for a bar in a Jerry Lewis movie, so especially wacky dogs are at home here. One canine customer, a pit bull/bulldog–mix that the owner calls a "big drooly dog," is honored with his picture behind the bar. Sadie, another four-legged regular, agrees this place has great people watching. 2319 W. Belmont Avenue; (773) 935-2118.

Wrigleyville/Lakeview

The Ginger Man Located within walking distance of Wrigley Field, this tavern has been a neighborhood treat for more than 30 years. Bartender Gary Barnes loves bringing his Akita, Glacier, to work every day. When Jay Shields, another bartender, brings her miniature pinscher, Chen, Gary sneaks both dogs beef jerky! These dogs truly have the dog's life! Canine companions are always welcome, although when the Cubs are in town, it can get extremely crowded, really noisy, and conceivably even dangerous for your dog. The staff looks kindly on dogs and always makes sure they have water. And if Gary is working, they may also get some treats on the house. 3740 N. Clark Street; (773) 549-2050.

Joe's on Broadway It seems that many patrons at Joe's are merely waiting for a table at Angelina Restaurant next door. Sorry, the bartender will not "dog-sit" while you dine. In any case, dogs are welcome at this unadorned tavern. 3563 N. Broadway; (773) 528-1054.

The following bars allow dogs only in their outdoor seating areas:

Bernie's Tavern Location, location, location! This bar is right across the street from Wrigley Field. The staff encourages people to leave their dogs at home on game day, when it's standing room only. Unless you have a Chihuahua that fits in your pocket, it is not safe for four paws to be competing for space. When the Cubbies are away, the pups can come and play! The menu is written on a big board and includes standard bar fare. The most popular item is the cheeseburger and fries. 3664 N. Clark Street (Wrigleyville/Lakeview); (773) 525-1898.

Ginger's Ale House This Irish pub offers a few tables outside at which to sit and enjoy a drink with your dog. They offer an extensive variety of both domestic and imported beers. There are trees, flowers, and lots of space for canines to stretch out. The relaxed atmosphere makes it a comfortable place to meet your neighbors and maybe find some four-legged friends for your pup. 3801 N. Ashland Avenue (North Central); (773) 348-2767.

JT Collin's Pub The outside seating area is a jolly place to enjoy a meal on a nice day. More than just a pub, JT Collin's has an extensive menu. From baked goat cheese in marinara to the Black Angus beef burger, you and your dog are sure to find something delicious. The patio is a comfortable place where you'll want to linger. 3358 N. Paulina (Roscoe Village); (773) 327-7467.

Kelly's Pub Every two minutes, the trains zoom overhead, so many dogs are too nervous to have a good time. One patron hollered out an order from the bar menu as the trains roared by: "A chicken sandwich and two aspirin!" 949 W. Webster Avenue (DePaul); (773) 281-0656.

Lucky Strike Even though your dog can't join you on the bowling lanes, she can sit outside and cheer you on from the patio. Lucky Strike is a bar, a restaurant, and a great place to experience some old-fashioned bowling. Real live "pin boys" set up the bowling pins instead of the machines we're all used to. In addition to character and charm, you get fabulous. The homemade fries are famous. 2747 N. Lincoln Avenue; (773) 549-2695.

McGees Tavern and Grill This Irish pub boasts more than 30 beers on tap and will check your dog's ID before serving him. They have no reservations about bringing out water in a bowl, however. Surrounded by a few trees and flower boxes, you'll notice that the leaves shake and rumble when the nearby train zips by. Don't miss brunch or the Bloody Mary bar on weekends. 950 W. Webster Avenue (DePaul); (773) 549-8200.

Mickey's Grille and Pub Among a herd of restaurants on Broadway with outdoor patios, Mickey's stands out as the place to be to watch sports. Even if you're sitting outside, the TVs are still in view; at the very least, your server will tell you the score. The food here is typical bar fare, with highlights including the skirt steak sandwich, the burgers, and the fresh-cut fries. 2831 N. Broadway (Lincoln Park); (773) 929-2830.

Slugger's World Class Sports Bar It's just down the street from Wrigley Field. You don't want to subject the dog to the masses of tipsy fans who hit the bar after the games; however, when the team is on the road, pooches are welcome to sit inside the wood fence for pizza, burgers, and beer. 3540 N. Clark Street (Wrigleyville/Lakeview); (773) 248-0055.

Tavern on the Pier With three televisions outside, you won't have to miss seeing the Bulls win or the Cubs lose. There are 20 tables, all available for people and their pups. At North Pier Terminal, 435 E. Illinois Street (Streeterville); (312) 321-8090.

Restaurants

Chaser, Lucy, and Luna dine all over town—and we do mean all over town, from munching on the biker brunch at the Twisted Spoke in East Village to sipping tea at Coffee Chicago in Uptown.

At lots of places, the dogs were lavished with special attention. Many restaurants offer dogs a personal water bowl, and some provide biscuits. At the Clark Street Bistro in Lincoln Park, dogs celebrating birthdays receive a free dessert, which they may or may not split with their people. Cucina Bella, also in Lincoln Park, has a separate menu for canine clientele. Instead of a wine steward, this place has a dog steward.

After the first edition of this book was published, some inspectors from the city's health department threatened to withdraw the food license of some restaurants that allow dogs outdoors. Dog-loving Cucina Bella was not about to roll over and play dead. The restaurant's publicist called me for advice.

When I phoned the city, I was told inspectors were only following the health code. Well, that's not right. I learned that the law was not on their side. What restaurants do outdoors on their own property is their business. There is no city or state health code that implies dogs cannot dine outdoors.

I spoke about the issue on my radio show and as a guest on several TV stations. Meanwhile, the *Chicago Sun Times* and *Lerner Newspapers* also wrote prominent stories addressing this "dog discrimination." It was a column written by my colleague John Kass in the *Chicago Tribune*, however, that forced Mayor Daley to address the issues publicly. He explained that he has no problem with dogs eating outside, along sidewalks, or in patios. "This is a city where we all can enjoy wonderful restaurants, as long as the dogs don't create a disturbance." He continued, "I like dogs. Dogs are good companions."

As if by magic, the inspectors left the restaurants alone, and there are now more listings in this edition than there were in the first. Of course, any dinner guest is expected to act properly, even those with four legs. It isn't considered proper to steal food from the next table, bark at those who pass by, or run into the kitchen to snatch a few table scraps. In all, we personally visited more than 70 restaurants and coffeehouses. And not once did we witness obnoxious canine dinner etiquette serious enough to disturb others.

One puppy did whine a bit and continually tried to get up from the down command. That was our puppy, Lucy. At the time she was only about four months old. Because Lucy, Luna, and other city dogs begin their alfresco experience at a young age, they quickly learn the ropes.

It's easy to control your pup when he or she is right there at your table. However, some restaurants prefer tying dogs to the rope, chain fences, or posts that are on the border of the outdoor eating area. Not only can't you control your dog, but sometimes the pooch may be a nuisance to pedestrian traffic. While some dogs will lie down patiently, tying up a dog nearby is still not our preferred way to dine with doggies.

Another problem is inconsistent canine policy. In most instances, canine researchers actually ate at the places listed here. And in all cases, restaurants' canine-friendly policy was confirmed at least twice before going to press. Still, a snotty manager may decide not to allow dogs. Or perhaps on a crowded evening, when there's a wait, customers with dogs aren't considered worthwhile. At one restaurant, I'm absolutely certain we waited longer for a table just because we happened to have dogs with us. Of course, restaurants can do what they like— so it's always best to call in advance.

What follows is a list of restaurants by neighborhood. A separate list of places for quick bites—such as hot dog joints or spots for ice cream or bagels—follows. I've also listed coffee shops that allow dogs.

Bon appétit!

Andersonville

Andies Restaurant You may dine with your dog if you're lucky enough to get one of the four window seats, allowing your dog to sit beside you on the street. The weather must be nice enough to have the doors open. The restaurant does not take reservations for these special tables, but it's worth the wait; the food is fresh and filling. The focus is on Lebanese and Greek cuisine. Janice goes for the tabbouleh and the chicken gyros with the yogurt sauce. 5253 N. Clark Street; (773) 784-8616.

Pauline's This relaxing outdoor seating area surrounded by flowers was the scene of Luna's first restaurant-dining experience. The owner himself, Ron Messier, came out to greet her, sharing stories about his beagle. If your pup is thirsty, water is supplied faster than she can bark, "Waiter please." Luna was comfortably lying near the tree on the patio, basking in the attention being showered on her, when she was only 12 weeks old! Being more than a year old now, she continues to wag her tail here, even though it's Janice and Barry who are enjoying the home-cooked comfort food. The five-egg omelets, Pauline's potatoes, and the huge buttermilk pancakes are a Sunday favorite. For lunch, you can't beat the grilled cheese, chili-mac, or any of the homemade soups that are just like Grandma used to make. Janice and Barry have never had a bad meal here, though the weekend brunch hours can get frenetic. Don't miss the giant bowl of candy near the register for a sample of old-fashioned favorites such as Mary Janes and Bit-O-Honey. 1754 W. Balmoral Avenue (at Ravenswood); (773) 561-8573.

Bucktown/Wicker Park

Gallery Café Formerly the World Café, the Gallery Café exudes the same friendly atmosphere. Local artwork covers the walls, and a new menu tempts with a colorful sandwich list. If you're feeling creative, try the Picasso sandwich (tuna salad) or the Warhol (ham and cheese). Daily breakfast specials and an extensive coffee selection make this café a pleasing destination when you're out on a morning constitutional with Fido. The dog-friendly patio always has a full water bowl. Even when patrons aren't staying for a meal, the large glass container filled with doggie biscuits makes this a regular stop on many dogs' routes. 1760 W. North Avenue; (773) 252-8228.

Li'L Guys/My Pie When you're of two minds about what to eat, what could be more convenient than two restaurants in one? That's what you get with this unique combo. Li'L Guys features an assortment of small sandwiches, and smoothies. My Pie offers pizza in the pan and a healthy salad bar. The dog-friendly patio has two doggie bowls and a comfortable seating area with umbrellas. During the dog days of summer, shade is a must! Inside there are complimentary doggie biscuits which can be delivered to the tables of canine guests. 2010 N. Damen Avenue; (773) 394-6900.

DePaul

Athenian Room Greek chicken, Greek salads, and hamburgers are delivered to human guests, and water is delivered to the dogs. On-street parking. 807 W. Webster Avenue; (773) 348-5155.

Chicago's Pizza More than just pizza, this restaurant dishes out sandwiches, chicken, and burgers. Many dogs have been known to convince their people to order the chicken-wing appetizer while waiting for the stuffed pizza to arrive. If your dog isn't afraid of the trains, the outdoor area is a relaxing place to eat. When you and your pup get the late-night munchies, keep in mind that Chicago's Pizza will deliver until 5 A.M. 3006 N. Sheffield Avenue; (773) 477-2777.

John's Place Lots of dogs take their people here, especially for Sunday brunch. During our visit, while the 30-minute wait for a table dragged on, Lucy and Chaser got to chew the fat with other canines. For those seated outdoors, elephant-size double doggy bowls are filled with water.

The breakfast was good, featuring French toast nearly too thick to cut, Mom's buttermilk pancakes, and a smoked-salmon omelette. Juices are freshly squeezed, and our breakfast guest—coffee maven Jan Motley—did cartwheels over the java. On-street parking and a bike rack make coming and going convenient. 1000 W. Webster Avenue; (773) 525-6670.

Leona's This large outdoor seating area holds about 40 people and is big enough for any family dog. There are flowers all around, though the restaurant has had problems with their disappearing. Luckily, they're not accusing any of the dogs of eating them; they believe it's an outside job! Noise-sensitive pups may be disturbed by the nearby trains. This family-owned restaurant has a large menu; pizza and pasta specials are bestsellers. 3215 N. Sheffield Avenue; (773) 327-8861.

Robinson's No. 1 Ribs Robinson's maintains that its slow-cooking process removes most of the fat, so these baby backs are relatively low in calories. Right.

The dogs don't seem to care about that. Canines who have the good fortune to get tossed extras agree that these ribs are indeed number one. Canine guests are welcome in back and on occasion are offered dog treats. That's nice, but they prefer the ribs. There's on-street parking, but it's hard to come by in the evening due to resident-only parking restrictions. 655 W. Armitage Avenue; (312) 337-1399.

Food for Thought

So, you decide to dine at one of the restaurants listed in these pages. Naturally, your dog will want to dine too.

Veterinary nutritionist Dr. James Sokolowski says that the challenge is to keep the total number of snack food, junk food, and people food calories to less than 10 percent of the dog's usual calorie total.

It sounds easy, but Sokolowski points out that for a 30-pound dog, two potato chips a day might meet the limit. If you do offer people food while dining alfresco, try sticking with steamed vegetables. They have fewer calories and are much healthier than potato chips. Although Sokolowski concedes that if you usually feed your dog a balanced dog food diet with a minimum of snacks and people food, pigging out occasionally on a slice or two of pizza, a hunk of steak, or pasta with meat sauce isn't going to throw the dog into a nutritional tailspin. Just keep in mind that too much of a good thing can make a pooch sick.

Shine Garden Sichuan and Mandarin Chinese is served at this sidewalk garden with seats among flower boxes along Freemont Avenue. 901 W. Armitage Avenue; (773) 296-0101.

Downtown/The Loop

Brasserie Jo If your pup is really lucky, he or she may get to meet one of the most famous chefs in the country. Chef Jean Joho is a dog lover, and it shows. Being a French dude, he isn't reticent about lavishing affection on canine guests seated within the brass railings set along the sidewalk. The Brasserie buzzes, so your pooch better be used to lots of action. Servers may whiz by with Alsatian onion tarts, steamed mussels, or coq au vin. Valet parking. 59 W. Hubbard Street; (312) 595-0800.

Corner Bakery Sit at one of a handful of tables along the sidewalk on Clark Street. The petite outdoor café is usually busy, and it's a tight squeeze. They don't have table service here, so you must leave the pooch outside while choosing your pizza, muffins, or any of the 10 to 15 home-baked breads indoors at the counter. It's no stumbling block if you're with someone who can watch the dog while you order. 516 N. Clark Street; (312) 644-8100.

Emilio's Tapas To experience summer in the city while enjoying a delicious meal, this elegant outdoor seating area is the place to be. While you're dining at a table appointed with white linen and fresh flowers, your dog can be lying next to you sharing your night out on the town. This is a great place to go with an entire pack of amigos, so you can sample a variety of dishes. The grilled calamari and grilled octopus, goat cheese baked in tomato sauce, and Spanish omelette are some of the most popular items. Your dog may want to whet his whistle at the decorative fountain, but the wait staff will bring out his very own water bowl, instead. Sorry, dogs aren't allowed to sip sangría. 215 E. Ohio Street; (312) 467-7177.

Mambo Grille Here's a fusion of South American, Puerto Rican, and Mexican; all in all, food with an attitude. But beware: many items are way too spicy to share with a pooch. There are seven tables outside.

Entrees include arroz con pollo (chicken and rice), zarzuela de mariscos (seafood Creole stew), and chiles rellenos. Robin and I can highly recommend the Cuban sangría, and I hear the margaritas are great.

Parking in nearby lots. 412 N. Clark Street; (312) 467-9797.

Nick & Tony's Nick & Tony's happens to be smack-dab in the heart of downtown Chicago, with wrought-iron furniture set along Wacker Drive across from the Chicago River. Even though there are 195 outdoor seats, tables may be hard to come by at the noon hour. Because of the nearby train and general downtown lunchtime frenzy, Chaser, who can be a nervous Nellie, stayed home. With Lucy, the short walk from our parking space to the restaurant took more than 20 minutes. For friendly passersby, seeing a nine-pound puppy stroll confidently down Michigan Avenue isn't a common occurrence.

Finally, we arrived to do lunch with Donna Marcel, editor of *Dog World* magazine. Lucy performed a perfect sit and then politely offered a paw to "shake" while Donna reached down to pet her. That's when Deanne E. Gloppen, a vice president at Draper and Kramer Inc., came by. "I can't believe this trained puppy," she raved. "I have two untrained dogs at home driving me crazy." She added that one trainer recommended against enrolling one of her dogs because it was only six months old. Marcel returned to the office inspired to write an editorial on the importance of early training. Lucy's impeccable training failed, however, when she decided to box with a shadow under Gloppen's Victorian dress.

Nick & Tony's is a loosen-your-belt-buckle kind of place. Generous portions of home-style pastas are prepared like Grandma used to (if she happened to be Italian). Even the salads are large.

Walking back to the car, we felt like celebrities. Among Lucy's on-street admirers was a woman visiting Chicago on business who sorely missed her own dog. When asked how long she'd been away, she answered, "All day." And then there was the couple from Finland who didn't speak a word of English. Lucy understood their affections just the same. Parking in downtown lots. 1 E. Wacker Drive; (312) 467-9449.

Tattoria Parma We're told that only well-behaved dogs are welcome at this quality Italian restaurant. Green tables are covered with salmon tablecloths under umbrellas, amid fresh flowers and ivy-filled planters. Entrees include linguine with roasted garlic and zucchini; grilled pork chops with spinach and ricotta cheese; and penne bolognese. Valet parking. 400 N. Clark Street; (312) 245-9933.

East Village

Twisted Spoke At this former site of a 1960 gas station, the sign now has a revolving motorcycle instead of the original dinosaur. They're open for lunch and dinner, but the real hoot is the biker brunch. For pooches spooked by the whir of a Harley, the Twisted Spoke brunch isn't a good choice. The motorcycles pull up with a roar. If you don't happen to be sitting on a Harley, you can park yourself at one of eight picnic tables surrounded by trees planted in steel drums.

Canine customers get a bowl of water and a bounty of biscuits. Brunch choices include a breakfast burrito and corned beef hash and eggs. On-street parking. 501 N. Ogden Avenue; (312) 666-1500.

Gold Coast

Carmine's This large, albeit somewhat cramped, outdoor dining area has 20 tables. Ten of them are available for you and your pup. Here you're in the center of the Gold Coast, and Rover will be grateful for an evening on the town. The food is definitely worth coming out for. The oysters are fresh, and the radiatore pasta with vodka sauce is excellent. This Italian restaurant will not let you go home hungry. In fact, you will most likely leave with a doggie bag, with no complaints from your four-legged escort. 1043 N. Rush Street; (312) 988-7676.

Chicago Rib House This large outdoor area has 14 tables from which to choose, making it an easy place to dine with your dog. The menu reflects the management's laid-back attitude, stating, "If you're looking for good food and a friendly face . . . Don't move!" Your pooch will no doubt be drooling over the smoked baby back ribs and the rib tips, but be careful if you share: rib and chicken bones are very soft and can easily get stuck in dogs' throats. Rover may be willing to settle for licking the BBQ sauce off your fingers. 800 Dearborn Street; (312) 751-2233.

Fuzio The friendly staff at this restaurant have a soft spot for dogs. According to a server, "huge" dogs such as Saint Bernards and Great Danes may have trouble dining comfortably outside with their owners. And when it's crowded, their presence makes it difficult for the servers to maneuver around all those big paws. Otherwise, "normal"-size dogs such as Labs, golden retrievers, and smaller breeds are usually accommodated. The global menu offers dishes from Thai to Italian. Each meal is prepared in the open kitchen for guests to see. 1045 N. Rush Street; (312) 988-4640.

Yvette Human customers will have to pay for their pâté at this French bistro, but a single serving is delivered to canine clientele gratis at the few seats adjoining the sidewalk where dogs are allowed. The pâté is cut in a rectangle and served with fresh greens. "We are a French restaurant; of course you get served first," said the waiter as he knelt down to present the plate to Chaser.

Nan Mason, a piano bar performer, returned from a break and asked for requests. On Chaser's behalf, we offered "How Much Is That Doggy in the Window?" Mason complied.

Deep in the heart of the Gold Coast, Yvette is great for people—or dog—watching. One passing standard poodle (no doubt familiar with this French eatery) stopped for a tentative sip of Chaser's water but then quickly walked off. We figured she must prefer bottled water, which is available here for dogs. Open since 1982, Yvette is a bustling Chicago mainstay. And the live music is among the best in the city. There's no cover charge. Parking is in the lot across the street or on-street. 1206 N. State Parkway; (312) 280-1700.

Hollywood Park/Peterson

Martino's You may dine with your dog outside as long as no customers object to eating next to a four-legged, furry guest. You can always tie your dog to the other side of the fence, but for dogs who must be within a paw's reach, this may be a tad too far. Five tables are covered by an awning to keep you and the pup cool in the hot sun. Specials include the pasta del mare, the chicken Vesuvio, and the fried calamari. 3431 W. Peterson Avenue; (773) 478-5410.

Via Veneto If your shy pooch enjoys privacy, you'll be glad to know that canine guests dine behind an iron fence and a Plexiglas barrier at this regional Italian restaurant where the specialty is seafood. Away from the competition, Via Veneto offers a good value. On-street parking. 3449 W. Peterson Avenue; (773) 267-0888.

Lincoln Park

Ann Sather This pint-size location has about six outdoor tables on Drummond Avenue. Naturally, you can still order the excellent Swedish pancakes or cinnamon rolls. On-street parking. 2665 N. Clark Street; (773) 327-9522.

Big Shoulders Cafe Located at the south end of the Chicago Historical Society, the café is only inches from Lincoln Park. Canine guests aren't only welcome—they're expected. An especially popular place for weekend brunches, and great salads at lunch. Dinner is not served here. 1601 N. Clark Street; (312) 587-7766.

Bordo's Eatery and Sauce Owner Todd Bordenaro and his friendly staff have an affinity for dogs. You even receive 15 percent off your bill, Monday through Thursday, if you show the wait staff a picture of your dog (or any pet). The patio has 10 tables and four water bowls. Many neighborhood dogs stop by for a drink, and the regulars know that dog treats are available upon request. Dining on busy Lincoln Avenue can be interesting; sitting among the parking meters adds to the urban atmosphere.

Bordo's is a proud sponsor of Wiggly Field and generously hosts various Dog Advisory Work Group committee meetings and events. Janice is a regular. She makes it a point to take Luna along to dog-related meetings in the summer when Luna can sit outside. In the winter, she only takes pictures of Luna. She and Luna usually schmooze over appetizers and highly recommend the quesadillas, the black bean and hummus platter, and the artichoke and spinach dip. When Luna is staying for dinner, her favorite is the Bordo's burger, and Janice likes the veggie rotolo, one of the many pasta selections. If you're too full to order dessert, you can indulge in a piece of Bazooka bubble gum or other penny candy from the jars scattered throughout the bar. Late in the evening, you can usually spot a line of young, single "beautiful people" waiting to get inside. Bordo's is definitely one of the North Side's places to be seen. 2476-78 N. Lincoln Avenue; (773) 529-6900.

Clark Street Bistro When it's your pup's birthday, take along proof and you can share a free dessert. One would expect no less from a French bistro with a tinge of Italian influence—perfect for a French poodle/Italian greyhound–mix. Chairs are lined up along Wrightwood Avenue.

Fido will appreciate steak aux pommes frites way more than the free dessert, but you'll have to pay for that. Other entrees include lamb shank, duck breast with wild mushrooms, and various pastas. On-street parking. 2600 N. Clark Street; (773) 525-9992.

Cucina Bella Indisputably the most dog-friendly restaurant in the city. This place is too classy to allow canines to chow down on the bare pavement, so place mats with caricatures of dogs are set out before the biscuit basket arrives. The for-dogs-only basket is filled with pig ears, doggy truffles, chew sticks, and real Italian bread.

Some restaurants have wine stewards; Cucina Bella has a dog steward. He offered recommended daily specials. "The spaghetti tossed in a light marinara is quite lovely today," he explained. The girls wagged their tails at that choice, which they agreed to share (there is no extra charge for dogs who share). Their pasta, garnished with a parsley leaf, was presented in ceramic dog bowls. Meanwhile, human guests enjoy Italian comfort foods such as country-style rigatoni; rosemary, lemon, and garlic–baked chicken; and spinach fettucine with fresh seafood.

We began to dine under clear skies, but ominous dark clouds quickly rolled in from the west. Chaser and Lucy both chose doggy doughnuts for dessert, but we didn't have time to indulge—the skies opened up, and it began to rain cats and dogs. This is the downside of dining with dogs. Finishing the meal in the dry dining room just isn't an option.

While there's no charge for items from the doggy biscuit basket, you have to pay for the special canine pastas. This is the ultimate dog-friendly restaurant because the dogs get to eat out, too. On-street parking. 543 W. Diversey Parkway; (773) 868-1119.

Four Farthings Tavern and Grill An ambitious menu offers more than standard bar food. The atmosphere, however, is strictly that of a neighborhood bar. Seating outdoors is across from a tiny park, which is handy for bathroom breaks. There's almost always at least one dog out here. We're told there never has been a dogfight for the best seat in the house—table number one, located near the fire hydrant.

Robin and I arrived with Lucy and Chaser in tow. The woman seated at the next table with her two-year-old commented, "I hope your dogs are well behaved; my child is sensitive." We assured her that once Chaser and Lucy are told to lie down, they stay until they're released from the command (most of the time). For the next 20 minutes, all we heard was that sensitive kid screaming, crying, and ranting, "I want dessert!" Naturally, the parents gave in and the brat got dessert. He finished Mom's dessert, too. We became worried when the kid eyed my burger. The burgers here are good, and so is the chicken Caesar salad. On-street parking. 2060 N. Cleveland Street; (773) 935-2060.

John Barleycorn Memorial Pub Inc. Once a speakeasy where John Dillinger hung out, this pub and burger joint does not allow dogs in the spacious patio. However, dogs are allowed at the tables located on the sidewalk on Orchard Street. They must be tied to the railing and seated on the outside of the railing. This works fine, since the dog can still hear, see, and smell you. 658 W. Belden Avenue; (773) 348-8899.

Lakefront Restaurant The kind of place for a quick salad or sandwich, and they have really good coffee. The seating space under the green awning used to be dog friendly, but the rules have changed a bit. The manager told me dogs can be tied to the fence or a post about three feet away but may not sit directly with the customers. Last year a customer got bitten by a dog, and the restaurant got sued. A prime example of why humans need to be in tune with how their dogs act in a crowd. 3042 N. Broadway; (773) 472-9040.

Lou Malnati's The deep-dish pizza here is arguably among the best in this city boasting the best deep-dish in the nation. The problem is that everyone knows this, and there are only a pawful of tables along Wrightwood Avenue. On our most recent visit here, the host told us that the wait—on that Friday night in September—would be 40 minutes. Perfect. We walked about two blocks down the street and let Lucy and Chaser burn off calories at Wiggly Field (see p. 28). After 20 minutes of park time, we returned to the restaurant and had to stand by for only another 5 minutes to be seated. The staff delivers water to your pooch, but not pizza.

On-street parking. 958 W. Wrightwood Avenue; (773) 882-4030.

Noodles in the Pot Dogs relax in a shady concrete garden behind an iron fence at this Thai restaurant. 2453 N. Halsted Street; (773) 975-6177.

Rizzata's This Italian restaurant is happy to have dogs and people enjoy a meal outside in the warm weather. Although the patio has only three tables, there is plenty of room for Fido to relax. Try the pizza, or one of the enormous meatball sandwiches. 953 W. Willow Avenue; (312) 640-1299.

Lincoln Square

Daily Bar & Grill Even on a busy night, the outdoor seating area on Lincoln Avenue is a comfortable and peaceful place to enjoy a meal. Tables with umbrellas are surrounded by a few trees, which your dog will appreciate. The menu ranges from standard appetizer items to classic comfort foods. The chicken potpie is a big seller, as is the macaroni and cheese. Water is offered to all visiting pooches. 4560 N. Lincoln Avenue; (773) 561-6198.

North Central

Gino's East Legendary deep-dish Chicago pizza is always worth the trip. The outdoor seating is at the edge of the parking lot, so make certain the pooch is tied in place. 2801 N. Lincoln Avenue; (773) 327-3737.

Little Bucharest Behind a wrought-iron fence, visitors are transported to Romania. With the fresh flowers and an occasional violinist playing tunes from the old country, the effect is just about pulled off. Of course, the genuine offerings such as goulash and stuffed pork chops help. On-street parking. 3001 N. Ashland Avenue; (773) 929-8640.

Que Rico! Dogs are warmly welcomed, but there isn't always a seat. Only a handful of patio tables and chairs are found at the entrance of this small family-operated Mexican cantina. On-street parking. 2814 N. Southport Avenue; (773) 975-7436.

Old Town

Fireplace Inn Restaurants may come and go, but this Old Town institution shows no signs of wavering. The primary product became barbecued ribs more than 25 years ago when the Novak brothers played a hunch that the idea would catch on. It did. In fact, Bill and Hillary Clinton once called in for a delivery directly to the president's airplane parked on a runway at Midway Airport.

Dogs dining outdoors are a relatively recent addition here. The restaurant is still reluctant to allow canines in the main section of the outdoor dining area, fearing complaints from grouchy non–dog lovers. Still, dogs can hop onto the deck where the bar is and where folks chomp on ribs while watching ball games. There are also several dog-sanctioned tables surrounding the bar. Valet parking. 1448 N. Wells Street; (312) 664-5264.

Fresh Choice This restaurant that specializes in healthy fast food also caters to four-legged guests and their humans. The outdoor patio seats about 20 people, with plenty of room for dogs. If you are dining with your dog and can't go inside to order without leaving her alone, Fresh Choice provides a bell you can ring for outdoor service. A server will appear to take your order, and in addition, water and biscuits will be brought out for your pooch. The highlight of partner Cara Board's day is when Cornflake, a teacup poodle, comes to visit, grabbing healthy snacks along with her mom, Audrey. Sit and sip a smoothie, while enjoying people-watching in Old Town. 1534 N. Wells Street; (312) 664-7065.

Hong Kong Bay Your leftovers may be too spicy for Fido if you order the favorite garlic or kung pao sauces with any of your entrees. The moo-shu is popular, as is the sushi menu. There are four tables on the sidewalk surrounded by lots of Old Town activity. 1531 N. Wells Street; (312) 222-2228.

Trattoria Pizzeria Roma A quaint spot to enjoy dinner alfresco with friends, family, and canines, just like they would in the old country. The flowers are abundant, and the umbrellas keep you and pups comfortable in the shade. The fresh menu changes daily. 1535 N. Wells Street; (312) 664-7907.

Uncle Julio's Hacienda This patio is large enough for nearly any dog to dine outside comfortably. On the busy corner of North Avenue and Clybourn, there is a lot to look at. Mexican specials include fajitas and enchiladas. Pooches with a full weekday schedule can come for the Sunday brunch. 855 W. North Avenue; (312) 266-4222.

Ravenswood

Zephyr Nearly any time you drive by this long-standing art deco restaurant, you will spot a crowd. Zephyr has something for everyone, including simple meals, but it's best known for ice cream, most notably banana splits and sundaes. Since Barry and Janice live in the neighborhood, this is one of Luna's favorite destinations on hot summer evenings. 1777 W. Wilson Avenue; (773) 728-6070.

River West

Club Creole A Louisiana Catahoula dog ought to be the mascot at this Cajun/Creole restaurant. The attitude is laid-back at this sparsely decorated sidewalk café. If you need to tone down a notch yourself, a Hurricane (a rum and fruit juice drink) or a Sazarac (Jim Beam rye, bitters, and anisette) will do the trick. Specialties include étouffée and gumbo. On-street parking. 226 W. Kinzie Street; (312) 222-0300.

Kinzie Street Chophouse Steaks are always a favorite for dogs. Of course, too much of a good thing isn't recommended. Again, we mean for the dogs. But one bite of steak can't hurt Fido, and the chops here are ample hunks of meat—large enough to cut off a piece for pooch.

There's room for 75 people, and at least a few dogs, on Kinzie Street perpendicular to the train tracks at Wells Street. However, the rattling and screeching trains may spook sound-sensitive pups.

On-street parking or in nearby lots. 400 N. Wells Street; (312) 822-0191.

Roscoe Village

Kitsch'n The retro brunch menu is a blast from the past. Unfortunately, your pup won't be able to check out the cool decor on the inside, which immediately evokes thoughts of the Brady Bunch and the Partridge Family. Fortunately, the outdoor café in the back is done up with pink flamingos and plastic flowers to inspire the same cheesy charm. There's also a tiki hut–style bar that serves coffee and the house specialty, a "Tang-tini"—a martini made with Tang (just like what the astronauts used to drink!).

After a night of partying with your dog, you may want to try the Chilaquiles "Levanta Los Muertos." The menu claims this is "the ultimate hangover breakfast to raise the dead," a spicy mix of scrambled eggs with lots of extras. The "Eggs in a Basket" is Janice's favorite, and her husband Barry always gets "Green Eggs and Ham . . . Sam," eggs scrambled with spinach pesto and other green veggies. Lunch and dinner items include yummy comfort food and "TV Dinner Entrees." Don't worry, no tinfoil trays are involved. The creativity at Kitsch'n goes beyond the names of the menu items. Be sure to save some room for dessert; try the "Twinkie Tiramisu" or the "Pop-Tart Sculpture." The latter is the most imaginative presentation of a Pop-Tart you've ever seen.

While waiting for your meal, you may play with an Etch-a-Sketch or a Mr. Potato Head toy. This restaurant does everything it can to ensure that your dining experience is a positive one. 2005 W. Roscoe Street; (773) 248-7372.

Piazza Bella Trattoria This neighborhood Italian restaurant is happy to make room for doggies wishing to dine alfresco. Luna and her friend Maggie, a shih tzu/poodle–mix that fits in the palm of your hand, enjoyed a beautiful summer evening together smelling fresh pasta and seafood. The tomato, mozzarella, and basil salad is good to the last drop, topped with fresh basil picked from the small herb garden that grows on the patio, on which dogs are not allowed to graze. Both dogs behaved well during dinner; Luna quietly chewed a rawhide she had stolen from Maggie, while Maggie slept in her mom's purse. At the end of the meal, Luna made a scene by proceeding to slurp from the decorative fountain for five minutes straight as other guests watched and laughed. Luckily, she didn't slurp up the pennies. 2116 W. Roscoe Street; (773) 477-7330.

Victory's Banner This quaint little outdoor eatery has just enough room for you and your pooch to sit inside the yellow wooden fence. If it's crowded, your dog may need to relocate to the other side of the fence. If it's sunny, you can seek shade under the umbrella, and hope there's a breeze. Breakfast specials include the Greek omelette and, for when you're feeling slightly decadent, chocolate chip pancakes. 2100 W. Roscoe Street; (773) 665-0227.

Village Cafe and Pizzeria This small patio offers a quiet place to relax and enjoy a leisurely meal. Big dogs may have a hard time sitting right next to you if it's busy, but they can remain reasonably close on the other side of the fence. For a tasty brunch, stop by on weekends until 2 P.M. 2132 W. Roscoe Street; (773) 404-4555.

Emergency Care

As with people, unforeseen injuries to pets happen all the time. Although Lucy, Chaser, Luna, Breathless, Bonnie, Bayla, Kalea, Sophie, and all the other pooches who participated in canine research for *Doggone Chicago* made it through the experience unscathed, we did witness injuries to other dogs.

In Libertyville, we were watching dogs playing what seemed like an innocuous game of fetch. Hank, a Labrador retriever, landed wrong after jumping for a tennis ball. He failed to walk off the injury, and the owner drove him to the vet.

On another occasion, in Lincoln Park, Robin noticed a guy with a rottweiler and a Siberian husky, both off-leash and both growling at passersby. Another guy innocently walked by with two huskies on-leash. Before her eyes, the off-leash rottie and husky lunged at and attacked his leashed dogs. We immediately took our dogs to safety and left the scene.

We also saw a dog run off from Oz Park into Lincoln Avenue, narrowly missing getting sideswiped by a car. The owner was more shaken than her dog. But what if that dog had been hit? Are owners prepared to play pooch paramedics?

Here are some first aid tips from Chicago vet Dr. Shelly Rubin.

Biting

Even your own dog may bite if the dog is in enough pain or is totally frightened, so muzzling an injured dog is a good idea. A necktie, a nylon stocking, a clothesline, an extra leash, or a belt can be tied over the muzzle of long-nosed dogs.

Dogs with short, pushed-in snouts can't be muzzled, but they can be restrained by taking the shirt off your back and slipping the dog through it. A towel can also serve this purpose. For maximum control, hold the dog around the back of the head with both hands. If you're dealing with a small dog, you'll probably need an extra pair of hands.

Bleeding

Profuse bleeding must be stopped. Create a tourniquet by using a necktie, belt, or rag. You can also try applying pressure with a towel or rag to halt the bleeding. See a veterinarian immediately.

Glass cuts are very common, particularly among dogs who swim along the rocks at Lake Michigan. Use gauze to bandage the cut. Glass cuts may be deeper than you think, and, in most cases, veterinary care is suggested. You may not see it, but the tendons between the foot pads may also be cut, and this must be treated by a professional.

For superficial cuts, clean the area with 3 percent hydrogen peroxide, and apply pressure. If bleeding stops, fine. However, see a vet if the bleeding continues.

Back Injury

Minimize your dog's movements by placing the pooch on a stiff board. If you can't find a piece of wood, use a collapsed box.

Broken Limb

Obviously, veterinary care is required immediately. If there's an open fracture, treat it with 3 percent hydrogen peroxide. Create a splint using a wooden board for a large dog, or a rolled-up magazine or a paint-mixing stick for a medium-size or small dog. Use rope, a necktie, a rag, or duct tape to tie over the splint. Don't encourage the dog to walk; gently lift him or her up.

Lameness

If the dog comes up limping from exercise, simply stop the activity and rest. If it worsens and/or the limb appears to be bearing no weight, call your vet. In most cases, the dog will bounce back within 30 minutes, and certainly within 24 hours.

Puppies often twist the wrong way; it hurts, so they scream as if they're in agony. Most often, the puppy is simply scared. By coddling too much, people train their pooches to be melodramatic actors who can solicit loving attention from an entire park. Most often the words "Let's play fetch" or "Do you want

continued

the ball?" are enough to bring down the curtain on their little performances. However, a pup could be seriously hurt. If the whining persists, or you simply have doubts, call the vet.

Animal Bites

Dogs biting other dogs is all too common. Carefully assess the injury. This isn't easy on dogs with heavy coats, but it's necessary. If there's enough bleeding for you to repeatedly wipe, or if the dog seems to be in pain, see a veterinarian immediately. Bites often do more damage beneath the surface than on the surface, and it takes an expert to check them out.

Strange as it sounds, the dog may begin to suffer up to 12 hours later. Seemingly out of nowhere, a previously invisible puncture wound can begin to bleed, and your dog may cry out in pain. Even if your dog appears to be fine, apply 3 percent hydrogen peroxide and keep a close watch on the wound. Don't bandage it. If bleeding does begin again, or if the dog is in pain, see a vet immediately.

Following is a list of emergency veterinary clinics. Some veterinary offices also offer emergency hours. For further information you can call the Chicago Veterinary Medical Association, (630) 325-1231.

Animal Emergency Center
1810 Frontage Road
Northbrook, IL 60056
(847) 564-5775

Animal Emergency of Lake County
131 E. East Town Line Road
Vernon Hills, IL 60061
(847) 680-8600

Animal Health Care and Emergency Clinic
4533 S. Harlem Avenue
Forest View, IL 60402
(708) 749-4600

Animal 911 Ltd.
9851 Gross Point Road
Skokie, IL 60077
(847) 328-9110

Chicago Vet Emergency Service
3123 N. Clybourn Avenue
Chicago, IL 60618
(773) 281-7110

Emergency Animal Service
118 E. Kirkland Circle
Oswego, IL 60543
(630) 978-1111

Emergency Veterinary Care
13715 S. Cicero Avenue
Crestwood, IL 60445
(708) 388-3771

Emergency Veterinary Services
829 Ogden Avenue
Lisle, IL 60532
(630) 960-2900

We're glad you want to visit destinations listed in *Doggone Chicago*, but be like a good Boy (or Girl) Scout, and be prepared. According to Rubin, the following items should be in a canine first aid kit and kept in the car or at hand at all times:

Duct tape

Gauze rolls

Sterile gauze pads

Scissors

An old magazine (*Cat Fancy* will do nicely)

A blanket

An old T-shirt

Rope

An extra leash and collar

Plastic bags

Streeterville

Bice Ristorante The crowd is sophisticated and stylish at this upscale contemporary Italian restaurant. Who knows, your pooch may become a star. This is where fashion photographer Victor Skrebneski has discovered several models. At the noon hour, rub elbows with local CEOs and the ladies who do lunch on the outdoor patio. A parade of chefs has resulted in a lack of dining room direction. Management prefers that dogs occupy the outer perimeter of seats. Valet parking. 158 E. Ontario Street; (312) 664-1474.

Bubba Gump Shrimp Company, Navy Pier Located near the entrance to the pier, the spacious patio is enclosed by iron fencing. Dogs usually sit here rather than at the adjacent karaoke bar, which is where the action is Thursdays through Sundays. The meal begins with a basket of homemade breads (dogs enjoy samples) and is followed by basic American fare and a smattering of pastas. All salads are made with fat-free dressings. Parking is at the pier or in nearby lots. 700 E. Grand Avenue; (312) 595-5500.

Charlie's Ale House, Navy Pier Discriminating dogs will be impressed with the wide selection of beers. Food is a tad overpriced, as is often the case with tourist places. Recommendations include burgers and Bernie's chili. Take your camera—the view of the city is spectacular, particularly with Fido posing in the foreground. The restaurant is at the south promenade at Navy Pier. Parking is at the pier or in nearby lots. 700 E. Grand Avenue; (312) 595-1440.

Wrigleyville/Lakeview

Ann Sather's A nice spot to have a hearty sandwich or a healthy omelette. A varying assortment of fresh breads is placed on the table. The zucchini bread is Janice's favorite. Ann Sather's is famous for the cinnamon rolls, and they are perpetual bestsellers. Luna didn't get her own, but she did get to lick the frosting from Janice's fingers. 3416 N. Southport Avenue; (773) 404-4475.

Bamee Noodle Shop White plastic chairs and tables are arrayed behind a green picket fence. Lots of specialties are pepper-laden for a fiery taste. Recommendations include ginger chicken, spicy basil leaves, and nam sod salad with lime juice, ginger, onions, and dried peppers. Tofu or vegetables can be substituted for any meat selection. On-street parking. 3120 N. Broadway; (773) 281-2641.

Bistrot Zinc It wouldn't be a French bistro if dogs couldn't sit outside. Water bowls are presented to any four-legged visitor. Should the pup require a refill, a waiter simply taps the street-side spigot. Voilà!

The accent here is on the national French sport of wine and cheese tasting while people-watching with your best friend at your side. But don't be an ugly American. On busy Southport Avenue, other dogs are bound to walk by, so your pooch must be well behaved.

Of course, Bistrot Zinc wouldn't be a truly authentic French bistro without the simple yet incredible food. Our sole complaint is that the outdoor menu is somewhat limited. Valet parking. 3443 N. Southport Avenue; (773) 281-3443.

Chicago's Renaldi's Pizza In addition to thin crust and pizza in the pan, Renaldi's is famous for its *spingione* pizza—a Sicilian special with a "light and fluffy" texture. The vast selection of toppings will task your decision-making skills. Luna was content to sit outside and gobble up errant crumbs and pieces of cheese or sausage. The seating area is cozy for both humans and canines. Lush vines crawl up the wooden trellis, and a few trees nearby add to the greenery. The menu also lists an extensive selection of Italian specials that looked appealing, but we were too full from the pizza to try any of them. 2827 N. Broadway; (773) 248-2445.

Cousin's After an exhausting evening at dog agility class, Luna joined Barry and Janice for dinner alfresco at this Middle Eastern establishment. About five tables are available on the sidewalk, with a view of retail shops and Border's bookstore on Broadway. Luna was so tired that she barely lifted her head to say hi to people passing by, and the waitress was extremely impressed at how well behaved she was. The trick is lots of exercise! The ezo gelin soup is excellent, as is the jajik yogurt dip. 2833 N. Broadway; (773) 880-0063.

Cullen's Bar & Grill Dogs are welcome at this Chicago version of an English pub decorated with umbrellas and large flowerpots. All pooches are offered water and dog treats.

The menu for people includes fish-and-chips and chicken potpies. Inside there's live Irish rock music (which can be heard outdoors) on Wednesdays and Sundays. No cover charge for people or their pets. Valet parking. 3741 N. Southport Avenue; (773) 975-0600.

Cy's Crab House The evening that Janice and Barry took Luna to Cy's for dinner, Luna practically had the run of the patio. The grassy area in front of the tables gave her room to stretch out. Janice's cousin Errol, visiting from Australia, was amazed and delighted to have the opportunity to dine with the whole family, puppy included. According to Janice, the seafood at Cy's is some of the freshest in town. The grilled swordfish was amazing. 3819 N. Ashland Avenue; (773) 883-8900.

D'Agostino Pizzeria Chairs are roped off behind a series of pickle barrels. Management prefers the dogs on the outside of the ropes. Old-style red-and-white-checkered tablecloths cover the outdoor tables and are held in place with Chianti bottles. This place hasn't changed much over the years. On-street parking. 1351 W. Addison Street; (773) 477-1821.

Deleece This outdoor seating area is just north of the corner of Southport Avenue and Irving Park Road. The setting includes a few trees for your dog to enjoy, and umbrellas for keeping things shady. The traffic gets heavy on days when the Cubs are playing at home, making the environment noisier than usual for dogs and making the trek more difficult for people. Good choices here are the traditional bouillabaisse and the flavorful oven-roasted half chicken with rosemary, thyme, and garlic. 4004 N. Southport Avenue; (773) 325-1710.

Dish Owner Patrick O'Dea lives upstairs with Nelson and Dyna, his two sociable basenjis who often come downstairs to greet customers. Although they're not happy about it, they watch as their dad unloads a pocket full of biscuits to all canine guests.

O'Dea calls the cuisine "progressive American." Nightly specials include at least three fresh seafood picks and assorted vegetarian dishes. Dish boasts an extensive wine list and a wide variety of microbrews. Open every night except Monday at 5 P.M. and for brunch on weekends. 3651 N. Southport; (773) 549-8614.

Las Mañanitas Mexican Restaurant Dogs are so common here that the sight of canines sprawled out along the sidewalk doesn't merit a second glance. The wait staff will usually provide water for the dogs and margaritas for their people. Chaser liked the water here, and I felt the same about the margaritas. 3523 N. Halsted Street; (773) 528-2109.

O'Donovan's We dig O'Donovan's, mostly because it makes a great hangout for Lucy and Chaser, but also because we're cheap. On Monday nights you can order a burger for a buck; Tuesdays it's 10 cents per chicken wing; Wednesdays it's meat-loaf-and-mashed-potato mayhem, $1.95; on Thursdays a full rack of ribs is $8.95, and that's with fries; fish and chips is the cheapo special Fridays, $4.95; Saturdays get more upscale—New York strip steak and potato for $9.95; and $7.95 for prime rib on Sundays is a steal. The food is really down-home good, and so is the canine hospitality.

People have two outdoor places from which to choose—though dogs have only one. There's a patio adjacent to the parking lot. That's right, a city restaurant with its own parking, and it's free. This is exceedingly important for people who are too cheap to pay for valet service. Dogs are not allowed on this flower-filled patio because the only entrance is through the dining room. However, dogs can rest in the shade of umbrella tables along the sidewalk. Dogs with late-night munchies will be happy to learn that this place is open until 1 A.M.

Robin figured, for a buck, why not? She sacrificed her burger to Lucy and Chaser, and then ordered another for herself. 2100 W. Irving Park Road; (773) 478-2100.

Once Upon a Thai Noodles Dogs and their people can sit inside a green railing held in place by flower-filled buckets. On-street parking. 3705 N. Southport Avenue; (773) 935-6433.

The Outpost Even if it's drizzling out, you can keep your hand on the neighborhood pulse from under the sprawling canopy. While you're savoring seared ostrich, tartare of tuna, or pizza with goat cheese, your dog will be busy watching the parade of canines pass by. Given the high volume of Cubs traffic, you should probably check the home schedule and do your dog a favor by not dining out during a game. 3438 N. Clark Street; (773) 244-1166.

Penny's Noodle Shop Tucked beneath the tracks, the seats on the sidewalk rumble whenever a train goes by—which can be every two minutes during the dinner hour. Dogs who aren't into reverberating trains should avoid this otherwise great stop for Asian noodle dishes. A sweeping golden canopy protects diners from the sun and rain. Specialties include pad thai (stir-fried noodles with egg, tofu, peanuts, bean sprouts, green onions, and cilantro); lad nar (wide rice noodles stir-fried with broccoli, carrots, chicken, and fresh ginger); and a surefire-cure-for-the-common-cold chicken soup. The outdoor seating begins at 5 P.M., and dogs must be tied up outside the fenced-in dining area. On-street parking. 3400 N. Sheffield Avenue; (773) 281-8222.

Pizza Capri Janice, Barry, and Luna are fans of the stuffed spinach pizza, and they make Pizza Capri a destination when they have out-of-town guests with two legs and/or four. The wait staff is friendly, and the server usually delivers water for Luna even before they ask for it. The patio, surrounded by flower boxes, is large enough to accommodate big dogs. 964 W. Belmont Avenue, (773) 296-6000; and also 1501 E. 53rd Street, (773) 324-7777.

Roscoe's Tavern and Cafe Flower boxes and plants brighten the awning-covered café along Roscoe Street, which is open only after 5 P.M. Fridays and Saturdays, and Sundays after noon. In the evening it's a predominantly gay nightclub. Great salads and basic burger and pasta dishes are the principal fare. On-street parking. 3356 N. Halsted Street; (773) 381-3355.

Samuel's Old-Fashioned Deli There aren't many seats, but there's enough room to share a pastrami sandwich and pickle with your pup. Before you do this, I recommend Cur-Tail, a product to curb canine flatulence. On-street parking. 3463 N. Broadway; (773) 525-7018.

Strega Nona The tables in the outdoor dining area are close together, and servers worry about stepping on tails. While you eat, your dog must be tied to the outside of the fenced-in area—a fact of life that some people and some dogs just won't tolerate. Shoot for a table on the perimeter, where your dog will remain close by. Water will be supplied for your best friend upon request. This Italian restaurant features a variety of fresh pasta, chicken, and seafood. 3747 N. Southport Avenue; (773) 244-0990.

Tango Sur This simple Argentine restaurant nestles at the north end of the hot Southport Avenue strip. Your dog will take a shine to the view, greeting lots of humans and dogs that promenade by while you eat. Make sure to leave room for some flan. Note: It's a tight squeeze for big dogs here. 3763 N. South-port Avenue; (733) 477-5466.

Taqueria Mamacita This is a surprisingly wonderful and inexpensive Mexican joint with great burritos. Also recommended are the chicken mole and various quesadillas. With two locations:

On Broadway, the outdoor café is along the sidewalk under a white trellis holding hanging baskets of flowers. Dog owners are typically seated near the end of the thin railing, where they can tie up the pooch in relative peace.

Chaser and Lucy preferred the small grated tables on Southport, because food falls through the spaces and into their waiting mouths. We've visited several times, and it didn't take long for them to learn how this works. Happily for them, I'm a sloppy eater. On-street parking. 3324 N. Broadway, (773) 868-6262; and 3655 N. Southport Avenue, (773) 528-2100.

Tarascas This upscale Mexican restaurant permits well-behaved dogs to join their humans in the outdoor café. Owner Jose Gomez is a dog person from way back and makes sure the water dish is always full. Even though he has experienced some missteps with the dog clientele, he remains open to allowing them entrance. He relies on responsible owners to decide if their dogs can cope with a crowded patio, and if they can sit quietly through a meal. Specialties include the salmon with mango-ginger dressing, guacamole, and margaritas. 3324 N. Halsted Street; (773) 281-5510.

Tuscany on Clark Watch out. This place is so close to Wrigley Field that a baseball just might land in your spaghetti. Dogs are welcome, but only tied outside the white picket fence along Waveland Avenue. It's not all that bad since the pooch can still see, hear, and smell you as well as your food—such as baked sausage with cannellini beans in tomato sauce, or seafood fettuccine. Valet parking, except on nights when there are Cubs games. 3700 N. Clark Street; (773) 404-7700.

Uncommon Ground Only a baseball toss from Wrigley Field, this cozy place with a full-service kitchen is more than a coffeehouse. Vegetarian offerings are the specialty. Breakfast is especially fun. Try Uncommon Huevos (two black bean cakes topped with two eggs and chili sauce, cilantro, and Chihuahua cheese), or Portabella Eggs Benedict. Even more fun than the breakfasts are the Beermaker Dinners, which are held periodically.

Dogs slurp from stainless-steel bowls and munch on complimentary treats. 1214 W. Grace Street; (773) 929-3680.

Wishbone Here at one of Janice's favorite brunch places, Luna is frequently included in the Sunday-morning ritual. While Janice sips coffee between bites of red eggs, Luna makes herself at home on a section of the newspaper that no one is reading, especially the help wanted ads. Due to the fabulous food and casual atmosphere, Wishbone can get very crowded. Expect a wait on the weekends. They do give you a pager to let you know when your table is ready, so instead of twiddling your thumbs, you can walk your dog! 3300 N. Lincoln Avenue, (773) 549-2663; and 1001 W. Washington Street, (312) 850-2663.

Quick Bites

Anthony's Homemade Italian Ice There are just a few seats outside at this street-side store serving about 15 kinds of enticing Italian ice. Ice cream and chocolate-covered bananas are also served. 2009 N. Bissell Street (DePaul); (773) 528-4237.

Athens Café This restaurant invites you and your pooch to dine outside as long as your dog is not "scary." This is what a staff person told Janice on the phone. When Janice showed up with her four-legged pal, the waitress had no qualms about Luna and observed, "She's a good dog; she doesn't bark." This woman never saw Luna poised in front of the picture window when school lets out! The small patio in front of the restaurant holds two tables. At rush hour, Ridge can get congested and noisy from all the cars. Specials include gyros and Italian beef sandwiches. 6757 N. Ridge Boulevard (West Rogers Park); (773) 743-5900.

Ben & Jerry's Get a scoop of the luscious Cherry Garcia (vanilla ice cream with chunks of cherries and fudge) or Chubby Hubby (chocolate-covered peanut-butter-filled pretzels with vanilla malt ice cream rippled in fudge) while sitting outside on a bench. It's not all that comfortable, but when you're in ice-cream ecstasy, it doesn't really matter. 338 W. Armitage Avenue (Lincoln Park); (773) 281-3150.

If you head south for your scoop, you and your best friend can lounge outside in style. This location boasts tables and chairs. 30 W. Chicago Avenue (Gold Coast); (312) 642-3424.

Café De Luca Nearly every morning, a parade of dogs and their owners can be counted on to stop by for coffee and dog biscuits. One day when a familiar pair of neighborhood pugs dropped in, a staff member realized that all the dog treats were gone. Thinking quickly, she offered the pups some biscotti. These dogs were in pug ecstasy. Later in the day, dogs bring their humans by for panini and bruschetta. A neighborhood Great Dane likes to stop by even if he's not staying for dinner, and drink from the extra-large water bowl that sits outside. Parking is available in the back. 1721 N. Damen Avenue (Bucktown); (773) 342-6000.

Chili Mac's 5-Way Chili Seats remain outside through early October, but staying warm is no trouble after a bowl of chili. The rule is that if another guest does not like eating next to a dog, you will have to leave. The owner says he's trying to avoid arguments. Be prepared to eat fast. 3152 N. Broadway (Wrigleyville/Lakeview); (773) 404-2899.

Costello Sandwich and Sides If you're looking for a sandwich that is truly a meal, you will not be disappointed. Costello brags that its oven-baked sandwiches are "crispy on the outside and melty on the inside." The side dishes are made from scratch; don't miss the red-skinned mashed potatoes. The outdoor sitting area is enclosed by a wooden fence and offers a quiet, comfortable place to chow down. If you're dining with your dog, you'll want to avoid leaving him alone outside. You can call in your order before you go, for faster service. 2015 W. Roscoe Street (Roscoe Village); (773) 929-2323.

Einstein Bros. Bagels They relate to dogs at this chain, but as with all restaurants, dogs aren't allowed indoors. You'll have to tie the pooch and go inside to order, which isn't always a practical idea. It doesn't take an Einstein to figure out that the best plan is to take along a human friend. Aside from assorted bagels for people, dog bagels are also sold. The bagels for dogs are really hard, a challenging chew for small dogs. It took little Lucy 10 minutes to put her bagel away; it took Chaser about 2 minutes.

2530 N. Clark Street (Lincoln Park); (773) 244-9898. This was once a parking lot, and it looks like it. At least there's lots of space on this concrete and definitely urban patio.

3420 N. Southport Avenue (Wrigleyville/Lakeview); (773) 281-9888. Nearly sharing space with the abutting Caribou Coffee location, dogs sit behind a wooden fence. There are lots of seats, but they're squeezed close together.

3455 N. Clark Street (Wrigleyville/Lakeview); (773) 529-1888. Just a bagel toss from Wrigley Field, the staff sometimes sneaks free bagels to dogs.

5318 N. Clark Street (Andersonville); (773) 506-9888. A staff member may also surprise a canine customer with a doggy bagel at this location.

El Porton There isn't much space, only two outdoor tables, at this quickie Mexican restaurant. It's possible you'll have to cool your heels if you show up with

Fido. Specials include enchiladas and fajitas. 3910 N. Sheridan Road (Lakeview/Wrigleyville); (773) 549-8232.

Enisa's European Bakery & Café Located in the heart of Lincoln Square, this small pastry shop is filled with delicious desserts as well as ice cream. The quaint patio has 10 tables, with plenty of room for canine guests to sprawl out under the large tree in the center. The bright blue umbrellas offer abundant shade when the sun is beating down. Luna and Janice stopped for a sandwich (both recommend the tuna) on one of the hottest days of summer after shopping at the farmer's market and were surprisingly comfortable. Maybe their satisfaction had something to do with the banana split that they ordered for dessert. 4701 N. Lincoln Avenue (Lincoln Square); (773) 271-7017.

Icebox/Soupbox At the Icebox, connoisseurs have 20 kinds of Italian ice from which to choose. You can cool off on a bench on Broadway and share your selection with your pup. In October this place transforms into the Soupbox and stays that way until the spring weather arrives. You can warm up with 12 different kinds of soup in the cold winter months. A perfect fit for the extreme Chicago weather. 2943 N. Broadway (Lincoln Park); (773) 935-9800.

Panera Bread Company With wrought-iron seats and tables set up along Diversey Parkway, this is a dandy place for eating outdoors. However, you'll have to go indoors to order the sourdough bread or any of the other freshly made breads, bagels, muffins, soups, or cookies. That entails leaving the pooch either alone tied to a tree (which we frown upon) or with a friend. 616 W. Diversey Parkway (Lincoln Park); (773) 528-4556.

Pompei Bakery Only a few outdoor tables are available here, so if you visit during peak hours, you may have to circle. Dogs who don't like loud noises may get frightened sitting so close to the train tracks. On the positive side, the cafeteria-style ordering makes it easy to see what looks good enough to eat. 2955 N. Sheffield Avenue (Wellington/South Lakeview); (773) 325-1900.

Rocco's Italian Sandwiches With only two outdoor tables, timing is everything. Your dog will be patient, though, knowing that leftovers may soon present themselves. The steak sandwich, burgers, and fries are the most popular items. 4900 N. Western Avenue (Albany Park); (773) 271-2480.

Southport Sandwich Company The sub, club, and Reuben sandwiches might be larger than the space outdoors. Still, dogs are allowed. 3501 N. Southport Avenue (Wrigleyville/Lakeview); (773) 325-0123.

A Taste of Heaven This sweet spot is a welcoming place to go any time of the day. Fresh sandwiches, soups, and pasta salads come highly recommended. Make sure you save room for dessert. The baked goods are the stars of this café. Choose from a variety of cakes baked daily, and an assortment of cookies, brownies, and macaroons. Luna sits transfixed while Janice snacks on café au lait and a slice of apple crumble, and it's not the café au lait that Luna's licking her chops for. If you do share with your dog, just make sure it's not the double-chocolate layer cake. Chocolate can make dogs very sick. 1701 W. Foster Avenue (Andersonville); (773) 989-0151.

Tom & Wendee's Homemade Italian Ice Don't serve the chocolate-flavored Italian ice to dogs (chocolate is toxic to canines). There are about 15 other flavors ranging from blueberry to watermelon. Dogs like sitting under the long bench for shade—and licking up what sloppy eaters have left behind. There are also a few white plastic seats. 1136 W. Armitage Avenue (DePaul); (773) 327-2885.

Toots This is more than a typical hot-dog place. Toots also offers sandwiches, cheeseburgers, and pizza puffs. But its claim to fame is the ice cream. Researcher Steve Karmgard's favorite is the Arctic Blast, vanilla ice cream with a choice of Oreo cookie, Butterfinger, or Heath Bar mixed in.

There are five picnic benches outside, and there's plenty of room. However, being at a busy intersection, Toots can get noisy. 4534 N. Central Avenue (Jefferson Park); (773) 736-7855.

Waveland Cafe The menu isn't much, but the location is prime doggy real estate. This café is situated just southeast of Irving Park Road in Lincoln Park, a chew toy's throw from "Dog Beach" (see p. 41) and just northwest of the rocks where dogs jump into the lake.

It's the perfect pit stop after running along the park's jogging path or taking a dip in Lake Michigan. In the summer months, you can almost always watch a softball game.

The menu is primarily limited to basic sandwiches, burgers, and salads. Parking is available in Lincoln Park, off the Recreation Drive exit from Lake Shore Drive northbound or off Irving Park Road from either north or southbound Lake Shore Drive. 3700 N. Recreation Drive (Wrigleyville/Lakeview); (773) 868-4132.

Wiener Circle This place is open until 4 A.M. Sundays through Thursdays, until 5 A.M. Fridays, and until 6 A.M. Saturdays. There are four red picnic benches for when you and Fido get the late-night/early morning munchies. 2622 N. Clark Street (Lincoln Park); (773) 477-7444.

Wrigleyville Dogs Even when the Cubs are in town, this is a fairly safe place to hit with your pooch. It may get crowded, but most Cubs fans eat on the run while headed north to Wrigley Field. The danger lies in tying your dog (the four-legged kind) up and leaving him alone while you run in to grab your dog (the all-beef kind). Take along some friends to watch your pup—you can pay them back in fries. 3737 N. Clark Street (Wrigleyville); (773) 296-1500.

Zoom Kitchen Searching for fresh and tasty "comfort foods"? If so, Zoom Kitchen is always reliable. From the down-home meat loaf sandwich to the macaroni and cheese, you and your dog are sure to find something to fill up on. When Luna goes with Janice, she always begs for her own order of grilled sliced sirloin steak, but all she gets is a plain old Milkbone. 620 W. Belmont Avenue, (773) 325-1400; and 1646 N. Damen Avenue (South Lakeview and Bucktown), (773) 278-7000.

Coffee Shops

Cafe Avanti All dogs get water and biscuits. For people, there are many kinds of coffee. 3706 N. Southport Avenue (Wrigleyville/Lakeview); (773) 880-5959.

Cafe Boost Talk about convenience: here you'll find a tree and six tables along Balmoral Avenue. The staff provides dog biscuits and water for your pooch so she can relax with a full tummy as you get your caffeine fix. 5400 N. Clark Street (Andersonville); (773) 907-8674.

Caribou Coffee All of Caribou's locations with outside seating are dog friendly. The fare includes both dark-roasted strong coffee and lighter blends. The husband and wife who founded the company got the idea to open these shops while they were in Alaska watching caribou; hence the rustic appeal. Here are dog-friendly Caribou locations:

3300 N. Broadway (Wrigleyville/Lakeview); (773) 477-3695. A stainless-steel doggy bowl quenches the thirst of canine guests, and sometimes dogs get day-old pastries.

2453 N. Clark Street (Lincoln Park); (773) 327-9923. Unwind and watch the yuppies with their puppies at outdoor wood-top tables adjacent to Arlington Street. There's also a bicycle rack.

1 S. LaSalle Street (South Loop); (312) 609-5108. This location is convenient for those who take the dog to the office.

1 W. Division Street (Gold Coast); (312) 664-6789. Even though this shop has no outdoor area, servers try their hardest to accommodate your pooch.

You can always get a cup of ice water to go and a dog biscuit for your furry friend. If you do run in for a cup of joe, please have another human to stay with your dog!

3424 N. Southport Avenue (Wrigleyville/Lakeview); (773) 529-4902. Ten tables are behind a wooden fence, and there's a dog bowl for canine guests, although there isn't much room to stretch long canine legs.

1561 N. Wells Street (Old Town); (312) 266-7504. While your pup chews on a Big Mac, available next door at McDonald's, you can sip on coffee. Ben, the team leader, assured us, "We like dogs!" And it shows when employees toss your pup a treat across the counter, in addition to providing a water bowl outside.

Coffee and Tea Exchange   They do their own roasting at both locations.

3311 N. Broadway (Wrigleyville/Lakeview); (773) 528-2241. Dismissing at least five other coffee places within several blocks, the manager touts, "Our coffee is the best!" Water is offered, and they often provide biscuits.

833 W. Armitage Avenue (DePaul); (773) 929-6730. There are only a handful of seats at this location, but the staff dotes over canine guests.

Emerald City Coffee Bar   Since the street is so close to the outdoor tables, some patrons like to tie their hounds to the nearby bike rack just to be on the safe side. Water is offered to canine visitors. 3928 N. Sheridan Road (Wrigleyville/Lakeview); (773) 525-7847.

Ennui Cafe   "Most certainly, we love dogs," gushes co-owner Kathy Sprattling, who personally offers canine guests "the best biscuits I can find" and water from plastic bowls labeled "Fifi" and "Fido."

The umbrella tables are on the sidewalk on Lunt Avenue. Special members of the wait staff are Jake, who is Sprattling's German shepherd dog, and Sugaree, co-owner Tenley Timothy's Doberman/greyhound–mix. 6981 N. Sheridan Road (Rogers Park); (773) 973-2233.

Higher Ground   Cats can sniff catnip. People can sip coffee. What is there for dogs? Ponder this question while sitting outdoors with Fido at this coffeehouse. 2022 W. Roscoe Street (Roscoe Village); (773) 868-0075.

Intelligentsia   Read the daily newspapers, which are available inside at no charge, while you rest your bones on wooden deck chairs outside. Water is offered to dogs. 3123 N. Broadway (Lakeview); (773) 348-8058.

Peacock Cafe There's only one table, but if it isn't occupied, you can sit outside the door of this neighborhood coffeehouse with the pooch. 5440 N. Sheridan Road (Edgewater); (773) 275-1224.

Seattle's Best Coffee Take a seat at one of the umbrella-covered tables decorated with a tiny square pot of flowers. Locations at 42 E. Chicago Avenue (Gold Coast), (312) 337-0885; 2951 N. Broadway (Lincoln Park), (773) 296-6086; 701 N. Wells (Loop), (312) 649-9452; and 1700 N. Wells (Old Town), (312) 649-1620.

Starbucks The shops of this chain are dog friendly, as long as they have space for their green chairs and tables outdoors, and most locations do. Here's a list of Starbucks locations that love dogs nearly as much as java:

1023 W. Addison Street (Lakeview/Wrigleyville); (773) 929-0945. The water bowls feature coffee stickers and a Starbucks logo at this locale across from Wrigley Field.

3359 N. Southport Avenue (Lakeview/Wrigleyville); (773) 975-2071. The water dish placed here is large enough for a pack of Irish wolfhounds, and sometimes packs do invade this doggy-happy locale. The back patio is a wonderful respite, offering seclusion and relative quiet.

Dogs are also welcomed at these Starbucks locations: 3358 N. Broadway Avenue, (773) 528-0343; 3845 N. Broadway Avenue, (773) 755-4176; 2529 N. Clark Street, (773) 296-0898; 5300 N. Clark Street (773) 728-2777; 555 S. Dearborn, (312) 922-8910; 1002 W. Diversey, (773) 665-1888; 2200 N. Halsted Street, (773) 935-2622; 55 E. Jackson Boulevard, (312) 786-9201; 2475 N. Lincoln Avenue, (773) 528-1275; 3356 N. Lincoln Avenue, (773) 871-6888; 4600 N. Magnolia Avenue, (773) 506-4280; 202 N. Michigan Avenue, (312) 541-1313; 210 W. North Avenue, (312) 867-0186; 10 S. Riverside Plaza, (312) 441-1919; 2023 W. Roscoe Street, (773) 281-6272; 932 N. Rush Street, (312) 951-5436; 828 N. State Street, (312) 751-1676; 150 N. Wacker Drive, (312) 704-0655; 100 S. Wacker Drive, (312) 759-5559.

Shopping

Running errands can be a way to accomplish two goals at once: Bowser gets to go for a walk while you get things done. This is particularly so on the city's Near North Side, where most folks walk rather than drive. It's also a great way to socialize young pups and exercise both yourself and your dog.

Dogs are welcome at many dry cleaners, video stores, and shoe-repair shops in that part of town. This section lists more than 30 retailers with open-dog policies—not including the obvious, such as pet stores and groomers. Many of these businesses not only allow pooches but also celebrate their appearances. However, as with anything else, store policies may change. Before charging in with Bowser, ask for permission.

Active Endeavors Wear and gear for the outdoors. This place can outfit you and your dog for just about anything, including a hiking trip in Antarctica. They'll find just the right backpack for you and will stock it with doggie power bones. 935 W. Armitage Avenue (DePaul); (773) 281-8100.

Armitage Ace Hardware Dogs accompany customers here all the time, especially when they have a vested interest, such as picking out a new Weber grill. The store boasts a 1,200-square-foot showroom for Weber grills.

On one occasion, owner Brian O'Donnell was called upon to muster all his hardware skills. WGN Radio personality Judy Markey showed up with her dog, explaining, "Mr. Hardware Man, my dog has a soup bone wedged in its mouth and it won't come out." O'Donnell carefully used a hacksaw to cut the bone, and then inserted a screwdriver to snap it. "We believe in answering the really tough problems, but it doesn't get any tougher than that," O'Donnell says. 925 W. Armitage Avenue (DePaul); (773) 348-3267.

Banana Republic Lucy and Chaser aren't much of a crime deterrent. While we were shopping for urban safari gear, a man was nabbed for shoplifting. Lucy and Chaser were absolutely oblivious to the crime, and to the tumult created after the police pulled up. One officer turned to the dogs and questioned, "What good are you?" They offered no reply. 2104 N. Halsted Street (DePaul); (773) 832-1172.

Barker & Meowsky: A Paw Firm   You won't believe what you'll find at this upscale gift store for pets and pet lovers. Paws down, this store is guaranteed to have something for the owner and pet you thought had it all. Check out hand-painted tiles (an assortment of 150 dog breeds), $25; antique dog prints, $50–250; canine yarmulkes (for the High Holy Days, Bark Mitzvahs, or Hanukkah), $10; velvet pet beds, $60–195; the Bettie (a trendy fetch toy you can also stuff treats inside), $20; and custom portraits of your pooch on slate, $95.

All dogs who visit can sample treats from Howling Hound Bakery, which owner Alice Lerman says she munches on herself. There is also a wide selection of outdoor wear, including booties, sweaters, and jackets—sort of a Nordstrom's for dogs. For big dogs you'll find water and food dishes raised from 2 to 12 inches off the floor.

You will also find coffee table books about dogs and learn the latest in Chicago dog news from the owner, who likes to bark out the gossip. Generally, if it's a new product for dogs you'll find it here. Visit their website at www.barkerandmeowsky.com, or stop by in person. 3319 N. Broadway (Lakeview); (773) 880-0200.

Big Bear's Hand Car Wash and Detailing   For Lucy it's like a horror movie come to life. Hopping out of the car, she found herself under the shadow of a carved wooden replica of a grizzly bear. This 12-foot-high incredible hulk was poised to attack. Though only a puppy at the time and all of nine pounds, Lucy was ready to do battle. Her high-pitched puppy barks didn't scare off the big bear. Fearlessly, she walked right up to the behemoth and mustered a mighty growl. Well, maybe not so mighty, since it sounded more like a songbird chirp. The wooden bear wasn't intimidated, but she earned a biscuit for her efforts.

It turns out that many neighborhood pooches visit to snarl at the bear on their daily walks and receive free dog treats for their labors. As for Chaser, she couldn't care less about the bear. Her single concern was to avoid getting her paws wet at this indoor drive-in car wash located in a garage. 2261 N. Clybourn Avenue (Clybourn Corridor); (773) 325-2334.

Bloomingdale's   The Michigan Avenue Bloomie's is not nearly as dog friendly as the original department store in New York City. You have to sneak your pooch in, entering on Walton Street instead of the main entrance on Michigan. That's because dogs aren't allowed in the mall.

If you're lucky, once you're in, you can usually go about your business with a pooch. Nevertheless, you should plan on disguising your dog as a fellow shopper; I know of one person who was tossed out of the store with a well-behaved Norfolk terrier—even though the store officially allows dogs on leashes. But don't even think about pulling this stunt at Bloomingdale's at Old Orchard in Skokie. Try walking with a dog from the car to the store, and you might as well be nabbed for carrying a dangerous weapon. Officials in Bloomingdale's corporate office blame the Skokie shopping center's dog policy. 900 N. Michigan Avenue (Gold Coast); (312) 440-4460.

Bombay Company You might think they'd be concerned about a dog's chewing on a table leg at this upscale furniture store, but there are no such worries here. 2052 N. Halsted Street (DePaul); (773) 348-3409.

Brown Elephant This resale shop has it all—clothing, records (vinyl and CDs), furniture, paperback books (especially trashy novels), and home accessories. Proceeds benefit the Howard Brown Health Center.

On one memorable visit, while Robin was perusing the paperback books (yes, the trashy novels), Chaser, Lucy, and Lucy's best friend, Sophie, were all lined up obediently at the door in a perfect sit/stay, having politely greeted maybe a dozen customers. When a 12-year-old boy named James walked in, Sophie couldn't take it anymore. She let out a "Whaooo!" and began to cry because I said she couldn't move. I turned around to see that the three dogs had an audience of five people watching and laughing.

At that moment, Lucy also began to wail. As I implored, "Quiet, Lucy," a man brayed in his best Ricky Ricardo accent, "Oh, Lucy, what have you done now?" By then, we had 10 people watching. On our way out, an employee serenaded us with the theme from "I Love Lucy." 3651 N. Halsted Street (Wrigleyville/Lakeview); (773) 549-5943.

Climate Home Owner Larry Ravenna takes his three-year-old Border collie, Taylor, to work with him at his home, gift, and accessory shop. "More customers come in to see Taylor than they do to see me!" Ravenna says. All three locations readily allow canine companions (and cats, if they're willing) to come and help their humans shop. Animal-themed items include trendy books, magnets, picture frames, food bowls, and a unique and very popular dog-Buddha. If you happen to stop by and Taylor isn't working, she's probably home watching TV. Ravenna says her favorite program is "Lassie." 1702 N. Damen (Bucktown), (773) 862-7075; 2462 N. Clark (Lincoln Park), (773) 327-7717; and 5408 N. Clark (Andersonville), (773) 878-4804.

Eco'Fields Inc. This store features agriculturally based, environmentally correct papers and products. You can purchase leashes, collars, and toys made out of hemp. Word has it neighborhood cats have enrolled in a 10-step program to overcome their addiction to the hemp-covered catnip mice. Owner Patricia O'Brien points out, "Dogs love the smell of hemp." She painted a sign in the window that says "Pets welcome," but she really didn't need it, since dogs are so intrigued by the odor that they pull their owners toward the door. She looks forward to meeting her four-legged customers and encourages them to stop by for a drink of water; she always makes sure the bowl is full. O'Brien sources unique pet products. Dogs groove on the special-order doggy beds made of hemp fabric, which are durable and easy to clean. 1708 N. Wells Street (Old Town); (312) 867-0624.

Elliott Consignment and Designer Collection This unusual store has two locations. One site houses furniture and collectibles, and just a few doors down is the apparel and accessories boutique. Both stores carry gently used items with style. If you're looking for a bargain, look here—and there. 2445 N. Lincoln Avenue and 2465 N. Lincoln Avenue (Lincoln Park); (773) 404-6080.

Erehwon Mountain Outfitter One of our best pet-related purchases came from this store: "Hank's water bowl," named for the inventor's own dog. This travel bowl folds up into a little ball and can be Velcroed to a leash, a belt buckle, or virtually anything else. The gadget is well worth the $17.95 investment; we take it everywhere. Erehwon (nowhere spelled backwards) has everything from rock climbing equipment to kayaking skirts, and also caters to active dogs. You have your choice of backpacks for dogs, as well as collars and leashes. 1800 N. Clybourn (Clybourn Corridor), (312) 337-6400; and 1600 W. 16th Street, Oak Brook, (630) 574-2222.

Father Time Antiques Instead of strapping on a newfangled watch, sift through the vast array of vintage timepieces. Father Time even has the kind of pocket watches that train conductors once used. Owners Jim and Chandra Reynolds are dog lovers, and they always point out the portraits of Curly, a husky/malamute–mix, and Alex, a collie/shepherd–mix, on their canine gallery behind the counter. They also refinish furniture. 2108 W. Belmont Avenue (Riverview); (773) 880-5599.

Dog Bakeries

"People are seeking to eat healthier, and they want the same for their dogs," says Jodi Jaunich, owner of Galloping Gourmutts, a bakery for dogs.

The offerings vary from bakery to bakery, but each of the places listed here uses few—if any—preservatives, no sugar, no salt, and no artificial sweeteners or colorings. Most prepare food on the premises. Some of the dog chefs are actually classically trained in the culinary arts but have chosen to bake for those who bark for their meals.

Fido's Food Fair is the original dog bakery, dating back to 1979. Owner Gloria Lissner concedes, "Back then, people thought I was totally off my rocker. Now those same people are my customers. The way we think about our dogs has changed."

Juliene Fryer, manager at Three Dog Bakery, says, "People love buying things for their dogs as much as the dogs enjoy eating them—well, almost as much."

Here's a roundup of dog bakeries, complete with revealing personality profiles.

Tres Bone Bakery and Boutique: 27 W. Chicago Avenue, Naperville, (630) 579-4979; and 508 N. Seymour, Mundelein, (847) 837-8901.

The store offers hypoallergenic dog treats prepared to order. The signature treats are peanut butter and carob or garlic chicken birthday cakes, frosted with mashed potatoes, $14.95 to $19.95, and beef and garlic cigars, $1 to $1.99.

The most popular item? It's the "peanut butter melt-a-way," a soft treat that's great for older dogs, 40 cents.

Dinger's Dog Bakery and Boutique: 105 W. State Street, Geneva; (630) 845-2650. In addition to offering 16 kinds of cookies, as well as four birthday cake flavors in four sizes ($13.95 to $16.95), Dinger's will prepare custom gift baskets.

The most popular item here is the "oatmeal man" cookie, made with raisins, cinnamon, honey, and oatmeal, 50 cents apiece or $6 for a barker's dozen.

If owner Bonnie Mackowiak were a dog, she'd most want to sniff out the "beef-o-juice" cookies, which are made with a base of beef stock, 50 cents apiece or $6 for a barker's dozen.

Fido's Food Fair: 5416 N. Clark Street (Andersonville); (773) 907-0305. Even the most finicky dog has got to salivate to something here, starting with two hundred kinds of cookies. How about a frozen dinner? Entrees are "chicken a la Fido," "steak and kidney ragu," and "muttloaf," $3.99. If calories aren't an issue, Fido's "cheesecake" is $10 whole or $1.50 per slice.

Fido's will also host birthday parties, graduations (from obedience school), or "bark" mitzvahs for dogs at a cost of $15 per pooch. Included is a "liver a la mouse" appetizer, your choice of entree, a cookie, and a doggy birthday cake, along with party favors. The Food Fair will also cater your doggy pool party or prepare picnic baskets.

The most popular choice around these parts is the "party kisses," which are soft, kiss-shape cookies available in five flavors, $4 per pound or five kisses for $1.

If Lissner were a dog, she'd most want to sniff out a garlic, cornbread, and honey birthday cake topped with low-fat cream cheese and freeze-dried liver, $15 to $25.

Galloping Gourmutts: 2736 N. Lincoln Avenue (Lincoln Park); (773) 477-K9K9 (5959). Owner Jodi Jaunich describes her bakery as a sort of Whole Foods for pets. Everything is made with natural ingredients, including 50 kinds of cookies.

The bakery's most popular item is "canine cannoli," a cookie filled with peanut butter and topped with carob, $1.

If Jaunich were a dog, she'd most want to sniff out the "barbecue squirrels"—chicken-flavored squirrel-shape cookies, 50 cents.

Pet Celebrations: 1812 Taft Avenue, Berkley; (708) 236-0321. Opened as a retail store in 2000, their claim to fame is Aunt Lee's recipe for all-natural hand-cut treats. Aunt Lee, now 85-years young, is owner Robin Sparacino's aunt who developed recipes for her late husband Gil's vet practice. There are more than 25 flavors of these treats, including liver, cheese, carob, garlic and parsley, banana, honey, and cherry. You can also host your pup's birthday party here. The parties include party favors and cake, and the cost is $50–60.

Pet Celebrations celebrates nearly every holiday. For example, on St. Patrick's day, they host Dog Days of Ireland. This festival includes free green shamrock biscuits for all dogs. On Valentine's Day, the store hosts a party that features a Barkacinno and biscotti for dogs, and free Starbuck's coffee

continued

for their people. On Easter, a free picture of your pet with the Easter bunny is offered and a prize is given to the dog who sniffs out the hidden Easter egg.

Three Dog Bakery: 2142 N. Halsted Street (DePaul); (773) 388-2599. Aside from the cookies, you can snap up hypoallergenic treats, 17 kinds of pastries for dogs, and even a water bottle called Cool Pooch that you can share with your dog, $7.50.

Three Dog's most popular item is "barbecued ribs," a garlic cookie with barbecue sauce baked into it, two for $1.50.

If manager Juliene Fryer were a dog, she'd most want to sniff out "boxer brownies"—carob muffins with low-fat buttermilk frosting and a carob-shape bone on top, $2.50.

Flower Flat Join the zoo. With Lord Chumley the bulldog; two lories named Barron and Flora; Salvador Maui, a rare blue-colored green iguana; Bart the red-footed tortoise; Thor the leopard tortoise; and the fully stocked saltwater aquarium, another dog or two would hardly be noticed. It comes as no surprise that this flower shop specializes in unusual blooms. In summer months, flowers are lined up against the building, the lories are chirping outdoors in their cage, and Lord Chumley oversees the canine traffic departing nearby Lincoln Park. 622 W. Addison Street (Wrigleyville/Lakeview); (773) 871-0888.

Framed Classics I returned from London toting a set of vintage English dog trading cards mounted in a beautiful frame. I used bubble wrap to protect my prize in transit, and cushioned it inside Robin's raincoat, placing it carefully between other clothes. Still, the frame broke into about a thousand pieces. Not only did the experts at Framed Classics reframe the cards, but they also doted on Lucy and Chaser. And recently one of the owners adopted a feral cat. Now, that's a quality business. They specialize in repairing antique frames and pictures, and they sell vintage prints. 2227 W. Belmont Avenue (Riverview); (773) 871-1790.

Frame Factory/Gallery 1909 "We frame everything!" is the motto at this dog-friendly store—especially pictures of your pets. When Luna and Janice arrived, they were offered a biscuit and a few pats on the head. Luna took advantage, while Janice declined. You might even get better service if you come with a dog; employees are keen on dogs, and some take time to play with the pooches. Store personnel pride themselves on living up to their slogan, successfully custom-framing even the most challenging objects. 3026 N. Ashland Avenue (Riverview); (773) 929-1010.

Gabby's Barber Shop The dogs come to watch their people get groomed. Despite one member of the gallery who barked at customers as they entered, owner Wayne Kauffman says that the dogs are good for business. There's a small, enclosed concrete area in back where dogs are allowed to dawdle, as long as the owners pick up. Despite numerous requests, Kauffman declines to cut dog hair, but he does distribute free jerky treats. 2860 N. Clark Street (Lincoln Park); (773) 549-8832.

Ha-Lo Office and Art Supplies The managers say that since they've begun to offer dog biscuits, business has improved. Perhaps canine customers got word about the treats and are leading their owners to the store. All guests are greeted with welcoming barks from Shaine, the resident miniature schnauzer. 3831 N. Broadway (Wrigleyville/East Lakeview); (773) 525-0272.

Hit the Road Dogs come here to help plan the family vacation. Manager Maureen Geoghegan answers questions about traveling with the pooch. Meanwhile, your pup can chomp on treats. Traveling pet bowls and books about traveling with pets are available here. They also sell maps, guides, luggage, and other accessories for people hitting the road. 3758 N. Southport Avenue (Lakeview/Wrigleyville); (773) 388-8338.

Hubba-Hubba Dogs can help their owners pick out unique clothing and high-quality vintage items. Lucy and Chaser are regulars at this busy store (that's because Robin is a regular). On one occasion Lucy bolted from her sit/stay and nonchalantly moseyed her way under a curtain into a dressing room. The voice behind the curtain asked, "The dog fits; is it for sale, too?" 3309 N. Clark Street (Wrigleyville/Lakeview); (773) 477-1414.

Johnny Sprockets Even if your dog can't ride a two-wheeler, she'll get a kick out of this bike shop. Employees give canine visitors treats and always take time out to say hi and pet their furry heads. Owner John Riordan often baby-sits for his sister's Jack Russell–mix, Cheri. This is Luna's favorite part about the visit. Luna really likes Cheri. In fact, I think she secretly hopes for broken spokes so that she can get in some romping time with her girlfriend. For athletic dogs, you can purchase a dog pack so the pooches can carry their own gear. Or, for the less ambitious animal, who's just along for the ride, John will fit your bike with a trailer for dogs. You pedal, and the pooch relaxes in style. 3001 N. Broadway (Lakeview), (773) 244-1079; and 1052 W. Bryn Mawr Avenue (Edgewater), (773) 293-1695.

Kinko's   For late-night reports, last-minute printing, and sales presentations that must be perfect in an hour, Kinko's is the ER of the business world. Given the huge variety of services, many business owners and self-employed people practically live at these stores, usually while on the pressure of a deadline. Billy Proctor, general manager of the store on Southport, says, "It relaxes people to have dogs around." He sees people working on the computer night after night who would not get to spend any time with their dogs if the pets weren't allowed on the premises. As long as the canines don't try to photocopy their paws, employees are glad to have them around. There's even a dog bowl filled with treats at the counter.

In 2000, Kinko's stores in the Midwest sponsored a fund-raising drive called "Pens for Pets." They donated a portion of the sales of pens to the Humane Society of the United States.

These two locations are extremely pet friendly: 3524 N. Southport Avenue (Lakeview), (773) 975-5031; and 3435 N. Western Avenue (Roscoe Village), (773) 755-9000. Call your local Kinko's for more information.

Midtown True Value Hardware   This is where Lucy accompanied me to purchase her long line (an extra-long leash to enforce the "come" command), which looks like an extra-long clothesline. Naturally, the merchandise also includes nuts and bolts, and all those hardware items; you can even buy some furniture. 3130 N. Broadway (Wrigleyville/Lakeview); (773) 871-3839.

Mosaic   Of the three ladies in my life, Robin is especially partial to this upscale women's shop—because as she has said many times, "If it's about to become a fashion trend, Mosaic will be carrying it." Chaser and Lucy remain unimpressed. 843 W. Armitage Avenue (DePaul); (773) 935-1131.

MotoPhoto   This store will take canine portraits. It's easy to get a dog to smile; just say, "Look at the birdie." 2420 N. Clark Street (Lincoln Park); (773) 477-6661.

Nationwide Video   Dogs are welcome at all locations to help nose out the hard-to-find videos in which these stores specialize. 843 W. Belmont Avenue, (773) 525-1222; 736 W. Irving Park Road, (773) 871-7800; 2827 N. Broadway, (773)

348-8311; and 3936 N. Clarendon Avenue, (773) 871-1882 (all Wrigleyville/ Lakeview).

Natural Selection "Hi, Chaser," sang out owner Karen Ishibashi at this small card and gift shop. She admitted that she often doesn't recall the names of her customers as readily as the names of their dogs. Karen and her mother, Florence, lavish canine customers with biscuits, sneaking them in when they think the dog's owner isn't looking. They even play hide-and-seek with canine regulars, concealing treats and then letting the dogs run through the store to search them out. 2260 N. Lincoln Avenue (Lincoln Park); (773) 327-8886.

OutSpoken This local bike shop is open to canine customers. Owner Kim Pierce always stops what she's doing to come over and say hi to your pooch. OutSpoken specializes in outfitting riders for long bike trips. Every year, the shop sponsors the Twin Cities AIDS Ride, and last year, the staff went all the way up to Alaska to support riders through six days of biking. Too bad they don't offer dog-sitting services for when you're away on a bike trip. 1113 W. Belmont Avenue (West Lakeview); (773) 404-2919.

Pagoda Red This unique store specializes in 18th- and 19th-century Chinese furniture and accessories. The antiques are delicate, and some items in the showroom are vulnerable to large tails. Co-owner Betsy Nathan thinks dogs are wonderful but understandably prefers that only small, well-behaved dogs come in to browse. We all know it's bad luck for a dog to break a pagoda. 1714 N. Damen Avenue (Bucktown); (773) 235-1188.

Rain Dog Books How could a place with this name refuse pups? They don't. Dogs are welcome at this antiquarian bookshop. 404 S. Michigan Avenue (South Loop); (312) 922-1200.

Scarborough Faire Being a Brittany, Chaser is a dog of French descent. And florist Ginnette Sorensen knew that the first time she saw her. In her delightful French accent, she chirped, "It's a Brittany! I love you! I love you!"

There isn't much room to maneuver indoors at this cramped European-style flower shop. That's why so many of the blooms are outside during the summer months. All dogs are free to inhale the exotic scents as long as they don't chew on the merchandise. However, French poodles, briards, and Brittanys get extra love. Sorensen never lets Chaser exit without giving her a kiss. She exclaims, "You are wonderful; au revoir, you wonderful dog." 2201 N. Sheffield Avenue (DePaul); (773) 929-2224.

Unabridged Books "We love dogs," exclaims book clerk Owen Keehnen. He rattles off the names of Barney the standard poodle, Linda the Shetland sheepdog, and Dana the Rhodesian Ridgeback among the regulars. He says their owners usually come by to look up the latest in canine literature. Meanwhile, clerks keep the dogs occupied with cookies. 3251 N. Broadway (Wrigleyville/Lakeview); (773) 883-9119.

Uncle Dan's When Luna goes to Uncle Dan's, employees often fight over who gets to give the canine customers pieces of the Zuke's Power Bone, an energy bar for pups. After her snack, Luna energetically heads to the water cooler, where the big dog bowl awaits with cold water.

While you shop for outdoor gear, your dog can do some browsing, too. Kong toys, tennis balls, and Frisbees are the most popular with the dogs. Owners gravitate toward items such as travel water bowls, leashes, collars, water bottles, and leash bags. If you're going on a camping trip, Uncle Dan's has everything you need, plus some stuff you had no idea you needed! Employees know that dog backpacks can be uncomfortable if they don't fit properly. They'll help you adjust the straps just right.

According to manager Mike Fowler, the policy of welcoming dogs to shop with their owners derived from the need to keep customers happy. He says, "Our suburban stores cater to parents shopping with kids, and the Lincoln Park store fills a need for people shopping with their dogs." Dogs and children are welcome at all locations. 2440 N. Lincoln Avenue (Lincoln Park), (773) 477-1918; 700 W. Church Street, Evanston, (847) 475-7100; and 1847 Second Street, Highland Park; (847) 266-8600.

Urban Outfitters Dogs can browse here for clothes for those owners who seek a retro feel but yearn to be fashion forward. The dogs—and the merchants—hope those owners will also purchase one of the many items geared to dog lovers. There are food bowls, place mats for under the food bowl (one is shaped like a bone, another like a Labrador retriever), picture frames with dog designs, and a leopard-patterned dog bed. There's also a small but unique selection of dog books. 2352 N. Clark Street (Lincoln Park), (773) 549-1711; and 935 N. Rush Street (Gold Coast), (312) 640-1919.

Vertel's Finally, a place to get real help choosing running shoes. The only way to be sure you get the shoes you want is to test them, and just walking around in the store isn't going to work. That's why Vertel's encourages you to run up and down the street as many times as necessary to simulate normal running conditions. For some people, normal running condition is with a canine. Vertel's understands, and that's one reason why dogs are allowed in the store. In fact, I couldn't think of testing running shoes without Chaser's input. They also sell running and fitness gear and clothing. Don't forget to run down some Bark Bars for your athletic pooch. 2001 N. Clybourn Avenue (Clybourn Corridor); (773) 248-7400.

Visual Effects Optical The focus here is on the newest and trendiest eyewear. Still, picking out specs is never an easy task; you almost always take someone along for a second opinion. Why not see what Fido thinks of those way-cool glasses? 1953 N. Clybourn Avenue (Clybourn Corridor); (773) 281-0200.

White Elephant Shop A resale shop, with the proceeds benefiting Children's Memorial Hospital. 2380 N. Lincoln Avenue (Lincoln Park); (773) 883-6184.

Women & Children First Sorry, not all that many titles about dogs. But here is Chicago's most comprehensive selection of books dealing with female subjects, including birthing, childcare, career plans, and the like. Along with a wide range of children's titles, readings for kids are offered regularly. Dogs on leashes can come and listen, too. 5233 N. Clark Street (Andersonville); (773) 769-9299.

Places to Stay

Claridge Hotel All guests, including those with four legs, can travel anywhere in the downtown area via the hotel's limousine shuttle service between 8 A.M. and 10 A.M. Your dog may choose to sleep in, however, snoozing on the hotel's brand-new mahogany dog bed with a special velvet cushion. There is only one dog bed available, so if your dog wants royal treatment, reservations are necessary. There is no fee for this privilege. Human amenities include on-site massages and aromatherapy. Dogs of any size are welcome at this quaint yet refined hotel only a block away from the bustling scene at Rush and Division Streets in the Gold Coast. Rates are $145 to $250. 1244 N. Dearborn Parkway; (312) 787-4980 or (800) 245-1258.

Four Seasons Hotel Ah, it feels so good to stretch out on a king-size bed. All people who stay here get king-size beds. Dogs used to get their own doggy beds, but unfortunately the hotel stopped offering them; no one at the hotel could say exactly why. Since not all guests are dog lovers, special rooms are designated for canines to lounge around in. The hotel says not to worry; they have never had to turn down a four-legged guest due to lack of space. Fetching the paper isn't much of a challenge, since one is left at the door each morning. All canine customers receive biscuits, bottled water especially for dogs, and their own bowl. For $10, the bellhop will walk the dog (and pick up) along Chicago's posh Magnificent Mile (North Michigan Avenue).

While some hotels with trashy lobbies and ripped carpeting forbid canine guests, dogs here are welcome to tread the imported marble floors and whiff the antique furniture and the splendid arrangements of fresh flowers. The only restriction is that they aren't allowed to drink from the ornate fountain. Rates are $395 to $875. 120 E. Delaware Street; (312) 280-8800.

Hilton Chicago This hotel welcomes four-legged friends of 85 pounds or less. A $50 deposit and a signature accepting responsibility for damage are required.

Housekeeping provides small blankets for your pup to snooze on, making the floor a more comfortable option, and perhaps trying to discourage Fido from taking that usual sleeping spot in the bed! Rates are $139 to $329. 720 S. Michigan Avenue; (312) 922-4400.

Hilton O'Hare At this establishment's informal doggy play area, owners and their dogs can watch the planes land. Rates are $99–475. At O'Hare International Airport; (773) 686-8000 or (800) 445-8667.

Holiday Inn Mart Plaza The hotel is adjacent to the Merchandise Mart and sequestered 15 floors above the Apparel Mart along the Chicago River. There is a grassy area outside where you can take your dog and, of course, pick up after him. Helpful hint: Avoid the cabana rooms off to the side of the sky-lighted pool; they tend to be smaller and noisier than the others. Rates are $159 to $265. 350 N. Orleans Street; (312) 836-5000 or (800) 465-4329.

House of Blues Hotel, A Loews Hotel When you check in with your pet, you receive a personal note from the general manager, listing pet services available at the hotel, and a map of the area with dog-walking routes highlighted. Rooms are stocked with place mats, food and water bowls, toys and treats, and a special Do Not Disturb sign to let housekeeping know that a pet is in the room. Pet-walking and pet-sitting services are available through the concierge desk.

If your dog gets hungry and knows how to dial the phone, ordering room service is no problem. Bow Wow Burgers and the grilled filet are just a phone call away. For pets that miss the comforts of home, Loews offers a "Did You Forget Your Closet?" service that loans dog and cat beds, leashes, collars, and even pet videos. Charlotte St. Martin, executive vice president of marketing, understands that "pets provide unconditional love, and people love their pets unconditionally." St. Martin adds, "At Loews we've found that taking care of pets is one of the best ways to build customer loyalty and give our guests—and their companions—a good night's sleep."

It can be argued that no hotel loves pets more than this group does. They even have a "Loews Loves Pets" program, opening their doors to four-legged guests at each of their 15 hotels in the United States and Canada. To kick off the VIP (Very Important Pet) program, the House of Blues Hotel hosted the "Take Your Dog to Work Day" First Annual Bark Breakfast. Admission was $20 for the owner and pet, helping this 14-city event raise more than $15,000 for animal charities, including the Anti-Cruelty Society in Chicago. The event featured a buffet for the dogs, complete with rice, eggs, and cupcakes for dessert. Guest speakers included Dr. Susan Ferraro, president of the Chicago

Veterinary Medical Association, who offered health and safety tips for traveling with pets. And all attending canines went home with treats, toys, Cool Pooch water bottles, and doggy briefcases. The media ate up the Bark Breakfast: there was coverage on nearly every TV station in town, on the radio, and in several community newspapers.

Let's hope other hotels catch on to this loving, pet-friendly policy. Rates are $169 to $1,200. 333 N. Dearborn Street; (312) 245-0333 or (800) 23-LOEWS (5-6397). Visit the chain's website at loewshotels.com.

Palmer House Hilton Chicago Canine guests receive a combination food and water dish that bears the hotel's logo. Treats and bottled water for dogs are delivered on a newspaper-lined plastic tray. Some hotels get flustered by handling canine guests, but around here they're used to dogs. The Palmer House played host to 630 dogs during the American Council for the Blind convention.

The Palmer House opened on September 16, 1871, just 13 days before the Chicago fire reduced it to ashes. Chicago real estate tycoon Potter Palmer immediately rebuilt a new hotel three times larger, at ten times the cost of the original. A recent $130 million restoration has succeeded in returning this classic hotel in the Loop to its rightful stature among the top choices for visiting canine executives. The lobby's intricately painted two-story ceiling may take your breath (or your bark) away. Guests must sign a waiver stating that they are responsible for any damage caused by their four-legged companions. Rates are $159 to $399. 17 E. Monroe Street; (312) 726-7500.

Radisson Hotel This converted condo complex just east of Michigan Avenue has no "official" weight limit for visiting dogs. An employee told me, "As long as they're cute, they can usually be accommodated." Our suggestion: Take Rover to the groomer before checking in, to guarantee he's looking his best! There's a $150 refundable deposit per stay. Rates are $149 to $279. 160 E. Huron Street; (312) 787-2900 or (800) 333-3333.

Renaissance Chicago Hotel According to Tom Ernsting, director of sales, pooches under 45 pounds are allowed at this first-rate hotel at the north end of the Loop, across from the Chicago River. The front desk told me pups under 10 pounds are welcome. I then spoke to Paige Kerbel, the hotel's manager, who has no idea what the weight limit is for dogs but who told me, "We've never turned down a dog yet."

Your canine companion will not go hungry at this hotel; if she knows how to dial the phone, you may want to put a block on the room-service extension.

House specialties include Fido's Fillet ($8), the Chuck Wagon ($4), and the chef's favorite, the Canine Dream—scrambled eggs on potato hash ($8). Dessert choices include Doggie Bagels ($3) and Doggie Cookies ($3). If a feline friend is with you, don't worry: the Renaissance also caters to cats, with a special Kitty Cuisine menu. There is a $45 nonrefundable pet fee. Rates are $270 to $325. 1 Wacker Drive; (312) 372-7200.

Residence Inn by Marriott Guests pay $15 per day per dog. This is a nonrefundable charge, not a deposit. Rates are $99 to $299. 210 E. Walton Street; (312) 943-9800 or (800) 331-3131.

Ritz-Carlton Chicago The Ritz rolls out the red carpet for pets. The only restriction is that pups must weigh in at less than 30 pounds. As canine visitors arrive, they're lavished with praise for just being dogs. They're also presented with treats—healthy top-of-the-line biscuits, of course. After all, this is the Ritz.

Amenities are no less ritzy once pets reach their rooms. An arrangement of treats and bottled water for dogs is displayed on a silver platter with ceramic water and food bowls.

Canine guests can stroll through the lobby and even join afternoon tea. If they get bored with the human conversations, the all-knowing concierge will offer his advice concerning the best of the neighborhood dog-friendly parks. Or, for $20, you can leave it to the doorman to dog-sit, walk your pooch, and handle feeding chores. Room-service delicacies prepared for pets are among the finest in town. Entrees such as the Lovable Chopped Filet Mignon ($12) or the Tail Wagging Good Grilled Breast of Chicken ($6) are just some of the specialties. Rates are $360 to $3,500. 160 E. Pearson Street; (312) 266-1000.

Sutton Place Hotel It used to be called Le Meridien, and before that it was 21 East, but the luxury hotel remains pretty much the same—including the canine policy. If dogs are less than 50 pounds, they're welcome. Usually a $200 deposit is required. Whether the pooch may join you for snacks in the outdoor café along the sidewalk depends on whom you happen to ask. We're told that plans are being developed for more canine-friendly amenities. Rates are $250 to $285. 21 E. Bellevue Place; (312) 266-2100.

Westin Hotel, Chicago When I spoke to Rick Wang, director of marketing for this recently renovated Chicago classic, he told me dogs under 30 pounds are welcome, with no other restrictions. When I called back and spoke to the front desk, I was told dogs had to be under 45 pounds and in a cage. Make sure you ask specific questions when you make your reservation, and have them update the computer file to avoid a potential problem when you arrive to check in, pooch in hand. The hotel is located a tennis ball's throw from dog-friendly Oak Street Beach (see p. 36). Rates are $179 to $329. 909 N. Michigan Avenue; (312) 943-7200.

2 SUBURBAN COOK COUNTY

Several awesome canine special events are held throughout the region, such as the renowned LaGrange Pet Parade. Likewise, only in suburban Cook County can dogs partake of Shakespeare in the high style offered at the Oak Park Festival Theatre. The area also includes some of the best canine-only beaches. When it comes to parks, however, while plenty of communities allow dogs, others have zero canine tolerance.

We infiltrated some of the south suburbs ourselves but relied heavily on researchers Lisa Seeman, German shepherd dog Bonnie, and keeshond-mix Bayla.

"With only a few exceptions, establishments that dogs can patronize—such as cafés and restaurants with outdoor seating—and special events for dogs just don't fit into a South Side mentality," says Lisa.

Before setting off for Orland Park parks with her canine pals, Lisa called the Park District. The first person to whom she spoke wasn't certain if dogs are allowed in the parks. Lisa was told to call back and speak with a communications supervisor. She did. She was told Orland Park absolutely welcomes dogs as long as they're on a leash and the owner picks up.

Lisa cruised a dozen Orland Park parks. In many places, she saw dogs playing, sometimes even off-leash. Curiously, at nearly every park, she saw signs reading "No Dogs Allowed" and also signs reading "Only Leashed Dogs Allowed." So, which is it?

Hoping to clear things up, I phoned the Orland Park Park District and inquired. After bouncing back and forth between several bosses who were afraid to answer definitively, I was told to call the police.

The police spokesperson said that dogs are allowed. When I commented on the No Dogs Allowed signs, she said, "Then, they're not allowed."

I asked, "How can you enforce the ordinance when you don't know what it is?" She told me to call the Village Hall person in charge of community codes and ordinances. I did. It turns out that dogs are not allowed in the parks. As for the signs that say "Leashed Dogs Allowed," they are posted at asphalt paths. But dogs are allowed on the paths only; they're not legally allowed on the grass or in the park space.

Orland Park wasn't the only confused south suburb. In Palos Hills, the Park District had no idea if dogs are allowed on their own spaces. One person at the office said yes; another said no. I was told to call the village's animal control officer for the official ruling. It turns out leashed dogs are allowed as long as their people pick up.

However, most south and southwest suburbs don't allow dogs in municipal parks. Among those that forbid canine traffic are Alsip, Bedford Park, Blue Island, Bridgeview, Evergreen Park, Hickory Hills, Justice, LaGrange, LaGrange Park, and Westchester.

Cook County's north and northwest 'burb parks aren't any dog friendlier. Dogs are not allowed in municipal parks in Arlington Heights, Des Plaines, Glenview, Kenilworth, Morton Grove, Niles, Skokie, or Wilmette. Lincolnwood allowed dogs until a few years ago. I was told by a village spokesperson, "Owners abused the privilege. They didn't pick up, and there were too many complaints about obnoxious dogs." Sadly, this was probably true.

One Park Ridge resident says, "Police have even stopped me on public parkways [the green spaces between the sidewalks and the streets]. Aside from your own backyard, dogs don't get out much. That's why if you live around here, you're always looking for places to take your dog."

There are dog beaches in suburban Cook, but they will cost you. Nonresidents have to fork over $50 to use Centennial Park Dog Beach in Winnetka, $150 for Gillson Park Dog Beach in Wilmette, or $50 to use the Evanston Dog Beach. If you live fairly close, the Winnetka and Wilmette locations could be worth the money.

Glencoe's dog beach is free. There's one major trade-off: it's available for canine use only in the off-season, from the day after Labor Day until Memorial Day.

Evanston has some wonderful places where dog owners mix and mingle and take their pups off-leash. But allowing a dog to run free is against the law. There's also an active antidog movement that would like to see Evanston added to the growing list of suburbs that forbid dogs in public parks. As I was taking notes at one park, a woman frantically came running up to me. She didn't see that I had two dogs of my own. Robin and the girls were off playing elsewhere in the park. I believe this woman thought I was with the FBI or the CIA. She feared I was about to blow the whistle on her canine play group. When I told her about the book, at first she looked relieved. But then she panicked and begged me not to divulge exactly where the covert canine group cavorts. Reluctantly, I agreed. About a month later, the same thing happened in Oak Park.

Both of these communities are filled with responsible owners who simply want more opportunities for their loyal companions. Unfortunately, a minority of irresponsible owners combined with a contingent of antidog extremists have created a "them-or-us" attitude. It's all the more distressing coming as it does from two communities that are, in most ways, so enlightened.

For those canines who reside in the many suburbs that don't allow dogs in municipal parks, the Forest Preserve of Cook County offers wonderful alternatives.

Dogs are not allowed to swim in lakes or rivers in the preserves, and they must be leashed. You'll see dogs off-leash, but as we learned, the Forest Preserve police don't cut offenders any slack. So, when you take a dog off-leash here, you do so at your own risk.

Unlike the Forest Preserve of DuPage County or the Lake County Forest Preserve, there are no off-leash places designed specifically for pups in Cook County preserves, at least not yet. However, the subject is apparently under consideration. There are several interested citizens campaigning, attempting to convince the county commissioners to make the change.

We were bowled over by the striking beauty and wide range of hiking trails inside the preserves. My guess is that too many Cook County canines never get to experience these places, and that also is too bad.

Cook County Forest Preserve District locations are described at the end of this section, following the municipal listings.

Alsip

Places to Stay

Baymont Inn Conflicting information seems to be the norm at this hotel. One person told me they will accommodate any dog with a $25 deposit. The next time I called, they told me it's a $50 deposit, for dogs under 50 pounds. When making your reservations, get a confirmation in writing. Rates are $70 to $85. 12801 S. Cicero; (708) 597-3900.

Days Inn This hotel allows dogs and has them coming and going when dog shows are being held nearby. One thing management doesn't appreciate is bathing dogs in the bathtubs. Housekeeping says it clogs up the pipes. Maybe that's why there's a $35 fee per night, per dog. Room rates are $67.50 to $85. 5150 W. 127th Street; (708) 371-5600 or (800) 329-7466.

Arlington Heights

Festival

Frontier Days The local patriotic festival includes a pet parade. The festival dates vary, but it's always held over the July 4 weekend.

Patriotic pooches must share the pet parade spotlight with all kinds of pets including cats, hedgehogs, tarantulas, and on one occasion even a duck. Among many other categories, ribbons are given to the most unusual pet—sorry, canines will never win this award.

This parade doesn't go far, from one side of the stage to the other, at the northwest corner of Recreation Park.

A strictly canine event held during the festival is "Dog Frisbee Catch and Fetch." The idea is to fetch the best, and snatch Frisbees. There's no fee to register for either the parade or the catching contest, and you may sign up as late as 10 minutes before the events begin.

Unfortunately, dogs are allowed to join in the Frontier Days fun only on the day of the pet parade and the fetching event. Other activities continue throughout the festival, including food booths, activities for children, and some pretty impressive musical acts, such as Three Dog Night. It's too bad the canine audience isn't allowed to watch a group like that.

There's free parking in all Village garages and free shuttle buses from the garages. The festival is in Recreation Park, 500 E. Miner Street. Admission is free. Call (847) 577-8572.

Places to Stay

Best Western The manager told me, "No big dogs."

I asked, "How big? Do you have a weight limit?"

"Less than a Great Dane, maybe a golden retriever or smaller," he said.

"OK, but do you have a specific size in mind to define a big dog?"

"Yes, I said it: smaller than a Great Dane," he reiterated.

We concluded: they don't like Great Danes.

Rates are $64 to $66. 948 E. Northwest Highway; (847) 255-2900.

La Quinta Inn Pets under 20 pounds are permitted, but they—and their owners—must suffice with a "pet room." I'm told, "These rooms are just as good as all the others; you won't be disappointed." Rates are $79 to $103. 1415 W. Dundee Road; (847) 253-8777.

Red Roof Inn Dogs under 80 pounds are welcome to stay here. Only one dog per room, please. Rates are $58.99 to $109.99. 22 W. Algonquin Road; (847) 228-6650.

Bridgeview

Place to Stay

Exel Inn Dogs under 25 pounds are welcome and even have their own small grassy area out back on which to leave their marks. Just be sure to scoop up afterward. If you're planning on staying longer than three nights, you will have to proffer a $100 refundable deposit. All dogs and their humans are assigned smoking rooms, no matter how long you stay, even if neither of you smokes. Rates are $58 to $77. 9625 S. 76th Street; (708) 430-1818.

Burbank

Place to Stay

Cezar's Inn Well, it depends on how classy you want to get. Stay in a $200 room, and you'll have to leave the dog home. However, if you're willing to accept $69 accommodations, the pooch is allowed. You'll still have to fork over a $25 surcharge, though. 5001 W. 79th Street; (708) 423-1100.

Chicago Heights

Parks

Dogs are welcome in all parks, as long as they are leashed and owners pick up. Parks are open from sunrise to sunset. Call (708) 755-1351.

COMMISSIONER'S PARK // ½ The crown jewel of the local Park District, this spacious park is a jock's paradise, with baseball and soccer fields, basketball courts, and an in-line skating rink. Lots of families picnic here, as proven by the overflowing trash cans, which researcher Lisa Seeman's dog Bayla thoroughly enjoyed sniffing.

A wood-chip trail twists through the park. Along the way, there are balance beams, parallel bars, and military-style monkey bars for people who want to work out. For dogs, this trail is a no-brainer. There isn't much shade here; a few mature trees outline the park's border, and a few more poke between the play areas and the open fields. For relief, you can cool off in the spray pool or under one of the two picnic pavilions.

Open sunrise to sunset. There's lots of available parking at Commissioner's Park, at Chicago Road just south of Holbrook Road. (708) 755-1351.

EUCLID PARK / ½   The park is L-shape, with the playground area filling out most of the base of the L. At the south end, past the field house, there's a small grassy area, well-suited for canine fun. That's where Lisa and Bayla hung out. Bayla liked the grass on this side of the park, and Lisa wanted to stay away from the group of guys drinking heavily.

Bayla, a keeshond-mix, was about 10 months old and hardly offered much protection. Aside from the party of guzzling guys, the park was completely empty. Lisa said, "It's too bad I didn't bring my German shepherd, Bonnie; maybe this place wouldn't have creeped me out."

After a quick look, Lisa and Bayla were more than ready to depart. Just then, more people arrived, a group of little kids and their parents. By now, Bayla was already nervous, probably because she sensed how nervous Lisa was. A perceptive dog can discern even the subtlest hints of discomfort.

One little boy ran excitedly toward Bayla, waving his arms—not exactly the way to approach any dog, let alone a nervous one. Bayla panicked and somehow slipped out of her collar. The boy continued to run after Bayla, who also continued running, with her tail tucked between her legs. Finally the boy's mother called him.

This is how children can get bitten by dogs. The boy should have approached Lisa and asked, "Can I pet your dog?" When he didn't, his mom should have intervened.

Luckily, all Bayla wanted to do was get away. She was so shaken that Lisa had to get down on one knee and quietly coax her to return. Lisa and Bayla won't be setting foot in Euclid Park again anytime soon.

Open sunrise to sunset. Euclid Park is at 21st Street at Euclid Avenue. (708) 755-1351.

LANDEEN PARK *(worth a sniff)*   A small play lot with little open space. A split-log fence doesn't do much to prevent a dog that's off-leash from bolting into Schilling Avenue.

Open sunrise to sunset. Landeen Park is at 10th Street and Schilling Avenue. (708) 755-1351.

SMITH PARK ✓   The good news is that the park is fenced in. The bad news is that no one had unlocked the gates on the Sunday afternoon Lisa visited. The park is supposed to be open daily from dawn to dusk.

From the car, Lisa noted the numerous amenities, including tennis and basketball courts, a picnic area, and a softball field. In the winter, the softball field becomes an ice-skating rink. There were a few kids playing in the playground area, apparently having chosen to jump the fence. Lisa and Bayla weren't up for that. The recreation building is under renovation and will reopen as a Park District Day Care Center.

Open sunrise to sunset—unless you happen to arrive when the gate is locked. Smith Park is bounded by 15th and 14th Streets at Ashland and Scott Avenues. (708) 755-1351.

SWANSON PARK ✓ ½   This park has a real retro feel. Next to the modern playground made of recycled plastics are relics from a bygone era, including a vintage horse from a merry-go-round. For water, you or the pooch will have to pump your own with an old-fashioned handle. The water pump sits in the middle of the playground. There's also a soccer field and a fenced-in baseball field. For picnics, you have two pavilions from which to choose.

Open sunrise to sunset. Swanson Park is at 207th Street at Travers Avenue, a few blocks east of Western Avenue, and a few blocks north of Lincoln Highway. (708) 755-1351.

WACKER PARK ✓✓   While Bayla had a wonderful time, this was a bittersweet trip for Lisa. Lisa and the dogs she had as a kid were once regular visitors to Wacker Park. She grew up only a few blocks away.

Lisa used to scamper up the monkey bars. They're gone. The drinking fountains were out of order. The baseball field was a mess. However, no one minded Bayla running about the infield. Except for the two entrances (one on the east side, the other on the west), the park is completely fenced in.

A rottweiler was tied to a tree as its family picnicked under a nearby pavilion. Bayla continued running around the ball field on a long line and into the mowed grassy area. She was having a wonderful time. The other dog wasn't pleased. It was frustrating for that rottie to watch Bayla. The jealous dog began to bark, whine, and cry. Lisa took her dog and her memories and hightailed it out of there.

Open sunrise to sunset. Wacker Park is located at 1025 Lowe Avenue at 11th Street, near West End Avenue. (708) 755-1351.

Crestwood

Place to Stay

Hampton Inn Canines are welcome, but the general manager says, "We trust those dogs are well behaved." Even so, four-legged guests must be crated at all times. Housekeeping will not clean a room with a "loose dog." When walking anywhere in or around the hotel, your dog must be on a leash. Rates are $90 to $95. 13330 S. Cicero Avenue; (708) 597-3330.

East Hazel Crest

Place to Stay

Motel 6 Dogs under 20 pounds are welcome. The room rate is $47.03. 17214 S. Halsted Street; (708) 957-9233.

Elk Grove Village

Parks

Dogs are welcome on-leash as long as their people pick up. Parks are open from sunrise to sunset. For more information call (847) 437-8780.

AUDUBON PARK //   A pleasant-enough place for a romp. Lots of children use the play area. You can warm a bench while your kid and dog run around. There are baseball diamonds and tennis courts as well. The highlight of the park for locals is the in-line skating and skateboard facility, which includes a ramp area. There is also an in-line skating rink, which turns into an ice-skating rink in winter.

Open sunrise to sunset. Audubon Park is bounded by Victoria Lane, Elk Grove Village Boulevard, Ridge Avenue, and Bianco Drive. (847) 437-8780.

LIONS PARK/JAYCEE PARK / ½   It's too bad dogs aren't allowed in the water park. They can, however, go onto the ball field when it's not in use. There are also tennis courts. In the summer, there are concessions. Chaser ducked once when a particularly low-flying airplane passed over. At this park, your pooch may not hear you, because of the planes going into and coming out of O'Hare Airport, so be careful.

Open sunrise to sunset. Lions Park/Jaycee Park is behind Queen of Rosary School, 690 W. Elk Grove Boulevard, and is bounded by Brandwood Avenue, Keswick Road, and Rev. Morrison Boulevard. Entrances are off Charing Cross Road and Cypress Lane. (847) 437-8780.

Places to Stay

Days Inn Calls to this motel leave me adrift. No one can give me a definitive answer regarding the pet policy. During one call, I ended up in a philosophical discussion with a gentleman about the definition of a "pet" versus a "dog." He told me that pets are welcome to stay for the night, but not big dogs. I told him I happen to have a moderately big dog that is also my pet. He didn't seem to think this is possible. His final decision was that small pets weighing "about 20 or 25 pounds" can stay, but "big dogs that weigh 40 or 50 or 60 pounds, we do not allow." The hotel did have a definitive answer on one rule: there is a fee of $10 per night per dog . Room rates are $59 to $129. 1920 E. Higgins Road; (847) 437-1650.

Exel Inn-O'Hare Pets under 25 pounds are in. Dogs must be attended at all times. Rates are $67 to $200. 2881 Touhy Avenue; (847) 803-9400.

Holiday Inn It's only those giant breeds that are discriminated against here— dogs under 50 pounds are welcome. Off the record, one employee told me she's seen retrievers and German shepherds check in with no flack. Room rates are $79 to $119. 1000 Busse Road; (847) 437-6010.

LaQuinta Inn There's a 25-pound weight limit, and the rates are $99 to $129 per room. 1900 Oakton Street; (847) 439-6767.

Motel 6 I'm told, "As long as the dog is under 30 pounds and keeps quiet, it's OK." The room rate is $41.99. 1601 Oakton Street; (847) 981-9766.

When the Owner's Away

For your dog, it's a nightmare come true. The entire family absconds without explanation. Leaving the pooch in safe hands while you're off gallivanting through Europe or stretching out on a Caribbean beach is no easy task.

"No matter what you do . . . the dog will be stressed," says Sherry Linning, the director of this region for the American Boarding Kennel Association.

From your dog's perspective, the least stressful option is to stay with familiar friends or neighbors whose dog you watch when they go on a trip. Assuming the dogs get on well, this is a wonderful option. It's certainly the least expensive. The downside is the responsibility you're thrusting on your friend or neighbor.

Of course, you can hire someone whose job it is to be responsible for your dog. Keep in mind, though, that when you're away for more than 24 hours, a twice-daily dog walker isn't enough. In most cases, a three-times-daily walker isn't enough either. You should have someone stay in your house, a place where the dog is comfortable even though the family is away.

Sandy Kamen Wisniewski operates a business called Pet Sitters of America, Inc., out of Libertyville. Here are her tips for choosing a pet sitter:

- The yellow pages can suffice, but you're better off finding a pet-sitter through your vet, a friend, or a relative who can offer a recommendation.

- If you reach an answering machine of the pet-sitting service, that's fine; leave a message. However, if your call isn't returned for several days, or ever, that isn't fine. Remember, you're searching for responsibility. Any signal of irresponsibility should be taken seriously.

- Be cautious about any company in business for fewer than three years. However, a new company may be considered if highly recommended.

- Don't hesitate to ask for references. If they refuse to provide references, forget about them. Of course, services won't offer references of any clients who have had a bad experience.

- Make certain the individual or company you hire is insured and bonded.

- Be sure that the sitter who will be staying at your home comes out to learn household instructions and, most important, to meet your dog before you depart. If your normally friendly dog feels uneasy, follow the dog's instinct. If you feel uneasy, for whatever reason, follow your instinct. There are lots of pet-sitters out there.

Pet-sitters are becoming increasingly popular, but kenneling is still the most common option. Boarding facilities abound in the Chicago area. Sherry Linning, who owns Bark 'N Town Kennels in Ingleside, notes that some are better than others. In fact, a few may be downright horrible.

With Linning's help, here are some tips for finding good kennels:

- Ask for a tour. If they don't want to give a tour, be suspicious. Some kennels offer tours at specific times simply for ease of scheduling, but it also could be because they allow conditions to get really bad before cleaning up. You may never know. "It's reasonable for you to see where your dog is going, and to ask as many questions as you like," Linning says.

- A general doggy odor may be prevalent; however, you shouldn't be overcome with stench, nor should you smell feces throughout. "The staff can't walk with a bucket in back of the dogs, so there may be some defecation. Still, there should be a limited amount, and dogs shouldn't be sitting in their own feces," Linning adds.

- All tenants should have fresh water.

- Most kennels have charts that keep tabs of elimination, play times, and other activities. Also, all dogs should be called by their names.

- A kennel is in violation of the law in most states, including Illinois, if it doesn't require proof of vaccinations for rabies and canine distemper. Proof of vaccinations for parvovirus and bordetella (canine cough) are optional.

- Kennels should allow you to supply your own food as well as any toys or blankets of choice. Some kennels charge extra if they're required to follow your feeding instructions, although some places may negotiate this point.

- A responsible kennel will ask if there are medical conditions of which the staff should be aware. However, if your dog is very ill, don't board. If you have any doubts, consult your vet.

continued

> • Arrange for a one-night "rehearsal" stay for dogs not used to being boarded, particularly before a trip exceeding two or three days. Linning says, "The dog will learn you're not leaving forever, and you'll feel better about kenneling the dog." Of course, this stay won't be free, though some kennels may discount the "practice" evening.

Evanston

Parks

Dogs are quite the controversy in Evanston, and (at least from an outsider's point of view) it's all very weird.

There are several places where renegade owners regularly take their dogs to gambol off-leash. That form of gamboling is against the law, and police will sometimes pounce. An angry contingent complains vigorously to the police about dogs, fanatical about creating a law to forbid canines from visiting any city park. Then there are the dog lovers, who prompted a fleeting move to establish an off-leash dog park in Evanston, which was summarily shouted down.

Some dog owners who live in the south part of Evanston travel to parks in the north because they feel those places are more dog friendly. On the other hand, many people in northern Evanston head to the south end because they believe those parks aren't as overzealously patrolled.

Further confusing matters, the Evanston parks are operated by several governing bodies. Their views on dogs vary, but all conform to the city law; dogs are allowed on a leash, and owners are required to pick up. Parks are open from sunrise to 11 P.M. For more information call (847) 866-2910.

CENTENNIAL PARK/DAWES PARK /// Signage at Evanston parks reads "No Dogs or Cats Without a Leash." At first, I laughed. At this point, I had visited maybe two hundred parks and forest preserves to research this book, and we never saw cats on a leash. That was until we met Lizzy, a six-month-old calico, at Centennial. The cat was in a harness and led with a leash.

On a second visit to Centennial, this time with Lucy and Chaser, we happened to be there as the sun was beginning to set over the lake. On the breakwater looking south, we sat and took a collective breath, basking in the beauty of the Chicago skyline.

North of the breakwater is a small field that leads to a beach for people. Dogs aren't allowed on this beach, but Dog Beach is just to the south. Don't take your dogs near this field. After simply stepping into the field, Chaser began to lick persistently at her rear end. It turned out Chaser had got four burrs stuck on her rear and two more on her hind legs. Lucy also had a few burrs on her. It took several minutes to remove them. A sympathetic police officer offered to help.

The real danger was that Chaser was trying to remove the burrs herself, and she would have got some of the needles in her mouth if I hadn't intervened.

When I removed the final burr, she jumped at me and began to incessantly lick my face, as if to say "Thank you."

Two trails zigzag through the park. One is asphalt, and the other is crushed rock. It's a busy place, filled with boaters, sunbathers, and joggers. Visitors are of all ages, including little kids, seniors, and students from nearby Northwestern University. At the center of the park is a large decorative pond with fountains. Despite the constant circulation of this pond, the corners are packed with debris, including feathers and general garbage. Of course, one of these corners is where Chaser chose to spontaneously dive in. I called her out immediately. For one thing, she dived into garbage, and for another, dogs aren't supposed to swim in this pond.

Dogs also aren't allowed in the field house. And we did witness one police officer issuing a warning to an owner with a dog off-leash.

Open sunrise to 11 P.M. The park is bounded by Sheridan Road, Forest Place, and Davis and Church Streets. (847) 866-2910.

CLARK SQUARE PARK //   Take a seat on the rocks along Lake Michigan, and count the sailboats as they pass. Canine swimming is not allowed, although some dogs do take the plunge. This demure, tree-lined park is lovely. A paved path stretches from the parking area at Kedzie Street about one city block to the end of the park and into a residential neighborhood.

American cocker spaniel Toby was running circles around trees with abandon, until he found Lucy and Sophie. Then he was running around German shepherd–mix Sophie. Soon Lucy joined in running circles around her best canine pal. It was sort of a doggy version of monkey-in-the-middle. Having worked up a thirst, Lucy and Toby took advantage of the step stool at the drinking fountain, no doubt created for children, not small dogs.

Open sunrise to 11 P.M. Clark Square Park is at Sheridan Road and Main and Kedzie Streets. (847) 866-2910.

LEAHY PARK // ½   It's a charming place with an impressive stand of trees leading into a golf course. One Evanston dog trainer prefers the golf course to the park itself. Both his Labrador retriever/white German shepherd–mix and his Siberian husky/malamute–mix can be seen running through the course. Just so long as the hounds stay out of the way of golfers, there's generally no hassle. "So far, we've had a good time. Sometimes we see other dogs. And we avoid the sand traps," he said. The best time to visit the golf course is late in the afternoon, when most of the duffers have completed their games. Just watch out for flying golf balls.

The park also has tennis courts and a children's play lot.

Open sunrise to 11 P.M. Leahy Park is on Lincoln Street just west of Ridge Avenue, bounded by Colfax Street. (847) 866-2910.

RAYMOND PARK /   This is a nice-enough park, just southeast of downtown Evanston. Office workers and moms and/or dads with kids fill the park during the day. It's not as crowded in the evening. There are lots of benches for sitting, and there's plenty of play equipment. Unfortunately, there's not much for a dog to do. On top of that, the small park borders busy Chicago Avenue.

Open sunrise to sunset. Raymond Park is on Chicago Avenue between Grove and Lake Streets and Hinman Avenue. (847) 866-2910.

ROBERT CROWN PARK / ½   Most of the space is taken by an indoor sports center and ice rink. Dogs are not allowed inside. Instead, the pooch may frolic in the surrounding ball fields, if there's no softball game. But you have to be careful, since this park is bounded by two major streets.

Open sunrise to 11 P.M. Robert Crown Park is at Dewy and Dodge Avenues on Main Street. (847) 866-2910.

ROBERT JAMES PARK ///   The point of interest here is what locals call Mount Trashmore. This sledding hill was literally a junk pile that no one knew what to do with. Today the area is quite an impressive park, and the view from the hill is actually pretty good. On a clear day you can see several Chicago landmarks. Dogs have been seen sliding down the snowy hill on their bellies and being held in children's arms as they descend together on sleds.

Unlike a walk through Leahy Park and the adjacent golf course, there's no worry here about getting beaned. A sign clearly states: "Hitting Golf Balls Prohibited."

There are tennis courts and an expansive area for soccer and baseball. Sports events are often held in the evening at this well-lit site, the largest park in Evanston.

Open sunrise to 11 P.M. Robert James Park is at Oakton Street and Dodge Avenue, with parking off Mulford Street. (847) 866-2910.

Beach

Dogs are forbidden on Evanston beaches, except for the Evanston Dog Beach. Dogs are welcome at Dog Beach, providing their people adhere to the rules.

Despite the prohibition, people take their dogs to the various Evanston beaches all the time, before and after hours during the beach season, which extends from the second Saturday in June through Labor Day. Beach hours are 10:30 A.M. to 8 P.M. Dogs also run unrestrained on the beaches in the off-season, from Labor Day through the winter and up until the beaches open again in June. Technically, this is against the law.

Concerning canines using the beaches in off-hours or during the off-season, the real-world enforcement is unclear. "What can the harm possibly be?" asked one Evanston parks official. "Let's face it: we can't patrol the entire lakefront anyhow." On the other hand, a Park District public information officer warned, "The law is the law. Residents don't want dogs using beaches. Dogs now have their own beach, period." She added that owners may be ticketed even for using the Dog Beach in off-hours. In any case, one might think the Evanston police have better things to do.

DOG BEACH //   Rule number one: Tokens are required. Residents pay $25 per season, nonresidents $50. The official Dog Beach season begins on May 1 and ends on October 31. The site, southeast of Centennial Park, opens at 7 A.M. and closes at 8 P.M.

I never would have guessed that a beach designed specifically for dogs could merit such a meager ranking.

This beach is only about 25 feet across. Depending on the wind direction, the property can also be transformed into a cemetery for stinky fish. The dogs appreciate this, but their people don't.

To add to the stew, the boat launch is next door, and boaters dump debris that washes ashore here. There's also a concern about oil pollution in this water.

Lucy and her best friend, Sophie, visited on two occasions, both pleasant but cool days toward the end of the season. And each time, they were the only dogs on the premises. We asked several people—whose dogs were romping in nearby Centennial Park—why they weren't using Dog Beach. Mary Rogers offered a typical reply: "It's too dirty, and the police are always asking to see your token. I just don't like it." She added that she sometimes takes Tulip to a nearby beach after hours or during the off-season.

Dog Beach isn't totally awful. For one thing, it's gently sloping, offering small dogs like Lucy a chance to wade without going in over their heads. On our second visit, a whopping pile of lake crud had washed ashore over a period of at least a week. If a city collects money for use of the beach, it certainly should maintain the property. Not knowing what was in this odious pile, I kept Lucy and Sophie away, which wasn't difficult. It had one of those rare stenches that even dogs are smart enough to avoid. Officials have since promised to improve conditions at the beach.

Here are the other rules for Dog Beach:

- Owners or their agents must be in control of their domesticated dogs at all times.

- Owners or their agents with dogs may enter the water to their knees and no farther.

- Dogs may enter the water within the designated buoyed area.

- All dog owners or their agents must pick up all waste from their dogs and place it in appropriate receptacles.

- Sunbathing is prohibited.

For more information, call (847) 866-2910.

Recreation Area

Northwestern University The main campus of one of the most prestigious universities in the nation is a great place to walk with a pooch. The vintage architecture is fascinating, there are sculptures to look at, and there are always flowers in bloom. In the winter, its dignified beauty is almost surreal.

A little-known fact is that the campus is also home to an enormous squirrel population. There may be more squirrels per square foot here than in any other place on earth. Now you understand—this is a great place to walk a pooch.

While the main campus is definitely worth checking out, the canine highlight has to be the landfill area east of the school along Lake Michigan, from the Norris University Center at the south end to Lincoln Street at the northern tip.

The asphalt path that meanders through the landfill area can get congested with students jogging, bicycling, and in-line skating. Fortunately, there's also space to walk off of the path. A retention pond is located at the center of the landfill, but canine swimming is discouraged. Posted signs warn against diving into the lake due to dangerous currents. These warnings should be taken seriously.

You can grab lunch at the Norris University Center, but dogs aren't allowed inside. When it's warm, there are seats outside, or you can walk to the lake for a picnic.

As you cross over the wooden bridge on the south side of the landfill, look over your shoulder. The view of the Chicago skyline is extraordinary. Take your camera with you.

Although taking a dog off-leash is against the law, some outlaws sneak their dogs around the hill at the very north side of the landfill area.

There's visitor parking south of the library, or near the performance arts buildings at the southeast corner of the campus; enter off Sheridan Road. More visitor parking is at the north side of the landfill; enter on Lincoln Street, east of Sheridan Road. The Northwestern University Campus is mostly east of Sheridan Road from Chicago Avenue to Lincoln Street. (847) 491-3741.

Quick Bite

Olive Mountain Specialties include chicken shawerma (marinated chicken on a rotisserie) and homemade hummus. The menu features lots of seafood and vegetarian offerings. Water is provided for dogs on request. 814 Church Street; (847) 475-0380.

Coffee Shops

Cafe Mozart Dogs may hear the Mozart music playing indoors, but if you're seated outside *you* won't. Flowers are scattered in planters behind a white fence. 600 Davis Street; (847) 492-8056.

Starbucks Two Evanston locations welcome canine traffic: 528 Dempster Street, (847) 733-8328; and 2114 Central Avenue, (847) 328-1369.

Glencoe

Park and Beach

Dogs are allowed in the local parks and on the beach from the day after Labor Day until Memorial Day. A leash is required, and you must pick up. Parks are open from 6 A.M. to 10 P.M. Call (847) 835-3030.

Lakefront Park and Lakefront Glencoe Beach ✓✓✓ ½ This rating is for both facilities combined and applies to the off-season when the beach is open to dogs.

This is a superlative beach, used by people from June 1 through Labor Day. As you stroll down a walkway toward the lake, there is a boat ramp on your left, and the beach is to the right.

I took a Frisbee, in which Lucy showed no interest whatsoever. However, Lucy's friend Sophie proceeded to leap into the air to snatch the Frisbee throws. She'd first run into the surf, then swing around and make a midair grab.

Hank Balas, whose golden retriever Rusty was eyeing the Frisbee action with envy, asked how I ever taught the dog to catch like that. I sort of shrugged. The truth is that she usually doesn't. In fact, when I arrived back home and told Sophie's owner, Karen Daiter, about Sophie's great catches, she didn't believe me.

Lakefront Park is also a lovely spot. You could even call it romantic. There's a swing built for two, but it's for people, not dogs. Lots of trees are a nice sight in the fall with Lake Michigan as a backdrop. Nevertheless, the real draw is the beach.

Open 6 A.M. to 10 P.M. The Lakefront facilities are at Park, Longwood, and Hazel Avenues. The beach is open for dogs from the day after Labor Day until Memorial Day. (847) 835-3030.

Doggy Doing

Summer Concerts in the Park This event's organizer loves Motown and old Supremes music. That's why at least one Motown cover act is booked each year for the summer concert-in-the-park series at Kalk Park, Park Avenue at Green Bay Road. Concerts are at 7:30 P.M. on the last Tuesday in June, the first Tuesday after July 4, and the last Tuesday in July. Food concessions usually offer pizza and hot dogs. Take your own blanket or chair. The tunes are free. Call (847) 835-3030.

Farmer's Market

Your dog is welcome to sniff her way to fresh veggies, flowers, and spices. She must be on-leash. 675 Village Court, next to village hall; Saturdays, 7 A.M. to noon, June through October. (847) 835-4188.

Festival

Fourth of July Festival Various events are held at this holiday celebration, and dogs are welcome to attend. The festival begins with a one-block fun run—even dachshunds can participate in this race. The run begins at about 10 A.M. at Kalk Park, Green Bay Road at Park Avenue. It ends about 10 minutes later. The race is followed by parent-and-kid team events, including relay races, an egg toss, and a "mummy wrap," in which kids wrap their mommies in toilet paper. However, there are no relay races for dogs, and there are no puppy wraps.

Close by is the Fourth of July Art Fair, held at Wyman Green, between village hall and the library, 320 Park Avenue, from 10 A.M. to 3 P.M. About 30 booths are on hand, and food is available. All canine art critics are welcome.

Dogs can also march in the annual July 4 parade, which starts at 2 P.M. at Central School (620 Greenwood Avenue) and continues for three whole blocks into the center of town. There's no admission fee for these events, or registration fee for marching in the parade. For more information call (847) 835-3030.

Coffee Shop

Starbucks Water is provided for dogs at this coffee place. The management plans on doing more in the future to welcome canines. 347 Park Avenue; (847) 835-8098.

Glenview

Place to Stay

The Baymont Inn and Suites Dogs can't go far: they're restricted to smoking rooms on the first floor at $79 per night. Dogs are not allowed to stay in the suites. 1625 Milwaukee Avenue; (847) 635-8300.

Glenwood

Park

Researcher Lisa Seeman was told the usual: dogs are allowed in the parks, as long as they're on a leash and their waste is picked up. Guess what? On visits to three of the four local parks, No Dogs Allowed signs were prominently displayed. When I phoned, I was told, "Dogs on-leash are OK, if people pick up." The following listing is for the one park that doesn't feature a sign forbidding dogs. But it's probably not worth the trip anyhow. Parks are open from sunrise to sunset. For more information call (708) 754-9516.

CALLAHAN-STRAND PARK ½/   A small neighborhood park with a kids' play lot and a pawful of picnic tables. Lisa and Bayla bopped over on a beautiful sunny Saturday afternoon, and the only company they had was a sparrow. And it flew off.

Open sunrise to sunset. Callahan-Strand Park is off Main Street at Rebecca and Rose Streets. (708) 754-9516.

Hazel Crest

Parks

Of the 13 municipal parks in Hazel Crest, only 4 offer opportunities for canines. Dogs on-leash are allowed at these places if owners pick up. The Village will rent you an entire park for a picnic—for people and dogs. Reservations must be made in advance; call (708) 335-1500. Parks are open from sunrise to sunset.

OAK HILL PARK ///   This 27-acre park offers plenty of space to find a private alcove for an afternoon picnic. There are also two picnic pavilions as well as several baseball fields and two children's playgrounds. The east side of the park is always in use, but it's still way less noisy than the west side, which is near the Tri-State Tollway. Fencing prevents dogs from running into traffic.

Open sunrise to sunset. Oak Hill Park is at 171st Street, just east of California Avenue at 170th Place. (708) 355-1500.

OAK VALLEY PARK ///   The Hazel Crest police department takes its canine unit here for exercise, and you can too. This 23-acre park is a natural water-retention area. What you see is what you get: no tennis or basketball courts and no playground, but dogs don't need any of that. When it comes to quality sniffing, this park is tops in Hazel Crest, particularly in the basin and at the nearby trees. You're not supposed to take a dog off-leash, but what a great place to play fetch. Let's just say this—you won't be alone if you do. The hilly area is used by sledders in the winter. There's a one-mile walking path around the park.

Open sunrise to sunset. Oak Valley Park is at 171st Street and Rockwell Avenue at Woodworth Place. (708) 355-1500.

SETNES PARK // ½   Although Setnes offers space, most of this 21-acre park is filled with human athletes playing football, baseball, soccer, or basketball. There isn't much territory left over for canine sports. On the bright side, it's a good place for a social dog to meet people.

Open sunrise to sunset. Setnes Park is at 2500 Crescent, just west of Western Avenue at 167th Street, also bounded by Circle Drive, Sunset Road, and 169th Street. (708) 355-1500.

STONE HOLLOW PARK / ½   It seems that all streets in Hazel Crest lead to this small triangular park. The park is only five acres, but it's not bad. It presents statuesque trees for sniffing, and a nearly half-mile asphalt path winding around them, leading to a children's playground. Bonnie, our researcher Lisa's German shepherd dog, didn't want to leave the sand volleyball court. Lisa had to drag her away, which is no easy task with a pooch that size. "She generally listens well, but when it comes to sand, she wants to stay all day," said Lisa. "She just loves the feel of sand."

Open sunrise to sunset. Stone Hollow Park is appropriately bounded by Dogwood Lane, and also Oakwood Drive, Ridgewood Drive, Stonebridge Drive, and Pebblewood Lane. (708) 335-1500.

Hinsdale

Park

KATHERINE LEGGE MEMORIAL PARK /// ½ (OFF-LEASH)   At designated times, you can take your pooch off-leash in the area north of the creek, and this is a fine park for such purposes because the grounds are about 80 percent fenced in. Still, if your dog has an undependable recall, I'd worry about the 20 percent not surrounded by a chain-link fence.

Canine lovers meet here regularly when dogs are allowed off-leash. The hours are: May 1 through October 31, 5 A.M. until 9 A.M., and 7 P.M. until 10 P.M.; and November 1 through April 30, 5 A.M. until 12 noon, and 7 P.M. until 10 P.M. When dogs are off-leash, they must be under voice command and in sight of owners at all times. All dogs must wear a collar, with a rabies tag and owner's information. Only two dogs per owner are permitted. Dogs are not allowed in KLM Park (as it's known to locals) during village-sponsored or -authorized events when a sign is posted. For drivers, there's a parking lot located at the south end. Dogs must be on-leash when walking through the park to get to the designated exercise area.

The rules are strictly enforced, but it's worth it. The manicured grass lends itself to playing fetch, Frisbee, or a game of chase, and to practicing the "come" command (see p. 338). You can try to call your dogs off squirrels. The squirrels dart among the mature oak trees. You can also stroll down a groomed path and a paved walkway at the perimeter of the park.

Open 6 A.M. to sunset. KLM Park is at 5901 S. County Line Road, on the east side of the street, north of Interstate 55, south of 55th Street. (630) 789-7090.

Hoffman Estates

Parks

Sure, dogs are allowed in parks if they're on-leash and owners pick up. Some of these parks are better than others. In any case, most dogs would prefer Hoffman Estates' sister city, Augouleme in France. Parks are open from sunrise to sunset. For more information call (847) 885-7500.

CHESTNUT PARK *(worth a sniff)* All that's here is a retention pond surrounded by homes. The retention pond is too dirty for swimming. There's hardly any grass, with only a flagpole for a dog to lift a leg.

Open sunrise to sunset. Chestnut Park is bounded by Warwick Circle, West Dexter Lane, and Gannon Drive. (847) 885-7500.

COMMUNITY PARK *(worth a sniff)* There's a small patch of grass—which (as Lucy and Chaser learned) remains uncomfortably mushy even two days after a rainfall. There's also a reservoir, in which dogs aren't even tempted to swim, and some playground equipment and a splash pond.

Open sunrise to sunset. Community Park is on Grand Canyon Parkway at Buttercreek Court, just north of Bode Road. (847) 885-7500.

HIGHLAND PARK ✓ ½ The setting is easy on the eyes, but there really isn't much to stir a canine spirit. The retention pond has been renovated and is cleaner than it used to be, but dogs should not swim here. There's very little grass around it. However, there are two benches where you can sit and contemplate world events while your pooch can ponder bigger and better parks.

Open sunrise to sunset. Highland Park is at 1755 Highland Boulevard at Haverford Court and Dennison Road. (847) 885-7500.

LOCUST PARK /   Maybe the six-acre park does attract locusts, but Robin and I didn't hear any. And as far as we know, neither did Chaser or Lucy. Most of this small park is cattails, which the dogs enjoyed running through. We made a wise decision to have them stop at the mucky swamp. There's one bench for watching the songbirds who periodically fly in for a concert. There's also a play area.

Open sunrise to sunset. Locust Park is at 345 Frederick Lane at Kent and Monticello Roads. (847) 885-7500.

SLOAN PARK ½/   Just a ball field—that's all that's here. If you hit a home run over left field, you may break a window on the house that sits nearby.

Open sunrise to sunset. Sloan Park is on Bode Road between Western Street and Flagstaff and Woodlawn Lanes. (847) 885-7500.

SYCAMORE PARK //   I didn't see any sycamore trees here. In fact, there aren't many trees of any kind. There are three baseball fields, but the football field is definitely the highlight, with bleachers for those who want to watch the game. On the day Robin and I visited, the only game in progress was a boy tossing a tennis ball to his golden retriever. There's also a handicapped-accessible children's play lot.

Open sunrise to sunset. Sycamore Park is at Freemont Road and Hillcrest Boulevard. (847) 885-7500.

VICTORIA PARK ½/   A small hilly and grassy corner is choice real estate for cross-country skiing. Some people ski with canine power. A paved walking path bisects the park.

Open sunrise to sunset. Victoria Park is on Wainford Drive at Bode Road. (847) 885-7500.

VOGELEI PARK / ½   Soak up the sunshine or toss a tennis ball on this 10-acre flatland. There are lots of trees around the perimeter, a soccer field, and some picnic areas. The Hoffman Estates Teen Center is also located here.

Open sunrise to sunset. Vogelei Park is at Higgins Road and Cambridge Lane. (847) 885-7500.

Places to Stay

Baymont Inn and Suites Pets are sequestered to smoking rooms on the first floor. Room rate is $79. 2075 Barrington Road; (847) 882-8848.

La Quinta Inn Dogs under 20 pounds are welcome here. The room rates are $89 to $109. 2280 Barrington Road; (847) 882-3312.

Red Roof Inn Dogs are welcome under the red roof. The manager who answered my call specified, "One small dog per room." When asked to clarify the word *small*, he said, "Dogs under 80 pounds are welcome"! Perhaps he's a pretty big guy himself and it's just a matter of perspective. In any case, we're not complaining. The rates are $52 to $70. 2500 Hassel Road; (847) 885-7877.

LaGrange

Doggy Doing

Pet Parade The dog doesn't wear a costume, but the kid dresses as a fireplug. It's a perennial favorite in the LaGrange Pet Parade, which originated in 1946. The event draws about a thousand human entries and about half that many pets. It may be the largest and oldest pet parade in the nation.

More than a hundred trophies are awarded at the end of the parade, including a grand prize of $1,000 in scholarship money. "The idea has always been to have lots of winners," said Bob Breen, the parade's assistant director and son of its founder, Ed Breen.

Typically, 40 to 50 volunteer judges decide on those winners. Sometimes celebrities judge, but most arbiters are local volunteers. An eclectic list of celebrities have marched in the parade, including Debbie Reynolds, Marlin Perkins (of "Mutual of Omaha's Wild Kingdom"), Lassie, Morris the cat, Lucy Baines Johnson (daughter of President Lyndon Johnson), Max Baer Jr. (Jethro on "The Beverly Hillbillies"), Spike O'Dell and Dean Richards of WGN Radio, and yours truly in 1999 and 2000.

Of course, the parade is all about the kids, their pets, and their costumes. Lemont trainer and behavior consultant Peggy Moran admits, "I get into the LaGrange Pet Parade a little too much; perhaps I'm a human with a little too much time on her hands."

Moran and her kids have won all sorts of parade prizes. Her favorite was for Lassie's Red Hot Doggy Diner. A Great Dane named Phoebe wore a harness to pull a wagon, which was covered with a cardboard table complete with two place settings and fake carnations as the centerpiece. Of course, there was a Chicago-style hot dog on each plate. Three little girls who were dressed as waitresses each held a hot-dog toy for dogs in a pair of tongs. Following the entire group was a little dachshund with a hot-dog toy in its mouth.

In recent parades, the most popular canine costume has been a sort of Dennis Rodman look, always with a boa.

Over the years, dogs have dressed to match whatever event happens to be in the news. During the Watergate years, more than one pooch dressed as Richard Nixon. Other one- or two-year wonders include Power Rangers and Cabbage Patch dogs as well as dogs done up as Beanie Babies.

Pets of all types have shared the parade route with canines, including cats, various kinds of birds, hamsters, gerbils, European ferrets, and Vietnamese potbellied pigs.

The parade begins at Cossitt Avenue at LaGrange Road and proceeds north to Burlington Avenue, west to Brainard Avenue, and then south back to Cossitt, ending in the Lyons Township High School North Campus parking lot (100 S. Brainard Avenue).

The LaGrange Pet Parade is always on the first Saturday in June, starting at 9:30 A.M. There is no registration fee. Call (708) 352-7079.

Lansing

Places to Stay

Days Inn Even the manager didn't know the exact rules for staying with a dog. One employee told me the charge is $10 per night per dog, but the manager told me $15. When I asked him about the $10 quote I got, he said it was a "minimum of $10, but sometimes they charge more." One thing is certain: you will be staying in one of the rooms in the back, akin to the hotel's doghouse. This is a place from which to get a written quote before you arrive with Fido. Rates are $75 to $89. 17356 Torrence Avenue; (708) 474-6300.

Red Roof Inn Canines are welcome to stay, but it's their people who are responsible for any damage. Rates are $44.99 to $79.99. 2450 E. 173rd Street; (708) 895-9570.

Matteson

Parks

Dogs on-leash are allowed, and people should pick up. Parks are open from 9 A.M. to dusk. All parks have access to electricity, and a few have picnic shelters with 10 picnic tables and grills. For information on reserving any of the parks or for general information call (708) 748-1080.

ALLEMONG PARK /// Dogs here could have a field day running on the 25-acre field or up and down the rolling hills, but few people allow their dogs off-leash. The leash law is enforced. Bonnie and Lisa were content to walk.

Lots of children use the playground, and oddly, all commented about Bonnie from afar, but no one asked to pet her. Lisa heard, "What a nice dog," and "That's the biggest dog." Bonnie shared the walking path with bicycles and in-line skaters. The three baseball diamonds get a lot of use.

Open 9 A.M. to dusk. Allemong Park is at Willow Road and Allemong Drive, just off Vollmer Road. (708) 748-1080.

GOVERNORS TRAIL PARK // Lisa couldn't help but notice the fresh aroma of skunk. Mercifully, Bonnie didn't come upon one in the flesh.

But perhaps some other dog did (see p. 228 for how to de-scent). There isn't a forested area, so maybe the skunks were checking out the trash cans.

Those garbage cans are filled to the brim with debris from the many picnickers who utilize this 20-acre park. Dogs aren't supposed to dig in the horseshoe pits. A wood-chip trail leads from the parking area into the playground, and to another trail that extends a bit into the park—but even for a toy poodle it's not very far. There are two baseball fields near the center of the park. A picnic shelter, tables, and grills are available.

Open 9 A.M. to dusk. Governors Trail Park is at 21402 S. Governor's Highway; the parking is at the north end. (708) 748-1080.

MEMORIAL PARK // Bonnie will always be remembered at this park. It was getting dark, and Lisa just didn't notice as her German shepherd dog walked right up to a couple who were getting intimate in the grass. Bonnie didn't bark; she just sniffed. But the intrusion was enough to scare them off.

There's a cemetery at the west end of the grove of picnic tables. It's pleasant during the day.

On one Halloween night many years ago, a terrier dug up an old bone. Ever since, he returns each Halloween to do the same, despite the fact that he died several years ago. We assume this is an urban legend. But just in case, you may want to skip visiting on Halloween.

Lisa was happy to enter the busier part of the park, where there are typical amenities, including lit tennis courts, three baseball diamonds, a soccer field, and a sand volleyball court—the nearest thing you'll find to a beach in Matteson. Lots of newer trees are planted in this area, which Bonnie appreciated. There's also a children's playground.

Open 9 A.M. to dusk. Memorial Park is at 212th Place and Tower Avenue. Head north on 212th Place until the road ends, then head west to the park. (708) 748-1080.

NOTRE DAME PARK // ½   This 11-acre park recently completed renovation. You get two lit tennis courts, a ball field, and a lovely gazebo. Your pooch gets exercise on the one-mile walking path that winds its way through the park, with three water fountains available in case she gets thirsty. The picnic area is especially nice, with grills, tables, and shelter. Open 9 A.M. to dusk. Notre Dame Park is at Notre Dame Drive and Central Avenue. (708) 748-1080.

OAKWOOD PARK // ½   This beautiful 10-acre park is linked to the Community Center and has something for everyone. Attractions include two lit tennis courts, two baseball diamonds, a volleyball court, and a walking path just under a half mile long that winds through the grounds. Also part of the package are a picnic area with shelter, grills, and tables. Your dog can follow the action of the kids in the playground. Open 9 A.M. to dusk. The park is at 4450 W. Oakwood Lane, two blocks north of Lincoln Highway. (708) 748-1080.

WOODGATE PARK // ½   At 17 acres, this is a smaller version of Allemong Park. It has a playground, two baseball diamonds, two lit tennis courts, a volleyball court, and a picnic shelter. A half-mile walking path winds through the park. There are plenty of benches along the way if you or your pooch should need a break.

Open 9 A.M. to dusk. Woodgate Park is at 112 Central Avenue, at Woodgate Drive, two blocks south of Vollmer Road. There's no parking on the north side of Woodgate, but you may park at Woodgate Elementary School (101 Central Avenue) across the street. (708) 748-1080.

Shelters

Statistics vary, but experts estimate that more than 50,000 dogs and cats are euthanized annually in the Chicago area. There's no shortage of canines seeking loving homes. Here's a partial list of shelters. * Denotes a no-kill facility.

Chicago

Anti-Cruelty Society
157 W. Grand Avenue
(312) 644-8338

Chicago Animal Care and Control
2741 S. Western Avenue
(312) 744-5000

Lake Shore Animal Foundation
225 W. Division Street
(312) 409-1162

Pets Are Worth Saving
2337 N. Clark Street
(773) 244-7853

Suburban Cook County

South

Animal Welfare League
10305 Southwest Highway
Chicago Ridge
(708) 636-8586

People's Animal Welfare Society
    (PAWS)
8301 W. 191st Street
Tinley Park
(815) 464-7298

South Suburban Humane Society
1103 West End Avenue
Chicago Heights
(708) 755-7387

Village of Forest Park Impound
7233 Madison Avenue
Forest Park
(708) 366-8156

North/Northwest

Evanston Animal Shelter/Community
    Animal Rescue Effort
2310 Oakton Street
Evanston
(847) 866-5080

Kay's Animal Shelter
2705 Arlington Heights Road
Arlington Heights
(847) 259-2907

Orphans of the Storm
2200 Riverwoods Road
Deerfield
(847) 945-0235

Save-a-Pet*
31664 N. Fairfield
Grayslake
(847) 740-7788

West

Animal Care League
6937 W. North Avenue
Oak Park
(708) 848-8155

Oak Park Animal Control*
123 Madison Avenue
(708) 358-5679

DuPage County
DuPage County Animal Control
120 N. County Farm Road
Wheaton
(630) 682-7197

Hinsdale Humane Society
22 N. Elm Street
Hinsdale
(630) 323-5630

Naperville Humane Society
1620 W. Deihl Road
Naperville
(630) 420-8989

Pet Rescue*
151 N. Bloomingdale Road
Bloomingdale
(630) 893-0030

Pets in Need Midwest*
(adoption by appointment at various
    locations)
(815) 728-1462

West Suburban Humane Society*
1901 W. Ogden Avenue
Downers Grove
(630) 960-9600

Kane County
Anderson Animal Shelter
1000 S. LaFox Road
South Elgin
(847) 697-2880

City of Aurora Animal Care and
    Control
600 S. River Road
(630) 897-5695

Will County
T.L.C. Animal Shelter
13016 W. 151st Street
(708) 301-1594

Mokena

Place to Stay

Super 8 Dogs can stay here, but they're not allowed to tour the hotel unescorted. If your dog starts to bark, you will be asked to pack your bags. There is a $50 deposit, which you will get back after your room is checked and found to be damage-free. Rates are $55.98 to $77.38. 9485 W. 191st Street; (708) 479-7808.

Mount Prospect

Parks

Dogs are welcome if they're on a leash, and if you pick up. The parks have different hours of operation, which change with the season, so check the signs at each site. Dogs are not allowed in the play lot areas at parks in Mount Prospect; they may only watch from afar. Open sunrise to 11 P.M. For more information call (847) 255-5380.

CLEARWATER PARK //   An optimistic sign greets park-goers, "Do Not Feed Wildlife."

Aside from geese, squirrels, rabbits, and songbirds, I'm not sure this park offers much in the way of wildlife.

Chaser and Lucy were also hoping for wildlife. But there was none to chase. As compensation, some children were bounding about the play area, and both dogs love watching kids. Dogs are not allowed in the play lot area, but some of those children came over to pet them.

Much of this park gets very muddy after a rainfall. But the rains are great for the beautiful display of flowers near the parking area.

This park is open from sunrise to 10 P.M. from April 1 through October 31 and from sunrise to 6 P.M. from November 1 through March 31. Clearwater Park is at 1717 Lonnquist Boulevard at Crestwood Drive and Busse Road. (847) 255-5380.

LIONS PARK / ½   Most of this park space is taken up by a recreational facility building. Still, there's a large soccer area with bleachers. A game of fetch is possible when there's no soccer action. Or you can just run around the field as we saw one 50-something-year-old man do. His dog just stood by and watched from the sidelines. Historic South Church is at the foot of the park.

Open sunrise to 10 P.M. year-round. Lions Park is south of Maple and Williams Streets and east of Lincoln Street. (847) 255-5380.

SUNRISE PARK /   A large soccer area becomes more like a small lake after heavy rains. Don't cross the street into the Des Plaines park area; dogs aren't allowed in Des Plaines parks.

This park is open from sunrise to 10 P.M. from April 1 through October 31 and from sunrise to 6 P.M. from November 1 through March 31. Sunrise Park is east of Sunset Road, south of Louis Street at Williams Street. (847) 255-5380.

Sunset Park / ½   Relax on the bleacher seats as you watch Fido snatch a Frisbee or cheer your favorite Little League team. There's also a grassy area and a kids' play lot, so owners must monitor their dogs.

This park is open from sunrise to 10 P.M. from April 1 through October 31 and from sunrise to 6 P.M. from November 1 through March 31. Sunset Park is at Can-Dota and Wapella Avenues, Sunset Drive, and Lonnquist Boulevard. (847) 255-5380.

Northbrook

Parks

Northbrook is a champion among dog-friendly suburbs. Dogs must be on a leash except for when they do the doggy paddle in Lake Shermerville at Wood Oaks Park or in the west fork of the north branch of the Chicago River at Meadow Hills/Meadow Hills South Park. Owners must pick up. Parks are open from sunrise to sunset. For more information call (847) 291-2960.

Meadow Hills/Meadow Hills South Park / / /   These two expanses, which are connected by a walkway, comprise a grand total of 80 acres. Combined, this is the largest park space in Northbrook.

Aside from oak trees, several uncommon species are found here, including Chicagoland hackberry and autumn purple ash. The park is just gorgeous in the fall, displaying a kaleidoscopic array of colors. The scene is equally as spectacular throughout the winter. The overall beauty doesn't particularly excite canines, although the tall trees and cross-country ski trails might. The popular ski path goes for nearly two miles.

Dogs are allowed to swim here, no matter how deep the water is. After one summer dry spell, the depth of the west fork of the north branch of the Chicago River could be measured in inches. That's perfect for pups who like to get only their paws wet. However, in some years the water moves pretty fast; a small dog could wind up at the mercy of the current.

At the entrance to the park there are baseball and soccer fields. Past this mowed area is the natural growth found in the retention basin, a dandy place for a dog run. It's also a cool place to run through a field of wildflowers with your dog.

Another favorite amusement is the sled hill, especially when there isn't any snow. But it's fun in the white stuff, too, all the more if your dog likes to pull a sled—with you in it!

There's also a partially covered picnic area here.

Open sunrise to sunset. Meadow Hills and Meadow Hills South Park are at 1700 Techny Road, between Waukegan and Shermer Roads. (847) 291-2960.

WOOD OAKS PARK /// ½   Hooray! There's a lake where the dogs can swim, and the residents, the local police, and the Park District personnel won't get upset. It's called Lake Shermerville, and it lies low inside this sprawling park. The lake is relatively clean and goose-free. Anglers also catch fish here.

Dogs who prefer to keep dry can hop aboard a canoe. Of course, their people have to row and are responsible for forking over the $6-per-day rental fee for Northbrook residents; $12 for nonresidents. You can call to prearrange canoe rental.

A footbridge crosses from the lake area into the park, which contains a steep sledding hill. Dogs can run their people ragged on this hill in the summer. There are also baseball fields and tennis courts.

Open sunrise to sunset. Wood Oaks Park is at 1150 Sanders Road, about a quarter mile south of Dundee Road, at Russett Lane and Walters Avenue. There's no admission fee. (847) 291-2960.

Place to Stay

Red Roof Inn Dogs aren't allowed in the rooms alone, particularly when the housekeeper wants to clean. Rates are $56 to $109. 340 Waukegan Road; (847) 205-1755.

Northfield

Doggy Doing

Northfieldians Only This eclectic dog show is open to Northfield canines only. Nonresidents can watch, but not partake. It's typically held on a Saturday morning in mid-June at Clarkson Park, 1943 Abbott Court. Ribbons include "Best Costume," "Best Trick," "Floppiest Ears," and "Best Behaved." Advance registration is not required; there is no fee. Call (847) 446-4428.

Oak Forest

Doggy Doing

Strut Your Mutt This annual dog walk, typically held on a Sunday morning in mid-September, benefits the Animal Welfare League. Walkers are encouraged to collect pledges. Any canine-person team with more than $50 in pledges is eligible for really good prizes, which vary from year to year. Registration is $20 in advance, $25 the day of the walk. The three-mile walk is at Yankee Woods, 162nd Street and Central Avenue. For more information call (708) 636-8586.

Oak Lawn

Park

No dogs are allowed in city parks, with the sole exception of Wolfe Wildlife Preserve. Here dogs must be on-leash, and their people must have evidence of a pickup device, such as a scooper or plastic bag. The police patrol the park, and they don't hesitate to issue $50 fines. For more information call (708) 857-2200.

**WOLFE WILDLIFE PRESERVE /// ** There is an arched metal-and-wood bridge at the entrance over Stony Creek (where dogs aren't supposed to swim). A 1.6-mile pathway winds through all 46 acres of this park. It's well lit at night and heavily used at all hours by people and their dogs. This is the only park in town where you can take a pooch.

South suburban researcher Lisa Seeman was struck by the contrasts in this park. She noted at one moment the splendor of nature—rabbits hopping about, baby chicks calling for mama birds, a hammering woodpecker, and a natural bed of wildflowers. To her left, she saw an electrical box, discarded litter, and a parked bulldozer.

There are two playgrounds, on the southeast and the northeast corners. Strategically plan where you will be thirsty because there's only one drinking fountain. Or you can follow resourceful Lisa's example: cross the street for a visit to the White Hen and pick up bottled water.

Bonnie, Lisa's German shepherd dog, particularly liked sniffing the wooden signpost that reads "Pick Up After Your Dog." Unfortunately, not everyone complies. The scoop is that if people don't begin to pick up, this park will go the way of the other parks in this community in not allowing dogs. That would be a dirty shame.

Open sunrise to 11 P.M. Wolfe Wildlife Preserve is at 109th and Laramie Streets. The easiest access is to take Cicero Avenue to 109th, and turn west. You can also access the park from 107th Street off Central Avenue. (708) 857-2200.

Oak Park

Parks

Residents pushed hard for an off-leash dog area, and their efforts finally paid off. They were granted (very) early-hour off-leash privileges at Lindberg Park. It's not exactly what dog owners were hoping for, but it is a definite step in the right direction. Meanwhile, members of the antidog contingent continue to wish that dogs weren't allowed in the parks at all. That's why several secret places (which I won't reveal here either) exist where people allow their dogs to run. Despite the code of silence, police show up on occasion to enforce the leash law, and violators may be ticketed. People are also required to pick up. Open sunrise to 10 P.M. Call (708) 383-0022.

LINDBERG PARK ///   This locale is a favorite among early-morning risers. From sunrise to 8 A.M., dogs are permitted to run off-leash. While their people are still squinting and waiting for the Starbucks to kick in, the dogs are having the time of their lives at an early play party. Plumb in a posh neighborhood filled with historic Frank Lloyd Wright homes, these grounds are stomped by the most cultured of dogs. This large space encompasses a baseball diamond, a couple of soccer fields, and tennis courts. There are plenty of trees, many of them named after prominent citizens. To date, no trees are named after dogs.

An asphalt path winds through the park, which offers lots of shade. There's also a drinking fountain along the way.

The most famous dog hereabouts is Barkley, who was once a cover dog in a *Chicago Tribune* Friday section story on dog-friendly places. Barkley is a yellow Lab whose friends call him the official park canine greeter. Indeed, there are often lots of dogs here to greet, especially on Saturday and Sunday mornings. Barkley and many other dogs hang out in an open area near the soccer field. Researcher Steve Karmgard says lots of people in the park greeted him as well. "It's the friendliest park I visited," he asserts.

Open sunrise to 10 P.M. Lindberg Park is at Greenfield Street and Le Moyne Parkway between Forest Avenue and Marion Street. (708) 383-0002.

MILLS PARK /   Researcher Steve Karmgard called this misshapen park "goofy." If you run with your dog, it seems that you have to stop and turn every 30 feet.

Then again, it's a serene, quiet park, with plenty of shade, and benches for contemplating the squirrels. Of course, your pooch won't be content to simply contemplate a squirrel.

Open sunrise to 10 P.M. Mills Park is at Pleasant Place and Randolph and Marion Streets. (708) 383-0002.

SCOVILLE PARK / ½   You can go window-shopping in downtown Oak Park or dine across the street with Fido at The Green Onion (733 W. Lake Street), then stroll through this quaint park. Afterward you can sack out on a bench while Fido romps around the small stretch of ground. Check out the statue dedicated to the soldiers, airmen, and sailors of World War I. There are also tennis courts.

Open sunrise to 10 P.M. Scoville Park is bounded by Ontario, Grove, and Lake Streets and Oak Park Avenue. (708) 383-0002.

TAYLOR PARK //   Another friendly neighborhood park. This location is also very clean and well maintained.

Just be careful that your pooch doesn't break free, since you're near the major intersection of Division and Ridgeland Streets.

Maple and oak trees dot this park, and there are picnic tables and some benches. Athletes can avail themselves of the soccer field and a few tennis courts.

Open sunrise to 10 P.M. Taylor Park is at Division, Ridgeland, Berkshire, and Elmwood Streets. (708) 383-0002.

Doggy Doings

Shakespeare in the Park   Thespian hounds can watch the Oak Park Festival Theatre summer productions. Shows are held Tuesdays through Sundays at 8 P.M. (except occasional scheduled Sunday matinees) from the last Tuesday in June through the last weekend of August at Austin Gardens, Lake Street and Forest Avenue. Each year, the company performs one classic play, such as *Much Ado About Nothing* or *Hamlet*. People tote their own seats and picnic baskets, and dogs should be supplied with their own blankets and biscuits to enjoy as they contemplate to bark or not to bark. Chairs can be rented for $2. Admission is $17 to $19 for people; canines are free. Call (708) 524-2050.

The Wright Way to Walk   Canines interested in architecture will like the fact that Frank Lloyd Wright built his homes around mature trees. Dogs can admire these trees up close and personal while their people view the exteriors of Wright homes on self-guided walking tours. Cassette tapes are available at the

Gink-Go Tree Bookshop, 951 Chicago Avenue, for $9; $7 for seniors. You can also purchase a self-guided map for $3. Sorry, dogs are not allowed in the bookshop. Most of the Wright homes are within walking distance of the bookshop. Thirteen of the 26 Wright-designed buildings in Oak Park are in a six-block radius.

Perhaps the most famous building is the first prairie house designed here by Wright, the Frank Thomas House (210 Forest Avenue), which has several trees in front. Across the street is Austin Gardens Park, which has even more trees, some running space for a pooch, and a bust of Wright. Dogs are welcome only if they don't bark on the doorsteps of the homes, their people comply with the leash ordinance, and owners pick up. For further information call (708) 848-1976.

Restaurants

The Green Onion   Grilled tuna is this restaurant's signature dish—just ask Fido. The seating area consists of six wrought-iron tables with potted flowers, overlooking Scoville Park (see p. 157). The squeeze in this space can be tight for hefty hounds. 733 W. Lake Street; (708) 386-2555.

Poor Phil's   Their slogan is "summer on the sidewalk," and they welcome canines to party. But dogs must sit along the iron fence that surrounds the tables. Canine clientele are allowed to sniff, but not to search the flower beds for discarded lobster parts. Patrons follow an "ate"-step diagram that describes how to eat a lobster. Canines don't especially care that lobster is a costly delicacy. Given the chance, most would follow their own two-step diagram: crunch, then swallow. Surprisingly, some canines do get the chance; some generous (really generous) folks offer morsels to their drooling pups.

Other seafood choices include Cajun calamari, fish-and-chips, and both snow and king crab. For dessert, indulge yourself with Oak Park's famous Peterson's Ice Cream. 139 S. Marion Street; (708) 848-0871.

Puree's Pizza & Pasta   We're told that barbecued chicken pizza is the most popular choice among canine guests. Dogs can sit outdoors, where three tables are usually set up. If the tables aren't up, all you have to do is ask. Pastas and sub sandwiches are also offered. 1023 W. Lake Street; (708) 386-4949.

Coffee Shops

Minou Cafe   Eight outdoor tables with plenty of elbow and paw room. Sandwiches, pastries, and salads are offered. 104 N. Marion Street; (708) 848-6540.

Starbucks Canine customers sit outdoors at five round tables with heavy wicker chairs. Water is available on request. Located at 1018 Lake Street; (708) 848-5051.

Palos Hills

Parks

Dogs are allowed in Palos Hills parks if they're on a leash and if owners pick up. Open sunrise to sunset. Call (708) 430-4500.

CALVARY PARK ½ ✔ You won't hear a cavalry charge, but you'll certainly hear the charging children. This barely one-acre park is a fenced-in play lot, and a very busy one at that. This is not a place for dogs who don't adore children.

Open sunrise to sunset. Calvary Park is located off 111th Street and Roberts Road, although access is also available through the Calvary Memorial Church parking lot, 11111 Roberts Road. (708) 430-4500.

INDIAN WOODS ✔✔ This park has been renovated, so flooding is no longer the plague it once was. Some dogs may miss the wet grass and the mud, but the humans prefer to stay dry. There is a baseball field at the south end, and a half-mile trail that skims this nine-and-a-half-acre spread. Visitors can also make use of a playground as well as a picnic shelter with tables. Open sunrise to sunset. Indian Woods is at 100th Street and 82nd Avenue. The easiest route is to take 103rd Street to 82nd Avenue and go south to 100th Street. (708) 430-4500.

KRASOWSKI PARK ✔ ½ Krasowski must have been a ballplayer. (In fact, semi-pro baseball is played here in the summer.) There are five baseball diamonds. The large one is on the west side of the park, near the playground and an open field. The other four ball fields are on the other side of a small creek, accessed only by an old, rickety bridge, which Lisa was afraid to cross. Despite the beautiful weather, Lisa and Bonnie had the park to themselves. The only other sound was the constant buzzing of the overhead power lines. Lisa was worried she might begin to glow in the dark.

Open sunrise to sunset. Krasowski Park is at 104th Place at Todd Drive. The easiest way to locate the park is to turn off 103rd Street onto a gravel road with the sign indicating Bill Dunnett Field. There's lots of parking—just don't park too close unless you want a foul ball to land on your dashboard. Call (708) 430-4500.

Park Ridge

Dogs are not allowed in Park Ridge parks, except for one noteworthy destination called Paws Park. This off-leash place is open dawn to dusk.

Park

PAWS PARK **////**　This "woodsy" area is completely fenced in, and offers the perfect safe space for a game of fetch or Frisbee. Park Ridge's Board Commissioner Lauren Streff is among the happy dog owners who frequently visit the park. "We have a yard that's fenced, but he will have to learn how to socialize with other dogs, too," Streff says. So far, that hasn't been a problem for Duffy, her two-year-old yellow Labrador retriever. Duffy loves nothing more than joining his four-legged friends for a canine version of shaking their Bon Bons.

Paws Park is over one-third of an acre, with plastic bags, a pooper scooper, and garbage cans provided. The Park Ridge resident–organized Dog Park Committee, which was instrumental in the park's creation, is currently raising money to add benches, a doggie drinking fountain, and even exercise equipment for the playful pooches. If you're heading out there with the entire family, be aware that no one under six is allowed in the park, and six to twelve-year-olds must be accompanied by an adult. This is an especially congenial dog park, where discussions range from what stocks to invest in to how to teach a greyhound to come when called (good luck). Lots of friendships have been forged as a result of the dogs.

Open dawn to dusk. Paws Park is at 2800 W. Oakton, in the back of the Oakton Sports Complex, on the east side of the indoor ice rink building. (847) 692-5127.

Coffee Shop

Starbucks　Dogs are welcome at 15 S. Prospect Avenue. (847) 292-5678.

Prospect Heights

Place to Stay

Exel Inn　Dogs under 25 pounds can stay. The room rates are $45.99 to $90. 540 N. Milwaukee Avenue; (847) 459-0545.

Rolling Meadows

Parks

Dogs are welcome in the parks, at least if they're on a leash and when owners pick up. Open sunrise to sunset. Call (847) 818-3200.

CAMPBELL PARK // ½   Hey, there really are rolling meadows here, which make an idyllic setting for a picnic. The picnic area is under a canopy of trees. Paved walkways bisect the park. The centerpiece of this park is the Rolling Meadows skyscraper—the town's water tower.

Open sunrise to sunset. Campbell Park is just north of Campbell Street at Cardinal Drive. (847) 818-3200.

GATEWAY PARK *(worth a sniff)*   A triangular green space at a very busy intersection. If your pooch really has to go, fine. Otherwise, stay in the car.

Open sunrise to sunset. Kirchoff Road at New Wilke Road. (847) 818-3200.

KIMBALL HILL PARK // ½   On our visit, Little League baseball was about to begin, and the families were arriving in droves. It's a pity Chaser and Lucy couldn't use the ball fields to play their game of tag. For them, watching Little League is boring, so we moved on to the small pond. Some dogs dive in, but the practice is discouraged. There's a pavilion for picnics. There's also a play lot for kids.

Open sunrise to sunset. Kimball Park is off Meadow Drive at Sigwalt Street, south of Campbell Street. Parking is off Cardinal Drive. (847) 818-3200.

SALK PARK ///   Drop the kids off at the sports center, and then take the dog for a walk. This long and narrow park follows a creek and crosses it in two places, on a wooden bridge and on an iron bridge.

Robin and I played our favorite "Let's exhaust the dogs" game. She stood at the top of the sledding hill with the dogs, and I ran to the bottom to holler, "Come!" They get a treat for arriving, and then Robin calls, "Come!" The dogs charge up the hill for a goodie. Now I yell, "Come!" And it's back down the hill. It doesn't take much of this to wear them out. In winter this hill is used for sledding.

There are a trio of playgrounds and a gazebo.

You share a bumpy paved pathway with in-line skaters. Chaser and Lucy had no sweat walking the path, but the skaters sure don't take kindly to the bumps.

Open sunrise to sunset. Because of the adjacent sports complex, parking gets tight on the weekends. Lots of cars intruded on the grass, ignoring the signs that threaten to tow. Salk Park is between Kirchoff and Central Roads on Pheasant Drive. Parking is at Owl Drive and Pheasant Drive. (847) 818-3200.

Rosemont

Places to Stay

Hotel Sofitel Naturally, dogs are welcome at this French-owned hotel. In fact, canines have unparalleled freedoms. Except for the restaurants, your dog can go anywhere you do. Ideally located near the Rosemont Expo Center. Room rates are $99 to $245. 5550 N. River Road; (847) 678-4488.

Marriott Suites A cheery voice says, "Yes, of course; we love dogs!" Too bad that woman is not setting the rules. If you check in for less than a four-night stay, the fee is $50 per dog per night. If you stay longer, there's a flat fee of $100 per dog. When it comes to how big of a dog you can bring, as with many hotels, the answer varies on who happens to answer the phone. One front-desk employee told me there was a 50-pound limit, and one employee told me there was no weight restriction. Get confirmation in writing. The rates are $139 to $209. 6155 N. River Road; (847) 696-4400.

Schaumburg

Park

Schaumburg parks require that people pick up and dogs be on-leash. Open sunrise to sunset. Call (847) 985-2115.

RAY KESSELL PARK ✓ ½ Nearly color-blind, dogs aren't impressed with the bright yellow and green play lot equipment. But the tots seem to be. This spot is well-traveled by nearby kids. A babbling brook surrounds the park. Dogs sometimes splash in the creek, despite the fact that it's dirty. You also don't want Fido running into the small retention pond: there's goose poop everywhere. A paved walkway makes it easier to avoid the goose waste.

Open sunrise to sunset. Kessell Park is at Jones Road at Highland Boulevard. (847) 985-2115.

Places to Stay

Drury Inn Canine companions weighing less than 35 pounds may share your bed. But, only one dog per room—the beds aren't that big. Rates are $65.99 to $97.99. 600 N. Martingale Road; (847) 517-7737.

Homewood Suites by Hilton The enthusiastic response "We love pets!" is music to the ears of the person on the other end of the phone line. The "official" policy states that only dogs under 30 pounds can stay the night, but off the record, I'm told it is not strictly enforced. So, you may be able to slip by if the front desk doesn't ask to inspect Fido, or if you explain that he is on the Atkins diet and will soon be a trim 29 pounds. In any case, I am not officially suggesting you sneak around the rules. There's a $10 per night fee, and a $75 deposit, refundable at the end of your stay. There is a pet run outside. Rates are $99 to $169. 815 American Lane; (847) 605-0400.

La Quinta Inn Dogs under 20 pounds are allowed at $69 to $129 per room. 1730 E. Higgins Road; (847) 517-8484.

Marriott Hotel Hotel guests must sign a waiver accepting responsibility for any damage their pets may do, and pay a one-time $25 fee. I am somewhat in limbo when it comes to the size of the dogs allowed to spend the night. First call, any dog is welcome. Second call, dogs under 40 pounds are welcome. On the third call, in response to my question about the possibility of staying with a Saint Bernard, the employee advises me to "tell them it's a shi tzu and sneak him in the back door!" Call ahead, and get your reservation in writing. Room rates are $79 to $174. 50 N. Martingale Road; (847) 240-0100.

Summerfield Suites Hotel by Wyndham Here we go again. Dogs are welcome, but how big, no one knows exactly. From a few conversations, Janice figured, "a Saint Bernard is too big, but anything smaller than a collie is OK." When Janice asked if the hotel has a written policy, an employee read it to her, and it stated that dogs under 75 pounds are accepted. She seemed surprised to read that, and she quickly added, "We like to keep the dogs about 35 pounds." When Janice asked her why the hotel doesn't follow the written policy, the employee referred her to a clause that said they reserve the right to refuse certain animals, such as goats and pigs, and vicious dogs. Janice started to protest that big dogs are not necessarily vicious, when Luna spoke up with a loud bark, right on cue. The woman did not find any humor in it. No one at the hotel seemed vague about the $200 cleaning fee that all humans have to shell out for their dogs. Or the added 10 bucks per day per dog. Room rates are $169 to $269. 901 E. Woodfield Office Court; (847) 619-6677.

Schiller Park

Place to Stay

Motel 6 Only dogs under 25 pounds are allowed. Your canine must be with you at all times and absolutely may not be left alone in the room unattended. Rates are $55.99 to $61.99. 9408 Lawrence Avenue; (847) 671-4282.

Skokie

Places to Stay

Holiday Inn Dogs get the best views, since canines are allowed only in the rooms facing Niles Center Road. Rates are $129 to $165. 5300 Touhy Avenue; (847) 679-8900.

North Shore Doubletree Pets are very welcome, although there is a hefty $250 refundable deposit. Still, as long as the pooch is a model citizen, it won't cost you an extra sou. Rates are $99 to $400. 9599 Skokie Boulevard; (847) 679-7000.

South Holland

Place to Stay

Red Roof Inn Small dogs, "around 25 pounds or less," can vacation under this red roof. The front-desk employee told me that dogs are welcome as long as employees "don't have to go outside and pick up big stuff." That rule may not really be a good one, considering small dogs may deposit some nice-size packages. 17301 S. Halsted Street; (708) 331-1621.

Tinley Park

Park

Of all the parks in Tinley Park, only Siemsen Meadow allows dogs; they must be on-leash, and owners must pick up. For more information call (708) 532-8698.

Siemsen Meadow **//** As its name imparts, this is a meadow, plain and simple. There is a sort of mowed path. Researcher Lisa said, "It looks as if someone hopped onto a riding lawn mower and went for a zigzag ride all over the place." Naturally, the places with shorter grass are easier for small dogs to negotiate.

If you dutifully pick up as the law indicates, there's nowhere to toss the trash. Lisa crossed 167th Street to beautiful Centennial Park—with its lake, playground, and paved path—and deposited the bag in a can next to a sign that reads "No Dogs Allowed."

Open sunrise to sunset. Parking is scarce. Siemsen Meadow is on 167th Street between Harlem Avenue and 80th Street.

Wilmette

Beach

It's very sad—dogs aren't allowed in the parks in this North Shore suburb, but as a consolation prize, dogs have their own beach at Gillson Park.

Gillson Park Dog Beach **///** Residents' hounds can comb this beach for a fee of $25 a year ($5 for each additional dog). Nonresidents will have to shell out $150 for one dog ($50 for each additional dog). At these prices, it's not hard to see why only twelve nonresident pooches are members. There are 423 resident hounds who fill out the guest list.

At the green-gated entrance, you'll notice a three-foot-high sign with so many rules that it takes 10 minutes to read through them. Once you enter, you'll notice the trees—making this more than a beach. On the day we stopped by, one poor squirrel was trying to bury a stash for the winter, until Chaser and Lucy arrived. The terrified squirrel scampered up the tree and wasn't seen again while we were around. It seems a beach for dogs is a dangerous home for a squirrel.

Beyond the trees is the V-shape beach area. At one side, two fishermen were casting their lines, oblivious to the dogs. As a result of high water, the beach itself is now smaller than it was when it opened in 1996. Weather will determine if the beach continues to shrink. Regardless, dogs can also play on the large rocks extending into the lake, and around those squirrelly trees, as well as on the beach. All in all, there's enough space and plenty to do.

The beach is clean. People apparently pick up, not only dog waste but also their own trash.

The area is fenced in during the beach season, but a part of the fence is removed after September 1. This offers dogs the chance to run past the usual boundary of the dog beach and continue north along the lake. However, you have to be vigilant with so much freedom. I allowed Lucy and Chaser off-leash. Chaser turned the corner and ran way beyond where the fence once was. Not realizing the potential problem at first, Robin and I were playing with Lucy. Then Robin noticed that Chaser had taken off. She was too far gone to hear me calling. I wasn't worried about her running into the nearby drive, which could be a real concern; she was too busy rolling in dead fish. Among the four hundred rules and regs listed, there should be a warning that the fence may be partially removed. Additionally, dogs not reliably trusted off-leash shouldn't visit in the off-season.

By the way, as you walk to the beach, be sure to stay on the paved driveway. Should you dare to step on the grass, you may be ticketed. Dogs are not allowed in parks here, not even in this park where the dog beach is located. There was quite a fuss about whether or not to open this beach to canine traffic. A large constituency apparently felt dogs would be a nuisance and a potential danger. That hasn't been the case.

The long list of rules includes a warning that dogs must wear an official beach tag and a rabies tag, and owners must clean up and stay in designated areas. One rule I love is that aggressive dogs may lose privileges. Another interesting rule is that the owner/handler must be at least 14 years old or a freshman in high school.

From Memorial Day through Labor Day, beach hours are 6 A.M. to 10:30 A.M. and 5:30 P.M. to 9:30 P.M. Labor Day to Memorial Day, hours are 6 A.M. to 9:30 P.M. Gillson Park Dog Beach is at the southeast corner of Gillson Park, east of Sheridan Road, north of Linden Avenue, and south of Forest Avenue. (847) 256-9607.

Winnetka

Park and Beach

Centennial Park is the sole Winnetka park that permits dogs. While on the park grounds, dogs must be on a leash; when they get to the dog beach, they can be taken off-leash. For more information call (847) 501-2040.

CENTENNIAL PARK AND CENTENNIAL PARK DOG BEACH //// Paws down, this is the best all-dog beach in the book. Residents pay $25 a year for canine beach privileges and $5 for each additional dog. Nonresidents are nicked for $50, and $50 for each additional hound. There's also a mandatory $100 parking sticker fee for nonresidents. Resident-only parking (or nonresident sticker) and beach-use permits are strictly enforced. It's like a private club—users need a key card to enter.

The beach is below a bluff. No question, this spacious tract is nice enough for people to use—and you can't say that about the cramped and sometimes dirty dog beaches located near boat docks. This stretch of waterfront is longer than Elder Street Beach, the local beach for people. While the water level varies, when I visited, the south end was a super place for pups to wade without going over their heads; the slope is gentle. The center and northern sections get deeper faster and are more for major-league dog paddlers.

On our sojourn, Sophie and Lucy met a new pal from Buffalo Grove. "There's no water in Buffalo Grove; you bet this is worth the drive," said the dog's person.

Jane Karr is a Winnetka resident who arrives daily with her Airedale terrier named Peter. "I met a close group of friends here," she said. When Karr broke her leg, her beach friends went to her home to pick Peter up so he wouldn't miss his daily dalliance on the sand. Another woman credited her dog beach friends (as well as her dogs) with helping her to keep going after her husband passed away.

Sophie, who is a German shepherd–mix, is usually not a swimmer. But at this beach she bounded into the water, if ever so briefly. Sophie and Lucy were joined by two other visitors, a golden retriever and a Labrador retriever, for the ultimate game of tag. After 20 minutes, Lucy came running to me and began to cry. At first, I just assumed she was exhausted from racing around with the big dogs. Upon closer inspection, I noticed two burrs stuck on her flank. Once I removed them, she was back in high gear.

The only other drawback happens in the fall when the sweet bees get a sour disposition. Some years are worse than others.

Other dog beach rules include a ban against people swimming. In addition, any dog that is proved to be aggressive may have beach privileges revoked. To date, no aggressive incident has been reported.

Centennial Park is a delightful place to either dry off or catch some shade under the trees. It's a nice-enough park, but the dog beach is the real draw.

Open 6:30 A.M. to 10 P.M. Centennial Park and Centennial Park Dog Beach are located one driveway south of Elder Lane, east of Sheridan Road. (847) 501-2040.

Chenny Troupe

Petting programs have been taking pups to nursing homes and children's wards for years to help residents and patients feel better. Chenny Troupe, an organization unique to Chicago, takes therapy to another level: helping patients to *get* better. Chenny Troupe's volunteer dog handlers work with the therapists as well as with the dogs—taking an active role in the recovery process. The idea is for clients to benefit from canine assistance in achieving specific goals set by medical professionals.

Chenny Troupe was founded by Cathy Lawler and her business partner, Ann Rohlen. The group was named for Lawler's Labrador retriever, who often accompanied her to the nursing home when she visited her mother, who had multiple sclerosis.

"When I took Chenny to visit my mother, I noticed how intently people were motivated to interact with her," Lawler says, "even if the only interaction came from someone sitting in the corner who would say, 'Get that fleabag out of here!' At least Chenny motivated her to say *something*."

Both Chenny and Lawler's mom since have passed away, but the spirit of Chenny's impact lives on through the troupe. With sponsorship and volunteer help from the Junior League of Chicago, the Chenny Troupe idea came to fruition in 1991 and began to grow faster than a Great Dane.

Time and time again, Lawler has seen this amazing canine corps break through mental armor too tough for therapists, doctors, or family members to breach. At least one Chenny Troupe dog actually has "awakened" someone from a coma when previous efforts had failed, and many of the 45 Chenny dogs have helped victims of strokes and spinal cord injuries to increase mobility with assistance and direction from physical therapists.

The troupe's involvement with Somerset Place began when Lauryn Pappas, who had been volunteering at Somerset while conducting research for her master's degree in social work, approached troupe members in February 1998. She believed the Chenny dogs could prove beneficial to residents. The Somerset management agreed, despite the fact that no one could find a precedent—an organized program to help patients with severe mental illnesses, such as schizophrenia, depression, and other conditions. The troupe was barking up a new tree.

The success of the Somerset project has proved just how versatile this therapy group can be—and the wide swath of healing that dogs can effect. One reason for the troupe's accomplishments is the diversity among its membership. Chenny dogs have ranged from a miniature dachshund to Great Danes. Dogs have included the unexpected rottweilers to the expected golden and Labrador retrievers, as well as a petite Pomeranian, a shi tzu, standard poodles, and mixed breeds.

Some breeds are better suited for work in certain facilities. For example, a Maltese is perfect for hopping onto a gurney with a little child. Large breeds may be more fit for therapeutic training programs at substance-abuse rehabilitation centers. The overall impact is the same. "The breed doesn't mean a darn thing," says dog trainer Kathy McCarthy Olshein, director of programs for Chenny Troupe. "It's what's inside the dogs' hearts that counts."

McCarthy Olshein is also the program leader at City Girls, where dogs work with clients recovering from chemical dependencies. "By working with the dogs, the clients gain self-confidence," she says. "They learn how to achieve without resorting to violence." She notes that for the overwhelming majority of these young women, their preconceived notions about dogs are anything but Lassie-like. They've grown up around dogfighting, gang-bangers using dogs as weapons, and junkyard dogs. If nothing else, they learn about the unconditional love that dogs bestow.

Clearly, Chenny Troupe has taken animal-assisted therapy to a new level.

"It's magic," says Lawler. "These dogs are proving every day that they can change lives more than anyone ever dreamed. Our next step is to figure out how to document exactly why and how this happens."

At Grant Hospital in Lincoln Park, where Chenny dogs help with physical therapy, many patients are victims of stroke. One such patient was William. At 35, he was surprisingly young to be a stroke victim and was also suffering from depression. He was fond of dogs and liked the idea of meeting Wylee, a six-year-old Pembroke Welsh corgi. William had no feeling whatsoever on his left side, and therapists suggested that Sally Weiner—Wylee's owner—encourage William to attempt to use his right hand to place his left hand over Wylee to pet him.

William didn't understand the point of the exercise, but he reluctantly cooperated. Suddenly, he stopped petting. Weiner looked at William. A single

continued

tear dripped down the side of his cheek. She didn't say anything, and William didn't either. He seemed to be wallowing in a personal and very private joy. The smile on his face was wider than the room.

Then he blurted, "I felt something!" It was the first time he could feel on his left side. He went on to articulate that feeling with inconceivable detail, describing Wylee's soft inner coat hair by hair, then his coarser outer coat. William said one more thing before he left for that night—and he said it directly to Wylee: "Now I have hope."

"Hope, changing lives—that's what Chenny Troupe dogs do all the time," says McCarthy Olshein. "The dogs sneak under all the anger and fear and engulf them with unconditional love. It's just something they do, and something people can't equal. It's better than magic: it's real."

To become a Chenny Troupe dog, a canine must pass challenging obedience and temperament tests. Among other qualifications, the obedience portion requires owners to exhibit verbal control; dogs must be able to heel on-leash, maintain a one-minute sit/stay, and maintain a three-minute down/stay.

During the temperament portion of the testing, the dog must submit to a stranger's squeezing the dog's paw and must ignore the presence of other canines. In addition, the dog must respond positively to encounters with new people (including children) and with wheelchairs and other medical equipment. All dogs are observed for five minutes as their owners leave the testing room. Dogs are allowed to complain a bit when their owners depart, but expressing severe anxiety means failure. In fact, missing just one component of either the obedience or temperament section disqualifies the dog.

As a result, more than half of all applicants fail the first time around. Dogs showing even a hint of aggression toward people or fellow canines are given a permanent pink slip. Other pooches may be told that they aren't ready for the big leagues but that they can attend another spring-training session in hopes of passing on a second try. Many dogs succeed on the repeat effort, but some take three or four tries; other dogs never pass. As prospective Chenny Troupe dog owners are told before the test commences, "After all, not all dogs are destined for Chenny Troupe. But those dogs who make it can make a difference in a life."

If your dog likes the parks, does the doggy doings, and can share street space at festivals, then perhaps Fido is a candidate for a graduate degree of the dog world—to be a member of Chenny Troupe. For further information visit Chenny Troupe's website at chennytroupe.org or call (312) 280-0266.

Doggy Doing

Beach Party An annual beach party is usually held from 2 P.M. to 4 P.M. on a Sunday in late July at the Centennial Park Dog Beach. The party is sponsored by Iams (a dog food manufacturer), and all canine guests get a free goodie bag that includes food samples and treats. Snack food is provided for people, too.

Only members of the beach (see the preceding listing) may attend, and admission is free. At a recent party, Hazel greeted all guests and checked IDs. Hazel is the black Labrador retriever accompanying Liza McElroy, superintendent of recreation in Winnetka.

McElroy sought out the Beach Boys or at least Three Dog Night, but neither group was available. Instead, a woeful basset hound named Walter sang the blues. Despite an impressive turnout, McElroy said that not a single incident of canine aggression was reported. However, one person was seen snatching pretzels. (847) 501-2040.

Quick Bite

Panera Bread Company Up to 20 kinds of bread are offered daily, including Asiago cheese bread, olive bread, sun-dried tomato bread, and sourdough bread. Lots of dogs frequent this location when weather permits. 940 Green Bay Road; (847) 441-8617.

Forest Preserve District of Cook County

All forest preserve locations are listed here together because most span several communities.

Dogs on a leash are welcome—that's the law. But while doing our research, we saw many dogs off-leash. Most were innocently playing fetch or hunched under a picnic table waiting for dropped snacks. They were hardly a nuisance.

But then, there's always the dog that ruins it for everyone. At Busse Woods, an angry dog came running up to us. We had Lucy and Chaser on a leash, and they weren't able to get away. The owner called his dog back, but the dog totally blew him off.

Not seeing much of a choice, I got between this 60-pound mixed breed and my dogs. I hollered, "Get away!" My bluff worked. Still, instead of returning to his owner, who obviously had no control whatsoever, the dog continued to run in the opposite direction.

For counterpoint, there were Buddy and Sally, two little American cocker spaniel puppies who wanted desperately to play with Lucy and Chaser.

Chaser was sniffing the grass so intently that I doubt she was even aware of the pups. Lucy was lying in the grass, too pooped to play. The dogs wailed, cajoled, and pawed at Lucy.

Lucy could be a snob for only so long. Finally she got up, knelt into a play bow, and began to roll with these little pups as she rolls around at home with her cat, Ricky.

In some places, people were diligent about picking up. In other places, they obviously ignored the rule—as our shoes attested.

To date, there is no off-leash canine recreation area in the Forest Preserve District of Cook County. However, that possibility is being considered.

Forest Preserve of Cook County parks are open from sunrise to sunset. Call (708) 366-9420 or (773) 261-8400.

DES PLAINES DIVISION /// ½ Includes Iroquois Woods and Algonquin Woods (Des Plaines, Park Ridge); Lake Avenue Woods (Glenview, Mount Prospect); Allison Woods (Mount Prospect); and Potawatomi Woods (Wheeling).

This enormous stretch (more than 20 miles) of continuous forest preserve, which begins in the city, continues just west of O'Hare International Airport and extends along the Des Plaines River up to the Lake County border.

Fall colors sparkle with particular vibrancy at Algonquin Woods, south of Oakton Street; southwest of Beck Lake, north of Central Road; just east of the Des Plaines River south of Dundee Road; and in Potawatomi Woods north of Dundee Road. Wildflower beds with marsh marigolds brighten the wet places in the woods south of Che-Che-Pin-Qua Woods.

Some of the marked trails are flat and simple; others are surprisingly challenging, great for hiking. Even more surprising is the nature you might happen upon, including white-tailed deer, raccoon, and foxes. Canada geese are abundant in the northern suburbs. Garter snakes and various kinds of frogs often appear along the river. Dogs are not supposed to swim in the river, but some jump in willy-nilly. Similarly, dogs aren't supposed to swim in the various small lakes, but many do.

Just north of Lawrence Avenue and west of East River Road is an Indian cemetery that bears the graves of valiant Chief Robinson and his family.

It's amazing that those graves haven't been washed away. This preserve is a floodplain for several miles along East River Road. In some years, the water has flooded onto the streets and into nearby homes, creating serious damage. But even after an average rainfall, there are places where you won't want to walk—it's way too muddy.

Our favorite spot of all is just north of Irving Park Road and west of Cumberland Avenue, where the wells spew water that supposedly will keep its users forever young. And no, you can't bottle it and take it home.

As in all the other places we toured in the Forest Preserves of Cook County, we saw many dogs off-leash. The truth is that Forest Preserve police will enforce leash laws, but they can't be everywhere. To leash or not to leash: it's up to you.

Open sunrise to sunset. This series of preserves is bounded by Addison Street at the south; Thatcher, East River, Dee, and Talcott Roads on the east; Des Plaines, River Road, and Milwaukee Avenue on the west; and Lake-Cook Road on the north. Among the cross streets cutting through the preserves are Irving Park Road, Lawrence Avenue, Devon Avenue, Touhy Avenue, Oakton Street, Algonquin Road, Ballard Road, Rand Road, Golf Road, Central Road, Euclid Avenue, and Dundee Road. (708) 366-9420 or (773) 261-8400.

DWIGHT PERKINS WOODS (EVANSTON) //
This square block of lush Cook County Forest Preserve was particularly beautiful in the fall when we visited. The trees present a veritable rainbow of colors in this dense plot. A narrow asphalt path leads through the woods.

Open sunrise to sunset. Dwight Perkins Woods is at Colfax Street and Bennett Avenue. (708) 366-9420 or (773) 261-8400.

HARMS WOODS (SKOKIE, MORTON GROVE, AND GLENVIEW) // ½
Canines must be accustomed to picnics, horses, and bicycles. It's a mostly open area—lots of room for fetch or Frisbee. Picnic shelters and benches are everywhere. Come winter, cross-country skiers and their dogs make the most of these fields.

You'll encounter some forest and some walking paths along the north branch of the Chicago River.

Nearby stables are busy. The horses in Harms Woods often outnumber the dogs.

On our visit, we caught a stinky whiff of skunk. Large populations of raccoon and opossums also live around here. Continuing north, Harms Woods leads into the Skokie Lagoons.

Open sunrise to sunset. Harms Woods is bordered by Golf Road to the south, Lotus Avenue (south of Old Orchard Road) and Harms Road (north of Old Orchard Road) to the east, and Lake Avenue and the Wilmette Golf Course to the north. (708) 366-9420 or (773) 261-8400.

NED BROWN FOREST PRESERVE/BUSSE WOODS (ELK GROVE VILLAGE, ARLINGTON HEIGHTS, ROLLING MEADOWS, AND SCHAUMBURG) /// ½   Here are four thousand acres with lots of water, including the large Busse Lake. The beauty is spectacular. In fact, the 427-acre Busse Woods (which is in the preserve) is on a list of registered national landmarks. Don't expect to have this place to yourself; more than two million people visit each year. No one has counted the canine guests.

There are several entranceways off main streets, including Higgins Road (Illinois Route 72). Driving under the canopy of forest is dreamlike. A labyrinth of access roads wind through the preserve.

Robin was driving, Lucy and Chaser were barking orders, and I was taking notes. Glancing in her rearview mirror, Robin saw a Forest Preserve police car on our tail. There was nowhere to pull over. We figured he wanted to get around us, so we sped up. He sped up too and continued to drive only inches from our rear bumper.

Now he turns on his flashing lights and signals us to pull over. But where? We keep driving until we see a parking area, and we do pull over.

The officer told us we were going 40 in a 30-mile-per-hour zone. We said, "Yes, we were speeding when you were tailgating us. Before that, we were going 30."

He asked to see Robin's license and asked why we were so far away from home.

I thought to myself, "We're not really that far from home, and that's not really his business. The forest preserves are open to all residents of any county, particularly Cook County, where we live and pay taxes for the preserves." But I kept my mouth shut, which is more than I can say for Chaser. Whenever the officer said something, she barked. Chaser doesn't usually do that. Maybe she sensed how upset we were. Of course, whenever Chaser began to bark, Lucy would join in.

The officer replied, "Next time, drive slower." And he left us with a warning. During the time he wasted with us, a car filled with kids sped by doing maybe 45 or 50.

Even speeding Border collies aren't allowed to herd the elk on Arlington Heights Road, north of Higgins Road and south of the Northwest Tollway in Elk Grove Village. Members of this herd are descendants of elk from Yellowstone National Park, which were delivered to nearby Arlington Heights in 1925. People and their dogs are welcome to watch the species of deer for which Elk Grove Village was named from outside the fenced 14-acre enclosure.

Take Higgins Road west of the elk pen for Busse Lake and the nearby north and south pools. Ice fishing is not allowed. Dogs aren't permitted on ice-covered lakes. More to the point, dogs aren't allowed in the lakes at all—including in the rental boats ($5 per hour, $15 per day)—but they can look on as their fishing buddies reel in largemouth bass, bluegills, brown bullheads, crappies, or catfish from the fishing walls.

Some places are cleaner than others. It looked as if no one picked up near the upper Salt Creek area. One dog was playing fetch off-leash, and another was catching Frisbees off-leash. Dogs were all over off-leash, not bothering anyone. Even so, the Forest Preserve officers won't hesitate to fine violators of the leash law when they come upon them.

We decided to move away from the lawbreakers and head into the forest. The hiking is a full-fledged workout, quite challenging at times. We didn't spy many songbirds, but they weren't shy about performing. Those who prefer a more leveled walk can follow the 11-mile asphalt bike trail.

Open sunrise to sunset. Ned Brown Forest Preserve/Busse Woods is bordered by Illinois Route 53 on the west, Golf Road and Northwest Tollway (I-90) on the north, Arlington Heights Road to the east, and Biesterfield Road to the south. Higgins Road (Illinois Route 72) runs through the preserve.

Parking is available at various locations: on Golf Road just east of Illinois Route 53; off Higgins Road (Illinois Route 72) west of Arlington Heights Road; at Bisner Road and Cosman Road north of Biesterfield Road; and at Higgins Road (Illinois Route 72) at Illinois Route 53. (708) 366-9420 or (773) 261-8400.

NORTH BRANCH DIVISION /// Includes Bunker Hills Woods (Chicago, Niles); Miami Woods (Morton Grove, Niles); and Saint Paul Woods, Linne Woods, and Wayside Woods (Morton Grove).

Once an Indian trail, this is now a very busy 19.1 miles of bicycle trail (some extending beyond the Forest Preserve area listed here). The North Branch is the most intensively used division in Cook County. On weekends, walking these bike trails is a chore; there's more congestion than on Dempster Street.

As the people at the Forest Preserve District point out, "Walking is the best and cheapest form of recreation." And you can certainly get your money's worth here, but you're best off on the many miles of forest trails. Most of the trails are alongside streams or the north branch of the Chicago River. Canines can try to catch frogs, but mosquitoes may catch you. Dogs with horse sense will do fine on the trails shared with equines.

Dogs are not allowed in the river, near the Whelan swimming pool, or on the Edgebrook or Caldwell golf courses.

It's unclear whether or not golfers are allowed to practice in open spaces. At Saint Paul Woods, Lucy came within inches of a flying golf ball.

People picnic everywhere; groups must obtain permits from the clerk at the Forest Preserve District office in the County Building, 118 N. Clark Street, Room 608, in Chicago or at Forest Preserve District Headquarters, 536 N. Harlem Avenue in River Forest.

Open sunrise to sunset. This branch can be accessed east of Caldwell Avenue between Main and Oakton Streets; at Caldwell Avenue south of Touhy Avenue; at Lehigh Avenue at Dempster Street, east of Lehigh and Lincoln Avenues; and at Gross Point Road at Touhy Avenue. (708) 366-9420 or (773) 261-8400.

3 DuPAGE COUNTY

It's a great feeling to unhook Chaser or Lucy from the leash and not worry about being grabbed by the strong arm of the law. DuPage County offers the most off-leash havens in the greater Chicago area.

The Forest Preserve of DuPage County has off-leash dog training and/or exercise areas in Glendale Heights, Hanover Park, Naperville, Oak Brook, Warrenville, and Wayne. In addition, the progressive-thinking village of Oakbrook Terrace allows dogs off-leash in its parks. Fermilab, the sprawling research center in Batavia, also offers dogs space sans leash.

Off-leash places receive higher marks because Chaser and Lucy tell us dogs like them better. Watching Chaser chase down a bird at Springbrook Prairie in Naperville, then stop and hold a classic point, or a pair of Labrador retrievers running at breakneck speed through tall grass, is a special life experience, and one that just can't happen with the restriction of a leash.

With the leash off, dogs clearly feel less encumbered. But that doesn't mean they should be less obedient. So, if you're going to allow your dog off-leash, a dependable recall is absolutely required (see p. 338). Taking your dog off-leash is a romantic notion. And I'm all for it. I support having more places like those in DuPage County. But here are some other realities of taking a dog off-leash: Dogs have drowned and/or suffered hypothermia by running in the wrong direction on thin ice, dogs have been hit by cars while chasing squirrels or rabbits, and, less traumatic but still to be avoided, dogs have run off into forested areas following their noses—and it turns out to be a skunk they find at the other end.

Overly aggressive and/or poorly trained dogs are yet another curse. Sally Markus of Oakbrook Terrace has a terrier-mix that she allows off-leash only in the early morning. "I'm not worried about Sadie's running off," she says. "I'm worried about other dogs, crazy dogs."

Carol Truesdell, my DuPage County researcher, noted the same problem at several of the parks she visited. "Too many dogs that are off-leash aren't very nice, to either other people or other dogs. It's irresponsible to allow those dogs off-leash."

The biggest challenge is keeping an off-leash dog in sight, particularly if it happens to be a smaller dog. Of course, safety is the main issue, but it isn't the only concern. Carol often had three dogs in tow. It's not that she didn't try—she always had plastic bags to prove her sincerity—but if you lose sight of a dog, how can you tell when it's, pardon the vernacular, taking a dump?

Some of the off-leash places were absolutely filthy from the four-legged dumpsters. One explanation is that owners might have momentarily lost track of the dog. Also, in most of these facilities, trash containers exist only near the parking lot. Still, there's clearly a more pervasive "who cares about cleaning up" mentality at off-leash locations compared with other parks. Ultimately, if people want more places where dogs can have the freedom to be dogs, people will have to police themselves, requesting that others pick up.

Meanwhile, I suggest you wear old shoes, and wipe your pup's foot pads before returning to the car when visiting the Forest Preserve of DuPage County off-leash locales.

I don't want to give the impression that it isn't worth the visit. Quite the contrary, these off-leash areas are among the highest-rated parks in the book. Aside from allowing dogs an unparalleled opportunity to socialize and exercise, many of these parks are also quite picturesque. Because of these qualities, they draw visitors from all over. Jackson Palmerri says it can take him about an hour to drive to Springbrook from his Dearborn Park neighborhood. "There's nowhere around my house for Lady (a sight hound/retriever–mix) to really let loose," he says.

Just be sure to allow the dog to let loose in a designated off-leash place. The officers of the Forest Preserve of DuPage County (as well as many of the suburban police departments) are known to enforce the leash law to the letter. As we found out, you can be a mere 20 yards from an off-leash area, and an officer may issue a citation. In the Forest Preserve of DuPage County, the minimum fine for taking a leash off of a dog is $75. And don't try surreptitiously slipping that leash off in the woods—Officer Not-So-Friendly may be hiding behind a tree.

Here are the DuPage County Forest Preserve rules for pets being off-leash:

- Though a leash is not required, dogs must be under control at all times.

- Use of birds or animals, alive or dead, is prohibited.

- Only blank ammunition may be used for training purposes.

- Training devices using any kind of explosive force to propel retrievable objects are prohibited.

The forested areas of DuPage County are absolutely beautiful. Just keep in mind that they have their hazards, as do most of the other forests in the book. Please protect yourself and your pet from ticks and mosquitoes (see p. 30). And the hitch isn't only insects—coyotes can also be a threat to small dogs. Even goose poop can create a problem. Tracey Smith, an assistant at the Forest Preserve District of DuPage County, reports that her shih tzu Reggie got very ill from sampling goose droppings in a forest preserve. It's also best to keep dogs out of water overpopulated with geese. The DuPage Forest Preserve website, dupage forest.com, is an excellent source for information.

As for municipal parks, many won't allow dogs, including Bensenville, Clarendon Hills, Itasca, and Oak Brook. Other communities allow leashed dogs, as long as owners pick up. Happily, some are downright dog friendly. In Bartlett, there's the Annual Dog and Cat Pet Show at Bartlett Bonanza Days; in Downers Grove, canines have enjoyed movies in the park, such as *101 Dalmatians*; and in Wheaton, dogs may participate in two seasonal festivals.

These DuPage County dogs aren't couch potatoes. Dogs hurl themselves down snow tubes on Mount Hoy at the Blackwell Forest Preserve in Warrenville, and they have been spotted in rowboats on Herrick Lake in Wheaton.

Carol Truesdell, her husband, Mike, and Tibetan terrier Breathless were assisted by 12-year-old Danny, his beagle named Pork Chop, and his friend Snowball, a Maltese, in researching DuPage County.

Addison

Parks

Addison Park District parks welcome canine pals on a leash when owners pick up. These parks are open from sunrise to 11 P.M.; call (630) 833-0100. In addition, the county's Cricket Creek Forest Preserve is located in Addison.

ARMY TRAIL NATURE CENTER // ½   This is a quiet place to observe nature. Follow an asphalt and then wood-chip walking trail in the 22 acres of forest. You can't miss the five-acre pond, and if you do, your pooch will find it. Canine swimming is allowed here. As long as dogs are well behaved, Park District officials look the other way. However, ducks and geese are highly offended by canine interlopers. There are observation decks that serve as diving boards for dogs, as well as fishing platforms and places to bird-watch. If you don't have a barking hound, you may catch a glimpse of a blue heron. Foxes and white-tailed deer have also been seen here.

Open sunrise to 11 P.M. Across from Addison Trail High School on Lombard Street at Army Trail Road. (630) 833-0100.

CENTENNIAL PARK // ½   A pond attracts dogs, who like to jump in. It also attracts geese. In December, when researcher Carol and her dog Breathless visited, this was no problem. However, in June the adjacent half-mile asphalt trail gets bombarded with goose remains.

Bill Tookey, director of the Addison Park District, takes afternoon strolls at this park with his boxer, Gracie. He says that he wouldn't be setting a proper example if he let Gracie off a leash and into the water. That's because dogs are supposed to be on a leash. (Officials don't mind when well-behaved dogs jump into a pond or play fetch in a grassy area.) "Besides, Gracie doesn't like the water," he said. If your dog doesn't jump in, you can still cast a fishing line. Tookey said that he isn't sure what people catch.

There's an adjacent recreation center (where dogs are not allowed) and a playground area where dogs can visit.

Open sunrise to 11 P.M. 1776 W. Centennial, south of Lake Street on the east side of Route 53. (630) 833-0100.

COMMUNITY PARK // ½   Located on the opposite side of town, this is pretty much a mirror image of Centennial Park. At least one little cairn terrier joins the kids in the sandbox. The terrier—whose owner calls him a "terror"— does a better job of digging than her two children. There are a fair number of trees, but there's little shade. The park is new, the trees are young, and they don't offer much relief.

The busiest places are the athletic fields. Community Park also features a forested enclave. This is the least used part of the park. You can walk through the preserve if you can find the narrow makeshift path. Salt Creek runs alongside this forest, which connects to Cricket Creek Forest Preserve south of Lake Street.

Open sunrise to 11 P.M. Community Park is at 120 E. Oak Street, north of Lake Street and east of Addison Road. (630) 833-0100.

CRICKET CREEK FOREST PRESERVE //   There's a lot of water, but we kept Chaser away, because dogs aren't allowed in the water. Of course, trying to convince Chaser was another matter. The Salt Creek flows around the preserve, which is a natural floodplain. Following heavy rains, the ponds grow. Although there are no dogs in the water, there are plenty of fish. Anglers might catch bass, crappies, or sunfish.

Cricket Creek is a popular neighborhood destination for lunchtime picnics. Chaser felt unloved because we didn't allow her to crash any of them. The picnic shelter is just past the main entrance. There's also what the Forest Preserve District of DuPage County calls a tiny-tot play lot, ideal for kids in their "terrible twos" who yearn to explore.

Chaser forgave us when we walked her down the 1.8-mile trail that winds around the three ponds, just south of Fullerton Avenue. Lots of joggers use the trail. With the heavy usage and nearby Illinois Route 83 (to the east), this preserve isn't exactly a tranquil place.

The south side of the preserve contains a model boating area. A county permit is required.

Open from one hour after sunrise to one hour after sunset. The main parking entrance is north of Fullerton Avenue, west of Addison Road. (630) 933-7248.

Festival

Fourth of July Festival   Yes, this fest is on the Fourth, at Community Park, 120 E. Oak Street, north of Lake Street and east of Addison Road. Starting at 6 P.M., there are games for children and lots of food. Local lifeguards are victims in the dunk tanks. Labradors need not come to the rescue. Live bands also perform. The fireworks begin at about 9 P.M., and this is when most dogs will want to leave. Admission is free. Call (630) 833-0100.

Bartlett

Parks

Dogs are welcome in the Bartlett municipal parks. Dogs must be leashed, and handlers must pick up. Parks are open from dawn to dusk; call (630) 837-6568.

BARTLETT PARK // ½   It's like walking into a scene from *Little House on the Prairie*. There's even a historic log cabin that is used for Park District classes. Dogs aren't allowed inside the cabin, but they can run through the classic gazebo. At twilight, the old-fashioned streetlights brighten the park, which dates back to 1946.

Dogs can savor the decades of smells around the hundred-year-old hickory and oak trees. There are also interesting young whippersnapper trees, including Kentucky coffee, white ash, and cork.

There's a grassy space on the north side of the park. These four acres hold a charm of their own.

Open dawn to dusk. Bartlett Park is at 102 Northeastern Avenue, at Oak Avenue. (630) 837-6568.

SUNRISE PARK // ½   A natural pond is the highlight of this 43-acre park. It's a beautiful setting as weeping willows hang over the water and waterfowl peacefully paddle. Then the canine swimmers come along. One Labrador swims here on a regular basis and terrifies the ducks and geese in the process. Of course, from her point of view, that's the whole idea.

A wooded area thick with maple and ash trees beckons on the south side of the park, but there's no path. Another Lab regularly runs through here and terrifies the squirrels.

There are a couple of asphalt trails in the park for jogging with the pooch, and a spacious grassy place for playing catch.

Open dawn to dusk. Sunrise Park is north of Struckman Boulevard, just east of Illinois Route 59. (630) 837-6568.

TRAILS END PARK / ½   Looping through the middle of the park is a quarter-mile asphalt path that is handicapped accessible. There are also some picnic spaces and baseball fields. The large grassy area is just right for flying a kite or playing Frisbee with your dog.

Open dawn to dusk. Trails End Park is at Millwood Drive and Longford Road, northeast of Newport Boulevard. (630) 837-6568.

Doggy Doings

Free Concerts   Twice each month, on summer nights from May through August, free concerts are given at the gazebo in Bartlett Park. There are no concessions, so if you want food or dog biscuits, you'll have to carry them with you. You'll also want to take something to sit on. Concerts start at various times. The park is at 102 Northeastern Avenue, at Oak Avenue. For a schedule and more information call (630) 837-6568.

Pictures with Santa   Brush those pearly whites before visiting Santa for a family photo. Sorry, these photos are for animal members of the family only. Santa's knee takes a beating during this session. Santa's "manager" explained that Saint Nick was plenty jolly bouncing a little Yorkshire terrier on his knee, but after the family with three rottweilers had their "pups" hop onto his lap, Santa's arthritic joints began to act up. Photos can be made into magnets, buttons, or key chains.

The fee ranges from $7 to $15, depending on the package. The photo shoot is organized by veterinarian Dr. Jennifer Hart to raise funds to benefit the

Bartlett Neighborhood Assistance Spay/Neuter Program. The photo shoot takes place on the first Saturday in December, from about noon to 3 P.M. at the Heartland Animal Hospital, Bartlett Commons, 874 S. Route 59. Reservations are required; call (630) 372-2000.

Festival

Bartlett Bonanza Days   Play musical mats, a canine version of musical chairs, at the Annual Dog and Cat Pet Show. When the music stops, dogs must find a free mat and sit. Wandering dogs left without a mat are disqualified. The winners get a special prize, and all entrants are awarded treats and a bandanna.

Cats are judged by local luminaries for "Longest Whiskers," "Most Beautiful Color," and "Longest Tail." Dogs get judged in lots of categories, so there are plenty of winners. Some of the awards go to "Most Friendly," "Most Beautiful," and "Best Costume."

Capture the moment on film for $5 per picture. Proceeds from the photos benefit the Four Paws Animal Foundation in Bartlett.

When the weather cooperates, more than a hundred canine entrants show up, and all competitors are encouraged to enlist a large barking and/or cheering section. Barking fans get dog treats, and cheering fans can purchase home-baked cookies.

Participating animals must be at least six months of age. The three-day festival is held from noon to 4 P.M. on the second weekend in August at Bartlett Park, North and Oak Avenues. Registration for the pet show begins at 10 A.M. on Saturday. You pay $1 per pet. Call (630) 830-0324.

Batavia

Recreation Area

FERMILAB DOG EXERCISE AREA AND BIKE PATH //// (OFF-LEASH—DOG EXERCISE AREA ONLY)   Here is a little-used place, and one of the best finds of the book. Aside from a pleasant-enough 3.6 miles of walking/bike trail through 6,800 acres, the real thrill is the off-leash dog exercise area, which is about one square mile. As a backdrop is Fermilab, a private facility where world-renowned scientists focus on high-energy physics. Perhaps the dog area is there so they can study the physics of a canine catching a Frisbee in midair.

Because there's so much space, and because it's relatively undiscovered, privacy is rarely a problem. You can do serious work free of bratty barkers and other distractions.

An adept recall (response when you call your dog) is a good idea. Coyotes could theoretically be a threat to small dogs (it's probably a Fermilab urban legend, though—to anyone's knowledge, no coyote has ever scared a small dog here), or the pooch could chase after a fox, raccoon, squirrel, or, worst of all, skunk.

A large lake graces the southeast border of the dog exercise area. Dogs are welcome to dive in.

All in all, the location is extraordinary.

The best news is that people pick up. Fermilab officials were wary of my writing about this find. They figure that if the place becomes popular, it could become littered with doggy waste and debris from careless users.

Dogs must be on a leash on the asphalt bike path (which connects to the Illinois Prairie Path Batavia and Aurora branches). There's also a concrete sidewalk to the west along Batavia Road.

Your first or last stop—whatever the case may be—will most likely be Wilson Hall, which is a good hike east of the exercise area. Here you can use rest rooms, grab a bite at the cafeteria, or learn more about Fermilab. However, dogs aren't allowed inside.

There's a lot to see on this path—natural tallgrass prairie, an explosion of seasonal wildflowers, and more than 250 species of birds. On top of that, abstract sculptures keep popping up along the route, and your dog will have no better idea of what they represent than you do. The culmination is the pasture filled with 35 American bison. The buffalo roam northwest of Wilson Hall and east of the exercise area. When the wind is blowing in the right direction, you won't need a canine snout to find the buffalo.

Just north of Wilson Hall is the main parking area, and north of that are two winding prairie walks, where dogs are allowed on a leash. One path is nearly a mile, and the second is twice that long. Both are interpretive trails with signage that points out highlights and gives information about that plant, tree, or critter you might encounter.

Buzzing insects around these trails and near the wetlands can become overwhelming. Protect yourself and your pooch.

Open 9 A.M. to 5 P.M. Parking is on Pine Street off of Kirk Road. The area is one and a half miles south of Illinois Route 38 (Roosevelt Road) and one and a half miles north of Illinois Route 56 (Butterfield Road), just west of Illinois Route 59. (630) 840-3351.

Bloomingdale

Parks

Dogs aren't allowed in Bloomingdale municipal parks, but there are two significant DuPage County Forest Preserve areas here.

MEACHAM GROVE FOREST PRESERVE //   The wooded, mile-long looped trail on the west side of Roselle Road can be a sight to behold in spring, with its blanket of red and white trillium, and in the fall, with the dazzling display of colors on the sugar maples. This preserve is particularly strict about keeping dogs on trails, due to the county's concern about maintaining the natural setting and keeping the rare plants from being trampled.

Carol, Danny, and Pork Chop checked out this preserve in the fall. Pork Chop's beagle snout never saw daylight as he plowed through the crunchy layers of autumn leaves on the forest floor. Pork Chop slept for hours after this olfactory overload.

Open from one hour after sunrise to one hour after sunset. The main entrance is on Roselle Road north of Illinois Route 20 (Lake Street). (630) 933-7248.

SPRING CREEK RESERVOIR FOREST PRESERVE // ½   Our researcher Carol's pooch is truly an uptown girl. Breathless pulled ahead on her leash to investigate the 1.1-mile asphalt trail. That hard surface has a city feel in more ways than one. It attracts packs of in-line skating teenagers. It couldn't be described as a quiet forest preserve retreat, but that's the way Breathless, a city slicker if ever there was one, prefers it.

This trail is a good choice for people with physical disabilities. It is plowed throughout the winter. Summer brings a yellow and pink carpet of goldenrod and clover between the trail and the banks of the reservoir.

The preserve is shaped like a big bathtub, with the trail encircling the 38-acre reservoir tub. The reservoir has an average depth of 15 feet. Some dogs wade in, but the water isn't very clean.

Open from one hour after sunrise to one hour after sunset. The main entrance is on Illinois Route 20 (Lake Street) between Medinah and Glen Ellyn Roads. (630) 933-7248.

Carol Stream

Parks

Municipal parks do allow dogs, just so they're leashed and owners pick up. Parks are open from sunrise to sunset. Call (630) 665-2311.

ARMSTRONG PARK // ½   "On your left!" "On your right!" "On your left!" Your neck gets more exercise than the dog as mobs of in-line skaters swish by on the asphalt trail. This trail connects with other community paths, so skaters can glide along more than three miles of winding turns. If you don't mind the skaters rolling by, it's a peachy place for a jog with Fido. If you do mind them, you'd better wait until it's too cold for the skating crowd.

This 74-acre park is full of biped activities, including several lit baseball and soccer fields, outdoor tennis courts, and an indoor pool at the recreation center. Picnic areas, complete with pavilions, are available by reservation. Fishing is permitted in the 15-acre lake, but dogs are supposed to walk only up to the banks—not into the water.

Open sunrise to sunset. Armstrong Park is on Illini Drive west of Hiawatha Street; at Bluff Street it connects to Mitchel Lake Park. (630) 665-2311.

BIERMAN PARK AND HERITAGE LAKE // ½   Leashed dogs are welcome at this 48-acre park. The one-mile jogging trail is paw comfortable and loops around two-acre Heritage Lake. Dogs aren't supposed to dive in, but they do anyway. You'll find shade near the subdivisions. The gazebo can be reserved for picnics, although you may have to boot out the geese. Bierman Park also has a baseball field and a roller hockey court. Fishing is permitted in the lake, but dog swimming is not.

Open sunrise to sunset. Bierman Park is on Woodlake Drive between Lies and Army Trail Roads. (630) 665-2311.

HAMPEE PARK //   This 22-acre park has so much going on that your dog won't know what to do first. The athletic pooch may lean toward the soccer field, one of the basketball or sand volleyball courts, or the roller hockey rink. Your dog is welcome to suit up only when these areas are not being used by athletes with two legs. A pathway connects to the trail system of nearby Mitchel Lake and Armstrong Parks, creating a five-mile hard-surfaced path. Local kids beat feet to the playground, and lots of families both with dogs and without lay a spread in the shelter area for picnics. Bathrooms are another bonus.

Open sunrise to sunset. Hampee Park is on Lies Road, just west of Gary Avenue. (630) 665-2311.

MITCHEL LAKE PARK // ½   This 22-acre tract has a rip-roaring running area. The land is undeveloped, but the grass is cut, so even small dogs can make it through. Of course, dogs take pleasure in jumping into Mitchel Lake, although that practice is frowned upon.

Open sunrise to sunset. Mitchel Lake Park connects to Armstrong Park off Bluff Street, one block west of Gary Avenue, off Hiawatha Street. (630) 665-2311.

SUNDANCE PARK / ½   The best thing about this park is that it's shaped like a bathtub: once you're in, it's not easy to get out. Locals sneak their dogs off-leash, secure that the pups can't run off. However, if you're caught by the local police, you'll have to pay the piper. The football field here is heavily used, so most illegal dog walkers appear early in the morning—before the football players wake up. Otherwise, this three-acre park leaves dogs luke-warm.

Open sunrise to sunset. On Kuhn Road at Yeardly Drive. (630) 665-2311.

TIMBER RIDGE FOREST PRESERVE // ½   Gravel trails wind through natural prairie land for six miles. This setting is a draw for no-nonsense hikers, joggers, and bicyclists. To the south, Timber Ridge leads to the Illinois Prairie Path, which extends west to Elgin and Aurora. To the north, the Great Western Trail goes as far as DeKalb. You can pick up either trail at Timber Ridge.

Bill Weidner, public affairs director for the Forest Preserve of DuPage County, told me that some people practice marathons here. The trails are mostly flat—easy running for people and their four-footed partners.

Weidner ought to know about this trail, since his dogs have joined him on jogs for years. And they're not alone. It gets surprisingly busy with folks who are serious about their workouts. No time for visiting with other dogs. The courteous thing to do here is to run right on by.

Open from one hour after sunrise to one hour after sunset. The main entrance is west of County Farm Road, north of Geneva Road, south of Illinois Route 64 (North Avenue). (630) 933-7248.

VOLUNTEER PARK ½ /   There is some open space for stretching legs at this busy park. Sometimes there are so many people here, usually playing soccer or using the kids' play lot, that dogs have to navigate around the traffic. Plans call for adding 14 acres of wetlands adjacent to the park. A trail system is also being implemented to connect Volunteer Park to the Regional Trail System, allowing for miles of trail to be accessible.

Open sunrise to sunset. On Kuhn Road, just north of North Avenue. (630) 665-2311.

Illinois Prairie Path

The Illinois Prairie Path (IPP) is 55 miles of trailways that extend into Cook, DuPage, and Kane Counties.

Naturalist and author Mary Watts had the idea back in 1963 to convert the abandoned railroad right-of-way into a trail through the western suburbs. Two years later, the IPP became a not-for-profit agency. In 1971 a part of the path became the first place in the state to be included in the National Trail System. Various municipalities, forest preserve districts, and volunteers participate in the maintenance of the trails.

The main drag extends for 15 miles from Maywood into downtown Wheaton. The trail passes through or near Berkeley, Elmhurst, Villa Park, Lombard, and Glen Ellyn. Once in Wheaton, it branches to the north through West Chicago, Wayne, and Elgin and to the south through Warrenville and abutting Fermilab and its off-leash area (see p. 183) in Batavia. It continues south to Aurora, where yet another branch makes its merry way to Elgin. This especially picturesque branch goes through Geneva and St. Charles along the Fox River.

The IPP is the best place to practice long-distance running. A two-mile morning sprint won't do it for Calvin the golden retriever and his person, Jim Evans, who live in Elmhurst; they typically run six to eight miles daily. Sometimes they run to the IPP entrance located near their home, but often they drive to another location to begin, so they can see something new and different each time.

Evans has been running with Calvin on the path for about five years. He says, "No two runs are alike."

They've seen lots of kinds of birds. "I don't know anything about birds, but I like to know that I'm surrounded by nature," he says.

Dogs are welcome on the prairie path, as long as they're on a leash. When the path intersects or crosses into a county forest preserve, the same rule applies. In these places the rule may be rigorously enforced. Evans says that on occasion he's seen people bicycling on the path with a special hookup so the dog can run along; others merely walk with their pups.

Keep an eye on the dog. While the majority of the IPP passes through prairie land, as well as some forest preserve and marsh, the paths also cross some busy streets.

Here are some IPP highlights:

- In Elmhurst, you're among six acres of restored tallgrass prairie from Salt Creek to Spring Road. There's also an interpretive garden, where plants are labeled.
- As the path enters Villa Park, check out the Historical Society Museum and Illinois Prairie Path Visitor's Center at Villa Avenue. Sorry, dogs aren't allowed inside.
- From the Wheaton trailhead at Liberty Drive and Carlton Avenue, a pathway heads north over what's now called Volunteer Bridge. The 160-foot-long iron-truss bridge is named for the volunteers who helped restore it in 1983.
- The Elgin Branch of the IPP spans 15.7 miles to Elgin, where it connects with the Fox River Trail. From the observation platform at the 0.7-mile mark, you can cast around for the waterfowl that fly in to the Lincoln Marsh Natural Area for pit stops on their spring and fall migration routes. The platform even has benches, and stairs lead down to the water's level. Dogs are not allowed to dive in after the assorted ducks or Canada geese. In other places, beaver dams, and perhaps even their residents, may pop up along the river.

Easy access and the best parking are found at the following locations:

Elmhurst: East of York Road between Vallette Street and the IPP, enter from Vallette. Or west of Spring Road north of the IPP.

Villa Park: West of Villa Avenue on Central Boulevard. Or west of Ardmore Avenue on Central Boulevard.

Lombard: West of Westmore Avenue along Broadway on both sides of the path.

Wheaton: Free parking is readily available at the County Courthouse, 505 N. County Farm Road, off Manchester and County Farm Roads.

Elgin: County Farm Road at Geneva Road.

West Chicago: National Street near Arbor Avenue, at Reed-Keppler Park.

Parking is also available at municipal and county forest preserves located next to or near the IPP. For further information, including membership material, a free trail map, or a more detailed map for $3, write the Illinois Prairie Path, P.O. Box 1086, Wheaton, IL 60189. Or call (630) 752-0120.

WEST BRANCH FOREST PRESERVE /   The 1.5-mile trail is so poorly marked that our poor assistant Carol had a heck of a time even finding it. Plans are in the works to mark trails with posts for easier navigation. Breathless and Carol trampled through mounds of goose and duck dung before they finally discovered an overgrown path leading through the woods west of Deep Quarry Lake. A more obvious half-mile path cuts through the prairie grass along the east side of the lake.

After all that, it turned out to be a pretty boring walk for Breathless. She preferred watching two little girls falling in goose poop. Take the extra five minutes and head west to Pratt's Wayne Woods in Wayne. It's a better choice.

Open from one hour after sunrise to one hour after sunset. The parking entrance is on the south side of Army Trail Road between County Farm Road and Illinois Route 59. (630) 933-7248.

Clarendon Hills

Doggy Doings

Christmas Walk   A lot goes on outdoors during the Clarendon Hills Annual Christmas Walk on the first Friday in December. Leashed dogs are welcome to do their Christmas window-shopping. Unfortunately, most retailers don't allow dogs inside their decked halls.

Ice sculptors, carolers, and a special appearance from Santa himself can be enjoyed from 6 P.M. to 9 P.M. in downtown Clarendon Hills, between Walker, Prospect, Park, and Railroad Avenues. Horse-drawn carriage rides are a prime family activity. Lapdogs are welcome to rest merry, assuming they don't bark at the horses. The rides are $2 per person, $1 for children under 12 years; both two-legged and four-legged children can ride on laps for free. Call (630) 654-3030.

Pet Parade and Costume Contest   The winners of this pet costume contest receive gift certificates from local merchants. The contest commences following the pet parade, which starts at 9:15 A.M. on the third Saturday in June. (The parade kicks off at Walker School, 120 Walker Avenue, and proceeds to Railroad Avenue, east to Prospect Avenue, and then south into downtown Clarendon Hills.) There is no registration fee for the parade. Some kids march with stuffed animals or Beanie Babies, and one little girl even had a make-believe pet on a leash. However, only living pets may be judged in the costume contest. Winners are based on creativity.

The pet parade and costume contest are a part of Daisy Days, held 9 A.M. to 10 P.M. in downtown Clarendon Hills on the third Friday and Saturday in June between Park and Burlington Avenues. There are sidewalk sales and activities for children, where pooches are also welcome. Call (630) 654-3030.

Coffee Shop

Quinn's Coffee House In order to dine with your dog, you must phone this unique coffee house before you arrive to make doggy reservations. The village does not allow the establishment to keep tables outside all the time, and they are set up only on request. The outside area accommodates about six people and a pawful of pooches. Customers overheard talking about the coffee say it's the "best." 2 S. Prospect Avenue; (630) 323-3027.

Darien

Parks

In addition to sprawling DuPage County Waterfall Glen Forest Preserve, there are several neighborhood parks. In all parks in Darien, dogs on a leash are allowed as long as owners pick up. The Darien Park District facilities are open from sunrise to sunset. For more information call (630) 655-6400.

DARIEN COMMUNITY PARK // This park really seems to represent the community. Lots of seniors and lots of elderly dogs stroll down the easy-to-walk asphalt path. There are few in-line skaters or bicyclers to dodge. Most of the in-line skaters stick to the parking lots, so be careful when you let Fido out of the car.

There's no shortage of places to stretch canine legs, at least when the soccer and ball fields aren't in use. There are also sand volleyball, tennis, and basketball courts. This 20-acre park is the largest in Darien.

Open sunrise to sunset. Entrances are off Plainfield Road west of Clarendon Hills Road and on 71st Street at Clarendon Hills Road. (630) 655-6400.

MEYER WOODS // ½ Walk toward the back of the preserve. It's a relatively secluded spot and a top-flight place to watch red-tailed hawks, white-tailed deer, and assorted songbirds. At dusk you may spot bats. The Park District has plans to construct a boardwalk over the marsh so that people and their pups can get even closer to the wildlife.

A small oak forest supplies ample and sometimes much-needed shade. Several years ago when a power shortage hit the community during a heat wave, residents and their dogs came to picnic under the trees to cool off. There's also a sheltered picnic area.

Open sunrise to sunset. Meyer Woods is on 87th Street, northwest of North Frontage Road and southeast of Lemont Road. (630) 655-6400.

WATERFALL GLEN FOREST PRESERVE /// This 2,470-acre preserve is a celebration of ecological diversity. The park encircles Argonne National Laboratory, one of the largest federally funded scientific research facilities in the nation.

Make sure you don't kill any dragonflies. This is where entomologists discovered the rare emerald dragonfly that is now protected by law. There are also 10 endangered plant species, and more than 150 bird species have been sighted.

Not content with the preserve's neatly mowed trails, thrill-seeking canines may prefer the hilly and rocky paths. Chaser was in shape for these, but I wasn't.

Carol, our researcher, had a tough time here, too. For one thing, she was obliged to hang on to a plastic bag filled with "stool samples" from Pork Chop and Snowball. There are few containers for disposing trash. Carol chose one trail that doubled as a service road, so cars were an annoyance.

Pork Chop and Snowball were offended that most dogs weren't on a leash. After all, they both were leashed only because that's the law in this preserve. Adding insult to injury, some of the off-leash dogs were big show-offs. They ran in circles and barked incessantly at Pork Chop and Snowball.

It's one thing for the dogs to be off-leash, it's another when owners don't have control, and it's even worse when the dogs are aggressive. Carol was amazed that people would disregard the law with such unruly dogs.

My visit to Waterfall Glen wasn't nearly as comprehensive as Carol's, but we shared similar experiences. One little terrier-mix, about half the size of Chaser, pulled to the end of his leash, growling and snapping. The owner didn't appear fazed. Chaser and I exchanged looks of disgust.

Aside from the barking of unsociable canines, the preserve remains relatively serene. The Des Plaines River flows through the south border, but it's too filthy for swimming, even for dogs who are willing to traverse the cattails. Some people allow their dogs to swim at Sawmill Creek, just south of the waterfall. Here you must beware of the broken glass and pollution—it's not the best place for the dog paddle.

Contrary to popular belief, the preserve is not named for the man-made waterfall, but rather in honor of Seymour "Bud" Waterfall, who was a president of the District's board of commissioners.

A word of warning: Heed the signs that ask visitors to stay away from the Lemont Police Department shooting range at the far southwest corner. In addition to the real danger of being inadvertently shot at, the noise can disturb canine ears.

Instead, cross the trail at the Poverty Savanna. Don't worry; it's not named for the relative wealth of those who use the trail. The name derives from poverty oat grass that grows in the adjoining two-hundred-acre prairie alongside pussytoes and mountain mint.

On the south side of the preserve you'll find concrete walls and scattered shells of old buildings. These are the remains of the Lincoln Park Nursery. At one time, plants grown here were shipped to Lincoln Park on the Near North Side of Chicago. A loose gravel trail nearby leads to an old sawmill.

Be careful as you reach the high bluffs near the waterfall. The view is spectacular—but so is the drop. Make sure Fido is on a tight leash.

Over the winter, some of the hillier trails offer a supreme workout for cross-country skiers. During the summer, it's one of the best local destinations for mountain bikers.

Open from one hour after sunrise to one hour after sunset. The north parking area is west of Cass Avenue at Northgate Road, south of Interstate 55. The south parking area is near the waterfall, located south of Cass Avenue and south of Bluff Road (99th Street), west of Clarendon Hills Road. (630) 933-7248.

WESTWOOD PARK ½ ✦   Forget about allowing the pooch to play in the natural wetland: there are too many thickets. The outfield grass and soccer fields are better choices to gear up canine legs.

Open sunrise to sunset. Westwood Park is at 75th Street and Fairview Avenue; parking is off Fairview. (630) 655-6400.

Downers Grove

Parks

Municipal parks in Downers Grove allow dogs on a six-foot lead when owners pick up. These parks are open from sunrise to 11 P.M.; call (630) 963-1300.

59TH AND MAIN STREET PARK ∕ ½   You can run or walk the quarter-mile asphalt trail, and you can keep on going to the sidewalk that borders the 19-acre park to continue your workout. There's a small area of natural wetland, but there's not enough water for a dog to swim; it's just mush. Dogs are not permitted in the playground area.

Open sunrise to 11 P.M. 59th and Main Street Park is at 59th and Main Streets. (630) 963-1300.

FISHEL PARK ½ ∕   Most of this two-acre park is taken up by the band shell, so dogs have to get by with a small grassy patch outlining the structure, and some beautiful mature oak trees. There's also a play lot. The park is located near downtown Downers Grove.

Open sunrise to 11 P.M. Fishel Park is west of Maple Street on Grove Street and North and Maple Avenues. (630) 963-1300.

MAPLE GROVE FOREST PRESERVE ∕∕ ½   Even Lucy and Chaser seemed to mellow out in this heavily wooded, tranquil setting. At least during our visit, few people or dogs could be seen. A camera should be required gear in the fall, when the sugar maple leaves turn a stunning yellow and red. The 82-acre preserve is set far back from Maple Road; car traffic can't be heard, except by canine ears.

Open from one hour after sunrise to one hour after sunset.

Maple Grove Forest Preserve is bounded by Gilbert Avenue to the north and is nearly a mile west of Main Street. The main entrance is on the north side of Maple Avenue, west of Main Street and south of Illinois Route 34 (Ogden Road). (630) 933-7248.

McCOLLUM PARK ∕∕   crushed-limestone path loops around this 50-acre park. It's a well-used and easy-to-traverse walkway. Pups can run around on the green space near the softball fields.

Dogs aren't allowed on the 18-hole miniature golf course, the horseshoe court, or the playground area. But they may get lucky and find some scraps at one of the five BBQ grills.

Open sunrise to 11 P.M. McCollum Park is at 6801 S. Main Street, between 63rd and 75th Streets. (630) 963-1300.

PATRIOTS PARK ∕∕   The standout of this 27-acre park is Barth Pond, which flows into a nearby marsh. Canine swimming is discouraged, but there's a deck from which to observe wildlife where the two bodies of water connect. Benches are located around the pond. Another plus is the sensory garden, where visually impaired visitors can easily touch and smell the greenery. Dogs are allowed to smell but should not touch or trample the plants. The park also has a picnic shelter and grills for barbecuing.

Open sunrise to 11 P.M. Patriots Park is at 55th Street and Grand Avenue. (630) 963-1300.

Doggy Doings

Movies in the Park Not a drive-in movie, this is more of a walk-in movie. The flicks are presented once a month, June through August, at the Fishel Park band shell. You'll have to pop your own popcorn, as none is offered in the park. Movies are geared toward kids, such as *The Hunchback of Notre Dame* and *101 Dalmatians* (dogs loved this one). The most popular showings so far were *Space Jam*, starring Michael Jordan, and *Toy Story*. The movies begin at 8:30 P.M. and are free. For a schedule call (630) 963-1300.

Summer Concerts Enthusiastic dogs are tempted to bark musical requests at the Tuesday-night summer concerts at the Fishel Park band shell, west of Maple Street on Grove Street at North and Maple Avenues. Tunes start at 7 P.M. from the last Tuesday in May through the first Tuesday in August. Concessions are available, including pizza and ice cream. Sorry, no dog biscuits. Take a lawn chair. Concerts are free. Call (630) 963-1300.

Places to Stay

Marriott Suites in Downers Grove A front-desk employee tells me "only small dogs" can stay overnight. When asked to clarify exactly what he means by "small dogs," he says there is no written protocol. He then adds that to his knowledge, the hotel has never turned a dog away, no matter what size it was. Thus, there's hope for your Saint Bernard; just make you sure you call first. Owners are responsible for any damage caused by Rover. Rates are $69 to $169. 1500 Opus Place; (630) 852-1500 or (800) 228-9290.

Red Roof Inn I'm told, "Dogs are welcome as long as they don't chew on the bedspread." Rates are $65 to $73. One pet per room. 1113 Butterfield Road; (630) 963-4205.

Elmhurst

Doggy Doing

Pet Parade and Contest Canines shed their winter coats in favor of spring finery for this pet parade and contest held annually on the third Saturday in May. Along with dressing up their pets, many kids also decorate their bicycles for the four-block parade. It begins at 1 P.M. at Ahlgrim Funeral Home (57 Spring Road) and continues to the Silverado Grill (447 Spring Road).

The competition is intense. After all, two hundred pets participate. What's fair is fair—cats are judged in their own categories, as are reptiles. Dogs can win for "Best Groomed," "The Dog That Looks Most Like Its Owner," and "Most Unusual Trick."

Lemonade is available for people, and there's water for the dogs. Face painting adds to the color, and a bike safety program for kids makes it educational. There's no fee, but registration is advised. Call DeVreis Animal Center, (630) 833-7387.

Place to Stay

Holiday Inn Barkers stay home; only quiet dogs are welcome. Rates are $59.50 to $119. 624 N. York Road; (630) 279-1100.

Glendale Heights

Parks

Dogs aren't allowed in the municipal parks, although we're told that people sneak them in. Still, we won't list any here. However, dogs are welcome at two Forest Preserve District of DuPage County areas. One includes off-leash training grounds.

EAST BRANCH FOREST PRESERVE // This 483-acre preserve has a lot of open prairie area. Trees are few and far between, so take a hat to shade yourself and bottled water to spritz Fido. Although it isn't allowed, some owners let their dogs cool off in either Rush Lake or Sunfish Pond. Rush Lake is nine acres and has a maximum depth of 22 feet. Sunfish Pond is about half that size and just over half the depth. Sunfish, channel catfish, and bluegills populate both bodies of water. In lieu of designated picnic areas, you get plenty of flatland on which to spread a blanket.

Open from one hour after sunrise to one hour after sunset. The main parking entrance is east of Glen Ellyn Road, south of Army Trail Road, and north of the Chicago, Central & Pacific Railroad tracks. (630) 933-7248.

EAST BRANCH FOREST PRESERVE DOG TRAINING AREA //// (OFF-LEASH)

Hooray! A place where dogs can swim off-leash and no one will fine you. Not only is the dog paddle allowed, but it's also the stroke of choice.

A spokesperson for the Forest Preserve District of DuPage County swears that new turf is constantly being installed, but the dogs rip it up. With all the canine traffic, he's no doubt correct. Still, the effect is that there's mud everywhere. The dogs aren't deterred. Just be resigned to the fact that any pooch visiting here for more than 10 seconds will require a bath. You'll want to remember to lay an old sheet over the backseat of the car in preparation for the ride home with a smelly, wet dog.

Unlike the other Forest Preserve of DuPage County off-leash places, which are considered exercise areas, this is a true dog training area. It was designed to facilitate the training of sporting breeds. People who are seriously into hunting teach their dogs the ropes at this location.

There's a five-acre field where retrieving groups meet, most often on Saturday mornings.

Keep in mind that the field can get scorching in the summer because there's no shade. Since the pond water is so muddy, thoughtful owners will take drinking water along for their pups. Tracey Smith says she won't take her shih tzu, Reggie, on hot days because he gets overheated.

Raja, a golden retriever, and Doug Littlejohn of Naperville are regulars here. Raja, who is 13, has a great time, but Doug says Raja enjoys swimming a bit too much. "I feel we've overdone it when he barely wobbles back to the car," he says.

What counts is how the dogs feel about this place. Suffice to say that Lucy and Chaser didn't want to leave. And when Lucy finally began to lumber back to the car, she walked with her head slumped down and whimpered all the way. And that old sheet came in handy. The dog exercise area is scheduled to be relocated in the near future, which should eliminate some of the aforementioned issues. The new area, on the east side of Glen Ellyn Road, will be fenced with a double gate for safety and will have additional parking to accommodate this popular spot.

Open from one hour after sunrise to one hour after sunset. The dog training parking lot is west of Swift Road and south of the Chicago, Central & Pacific Railroad crossing. (630) 933-7248.

Mourning the Loss of a Pet

Perhaps the secret way in which pets touch us so profoundly is the same secret that explains the intense grief we feel when we lose a canine family member.

Roxanne Phillips, a Chicago psychotherapist with a special interest in pet loss, says, "There's nothing in this world to compare to losing a child, except, in a sense, losing a pet. You are that pet's caretaker, or parent. It's not inappropriate or surprising to feel real pain."

Phillips and other experts agree that the best thing you can do is to express that pain in whatever method feels most comfortable. Some people write stories, others compile photographs, and kids can draw pictures; you can "talk" about your pet on the Internet or call friends. Other mourners are more comfortable calling a stranger, which is why pet loss support lines are now in existence all over the country.

Dr. Mary Baukert, a vet based in Skokie, helped to establish the Chicago Veterinary Medical Association Pet Loss Support Line. "What you need to realize is that what you're feeling is perfectly normal," she says.

Bill Hart, executive director at the Evergreen Pet Cemetery in Monee, goes one step further. "When people say to me, 'I'm embarrassed because it hurts so bad,' I reply, 'It's a magnificent emblem of your humanity, and your relationship with that pet. Be proud to express those emotions.'"

Baukert says people require some sort of closing, some type of ceremonial good-bye. She advises, "Even if you allow your vet to dispose of the body, which is the most inexpensive route ($35 to $50), say a final good-bye. Take your time. Hold hands, hug with any family members present, and say some final words."

You can also have the ashes delivered to your home in an urn. Cremation and an urn range from $65 to $400, the higher prices for a particularly decorative urn. Again, Baukert suggests, "Before you place that urn on your fireplace mantel, say something special about your pet."

For those who can afford it, having a funeral at a pet cemetery offers a ritualistic chance to say good-bye. It's a good way to allow the healing to begin. Many cemeteries offer payment plans that can start when the pet is young. Of course, the other advantage of planning early is that you don't have to make a hurried decision when you're in an emotional state.

If you're considering a pet cemetery, planning well in advance will allow you to meet the staff and acquaint yourself with the grounds. Also, make certain the facility has proper zoning, so the place can't be bulldozed to build a parking lot.

Still, according to Phillips, no matter what you do, it's almost inevitable that you'll go through the following five stages of grief. Some people take only a few days before beginning to feel better, while others take many months—most are somewhere in between. "There is no right or wrong about how fast you'll go through these stages," she explains.

1. Shock: Even people expecting a death are surprised when it happens.
2. Acknowledgment: Coming to grips with the fact that Fido is gone.
3. Sorrow: That hollow feeling in your heart that actually makes you feel sick.
4. Anger: Some people take it out on the vet, family, or friends. It's normal to get mad.
5. Resolution: You might have one final cry as you come to grips and deal with what happened.

If you get another pet, it's best to give it another name. Don't expect it to have the same personality as the one you lost. In time, you'll find there may be enough room in your heart for a new love.

Pet Loss Resources

Chicago Veterinary Medical Association Pet Loss Support Line:
   (630) 603-3994

Pet Loss & Rainbow Bridge: A website where you can post photos and write about your beloved pet. Bereaved owners are linked together for a virtual support session. For children and adults. www.rainbowbridge .tierranet.com/bridge.htm

Also check out these books for children: *When Your Pet Dies: Dealing with Grief and Helping Children Cope*, by Christine Adamec (Berkeley Books, New York, 1996; $4.99); *Dog Heaven*, by Cynthia Rylant (Scholastic Inc., New York, 1995; $14.95). Another wonderful book is *Coping with Sorrow: On the Loss of Your Pet*, by Moira Anderson (Alpine Press, Loveland, CO, 1996; $11.95).

Glen Ellyn

Parks

Lake Ellyn Park is the only local park of note, aside from the sprawling Churchill Woods Forest Preserve.

CHURCHILL WOODS FOREST PRESERVE // ½   This 261-acre preserve is bisected by St. Charles Road. Crossing it can be a major feat. The buzzing ComEd electric lines over the north side of the prairie area are another annoyance. Still, the 34-acre prairie is a sight to behold when wildflowers, such as England aster, bottle gentian, and prairie sundrops, are in bloom. A 2.3-mile trail loops through both sides of the preserve.

    The south side of St. Charles Road is a better choice. A combination of woods and wetlands, it's also where the picnic area is located. This area is known as Babcock Grove. The bur oaks and black maples date back 150 years. Think of all the dogs that have marked these trees before Lucy and Chaser added their signatures. Much of the south trail follows the east branch of the DuPage River. It isn't much for canine swimming, but crappies, bluegills, sunfish, and largemouth bass might be caught.

    Open from one hour after sunrise to one hour after sunset. The parking entrances are south of St. Charles Road, west of Interstate 355, and east of Glen Ellyn and Swift Roads. (630) 933-7248.

LAKE ELLYN PARK / ½   This is an 11-acre park where leashed dogs can take a stroll on the 0.6-mile trail that circles a lake. Dogs are not allowed in the lake, despite being tempted by the geese. Just as well, since the water isn't especially clean. However, the trail is free of goose droppings.

    A sweet 1986 film called *Lucas*, starring Charlie Sheen, Corey Haim, and Winona Ryder, was filmed here and at the adjoining Glenbard West High School football field. Canines are not supposed to sneak onto the famous field. It was once voted the most picturesque football field in Illinois. Sources at the Park District confirm the honor, but they don't know who decided the winner. Sure, it's nice, but to the dogs, it looks like any other football field.

    This Glen Ellyn Park District facility is open from sunrise to 10 P.M. Lake Ellyn Park is bounded by Lake Road, Hawthorne Street, Essex Court, and Lennox Road. Parking is on Lennox Road. (630) 858-2462.

Quick Bite

Einstein Bros. Bagels Only four tables are set up outside this popular stop for bagels, sandwiches, and monster cookies. On hot summer days, be sure to ask for water—the sun really beats down, and there's no shade here. 443-445 N. Main Street; (630) 790-8881.

Coffee Shop

Starbucks There are only three tables, but spaces open up fast. 536 Crescent Boulevard; (630) 858-5966.

Places to Stay

Best Western Four Seasons There's a $7-per-day charge. Room rates are $63 to $68. 675 Roosevelt Avenue; (630) 469-8500 or (800) 528-1234.

Holiday Inn This hotel does not allow any dog over 25 pounds. There's a $25 non-refundable fee per stay. Rates are $89 to $115. 1250 Roosevelt Road; (630) 629-6000.

Hanover Park

Parks

Leash laws aren't taken lightly in this community, where municipal parks are open from dawn from to dusk. Call (630) 837-2468.

COMMUNITY PARK / ½ Dogs share space with lots of little kids, baseball and soccer players, in-line skaters, and geese at this 40-acre facility. Picnic shelters offer shade, while sand volleyball will put you in the sun. There is a one-mile asphalt trail for jogging with the pooch.

Open sunrise to sunset. Community Park is at 1919 Walnut Street at Church Street. (630) 837-2468.

THE HARBORS / ½ This linear-shape park includes one and a half miles of handicapped-accessible asphalt trail. It's especially busy with joggers on week-ends. Fishing is permitted in the ponds, but dog swimming is not. There are picnic areas and benches throughout.

Open sunrise to sunset. The Harbors is at Woodlake Drive and County Farm Road. (630) 837-2468.

MALLARD LAKE FOREST PRESERVE / ½   This 928-acre preserve is a work in progress. The District's main brochure indicates multipurpose trails. At this writing, the only current trail was from the parking area to the rest rooms. It's not much of a hike. Forest Preserve District personnel told us there are plans for trails around the 80-acre Mallard Lake and the 7-acre Cloverdale Pond. A 200-foot landfill overlooks the lake. It's a steep hike for Fido. The summit is the Mount Everest of DuPage County.

Two of the fishing piers are handicapped accessible. Largemouth bass, channel and flathead catfish, bluegills, crappies, and northern pike are stocked in the lake and pond. Ice fishing is touted as excellent.

Open from one hour after sunrise to one hour after sunset. The main entrance is on Lawrence Avenue, near Cloverdale Road, west of Gary Avenue and Thorn Road, and north of Schick Road. (630) 933-7248.

MALLARD LAKE FOREST PRESERVE DOG TRAINING AREA /// (OFF-LEASH)
Opened in September 1997, this sectioned-off part of Mallard Lake Forest Preserve remains relatively undiscovered. It's especially quiet during the week.

Dogs can start their sniffing in the quarter-acre mowed area. Next, take the one-mile trail around the entire circumference of the dog training parcel. For lazy bones, there's a shortcut trail about halfway through.

Open from one hour after sunrise to one hour after sunset. The main entrance is on Lawrence Avenue, near Cloverdale Road, west of Gary Avenue and Thorn Road, and north of Schick Road. The dog training area is on the southwest end of the parking lot. (630) 933-7248.

Hinsdale

Park

Dogs are allowed in Katherine Legge Memorial Park (see Suburban Cook County), even off-leash at certain times, and the Forest Preserve of DuPage County's Fullersburg Woods.

FULLERSBURG WOODS FOREST PRESERVE ///   The displays at the environmental education center change often, but all foster enthusiasm for nature. Past exhibits have included such beasts as the woolly mammoth. Dogs aren't allowed in the education center. However, they are welcome on the trails—and they can learn a lot in this 221-acre preserve. If you arrive while school is in session, you'll have to share the trails with kids delivered by the busload. More than 222,000 schoolchildren visit annually. No count on the number of canine guests.

A 1.3-mile self-guided trail runs near Salt Creek and over a bridge onto an island. Over the course of the summer, a part of the creek dries up. For whatever the reason, Chaser found one of these dried-up tributaries to be a sniffer's paradise. Perhaps it was the odor of the fish that once called this stream home. We eventually had to pull Chaser away. Salt Creek is fairly clean, and some people allow dogs to bound into the water. Keep in mind that you may be fined if you're caught in the act without a leash on the dog.

Chaser learned some tidbits about native flora. After all, the signage, which is changed seasonally, was at her level. She learned that Salt Creek was named after a farmer's mishap many years ago. His wagon was loaded with salt barrels and got stuck in the water. The salt washed into the creek—hence the name. Now, at canine cocktail parties, Chaser will deliver this anecdote to impress her pals.

There's also the Wildflower Trail, which extends for about a quarter of a mile. In April and May, you can witness a mosaic of wildflowers.

Another easy stroll is the half-mile trail to the Graue Mill. The mill still operates, and there's an adjacent museum. Dogs aren't allowed inside the mill buildings. The mill is open daily 10 A.M. to 4 P.M. from mid-April through mid-November. Call (630) 933-7248.

A three-mile trail heads northwest from the mill through the woods and along the creek bank. This multipurpose trail is used by the occasional horse (the Oak Brook Polo Club is nearby) and bicyclists. Several duck species may be sighted, including the wood duck, which actually nests in trees. We spied one wood duck, Chaser barked, and we never saw another. They must have heard she was in the neighborhood.

This is a popular family destination. If you are looking for privacy, this isn't the place for you and your pooch.

Open from one hour after sunrise to one hour after sunset. The parking entrance is on the east side of Spring Road, south of 31st Street, north of Ogden Avenue and west of York Road. (630) 933-7248.

Doggy Doings

Fourth of July Parade One year, a patriotic beagle managed to wave a flag as it marched in the town's annual parade. The flag was fastened to the dog's tail. The one-mile parade kicks off at 10 A.M. on July 4. The route starts at Sixth Street and Garfield Avenue and finishes at Sixth and Grant Streets.

Floats, marching bands, and infantry units firing muskets also appear in the parade. Sound-sensitive pups might get spooked. After the parade, a crafts fair is held near Hinsdale Middle School at 100 S. Garfield Avenue. The sidewalks are narrow, so little dogs could have a tough time navigating through the masses. Then again, there are scrumptious scraps to be scarfed down, since food vendors are scattered throughout the fair. Registration for the parade is required; call (630) 789-7000.

Halloween Parade They love their parades in Hinsdale. Dogs are welcome to participate in the town's annual Halloween Parade, but it isn't much of a challenge to complete, even for a Chihuahua—it's only about a block and a half. It's still fun to dress up, though. Costumes have included a West Highland terrier wearing a Wicked Witch of the West costume and a Pomeranian dressed as Dennis Rodman. The hair on the pom didn't even require a dye job; it's already red. There are no prizes for canine costumes, but kids receive trinkets for best costumes.

The parade is held the Saturday before Halloween. Registration is at 12:30 P.M., and the parade begins at 1 P.M. at Second and Washington Streets. Following the short trek and the costume contest, participants can trick-or-treat at neighborhood retailers. However, dogs aren't allowed inside the stores. Call (630) 323-3952.

Quick Bite

Einstein Bros. Bagels According to her owner, a basset hound named Taffy has tried each of the cream cheese spreads (except chocolate chip, which is dangerous for dogs). She likes veggie-lite cream cheese, sun-dried tomato cream cheese, and cream cheese with chives, but lox and cream cheese is far and away her favorite. Taffy, whose picture has appeared in the *Chicago Tribune*, is a local celebrity and will give her paw-tograph to any interested party. There are three tables outside. 54 S. Washington Street; (630) 794-9888.

Coffee Shop

Starbucks For big dogs, this outdoor patio is a tight fit. This Starbucks used to leave water bowls outside for the dogs, but they kept getting broken or stolen. It's a pity a good thing had to end. But if your four-legged friend is thirsty, just ask for water inside; the dog-loving staff is happy to oblige. 45 S. Washington Street; (630) 655-9923.

Itasca

Parks

The bad news: no dogs in municipal parks. The good news: the Forest Preserve of DuPage County offers three alternatives.

SALT CREEK FOREST PRESERVE / ½   In addition to being a popular picnic locale, this 83-acre preserve is especially useful to nearby residents as a floodplain. A mowed loop trail borders Elizabeth Street. You might as well walk around your own neighborhood to see cars passing by. Only a small section of the trail disappears into the woods, where red-tailed hawks and great horned owls have been known to nest. Fishing is allowed in Salt Creek. Some folks allow their dogs to run into the creek. It's great if you can get away with it, but if the dog is off-leash, you're subject to a fine.

 Open from one hour after sunrise to one hour after sunset. The parking is accessed north of Elizabeth Drive, east of Addison Road, and east of Salt Creek. (630) 933-7248.

SONGBIRD SLOUGH //   An easy-to-walk one-mile asphalt path takes you past the slough (marshy area). This path is handicapped accessible. The downside is that service vehicles also share the path, so make certain to adhere to the leash law.

 Our assistant Carol and her pooch, Breathless, didn't see any service vehicles. Instead, they were nearly run over by in-line skaters. Traffic died out once they reached the wooded area. Then it began to rain. Had Breathless been marching on a typical forest trail, she would have required a bath afterward. But this asphalt trail is amenable to a rainy-day walk or jog.

 The preserve insists that dozens of species of birds have been sighted here, including yellowthroat warblers; tree, grasshopper, and savanna sparrows; and meadowlarks. That's not to mention an assortment of waterfowl. But a wet fly in the rain was the only wildlife witnessed by soggy Breathless and Carol.

 Open from one hour after sunrise to one hour after sunset. The main entrance is on Mill Road, south of Illinois Highway 19 (Irving Park Road) and east of Interstate 290. (630) 933-7248.

WOOD DALE GROVE FOREST PRESERVE //   A one-mile crushed-limestone trail encircles Grove Lake and leads into the woods. The lake is often wall-to-wall with Canada geese, and their remains aren't hard to find. Sometimes the honking of geese can even drown out the airplanes at nearby O'Hare Airport.

There are two handicapped-accessible piers at the lake, where bass, bluegills, crappies, and sunfish may be caught.

The walk is an easy one. Breathless kept her nose to the limestone and didn't tire, but when Carol decided to rest, she was glad to see benches along the path.

Wood Dale Grove Forest Preserve is located on the Tinley Morraine glacial deposit. Underlying the area is a layer of glacial till, sandstone, and gravel left behind by the Wisconsin Glacier more than ten thousand years ago. Today, Wood Dale Grove includes 168 acres of open spaces, where there's plenty of picnicking, upland forest, and wetlands.

Open from one hour after sunrise to one hour after sunset. The main entrance is on Wood Dale Road, north of Interstate 290, west of Highway 83, and south of Third Avenue. (630) 933-7248.

Place to Stay

Holiday Inn It depends on who's helping you. I called three times, and first the weight limit was 20 pounds, another time it was 15 pounds, and finally I was told, "anything pretty small, like 25 or 30 pounds." I must say the personnel were exceedingly polite. It's just that the handbook for the hotel reads, "small pets are allowed." Of course, the definition of small is dependent on individual interpretation. We're told that dogs as large as Labradors have stayed here. The room rates are $99 to $129. 860 W. Irving Park Road; (630) 773-2340.

Lisle

Parks

In Park District parks, dogs are welcome on a maximum six-foot leash, and owners must pick up. The parks are open from dawn to dusk; call (630) 964-3410.

ABBEY WOOD PARK / ½   A particularly pretty setting, with towering oak and elm trees scattered around the park and near a fishing pond. Asphalt trails also curve through the five acres. The park is generally quiet, a pleasant place to contemplate life while relaxing on one of the benches set around the lagoon. Dogs aren't allowed to swim here.

Open dawn to dusk. Abbey Wood Park is accessed off Abbeywood Drive, west of College Road and east of Naper Boulevard. (630) 964-3410.

BEAU BIEN PARK / ½   Nearly all of the eight acres is potential canine running space, over a grassy area and ball fields. There are also tennis courts. This park is named for an early Lisle resident who opened a tavern. There aren't many shady spots, so take water for the pooch or stop for a cold one on the way home. A concrete path runs through the park.

Open dawn to dusk. Beau Bien Park is at Beau Bien Boulevard and Old Tavern Road. (630) 964-3410.

COLLEGE ROAD PARK / ½   A large pond consumes about half of the park's 23 acres. You can fish, but you can't allow your dog to take a dip. There's still plenty of room to run dogs. There's also a play lot.

Open dawn to dusk. College Road Park is off College Road between Trinity Drive and Carriage Hill Road, south of Parksleg Court. (630) 964-3410.

COMMUNITY PARK // ½   There's a lot to do in this 110-acre park. Asphalt trails take you over and around two small lakes. The dogs were cautious when walking over the wooden bridges, but they had no quibble with the two brick bridges. They would have liked to jump into the lakes, but swimming is allowed only if you happen to be a duck or a goose. The paths are an obstacle course of goose droppings.

The view of the ponds, particularly near the picnic groves, is quite picturesque. From here, walk past the rolling hills north of Short Street (which divides the park) and up the sledding hill. Gary Johnson and his Labrador-mix named Chinx visit the hill several times a week just to run up and down. "It's cheaper than joining a health club," Johnson says.

There's more running space on the south end of the park, where the lit baseball and soccer fields are located. Community Park also boasts the District's largest handicapped-accessible play lot.

Open dawn to dusk. Community Park is on Short Street between Route 53 and Yackley Road. (630) 964-3410.

GREENE VALLEY FOREST PRESERVE // ½   *(see Woodridge)*

HITCHCOCK WOODS //   One wood-chip trail cuts through the narrow 18-acre stretch of forested area. We visited in the winter, and Chaser and Lucy had the serene setting to themselves. Unfortunately, we couldn't find the wildlife that is often sighted here. Residents were probably hibernating, or maybe they went to Florida.

Open dawn to dusk. Hitchcock Woods is west of Yackley Avenue off Hitchcock Avenue. (630) 964-3410.

KINGSTON PARK // ½　The second tallest sled hill in the village is the highlight of this seven-acre park. Dogs can run up the hill, then back down and across the baseball field. Of course, it's best if baseball games aren't going on at the time. It's also a good place to run around in a circle. If no one is on the tennis or basketball courts, you and your dog have free rein. A concrete path encircles a small pond. Dogs aren't allowed to take shortcuts through the water. There's also a play lot.

Open dawn to dusk. Kingston Park is on Kingston Avenue, south of Maple Avenue. (630) 964-3410.

OLD TAVERN PARK // ½　Mostly flat grassland for 23 acres, this park provides room to run amok. There are also some nice wooded areas to play in. Just don't run into the geese who may be crossing the path. They are oblivious to runners and even barking dogs. Over the winter, some people ice skate on the retention pond, but the Park District highly discourages it. The ice is sometimes thin and can be dangerous.

Open dawn to dusk. Old Tavern Park is on Old Tavern Road, north of Ogden Avenue. (630) 964-3410.

TATE WOODS SOUTH PARK / ½　A sidewalk crosses an open space and then continues alongside a small wooded area. The park is seven acres, and there are tennis and basketball courts, a baseball field, and a play lot.

Open dawn to dusk. Tate Woods South Park is on Yackley Avenue, split by I-88. People and dogs can safely cross the tollway through the wide underpass. (630) 964-3410.

Place to Stay

Radisson Hotel Lisle-Naperville　Dogs who weigh in at 50 pounds or less pass the entrance test. I am told there's *at least* a $25 deposit, but it varies depending on who happens to be behind the front desk at check-in, and on how friendly your dog looks. So, make sure Spike ditches the spiked collar before entering, it may increase your deposit. I am warned that in the past, dogs have been kicked out for excessive barking. If your dog likes to speak, this may not be the hostelry for you. Rates are $79 to $189. 3000 Warrenville Road; (630) 505-1000.

Lombard

Parks

The lovely Lombard parks are exceedingly dog friendly, although dogs are supposed to be on a leash, and owners must pick up. Also, dogs are discouraged from
entering play lots. Lombard parks are open from 6 A.M. to 10 P.M. unless otherwise noted. For further information call (630) 953-6000.

FOUR SEASONS PARK /// Soccer is a big deal out this way. A new soccer complex features six fields. Of course, dogs aren't allowed on the fields when games
are in progress. But when there's no soccer activity, there's plenty of green
space for fetching or pawing at a soccer ball, particularly in the winter.

Dogs are discouraged from swimming in the pond. For one thing, they'd
have to compete with Canada geese for the space. Boating is allowed, but you
have to bring your own. Fishing is also permitted. There's no beach at the
pond, but for those who want the next best thing, there's a beach volleyball
court.

The view of the pond is especially beautiful looking down from the sledding area in winter. Your dog is allowed to sit in your lap as you zoom through
the snow. In other seasons, running back and forth on the hill can exhaust the
dog, the kids, and you.

Open 6 A.M. to 10 P.M. The parking entrances are at Finley Road at 16th
Street and at Main and 16th Streets, south of Roosevelt Road (Illinois Route
38) and west of Highland Avenue. (630) 953-6000.

LOMBARD COMMON // ½ Its rolling hills, weeping willows swaying in the
breeze, and blossoming trees are gorgeous. Locals call a specific configuration
of trees near the center of the park "The Cathedral" because that's what it
looks like when the light hits just right.

Of course, the dogs don't give a bark about that. They're more interested
in joining you for a down-to-earth run on the jogging path.

The picnic shelter is always busy on summer weekends. On the day Robin
and I visited, the Windy City K-9 Disc Club was holding its annual party. Dogs
were flying in the air to snatch Frisbees. And I was honored by national Hall
of Fame member and club president Tom Wehrli with the Pawlitzer Prize for
my contribution to the sport. For a canine journalist, it's the same as a
Pulitzer—well, not really. But you take what you can get.

Wehrli and one of his dogs, three-time Alpo Canine Frisbee World Final-
ist Delta (now retired), stood by a tree as they presented the plaque to me and
Lucy.

The Big Itch

As recently as five years ago, pets routinely wore toxic collars and were dipped with chemicals strong enough to wipe out a city block. Nevertheless, the fleas persisted.

"That's all changed. Today there's no excuse for a flea infestation," says Chicago-based veterinarian Dr. Shelly Rubin. The best of today's products are much more effective and are not toxic to mammals.

Fleas are more than a mere nuisance. They carry tapeworms, and as many as half of all dogs have an allergy to flea bites; some scratch themselves raw. And dogs aren't the only victims. Fleas won't use people as hosts to continue their life cycles, but they won't hesitate to bite human flesh.

Once an infestation has occurred, you'll have to either spend money to treat the environment or move out. A variety of options can help you avoid this fate, but choosing the right course requires expertise.

Rubin says, "Even the most effective and safest flea products work differently from one another. Some may or may not be best suited for your individual needs. Consult your veterinarian before making your final choice." These products are available only through veterinarians:

PROGRAM: This monthly pill does not keep fleas from hopping onto your pup or stop them from taking a nibble. Instead, it works as a sort of birth control, halting their formidable reproductive cycle. Since it won't deter bites, this product is not suggested for pets with flea allergies. PROGRAM may best be used in conjunction with Advantage, Frontline, or with an over-the-counter topical product. (Used with Advantage, PROGRAM is extremely effective, but it's an expensive one-two punch.) Over-the-counter topical products with pyrethrins as the active ingredient are safe and effective enough for most household situations (to use in conjunction with PROGRAM).

Advantage: The primary advantage of Advantage is that it prevents adult fleas from hitting on your dog. It also kills nearby larvae. This topical product is applied monthly between the shoulder blades of your pet. Rubin has never had a complaint about Advantage not working, and it's somewhat waterproof.

Frontline Spray: This spray product can be applied about once a month. This is the most waterproof of the topical products, and Rubin recommends it for dogs who swim regularly. The main drawback is lack of convenience. The instructions say to spray one pump per pound. On a miniature schnauzer, that's not a big deal. But how about pumping a 50- or 75-pound dog?

Frontline Top Spot: A spot-on product (applied onto the pet itself, between the shoulder blades) that works for both fleas and ticks. Rubin recommends Top Spot for his woodsy clients, and it's easier to apply than Frontline's spray.

Revolution: It seems this product does it all, killing fleas, preventing heartworms, zapping ear mites and ticks, destroying roundworm and hookworm in cats, and fighting off the *Sarcoptes scabie* mite that causes sarcoptic mange in dogs.

Revolution is applied monthly from a squeeze tube between the shoulder blades. Studies show it's effective even if you bathe your pet two hours after applying.

Veterinary parasitologist Dr. Michael Dryden, an associate professor at Kansas State University College of Veterinary Medicine–Manhattan, explains Revolution's effectiveness on fleas is unquestionable. He recommends Revolution in conjunction with the Preventic collar at times when a pet's potential exposure to ticks is moderately high or greater.

Additional Flea Busters

Bombs and Foggers: Only if a house is totally infested and dramatic action is required, is this it. Try to be careful not to miss corners. Also, choose a product with an additional Insect Growth Regulator. And be sure to follow label instructions—this is heavy-duty stuff.

Dips: Use only when recommended by your vet, and absolutely follow the instructions. Dips are now nearly always unnecessary. Above all else, obey this rule: More is not better. Chicago vet Dr. Donna Solomon reports that a client gave two extra baths to a puppy—both within an hour—just to make sure the fleas were gone. By that evening, the puppy was dead. Also, do not use a dip meant for dogs on the family cat.

Flea Collars: Rubin says that flea collars tend to work better on small dogs than larger dogs and that their effectiveness varies from product to product. On large dogs, the rump is barely affected by the collar. So, what's the point?

continued

Also, a collar attached too tightly may create neck irritation. Keep in mind that it's potentially dangerous to touch some flea collars (particularly right out of the package) and then stick your fingers in your mouth. It's a real concern if toddlers are around.

Ultrasonic Flea Collars: Rubin has two words, "Forget it!"

Garlic: You may keep away vampires, and your friends may no longer want to kiss your pooch, but it probably won't discourage the fleas from hopping on board.

Dr. Michael Dryden, associate professor of veterinary parisitology at Kansas State University College of Veterinary Medicine, says, "There's no scientific documentation to prove garlic is effective. At best it seems to be hit-and-miss. Ultimately, when fighting fleas, deterring only a small percent is of little help."

Boric Acid: Rubin says, "Applied in the right places around the house, it certainly may play a role at preventing reproduction of fleas in the environment, but it won't keep fleas off pets. Also, there's a concern when children are in the home."

Here are 10 very scary flea facts:

- I'm not sure who did the measuring to figure this out, but the typical flea sucks more blood daily than the typical vampire bat.

- The typical flea consumes 150 times its body weight in blood daily.

- Fleas are pound-per-pound among the most powerful jumpers on earth; a measly flea can leap one foot.

- The three states most infested with fleas are Arkansas, Alabama, and Florida. The state with the fewest fleas is Alaska. Illinois is number 39 on the list; fleas are more prevalent in neighboring Indiana, number 22; and Wisconsin, number 35.

- In the Chicago area, August and September are the peak flea months. Fleas especially like wet and humid conditions.

- The cat flea (*Ctenocephalides felis*) is the flea species that plagues most dogs. Go figure. A close relative, the rat flea, which carries the bubonic plague, is responsible for killing more people on earth than all the wars ever fought.

- The cat flea also infests raccoon and opossums and other small wild critters. It's very possible for cat flea larvae to leave a wild animal, land in your grass, and find a new home on your pet.

- There are 64 trillion (cat) fleas in America.

- Americans spend $1.5 million daily on flea control.

- Fleas don't believe in birth control. Every single flea you see on your pet or in your home may represent two thousand offspring. They lay 50 eggs a day.

Jessica Ritchie, a 10-year-old canine disc prodigy from Lombard who placed seventh at the District competition in Lincoln Park, is a natural at teaching dogs how to catch Frisbees. She just has a way with dogs. She spent 15 minutes with Lucy and finally shrugged. She offered, "You know, not all dogs are great at this." Still, Lucy had a wonderful time meeting some of the finest disc dogs in the Midwest. And while her Frisbee-catching skills aren't the best, she can out-obedience nearly any dog at the park. So, she still held her head high.

Usually, each April or May at Lombard Common, on a designated Saturday morning, the K-9 Disc Club holds free canine Frisbee lessons for newcomers, or for those who want to sharpen their skills. For specific information call (630) 355-2777 or (630) 357-9663.

The park also features a nine-hole Frisbee golf course and lots of open places to practice Frisbee catching with a pooch.

Open 6 A.M. to 10 P.M. Lombard Common is at St. Charles Road and Grace Street. (630) 953-6000.

LOMBARD LAGOON // ½   The setting is inspiring; weeping willow trees overhang the lagoon, Canada geese fly off into the sunset, and joggers run around with their dogs. The lagoon is about half the size of this 11-acre park. Dogs do bound into the water, and no one seems to mind. Benches are positioned along the perimeter of the pond so you can sit and keep tabs on all the activity.

Open 6 A.M. to 10 P.M. Lombard Lagoon is at Marcus Street and Grace Street. (630) 953-6000.

MADISON MEADOW //   Athletic dogs who want to whip their owners into shape should check this place out. There are six baseball and three football fields—that adds up to a lot of running room. However, dogs aren't allowed in the infield. There are also basketball and tennis courts, as well as additional green spaces, but the highlight is the 18-hole Frisbee golf course.

After the workout, dogs might jump into the pond to cool off. This isn't a pond their owners will want to follow the pups into. Geese share the water.

Dogs must adhere to the signs that read "Keep Out of the Garden Plots," which are found on the northwest side of the park. The flat, unsheltered meadow gets particularly hot unless you seek out the trees at the edges of the 89-acre facility.

Open 6 A.M. to 10 P.M. The main entrances are at Madison and Ahrens Avenues, and at Wilson Avenue just east of Fairfield Avenue. The park is west of Westmore Avenue and north of Roosevelt Road (Illinois Route 38). (630) 953-6000.

OLD GROVE WOODS / This is perfect for an old dog who just wants to sniff for a bit and return home. For a dog yearning for more, there isn't much here. Nearly half of this nine-acre park is given over to a single ball field and picnic grounds. The remainder is a natural wetland area that is impossible for people or dogs to navigate. However, the Canada geese call this place home, as do various kinds of songbirds. It's too bad there are no nearby benches for watching nature or pathways leading to the wetlands.

Open 6 A.M. to 10 P.M. Old Grove Woods is bounded by Michelle Lane and Lewis, Morris, and Fairview Avenues. (630) 953-6000.

SUNSET KNOLL PARK // No one knows exactly why the sunset looks so good from this park, but it does. The best views are from on top of the sledding hill and on the east side of the park (facing west, of course). Just running up and down the hill with Fido is great fun. It's more fun when there's snow and you're racing the dog on a sled.

Lots of trees are scattered around the park, and folks come here to experience the colors in the fall. The trees notwithstanding, there's enough green space among these 37 acres for canine runs.

Open 6 A.M. to 10 P.M. Sunset Knoll Park is at Finley Road and Wilson Avenue. (630) 953-6000.

TERRACE VIEW // ½ This park is 48 acres, about half of which is in the form of a pond. Boating is allowed if you bring your own. Dogs can cool off in the water on hot days. An asphalt handicapped-accessible walkway surrounds the water and is a natural choice for walking or jogging with a pooch. Terrace View is larger than Lombard Lagoon Park but not as pretty. There are also picnic areas.

Open sunrise to sunset. Located at Greenfield Avenue and Elizabeth Street, west of Main Street and south of North Avenue. (630) 953-6000.

WESTMORE WOODS /   The northern portion of this narrow 21-acre stretch consists of unspoiled woods, a small meadow, and a pond. There is a small path, so dogs won't have any trouble in trekking along. Otherwise, toy pups can get lost in the sea of tallgrasses.

The only place dogs can visit on the south side of this park is a softball field. It's pretty, but for dogs, there's not much sport.

Open sunrise to sunset. Westmore Woods is on Maple Street at Highland Avenue. (630) 953-6000.

Place to Stay

Residence Inn by Marriott   Dogs are welcome as long as their companions cough up a $100 nonrefundable cleaning fee—that's more than what people have to pay for most rooms here. And there's more: There's also a $6-per-day-per-dog fee. If this isn't enough, humans must sign the "Pet Policy," accepting full responsibility for any damage pets may cause. On the positive front, you can walk your dog in the designated area outside, and you will receive a dog bowl and some biscuits at check-in—but for those prices you may consider buying your own biscuits instead. Rates are $89 to $139. 2001 S. Highland Avenue; (630) 629-7800 or (800) 331-3131.

Naperville

Parks

A champion community to dogs, but pooches must be on-leash, and owners must pick up. Most parks are open sunrise to sunset. Call (630) 357-9000.

ARROWHEAD PARK / ½   The 24 acres of wide-open space are sometimes used for soccer or football but are much better for playing fetch or chase the pooch. When there's snow, dogs join kids on sleds, flying down the hill at warp speed. There's also a children's play area.

Open sunrise to sunset. Arrowhead Park is off Iroquois Avenue near Columbia Street and east of Washington Street. (630) 357-9000.

BURLINGTON PARK // ½   With 51 acres and lots of wide trails, this is a hiker's heaven. Plenty of sun manages to hit the trails—this is good if you're hiking in March and not so good in July. Trails aren't marked, so be sure to toss bread crumbs. Aside from hiking, there's nothing else to do.

Open sunrise to sunset. Parking is difficult to find, and so is the park itself. Even a bloodhound might fail to sniff out Parkway Drive off Douglas Avenue, which is eight blocks west of Washington Street. (630) 357-9000.

DuPage River Park /// This beautiful three-hundred-acre park is split vertically by the DuPage River and horizontally by Washington Street (Joliet-Naperville Road). To the west of Washington Street are tennis courts and soccer fields, where there are always folks tossing Frisbees to pups. A beaten path weaves through a forested area where the fall colors are spectacular. Be on the lookout for deer, raccoon, and the many species of bird life that call this park home. The Naperville Park District occasionally offers guided walks through the preserve, and dogs (on-leash) are welcome. Call for scheduling information.

To the east of Washington Street is a picnic pavilion and more open space for running a stir-crazy dog.

DuPage River Park's southwestern border is adjacent to Knoch Knolls Park.

Open sunrise to sunset. Parking is located east of the DuPage River. DuPage River Park is bounded by Royce Road to the north and Boughton Road is about a mile south of the park. Take Washington Street (Joliet-Naperville Road) directly into the preserve. (630) 357-9000.

Gartner Park / ½ A fence beyond the ball fields prevents speedy dogs from running into busy 75th Street. A children's play area and basketball courts are the chief amenities. A series of pine trees helps to border the park's south and west sides. Dogs' noses are sure to be tickled by the scent.

Open sunrise to sunset. Gartner Park is at Gartner Road, Alder Lane, and 75th Street. (630) 357-9000.

Goodridge Park / ½ A densely wooded 14 acres. The wood-chip trails are fun to tackle if you're in good physical shape. A footbridge spans the stream, but it's usually not necessary, as the bed is often dry. This is an ideal place to witness fall colors.

Open sunrise to sunset. Goodridge Park is off Hobson Street, east of Oxford Lane. (630) 357-9000.

Heritage Woods / ½ This petite, heavily wooded area is located just south of an apartment complex. It offers a cinematic view of the DuPage River, which dogs can only admire from a distance. This 17-acre parcel is a smaller and quieter version of Burlington Park and is mostly utilized by nearby residents. The only available parking is on side streets.

Open sunrise to sunset. This park is located off 5th Avenue, south of Ogden Avenue and west of Royal St. George Drive. (630) 357-9000.

KENDALL PARK / ½   Local dogs love this small park. There's a ball field and a play lot. The west side is bordered with mature trees, sort of a living fence. Open sunrise to sunset. Kendall Park is bounded by Washington and Main Streets and 5th Avenue. (630) 357-9000.

KNOCH KNOLLS PARK // ½   Located just west of DuPage River Park, here are 183 additional acres. To the north of the river, there's a soccer field and bathroom facilities.

A picturesque footbridge crosses the river. The majority of the park lies to the south, and its forested area can be hiked on various paths. It's a beautiful place, home to a wide variety of flora and fauna. You can learn names of plants and meet unusual insects on Park District interpretive tours.

Dogs are welcome to join in on those walks. Call the Park District at (630) 357-9000 for dates.

While there's no formal place for picnics, families—dogs included—camp out on the grass.

Open sunrise to sunset. The park is off Knoch Knolls Road, west of Washington Street and west of DuPage River Park.

KNOCH PARK // ½   It's dismaying that the one fenced-in ball field has a No Dogs Allowed sign. But dogs are allowed on the other baseball diamonds, which are larger anyhow.

While I was playing fetch with Chaser, at one point she came bounding back from the outfield grass as if sliding into home plate. (I had liver treats.) Robin played umpire and called, "You're out." With that, a full squadron of geese landed, and Chaser sped back to third base. Honking with disgust, the geese were out of there. Only moments later, a golden retriever named Trooper appeared from nowhere, and now Chaser was playing a game of chase. This little park should win an award for exhausting Chaser faster than any other place we visited.

Open sunrise to sunset. Knoch Park is bounded by West and Washington Streets, Martin Avenue, and Brom Court. (630) 357-9000.

PIONEER PARK // ½   You can float on the DuPage River through the center of this 39-acre park—if you happen to have a canoe. Or you can walk the wood-chip trails and cross the river on a romantic wooden bridge. Some high school kids come to this bridge to do what high school kids do on dates. The Park District discourages too much making out. They also discourage dogs from jumping into the river.

The trails through Pioneer Park can be arduous, the insects are abundant, and the canopy can be dense. Perhaps that's why so many scout groups earn their badges here.

Open sunrise to sunset. Pioneer Park is bounded by Washington Street and Gartner Road and is north of Hobson Street. (630) 357-9000.

RIVER WALK PARK // ½   The brick walkway that roams along the banks of the west branch of the DuPage River is so romantic.

This picturesque park is relatively quiet, despite the location near downtown Naperville. Lots of young lovers stroll and picnic here. Robin and I walked hand in hand with Lucy and Chaser between us. My parents think something is wrong with this picture. However, the dog-bag dispensers on the River Walk make it very convenient to travel with dogs.

There are three trails. The Green Trail is 1.6 miles, and the Red Trail and Brown Trail are both 0.6 mile. None of them is difficult. Seniors are often seen walking the trails. Joggers who don't seek a challenge like to run here, too, often with a dog. However, bicycles aren't allowed.

At the south side of the river, a small lake lures visitors with paddleboat rentals and fishing. Small dogs are allowed in the boats. Boat rentals are available from May through September. Dogs are not allowed to swim in the lake.

Keep sound-sensitive dogs at home on Sunday mornings when the nearby gun club takes target practice.

On the west end of the River Walk (signage tells you where that is), the hours are sunrise to 10 P.M. For the east end of the River Walk and the remainder of the Naperville Park Districts, parks are open from sunrise to sunset. You can park at Chicago Avenue at Main Street, south of Highway 34 (Ogden Avenue), or at Mill Street at Jackson Avenue. (630) 357-9000.

SPRINGBROOK PRAIRIE DOG EXERCISE AREA /// (OFF-LEASH)   I'll always remember this place, and so will little Lucy. This is where, when she was about 15 months old, her herding instinct kicked in.

Near the parking lot, where we pulled up, is an area of mowed grass where maybe a half dozen dogs were romping off-leash. From there, we continued down one of several narrow paths and met up with a couple and their two Labrador retrievers. The Labs ran off into the high grass. Chaser did the same but would frequently return, while Lucy stayed on the trail with us.

This trail was too narrow to walk side by side, so the woman, her friend, Robin, and I walked single file in that order. We chitchatted about the park, particularly about the swampy area—sort of a pond—that was the couple's destination.

After about 10 minutes of this, Lucy began to whine. Running up to the head of the line, she'd look at the woman and bark as if to say, "Wait!" Then she'd run past the woman's friend, past Robin, and bark at me as if to say, "Let's move it!" She hated the fact that we weren't together. Lucy continued dashing back and forth in a futile attempt to keep us all amassed. At the point where the trail split, Lucy went ballistic when the other couple began walking down one path and we headed down another. We all stopped and laughed.

Just then, off in the distance in the middle of this prairie we see a four-wheel-drive vehicle. Turns out that it's an official police vehicle of the Forest Preserve District of DuPage County with a ranger inside.

He says, "Good afternoon, and why aren't these dogs on a leash?"

We explained that we were in an off-leash area.

He said, "Oh, no, you passed that about 20 yards back near those bushes."

He didn't ticket us, but he claimed he often does ticket people for going beyond the off-leash area—something the other couple said they and their dogs do all the time in order to get to the pond. They had no idea they were breaking the rules. How could anyone possibly know "those bushes" mark the boundary? While it's true that signage imposes on the natural beauty, it seemed to us that the Park District should have posted some warning, such as "You are now exiting the dog exercise area," or expand the area to a more obvious border.

Lucy is finally quiet as the other couple head toward the pond despite the officer's warning. Meanwhile, we walk back toward the actual dog training area. Once there, we're greeted by a barking Scottish terrier. The owner grabs the dog up in his arms and says, "I don't trust him around other dogs."

We ask, "Why are you here in an off-leash area where you know other dogs will approach?"

He didn't reply, although his dog continued yapping as we walked off. We took another trail back, and both Lucy and Chaser got thistles stuck in their coats. We got thistles stuck on our pants. Luckily, both Robin and I wore long pants, highly recommended in the forest preserves.

Arriving at another mowed area, we played dodge the poop. It's unfortunate that people shirk their responsibility.

Instead of chancing wandering beyond the boundary of the exercise area a second time, we stayed close by and found a spot where few dogs had left their marks. Within two minutes, four dogs appeared: two mixed breeds, a Dalmatian, and an English springer spaniel. Now, this is what dog play areas were made for. Chaser was actually taking chase. And whenever the entire contingent of canines would run in one direction, Lucy would run in the other. Apparently, she wanted to play her way.

On the way back to the car, we met a beagle named Scooter. Scooter didn't notice me, Robin, or our dogs. His owner told us Scooter had been in the park for about an hour and didn't lift his nose from the ground once. For a beagle, this park must be an orgy of odors.

Since our excursion, the DuPage Forest Preserve has announced plans to relocate the off-leash area to the southwest section of the preserve. It will be fenced in, with double gates for safety, which will prevent people and their dogs from wandering out of bounds. The site will also have access to the water, so dogs can keep cool in the hot weather. The move will be a blessing for ground-nesting birds, who are often invaded by off-leash dogs trampling through their homes.

Open from one hour after sunrise to one hour after sunset. Springbrook Prairie is one-half mile south of 75th Street on the east side of Naperville-Plainfield Road. (630) 933-7248.

WEST GREEN'S PARK / ½   The sled hill is small unless you happen to be a Chihuahua. There's also a play lot and a small forested area.

Open sunrise to sunset. West Green's Park is on Laird Street just south of Benton Avenue. (630) 357-9000.

Restaurants

El Centro   Famous for the giant burritos. Taking Fido will save you the trouble of carrying home a doggie bag. 1015 E. Ogden Avenue; (630) 355-8888.

Front Street Cantina   Known by locals as salsa heaven. Best of all, more than 70 kinds of beer are offered. Dogs sit beside small round tables; there isn't much room for extra-large canines. 15 W. Jefferson Avenue; (630) 369-5218.

Quick Bites

The Chocolate Key   Round tables perch on a narrow sidewalk. Don't be tempted to feed your canine partner the available array of chocolates; chocolate is toxic to dogs. 217 Washington Street; (630) 357-1360.

Cookie Dough Creations Envision eight flavors of cookie dough, including cho-colate chip, M&Ms, and peanut butter. They also serve traditional ice creams and phizzers (natural fruit-flavored syrups with sparkling water and ice cream). 22 W. Chicago Avenue; (630) 369-4833.

Einstein Bros. Bagels Tables are on both Chicago and Jackson Avenues. There's more action on busy Chicago than on the quieter and less-traveled Jackson. 22 Jackson Avenue; (630) 416-9888.

Nicky's Red Hots The manager says, "Our hot dogs are great." When asked why they're so good, he admitted, "I don't personally know; I don't like hot dogs." In any case, four-legged dogs are allowed to sit outdoors where a few tables are set up. 335 E. Ogden Avenue; (630) 527-1200.

Coffee Shop

Starbucks There are five tables, but finding a seat may be iffy at this jumping java stop. 42 W. Jefferson Avenue; (630) 778-8614.

Shopping

Someplace Else They call themselves a gift shop for kids from 1 to 101. It's a nifty place to shop with a pooch for "Sparky," "Weenie," "Bernie," and "Ringo," all popular canine Beanie Babies. In addition to collectible beanbag critters, you'll encounter lava lamps, T-shirts, and balloons. 19–21 W. Jefferson Avenue; (630) 357-4144.

Places to Stay

Exel Inn of Naperville Dogs under 25 pounds are allowed to stay in smoking rooms only. The rates are $49.99 to $69. 1585 Naperville-Wheaton Road; (630) 357-0022.

Red Roof Inn There is no additional charge when your canine checks in for the night. Call ahead to get confirmation in writing; there is conflicting informa-tion on what the weight limits may or may not be. Rates are $66 to $78. 1698 W. Diehl Road; (630) 369-2500.

Oak Brook

Park

MAYSLAKE DOG EXERCISE AREA /// ½   Opened in June of 2000, this is the newest off-leash dog area in the DuPage Forest Preserve. At press time, it was the only dog exercise area in the Forest Preserve District that is completely fenced in, has double safety gates, and features four acres of mowed grass. It is designated as an "exercise area" rather than a "training area," which means that blank ammunition and propulsion devices are not permitted. This is a good thing. The new facility is intended as a place where dogs can run and play, not as an official training location.

Janice and Luna visited on a hot summer day. A group of trees in the center shields two picnic tables, allowing canines and humans to cool off in the shade. Janice met up with a woman who was directly involved in helping to attain this facility. In 1998 the DuPage Forest Preserve District conducted a survey to assess support of a canine recreation area. The survey respondents expressed a strong desire for additional off-leash facilities, especially in Oak Brook. The woman told Janice, "After two years, a few petitions, and a lot of meetings, Mayslake is open for the dogs." Having fenced-in, mowed grass was a priority for the community; it helps people see where their dogs have gone to the bathroom and also makes it safer for the dogs. This site is too close to a major expressway for it not to be fully enclosed.

Neighborhood dog owners go the extra mile to make this an upbeat place for people and their dogs. The first Saturday of every month, animals gather with doughnuts, cupcakes, coffee, and juice and sing "Happy Birthday" to all the dogs celebrating a birthday that month. Not only is this a hoot for the dogs, but it's a golden opportunity for community dog owners to come together.

The area is big and allows dogs to run and play together easily. Luna had to elude two Welsh corgis, Amber and Brooke, who had designs on her pink floppy Frisbee. She also wrestled with Mary, a three-month-old golden Lab–mix, finally settling on sharing a big stick under the picnic table. When it was time to quench their thirst, Luna watched in consternation as little Mary chewed on the water bottle, then the plastic dish, instead of actually drinking the water! Puppies will be puppies.

Currently a few areas are blocked off with snow fencing to keep the dogs out. Bogs were discovered, and when it rains, they flood. They've been filled in, and new grass was installed and must grow in before the dogs are once again allowed to romp there. A circular gravel path within the fenced-in area is a good place to practice your heeling technique. There are plans to redo the layout, including the addition of scattered shade trees.

Once you leave the double gates, the parking lot is about a 30-second walk. Janice was cautioned twice to put Luna back on her leash before exiting. Apparently, rangers arise out of the "wood work" to write citations for dogs who may not be restrained for this minuscule walk. I suppose it's a way to raise revenue and the forest rangers have nothing better to do. After the outing to this dog exercise area, Janice was happy, driving home with a tired dog.

Mayslake is at the southwest corner of Route 83 and 31st Street. The entrance and parking lot for the dog area are off St. Paschal's Drive east of the mansion; (630) 933-7248.

Oakbrook Terrace

Parks

The municipal parks in this enlightened community allow unleashed dogs under voice control. The result is a haven for dog lovers, even though the parks are limited in size and number. Folks drive many miles from other communities to get here, leaving their own local parks and their restrictive dog laws in the dust. As Lee Murphy, director of marketing for the Oakbrook Terrace Park District, told me, "The Oakbrook Terrace Park District always welcomes responsible dog owners." As is the law in nearly every community, owners here must pick up. The difference is that in Oakbrook Terrace, they really do. The Park District facilities are open from sunrise to sunset; call (630) 627-6100 for further information. York Woods, part of the Forest Preserve of DuPage County, is also in Oakbrook Terrace; dogs are allowed only on a leash here.

DOROTHY DRENNON PARK // (OFF-LEASH)   Named for a former schoolteacher in the area, this six-acre park offers a small grassy plot for playing canine catch. It also has picnic facilities, a sand volleyball court, and a play lot. There are several garden areas where dogs aren't allowed. This is the smallest of the Oakbrook Terrace parks.

Open sunrise to sunset. Dorothy Drennon Park is at Nimitz and Eisenhower Roads. (630) 627-6100.

HERITAGE CENTER PARK // ½ (OFF-LEASH)   The vast majority of Heritage Center is flat and open, and most of the perimeter is bordered by trees and landscaping. This is where Lee Murphy, formerly of the Park District, trains Moses,

Common Hazards

When it comes to temperature extremes, Chicago's got 'em. It can get hotter than a summer day in Florida, and as anyone who has survived a Chicago January knows, it can get cold, real cold, with windchill factors below those typical of Alaska.

While the whole point of this book is to encourage people to take their dogs outdoors, it is our wish that people do so safely. In addition to overheating and frostbite, seasonal hazards include fishing gear—it's surprisingly common for dogs to get fish hooks caught on their lips—and street salt, which can make dogs dance in pain.

Veterinary toxicologists Dr. Ernie Poortinga and Dr. William B. Buck from the ASPCA National Animal Poison Control Center at the University of Illinois College of Veterinary Medicine, Dr. Lawrence Fox, and Dr. Shelly Rubin, both past presidents of the Chicago Veterinary Medical Association, offer the following advice on prevention and treatment of common hazards.

Summer Hazards

Fish Hooks: Attracted to the aromatic odor of fish or curious about wiggly worms, pooches often get hooked. If it's a single hook (as opposed to multibarbed hooks), you may be able to push it through the skin, cut off the barb with a wire cutter, and then pull it back out again. Before you attempt this, be sure to muzzle the dog, which may bite because of the pain. (See the "Emergency Care" sidebar for tips on makeshift muzzles.)

If the hook is multibarbed, or if it's stuck on the upper palate or tongue, it is much kinder to your pooch to let a vet anesthetize the area before removing the hook.

Tar: Tar is toxic and, if left on the skin, can damage red blood cells. Condo dogs wandering on roof decks can get this sticky stuff on their paws. Use a gentle dish washing detergent (Poortinga recommends Dawn) and clip hair where possible. Another option is Goo Gone, or De-Solv-it, citrus-based liquids that are safe for pets and readily available at hardware stores. In only the worst cases, paint thinner can be used to remove the tar. However, paint thinner is also toxic and potentially more damaging than tar—that's the catch-22. Immediately rinse following use of paint thinner.

Heat Stroke: Dogs die needlessly every summer. Too frequently, people leave Fido in the car while they run errands. According to the AAA-Chicago Motor Club, on an 85-degree day, the dashboard of a car will reach a blazing 170 degrees after only 15 minutes, even with the window opened a crack. No wonder trapped dogs suffer heatstroke.

Physically fit canines will tolerate jogs in the early morning or evening. But Fox warns, "In 90-degree-plus weather, anyone crazy enough to go running at midday will need both a vet and a psychologist. It's very dangerous for even the hardiest dogs."

Dogs with pushed-in noses (brachycephalic breeds), such as bulldogs, pugs, boxers, shih tzus, and Pekingese, are particularly susceptible to overheating.

Overexertion is often the cause of heatstroke. Some dogs know enough to stop running around an off-leash area with no shade; others don't.

On one 90-degree day, Chaser and Lucy had been running for maybe 15 minutes. There was no shade, and no drinking fountain. In this case, 15 minutes was plenty. I offered the dogs water, which we've learned to always take along.

Meanwhile, their playmate, a Labrador who was on the scene before we arrived, continued playing. He kept right on with a game of fetch. The dog's tongue was hanging, and he was panting hard. The owner concluded that he must be OK; otherwise he wouldn't still be playing. Some dogs will run until they drop, which is apparently what this owner was waiting for. We did offer water, which the dog guzzled.

Dogs aren't as efficient at releasing heat as people are. Panting is normal for canines; that's how they release the majority of heat. However, if your pooch appears spacey or acts exhausted, or if its gums become dry, Fox recommends taking the pet indoors immediately, and taking its temperature. A normal reading for a dog is 100.5 to 102.5. If your pup's temperature is 105 or higher, immediately soak the animal in moderately cool water (don't use cold water). Naturally, offer cold water to drink. If the dog's demeanor returns to normal, and its temperature falls within normal range, just keep the dog calm for several hours. If the dog does not recover, call the vet.

If the dog's temperature is 107 or higher, its life may be in jeopardy. Call the vet now!

continued

Bee Stings: It's easy for a single sting to go unnoticed by the owner. But just as people can have allergic reactions, dogs can too. If the pup's face begins to swell, the animal's ability to breathe may be impaired. Call your vet. An antihistamine will usually alleviate the symptoms. Ask your vet to suggest the proper dosage. You should also apply ice to any swelling.

Rodenticide: Poortinga says that often deaths could be avoided if owners only knew the name of the rodenticide used. If a landlord or pest control company sets poison bait for rodents, be sure to ask what the name of the product is. Different products require different treatments.

Dogs can be attracted to the poison. The ensuing symptoms usually don't occur until about 72 hours after ingestion. And most of those symptoms, which include internal hemorrhaging and renal failure, aren't easily observed. By the time the owner realizes something is wrong, it may be too late.

Poortinga says that if you know for a fact that your dog has ingested rodent poison, call the vet. Inducing vomiting may also help. To do this, give hydrogen peroxide (use one teaspoon per five pounds of pet) with a turkey baster or spoon. Remember also that some dogs eat their vomit—so you may have to whisk the dog away.

Lawn Pesticides: Throughout the summer, the National Animal Poison Control Center receives an average of 120 calls per day about lawn pesticides. If Fido rolls around in a treated lawn that is still wet, don't use flea shampoo to bathe the dog. You'll only add to the toxicity. Instead, use a gentle dish washing detergent to wash it off. Again, Poortinga recommends Dawn. Don't worry about your pet munching on treated grass if vomiting is the sole symptom. However, if your pooch is acting lethargic and is unwilling to eat, do call your vet.

Keep in mind that slug pesticides are particularly appealing to pets and particularly dangerous.

By the way, eating grass (free of pesticides) isn't especially dangerous, except to your oriental rug on which Fido will no doubt choose to throw up. As for the technical veterinary explanation of why dogs eat grass, Fox says, "Because it tastes good. It's not because they realize they need to throw up. That's an old wives' tale."

However, Rubin comments, "Sometimes grazing on greens is a canine version of popping a Tums and may indicate stomach upset."

Pools: Pets die every year because they're unable to get out of the pool. Even Newfoundlands and Labradors can't swim forever, so make certain they understand how to exit the pool.

Winter Hazards

Antifreeze: To dogs, this green molasses tastes like honey, but it's as lethal as arsenic. It takes only a couple of tablespoons to do in a large dog. If you know that your dog has ingested antifreeze, call the vet immediately.

"I'm very saddened at the increasing number of reports of antifreeze poisonings because it's one of those things that can be prevented," says Buck.

Buck also recommends using "pet-friendly" antifreezes. They contain a less toxic chemical called propylene glycol. These kinder and gentler antifreezes are sold under several brand names, including Sierra, Prestone LowTox, and Sta-Clean. These products aren't nearly as hazardous and will at least make your own garage and driveway safe. They are available at automotive stores.

Frostbite: When the temperature sinks to its lowest, even the strongest of nordic breeds require an indoor respite. Just as wind plays a factor in how we feel, the same is true for dogs. Therefore, riding in the back of a pickup truck—which is dangerous anyhow—is of particular concern in very cold weather.

To determine what's appropriate, a lot depends on the size and breed of the dog. In general, smaller dogs have a rougher time keeping warm than the giant breeds, such as Great Pyrenees or Saint Bernards. (It's just the opposite in the summer—small dogs don't overheat as easily as the giant breeds.) Whippets and greyhounds, for example, can barely tolerate 20 degrees without a doggy jacket, let alone 20 degrees below zero. Also, dogs that are acclimated to the cold do much better than those that rarely spend time outdoors. A German shepherd dog who seldom gets out may get as cold as a little Yorkshire terrier. Activity level also plays a major role. A Siberian husky may shiver and shake if it's just sitting out in a snowstorm. However, if the husky is active, sliding down a hill or pulling a sleigh, it's much less likely to feel the chill.

Dogs with long ears are particularly susceptible to frostbite, and paws may also become frostbitten. The first indication is a lack of sensation. If the skin turns pink or the foot pads become cracked, take the dog inside immediately. Simply warm the exposed area with human touch. Don't administer heating pads or hot water bottles. If the skin turns purple and/or black, call a vet fast.

continued

Snow and Ice: Street salt can burn when it gets imbedded in paws. Dogs can also suffer upset stomach from licking imbedded salt. For dogs who often walk on salt and ice, little booties may help. Realistically, most dogs—and even more owners—can't stand the idea of canines in galoshes. At least wipe the salt from the dog's paws before you go back into the house. Keep a towel in the car and another inside the door of your house for just this purpose.

Hypothermia: With subdivision retention ponds strewn throughout suburbia, dogs are falling through the ice with increasing frequency. Rule number one: If the dog falls through thin ice, you can too. Be careful.

Fox says that a shivering dog with blue gums may be suffering from hypothermia. Towel-dry the dog and call the vet. If you can't reach the vet, give the dog a lukewarm bath set at room temperature. If the bathwater is too warm, the dog may go into shock.

Home Remedies

For Removing Skunk Stink: Mix these ingredients in a bucket:

1 quart hydrogen peroxide
¼ cup sodium bicarbonate
1 teaspoon liquid dish washing detergent
Step 1: Thoroughly rub and/or brush this on your stinking pooch.
Step 2: Fill the bathtub with three parts water to one part tomato juice. Dunk
   your dog into the tomato juice mixture.

A product called Skunk Off is also available at many stores. Follow directions on the label.

For Removing Bubble Gum: With scissors, carefully cut out what you can.

Create a blend of peanut butter and enough vegetable oil to make it pasty. Rub the paste on the affected area.

If your dog licks the area, that's OK. Licking may help remove the remainder of the gum, and the peanut butter tastes good.

If this fails, use Goo Gone or De-Solve-it, nontoxic citrus-based products available at hardware stores and some pet stores.

his black Labrador retriever. "Because the park has no obstructions, I can always see the dog," he says.

With only eight acres, the space is somewhat confining. That limitation aside, you get plenty of grass for playing fetch or for training black Labs, particularly when the baseball diamonds aren't in use. If you're working on your backhand, hop over to the tennis courts.

Like Terrace View Park, Heritage Center is a happening place for a dog to forge new canine friendships. Canines are always around, particularly on a designated Saturday morning in April when instructors from the Windy City K-9 Disc Club teach Frisbee catching to novice pups. The instructional seminar is free and open to the public; for more info call (630) 355-2777.

Open sunrise to sunset. Heritage Center Park is at 1325 Ardmore Avenue, two blocks south of Roosevelt Road (Illinois Route 38). (630) 627-6100.

TERRACE VIEW PARK /// ½ (OFF-LEASH)   It was as if Chaser had arrived at a concert. She barged into the grass amphitheater. This area is large enough to seat three thousand people who attend the park concerts. When not in use for music, it earns applause as a dog run. At one point, Chaser interrupted her sniffing to take care of some dog business. Two other owners in the vicinity stared daggers until Robin whipped the plastic bag out of her pocket. One of the owners, an area resident, said, "We take our freedom seriously. When people begin to leave messes, they may force us to leash our dogs—we don't want that! Besides, it's great not to worry about stepping in anything." Amen.

A six-month-old mixed-breed puppy named Jake and his owner, William B. Standon, had driven in from neighboring Villa Park, where dogs are not allowed off-leash. Standon said he made the trip because here he can teach Jake the art of retrieving in natural wetland space. Standon stood at the edge of the wetlands (there's no path through there) and tossed what he called "a dummy" into the swampy area. Jake held a sit/stay until he was released to locate the dummy and then retrieve it. Chaser joined in. She also remained on a perfect sit/stay, then followed Jake to the left, and then turned with Jake just as if she knew what she was doing. But when Jake snatched up the plastic dummy in his mouth, Chaser kept right on going until we called her back. Mr. Standon laughed and called our lovable Chaser "a dummy." I countered, "She doesn't retrieve mere plastic objects; she usually brings back frogs." Naturally, Chaser arrived back wet and frogless.

The deficiency of the sprawling open space is a lack of shade. Dogs and their people have to migrate to the north side of the park to find relief from the sun under a small grove of mature trees. Of course, dogs can jump into Terrace Park Lake to cool off. The park's half-mile bike/jogging path encircles the three-acre lake and connects to Dorothy Drennon Park, with a total distance of 1.4 miles.

At the park's nature center, kids play nature-oriented games and learn about fossils. But dogs aren't allowed inside. There's also an outdoor playground where well-behaved pooches are welcome.

Open sunrise to sunset. Terrace Park is at Park View Plaza, Route 83 (Kingery Highway) at 22nd Street. (630) 627-6100.

YORK WOODS // ½   This is the oldest preserve in DuPage County. It was established in 1917. It's a shady place, since the footpath takes hikers through the woods, and the picnic areas are sheltered. The north and south picnic areas are interconnected with a wheelchair-accessible asphalt trail. This clean and well-maintained 75-acre reserve is popular with nearby residents year-round, to cool off in the forest on sweltering summer days or for cross-country skiing in the winter.

Open from one hour after sunrise to one hour after sunset. The parking entrance is west of Harger Road, south of Illinois Route 38 (Roosevelt Road), and north of 22nd Street. There's another entrance off Frontage Road, west of York Road, and northwest of I-88 (East-West Tollway). (630) 933-7248.

Places to Stay

LaQuinta Motor Inn Restricted to dogs under 25 pounds. Rates are $89 to $96. 1 S. 666 Midwest Road; (630) 495-4600 or (800) 221-4731.

Oakbrook Terrace Hilton Suites Cultured dogs can relieve themselves on the wall of the adjacent Drury Lane Oakbrook Theatre. Rates are $105 to $135. 10 Drury Lane; (630) 941-0100.

Roselle

Parks

Provided that dogs are on a leash and their people pick up, there's no contention about canines sharing park space. Parks are open sunrise to sunset. Call (630) 894-4200.

CLAUS RECREATION AREA //   The one-mile asphalt trail is clean and well maintained. If jogging wears you out, rest assured: there are plenty of benches along the route. There are also picnic areas. However, geese have made a mess of the soccer field, as Carol and Breathless learned the hard way.

Open sunrise to sunset. 555 W. Bryn Mawr Avenue at West End Road. (630) 894-4200.

GOOSE LAKE PARK / ½ Guess what this 44-acre park is named for? And the feathered residents never hesitate to sound off about that. Mostly an area of prairie and wetlands, here dogs sometimes jump into the swampy parts or the lake. Be prepared to battle the mosquitoes.

Open sunrise to sunset. Goose Lake Park is on Bryn Mawr Avenue between Glenmore Place and Dorchester Court. (630) 894-4200.

KEMMERLING PARK / ½ This 10-acre park is connected to a sidewalk that leads to Roselle Middle School. Lots of parents take the pooch here to meet their children when school lets out. The heavily used park also features two tennis courts, a playground, and a baseball field. Dogs aren't allowed in the community swimming pool.

Open sunrise to sunset. This park is at 400 S. Prospect Street, at Bryn Mawr Avenue. (630) 894-4200.

PARKSIDE PARK / An asphalt trail tools through the small park, where you'll come across baseball fields and two tennis courts. Dog training classes are sometimes held at the multiuse recreation building.

Open sunrise to sunset. Parkside Park is at 304 E. Pine Avenue just east of Rush Street. (630) 894-4200.

TURNER PARK // A shimmering pond is the centerpiece of the park, which is surrounded by an asphalt trail. Dogs are discouraged from chasing the geese in the water, but they do anyway. On some occasions, nosy neighbors have been known to call the cops. Imagine the police having to respond to such an emergency: "There's a dog in the park pond." Horror of horrors! But the police take exposed transgressors to task and will issue a citation.

Fountains in the pond prevent the water from becoming stagnant and, ideally, deter some of the geese. There are also basketball and volleyball courts, and a play lot. The picnic area features an old-fashioned gazebo. After dark, the setting evokes the olden days, with illumination compliments of antique-style wooden lampposts that encircle the pond.

Open sunrise to sunset. Turner Park is at Devon and Granville Avenues and Roselle Road. (630) 894-4200.

Villa Park

Parks

Dogs are more or less tolerated, just as long as they're on a leash and their people pick up. Parks are open from 6 A.M. to 10 P.M. (630) 834-8525. More information is on the website at invillapark.com.

LIONS PARK / ½   This is a park for those with hoop dreams: it's jumping with basketball courts. Lions also has a baseball field and a handicapped-accessible play lot. The remainder of park space is forested with mature ash and locust trees. It's well lit, so it's very popular in the evening. Dogs are discouraged from skating on the ice rink. But then, we're told the issue doesn't come up all that often.

Open 6 A.M. to 10 P.M. Lions Park is at 320 E. Wildwood Avenue near Villa and St. Charles Roads. (630) 834-8525.

WILLOWBROOK PARK //   Dogs and their owners can perfect their pecs on the one-mile fitness trail with seven fitness stations. A drawback is that the grass trail offers little shade. However, the trees are bountiful elsewhere in this 15-acre park, so you can always go sit under one to cool off. There are also three picnic sites and a playground area. The park is adjacent to Willowbrook High School.

Open 6 A.M. to 10 P.M. Willowbrook Park is at Ardmore and Highridge Avenues. (630) 834-8525.

Place to Stay

Motel 6   Sorry, only one dog per room, and only dogs under 25 pounds are allowed. Dogs cannot be left in the room unattended. Rates are $49.99 to $59.99. 10 Roosevelt Road; (630) 941-9100.

Warrenville

Parks

BLACKWELL FOREST PRESERVE ////   Breathless and Pork Chop charged up Mount Hoy with their snouts burrowing through the grass. All they wanted was to dig into the dirt. Carol and Danny finally learned what it was the dogs had discovered about Mount Hoy, which is nicknamed "Mount Trashmore" by the locals. The 150-foot hill is an engineering feat: it's a landfill. The dogs honed in on an aromatic scent that neither Carol nor Danny could detect. And Pork Chop and Breathless weren't alone. Dogs are drawn to Mount Hoy as if it has a magnetic attraction.

Snow tubing is allowed on Mount Hoy when there's more than three inches of snow. For three bucks, you can rent a tube for an entire day. Dogs are discouraged from joining the action.

This 1,312-acre preserve also includes more than seven miles of multiuse trails and a maze of side trails. The Regional Trail is 10 feet wide and made of crushed limestone. You can access this trail to the west of the parking area near the main entrance. It's the only trail in the park where dogs and horses are fellow travelers. It continues past Mount Hoy to Springbrook Creek. Dogs should not swim in this creek—it's located near a sewage treatment plant (the water could be unclean). The trail heads north past Mack Road and a not-so-scenic physical plant and continues to the very scenic McKee Marsh. It is almost guaranteed you will see at least some bird life around the marsh and the cattails. If your timing is right, you'll note the squeaky call of the endangered yellow-headed blackbird.

At McKee Marsh, the Regional Trail meets the Bob-O-Link Trail at the northeast and the Catbird Trail at the northwest.

The rugged Catbird Trail is a nearly one-mile loop that winds right back to the Regional Trail after extending to the west branch of the DuPage River. The Bob-O-Link Trail is also a loop. It extends for 1.4 miles out to a prairie and back to the marsh.

Back near the main entrance is Silver Lake, a man-made but triumphant lake for anglers. Bluegills, largemouth bass, rainbow trout, and northern pike are among the fish to be lured from the 63-acre lake. There are three handicapped-accessible stationary piers.

One way to get close to the fish is to rent a rowboat or canoe, or bring your own. Rentals are $5 per hour or $25 for the day. You can also rent a boat with a trolling motor for $10 per hour or $50 for the day. Dogs are allowed in the boats.

There's a concession stand near the boat launch, so dogs can eat dogs, as in hot dogs.

Dogs are also welcome to pull sleds when the two miles of marked dogsledding trails are snow covered. This is DuPage County's version of the Iditarod (although there are no organized races).

Ice-skating is allowed in designated areas.

Open from one hour after sunrise to one hour after sunset. The main parking entrance is near Silver Lake and is north of Illinois Route 56 (Butterfield Road), west of Winfield Road and northeast of the west branch of the DuPage River. There's additional parking south of McKee Marsh at Mack Road, west of Williams Road and east of the west branch of the DuPage River. (630) 933-7248.

BLACKWELL FOREST PRESERVE DOG EXERCISE AREA /// (OFF-LEASH)   There's about an acre of both mowed grass and natural standing tallgrass. The problem with tallgrass is finding small dogs. If it weren't for little Lucy's yelping, she would have become lost in the sea of prairie grasses.

A mowed path through the tallgrass makes it tolerable for people to get close to their dogs. But the dogs don't care much for staying on this path. They bound together in the tallgrass . . . and on occasion, terrify a wandering squirrel. Don't think about allowing your pup off-leash if you can't maintain control. There's no fencing or landscaping to keep dogs from the nearby parking area. It's natural for dogs to greet one another, but a parking lot isn't an appropriate place to say "howdy."

Open from one hour after sunrise to one hour after sunset. Parking for the dog exercise area is south of Mack Road, east of Illinois Route 59, and west of Williams Road. (630) 933-7248.

Wayne

Parks

PRATT'S WAYNE WOODS FOREST PRESERVE ////   This is a beautiful, all-terrain 3,432-acre preserve. It's particularly noted for its lakes and wetland areas.

Most of the fishing is done off 6-acre Catfish Pond, 30-acre Pickerel Lake, or 2-acre Horsetail Pond. Fido can take five on the flagstone (a kind of limestone) fishing ledges. Among the species populating the water are sunfish, bluegill, and flathead catfish. Recently, one catfish was reported to be larger than 18-pound Lucy—a lot larger: the fish weighed 28 pounds.

Birds also live along the lakes and the marshy areas. The pied-billed grebe and great blue heron can be seen snacking on fish and frogs. The stately, four-foot-tall herons weren't even concerned about researcher Carol, her pal Danny, and their canine entourage.

Look up, and you may spot a red-tailed hawk. Don't worry; even little dogs are safe. The hawks' smaller relatives, American kestrels, also reside here, as do skunks, beavers, coyotes, white-tailed deer, and red foxes.

And there's certainly no shortage of Canada geese. To avoid the goose goo, stay on the trails near the marsh areas of Brewster Creek, Norton Creek, and Fern Meadows.

The south end of the preserve meets with the Illinois Prairie Path. According to some reports, the sandhill crane may breed here.

There's a model airplane field located south of the Illinois Central Railroad tracks and east of Powis Road.

Equestrians share many of the trails at Pratt's Wayne Woods, which was no imposition for Pork Chop and Breathless. But Snowball the Maltese was a bit of a klutz. She somehow managed to trample in horse poop.

You can picnic in seclusion. With 100 picnic tables, there's no shortage.

Open from one hour after sunrise to one hour after sunset. The main entrance is on the west side of Powis Road, north of Army Trail Road, south of Stearns Road, south of the Illinois Central Railroad tracks. (630) 933-7248.

PRATT'S WAYNE WOODS FOREST PRESERVE DOG EXERCISE AREA /// ½ (OFF-LEASH)

Researcher Carol nearly lost tiny Tibetan terrier Breathless in the three-foot tallgrass. Carol was worried, calling out "Breathless!" However, true to her name, Breathless was breathlessly bounding—and bonding—with other canine visitors. Their owners were also calling out, "Sandy!" "Sparky!" Finally, Carol found Breathless, as well as Sandy and Sparky.

There's some shorter grass here, too, but for whatever reason, Breathless stayed among the tallgrass. This was unfortunate for Carol, who wasn't quite able to navigate where she was stepping. It seems that regular park users rarely pick up here.

Finally, Breathless traipsed over to one of three areas of mowed grass and watched as several people tossed tennis balls to their dogs.

For dogs who prefer not to fraternize or don't have the temperament to do so, there is enough space here to find a secluded alcove. However, consider getting to that space on a leash. Breathless and Carol were terrorized by more than one bad-tempered pooch. "At one point, we felt surrounded by growling dogs, all off-leash," Carol recalls. "These dogs shouldn't be in an off-leash place; it's not safe."

There are no trees to offer shade. And there's no lake, pond, or drinking fountain. So, take your own water.

The west side of the exercise area borders the E. J. & E. railroad tracks, which are rarely used. Still, when playing around the tracks, listen for the train whistle. Also keep in mind that some paths are shared with equestrians. There's one report of two dogs nipping at the heels of a horse. Let's just say the horse didn't lose the battle. The owner attempted to call her dogs back, but they ignored her. If your dogs might chase horses, keep them away.

Open from one hour after sunrise to one hour after sunset. The main entrance is north of Army Trail Road, south of Stearns Road, and west of Powis Road. Follow the brown District sign marked "Special Use" to an area east of Powis Road. That access road will go under the railroad tracks; the parking is to your left. (630) 933-7248.

West Chicago

Parks

MCDOWELL GROVE FOREST PRESERVE // ½   If you happen to have a white dog, you'll definitely want to keep its paws away from Mud Lake. The lake is appropriately named. When researcher Carol visited, all-white Maltese Snowball ventured in. In five seconds, Snowball looked like "Mudball."

The fact that poor Snowball also tripped over horse manure didn't help the situation. But when a flock of geese bombed the defenseless dog from the sky, Carol knew it was time to go. Since few trails have markers, take along either your sense of direction, a compass, or a guide dog with a compass.

Carol and Snowball might have been wise to stick to the cleaner trails in the 426-acre preserve. Those are on the east side near the picnic areas. The main trails are mowed grass or gravel. Rugged side trails are also available, but given Snowball's condition, Carol took a pass.

This preserve isn't as heavily used as others in the District, allowing for lots of privacy. Privacy was the operative word of this place during World War II, when it was a top-secret Army base used to develop new radar technology.

Open from one hour after sunrise to one hour after sunset. The main parking entrance is east of Raymond Road at McDowell Avenue between Interstate 88 and Ogden Avenue, south of Diehl Road. (630) 933-7248.

WEST CHICAGO PRAIRIE FOREST PRESERVE //   Many native plants flourish among these 313 acres. For example, the rare white-fringed orchid grows here.

Lots of flowering plants and the marshes attract butterflies (and other insects) in force.

The trails themselves aren't especially noteworthy from Fido's point of view. With the exception of the West Loop Trail, none of the paths offers a way to return to the parking lot unless you double back on the same route. That's boring, since you've seen it all before, and Fido has smelled it all. The other trails lead to the Geneva Spur, part of the Illinois Prairie Path. What's more, the trails have become overgrown. Some of the bushes have thorns—wear long pants. Small dogs will have a tough time, and all dogs may pick up burrs.

Spaghetti-shape power lines and the noisy planes from nearby DuPage Airport take away from the natural beauty.

Open from one hour after sunrise to one hour after sunset. The main entrance is west of Illinois Route 59 on Industrial Drive, between Western Drive and Down Road. (630) 933-7248.

WEST DUPAGE WOODS FOREST PRESERVE /// Slightly larger than West Chicago Prairie, this 460-acre preserve is a much better choice because it's more tranquil, and the paths are easier to negotiate. The woods manage to muffle the whir of traffic on busy Illinois Route 59.

The woods also provide shade for people and dogs and shelter for white-tailed deer. In the fall, this is a great place to watch the colors change and to allow the dogs to romp on layers of leaf litter.

The 1.1-mile Circle Trail is perfect for a 30- to 40-minute hike. It's a very pleasant walk through the forest and over gently rolling hills. Elsen's Hill Circle Trail runs through the woods into a marshy area and then along the west branch of the DuPage River. The trail surfaces are varied, depending on where you happen to be. But they're in good shape for the most part; just watch out for the rough spots in a few places near the wetlands.

Open from one hour after sunrise to one hour after sunset. The parking area for Circle Trail is off Illinois Route 59, north of Illinois Route 38 (Roosevelt Road). The parking area for Elsen's Hill Circle Trail is just off Gary's Mill Road, north of Illinois Route 38 (Roosevelt Road). (630) 933-7248.

Wheaton

Parks

The Wheaton Park District has earned three Gold Medals for Excellence in Parks and Recreation Management from the National Recreation and Park

Association. No word on whether any dogs contributed to the voting. Wheaton police are sensible in their enforcement of the following rules: Dogs must be on a leash no longer than six feet, owners are required to pick up, and dogs are not allowed in picnic areas. Park District parks are open generally from sunrise to sunset. For more information call (630) 690-4880.

In addition, canines can horse around at the DuPage County Danada Forest Preserve or watch nature at the Herrick Lake Forest Preserve, both also located in Wheaton.

COMMUNITY PARK ✓ ½   Community Park is split into two sections. Hardier park-goers may prefer the undeveloped area with high grasses on the west side. There are no trails, so be careful: your next step may land you in a marsh. Dogs love that, especially on 90-degree days.

The east side of the park is developed, with tennis and basketball courts and a kids' play area—leaving very little for a pooch to do.

The entrance is on Thornhill Drive at Prospect Street, north of Geneva Road and south of St. Charles Road. (630) 690-4880.

DANADA FOREST PRESERVE ✓✓ ½   There aren't many other places where dogs can join the family for interpretive hayrides. A brief history of the area is described as horses head down the wooded trails. "It turns out dogs listen to the commentary better than the people," says staff assistant Sandy Slazyk. The hayrides are $3 for adults, $1 for children 5 to 12 years, and free for kids under 5 and all canine passengers. The only drawback is that families often share rides with others, and those strangers must approve of your dog. "We don't want to offend other passengers," says Slazyk, who adds that so far no pooch has been rejected.

Dogs are also invited to join in the sleigh rides. It's your job to draw up the guest list. Rides may be arranged for scout groups, family reunions, or birthday gatherings. There's a 30-person (canines included) maximum load allowed. Eight inches of snow is the minimum required for the sleigh rides. The fee is $125 for the first 30 minutes and $75 for each additional 30 minutes.

The preserve includes 753 acres. The sole walking trail is a nearly one-mile wooded hike that loops east of the main equestrian barn. There's also a regional trail that meanders into the Herrick Lake Forest Preserve at the far west end. It's a challenge to visit this preserve and not encounter equine traffic. Dogs with a fear of horses should stay home.

The 19-room mansion on the grounds is something to behold. But dogs aren't allowed in. For that matter, people aren't permitted either, except for

Four-Legged Lodging

Doggone Chicago offers lots of places to stay with a pooch. In every case, pet etiquette is de rigueur. An unmannered owner and pet may get tossed out of the inn.

Here are 10 rules for proper canine conduct at hotels and motels. Always remember that not all guests are pet lovers.

1. The staff will feel more at ease if they're confident your pooch is well behaved. Remember, the biggest impression is the first impression. Introduce the dog at check-in.

2. If your dog is American Kennel Club Canine Good Citizen–certified (see p. 287), you may want to show off the certificate. You'll feel proud, and the staff may feel more confident.

3. Dogs should not attack the maid. Seriously, this is one of the primary reasons pets aren't welcome at so many hotels. Dogs really shouldn't be allowed to stay in rooms unattended. This is a firm rule at many hotels and motels. For one thing, an anxious pet may want to bolt as soon as the door is open. And dogs with questionable temperaments can threaten the housekeeping staff. Small and midsize dogs may be crated, but they still shouldn't cause a ruckus when the housekeeping staff arrives. If you must leave your dog during the day, place the "Do Not Disturb" placard on your door.

4. If you absolutely must leave your dog in the room unattended, do so at night when the housekeeping staff won't be entering. You should also take the hound for a brisk walk or a jog before you depart. A pooped pup will snooze while you're away.

5. The ice machine, the ping of the elevator arriving, or people shuffling down the hallway shouldn't cause your pooch to bark. No one appreciates noisy neighbors.

6. If your pet chews on furniture, be sure to take along rawhide or something else acceptable for chomping. Chewing will also curb barking. Ask the housekeeping staff to not leave those mints on your pillow. Chocolate is harmful to dogs.

7. If your pooch has an accident in the room, clean up thoroughly— so thoroughly that no one will notice. When walking your dog on the property, be sure to pick up waste.

continued

8. Please don't leave fleas behind for the next pet. You should also protect your dog against fleas, since the last guest may have left some of the little buggers behind.

9. Pack some tape or a lint remover to clean up dog hair. Consider brushing the dog before you check in.

10. Fair is fair. If your pooch chews on a chair leg or soils the carpet, you should offer to pay for any damages.

special events and corporate functions. People can visit the formal gardens, but canines are discouraged.

Danada Forest Preserve is open from one hour after sunrise to one hour after sunset.

The main entrance is on the east side of Naperville Road and south of Illinois Route 56 (Butterfield Road). For hayride schedules, sleigh ride reservations, or information call (630) 933-7248.

HERRICK LAKE FOREST PRESERVE /// ½   This 851-acre preserve is truly a refuge for flora and fauna. More than 300 plant species, more than 100 kinds of birds, 19 species of mammals, and 13 types of fish are found here. In the large marsh at the center of the preserve, for example, species include the Eastern tiger salamander, northern leopard frog, pied-billed grebe, mink, and muskrat. I saw a muskrat, but Chaser missed it.

Regional Trail crosses through Herrick Lake, and the fishermen work hard to earn a catch. They fish here year-round, on the hottest summer days and on the ice. Of course, it helps that the 22-acre lake is frequently stocked with sunfish, channel and flathead catfish, largemouth bass, and other species. Rowboats and canoes are available for $5 per hour, $25 for the day. Trolling motors can be rented for $10 an hour or $50 for the day. You may not take your own boat or canoe here. Dogs are allowed in the boats, but canine and people swimming is not permitted.

The one-mile Lake Trail surrounds Herrick Lake. Along the way, Chaser let loose on a 150-year-old white oak tree. I felt guilty. After all, these trees are valuable living monuments. Chaser, I suspect, felt good. This trail is a pleasurable walk, in part because those trees provide shade in the summer and break cold wind gusts in the winter.

Several trails emanate from Regional Trail and reconnect with it later. One wishes the highways around Chicago were as well thought-out as this trail system. Even Chaser, who usually scares off the birds, witnessed egrets and various songbird species, as well as a bobolink—an increasingly rare sight. Continuing east, the Regional Trail leads right into Danada Forest Preserve, also in Wheaton. When the equine traffic increases, you'll know you're getting closer.

There are secluded grassy picnic areas in abundance throughout the park.

Open from one hour after sunrise to one hour after sunset. The main entrance is on the east side of Herrick Road, south of Illinois Route 56 (Butterfield Road) and north of Warrenville Road. (630) 933-7248.

HURLEY GARDENS ✓ ½   These were once the formal gardens at a rambling estate. The main structure is long gone, but a restored gazebo and white stucco teahouse survive. The grounds sprout a rainbow of flowers outlined by well-manicured hedges. It's no wonder that weddings are often held here. Make sure Fido doesn't crash a wedding party. This is a nice place to just sit on a stone bench and let the world pass by.

Open sunrise to sunset. Hurley Gardens is just south of Illinois Route 38 (Roosevelt Road) at Adare and Creekside Drives. (630) 690-4880.

KELLY PARK ✓ ½   A new accessible-for-the-disabled play area attracts lots of young children. Moms and dads arrive en masse with a kid or two and the family pooch. There's a nice grassy field as well as a paved pathway. Dogs who don't care for children shouldn't bother.

Open sunrise to sunset. Kelly Park is at Main and Elm Streets, two blocks south of Illinois Route 38 (Roosevelt Road). (630) 690-4880.

LINCOLN MARSH NATURAL AREA ✓✓✓   Begin by picking up a free map at the kiosk in the parking area. Wood-chip trails wind through the marsh and eventually into the forest.

Despite the park's being a marsh, a perfect breeding place for mosquitoes, we encountered very few of these buzzers. It was later explained that you're more likely to be bothered by mosquitoes in your own backyard than in this natural place. That's because there are so many birds and frogs that dine on them. In fact, the marshes are a haven for various frogs and rare kinds of salamanders. Do not allow your dogs to chase them, though. Park District officials ask that you and the dog leave nature as undisturbed as possible. There are also several rare kinds of marsh plants here. Dogs aren't allowed to snack on them.

It's hard to believe this 130-acre placid place is so close to the heart of downtown Wheaton. You can also access the Illinois Prairie Path at this location. Lots of folks jog to the Prairie Path to continue their run.

Open sunrise to sunset. Lincoln Marsh Natural Area is at Pierce and Harrison Avenues, south of Jewell Road. (630) 690-4880.

MEMORIAL PARK //   Established more than 70 years ago, this is the oldest park in Wheaton. Antique-style lighting, mature maple trees, and a classic band shell create the feel of a bygone era.

Pathways take you around the gardens and through this three-acre setting. There are plenty of benches, but at lunchtime they can fill up with downtown office workers and dog owners. Barbara Eaton, public information coordinator for the Wheaton Park District, says that she sometimes lunches here just to watch the dogs.

Open sunrise to sunset. Memorial Park is bounded by Union, Hale, and Wheaton Avenues. (630) 690-4880.

NORTHSIDE PARK // ½   Cottonwood and maple trees gently sway in the wind at this stately park. Much of the 70 acres is shaded by mature trees. Chaser and Lucy seemed to appreciate the cool breeze created around the aged trunks.

A one-mile trail is ideal for a quick run. The path winds near the Northside Lagoon. There's no ordinance about keeping dogs out of the lagoon, but it's shallow, stagnant water with a floating layer of goose feathers. Somehow, even floating a canoe on the pond isn't inviting. (Canoes are available June through September, noon to 4 P.M., for $6 per hour.) Dogs are allowed in the canoes. Plans are in the works to renovate the park, including dredging the pond.

Chaser and Lucy preferred the thrill of running down Cohee Hill and across a large grassy field. At first glance, the sledding hill looks as if it's always been there. In reality, the Park District's first swimming pool is buried under Cohee Hill. The Northside Family Aquatic Center occupies the east side of the park, and dogs aren't allowed.

This park also features cabins that are used by local Girl Scout troops. We were told, "There's never been a reason to think about allowing dogs inside." Apparently, they don't understand how Chaser feels about Girl Scout cookies.

Open sunrise to sunset. Northside Park is at the north end of West Street at Prairie Avenue, accessed by Park Circle Drive off Main Street. (630) 690-4880.

RATHJE PARK //   The entire playground is made of recycled car tires.

Dogs who prefer to fish might jump into the pond. For those who like to stay dry, a footbridge crosses the water and leads to a series of tall elm and maple trees. This is one of the most popular places to take dogs in Wheaton, so there are almost always other canines around. The large grassy areas are the favorite meeting places in this seven-acre park.

Open sunrise to sunset. Rathje Park is at Illinois Route 38 (Roosevelt Road) at Delles Road. (630) 690-4880.

SEVEN GABLES PARK // ½   This is a jock's park, with eight soccer fields and zillions of soccer parents dropping off the kids. Traffic can get congested when several games begin or end at the same time.

There's a one-and-a-half-mile paved fitness course for working out with the pooch. And there's enough green space for the canine jocks to play fetch. When no soccer, football, or baseball games are in progress—usually very early in the morning—you have tons of running room. There are also tennis courts.

Open sunrise to sunset. Seven Gables Park entrance is at Danada Drive, north of Blanchard Avenue at Naperville-Wheaton Road. (630) 690-4880.

Doggy Doing

Tuesday Night Concerts   The music is free on Tuesdays at 7:30 P.M. from mid-June through August at the band shell in Memorial Park. Entertainment ranges from bluegrass to big band to pop. There are some benches, but most people take their own blankets. Dogs can lie anywhere. A concession stand offers soft drinks and not much more, so you'll have to pack a picnic. Memorial Park is bounded by Union, Hale, and Wheaton Avenues. Call (630) 690-4880.

Festivals

Cream of Wheaton   This is a one-day celebration of activities on the last Saturday in May or the first Saturday in June, held in and around Memorial Park, bounded by Union, Hale, and Wheaton Avenues.

It all kicks off with Run for the Animals, 5K and 10K races to benefit Cosley Zoo. Dogs may not participate in the runs, but they are welcome to watch and cheer. You can register by phone or at 7 A.M. on race day. The race is at 7:30 A.M. Runners depart from Memorial Park, wind through town, and then return to the park. The first 2,500 people to register receive a free T-shirt.

The festival includes the Taste of the Western 'Burbs, which takes place from 11 A.M. to 7 P.M. in the park and along Wheaton Avenue. About 20 area restaurants participate. Rounding out the action are live music, a crafts fair, and children's activities throughout the day. The Cosley Petting Zoo critters also make an appearance. Dogs aren't allowed in the petting zoo but are otherwise welcome to party in the park.

For further information call (630) 690-4880.

Fall Festival Demonstrations of various kinds of horses and riding styles are the highlights of this festival at the Danada Forest Preserve. There are also barn tours, so you can meet the thoroughbreds up close and personal. Dogs are allowed, but they should exhibit good horse sense. A dog that barks at the equine entertainers won't be appreciated.

The festival includes Civil War reenactors and an art show. The event is held from 11 A.M. to 5 P.M. on the second Sunday in October. The main entrance is east of Naperville Road and south of Illinois Route 56 (Butterfield Road). Call (630) 668-6012.

Coffee Shop

Caribou Coffee Sip one of the rustic Caribou blends, while your pup sips an old-fashioned H_2O. 280 Danada Square West; (630) 871-9713.

Willowbrook

Places to Stay

Baymont Inn and Suites Dogs under 50 pounds and their human companions are restricted to smoking rooms on the first floor. So, your dog can smoke 'em if he's got 'em. All canine visitors must be attended at all times. Rates are $69 to $90. 855 W. 79th Street; (630) 654-0077.

Red Roof Inn The conversation I had with Aisha, the front-desk employee, left me smiling. When asked if dogs can stay at the motel, she replied, "As long as you let us come down and pet it." Aisha told me about one woman who checked in with 12 dogs when a dog show was in town. This hotel is not just tolerant of animals but actually enjoys having them as guests. Rates are $55.99 to $81.99, with no additional pet charges. 7535 Kingery Highway; (630) 323-8811 or (800) 843-7663.

Winfield

Park

Dogs must be on-leash, and owners must pick up. Open sunrise to 9 P.M. Call (630) 653-3811.

OAKWOOD COMMUNITY PARK // Park District personnel strongly warn that owners with dogs must be responsible for their pets' actions. While the community hasn't had a gripe and the park remains clean, those officials are pretty nervous. I'm told, "The problem with appearing in your book is that nonresidents will invade our park." So, when you visit, pretend to be a native—learn the names of local officials and streets.

When you invade, here's what you'll find: A one-third-mile asphalt running trail that loops around the park and a small fishing pond, where dogs have been known to dive in. The water appears reasonably clean, and there isn't a goose in sight. There are lit tennis and volleyball courts. The new in-line skating rink tends to get flooded and, in the winter, transform into an ice rink. There are also a few picnic shelters. If this 10-acre park were larger, it would be terrific. But it's not bad as it is.

Open sunrise to 9 P.M. Oakwood Community Park is at Winfield Road, south of Geneva Road and north of High Lake Road. (630) 653-3811.

Woodridge

Park

The Forest Preserve of DuPage County operates the only notable park here.

GREENE VALLEY FOREST PRESERVE // ½ A good part of the 1,425 acres is flat and paw-comfortable. The east branch of the DuPage River spans the length of the east side of the preserve. The preserve is also divided by the north-west thoroughfare, Greene Road. The trails are mostly mowed turf, especially east of Greene Road, where there's flat open prairie. On the west side of Greene Road, a recently completed looped trail ambles through a wooded area. Signposts will test your knowledge of local trees. Chaser paused at one such sign, then aimed and hit a bull's-eye.

Picnic facilities are available.

The Greene Valley Forest Preserve is not named for the color, but rather for a family that originally settled here. Volunteers have restored and maintained the Greene Farmstead, which is at the north corner of the preserve near Greene and Hobson Roads.

Open from one hour after sunrise to one hour after sunset. The north entrance is on the east side of Greene Road, south of Hobson Road, north of 75th Street, and west of Illinois Route 53. The south entrance is south of 79th Street, west of Greene Road and east of Wehrli Road. (630) 933-7248.

4 LAKE COUNTY

Welcome to the land of Fluffy and Muffy. Hey, let's face it, you're unlikely to find a single dog back in Berwyn named Mirabelle or Rousseau. But in Lake County, those names are as chic as the embroidered sweater worn by a Maltese and personalized with the name "Louise." I also saw several dogs sporting $30 fleece outfits and even witnessed one wearing what the owner called a "tail warmer."

If you remember Mrs. Drysdale from "The Beverly Hillbillies," you'll be happy to learn that she now lives in Lake Forest. Just as we entered Lake Forest, a voice bellowed in the distance, "Claude, come back here instantly!" Claude, a striking white French poodle, was wandering off-leash.

"We don't want to muddy ourselves, do we?" she implored while waving a Technicolor rhinestone-laden leash. Despite his impeccable trim, Claude is, after all, a dog. (Oh, not that we would dare inform the owner of such a harsh reality. She probably couldn't take it.)

Claude was busy sniffing in the mud with a bourgeois terrier-mix. Mrs. Drysdale arrived to scold Claude, "You naughty boy. Now we'll just have to visit our friend the groomer and get a bath. This is just awful."

She put the leash on Claude and proceeded to blame the innocent little mixed-breed dog and its owner. "How dare you corrupt my poor Claude," she said as she walked off in a huff.

Of course, all of Lake County isn't quite so, how shall we say, over the top, about their canine companions. But the extreme attitude does have its advantages. Lucy felt like a million bucks in the North Shore. Lucy is a North American shepherd—a rare breed. And wow, did she get the attention here. Naturally, she exulted in every moment.

Wherever we went, from Lake County to Kane County, Lucy's blue-merle coat and sparkling blue eyes captivated people. And as those who have been lucky enough to hear them can attest, her frequent concertos add to her charm. On several occasions, folks have hit the brakes to pull over and ask about our little girl. One dog trainer drove the wrong way down a one-way street in order to inquire about Lucy.

Many North Shore–area dog lovers seeking the latest, most novel breeds were pulling pens out of their purses in order to get the name and phone number of the breeder. When Robin would explain that breeder Susan Sinclair, based in San Diego, was, in part, responsible for originating the breed, the entire notion became increasingly appealing.

Robin would say, "Lucy flew in from San Diego as a puppy." Well, that's apparently a pretty fashionable thing to do. People were impressed. In truth, that's not the ideal way to get a dog. It's best to actually see the breeder's facility for yourself.

People were so obsessed with Lucy that we soon learned to take Susan's phone number with us when visiting the North Shore.

Chaser, our Brittany, wasn't altogether ignored. One Lake Forest woman excitedly pointed to our pointer and exclaimed, "That's a Brittany! Oh yes, you should take your dog to Paris!" Then she proceeded to speak in French. Perhaps she assumed we understood because Brittanys originated in France. Robin and I just smiled and shook our heads. Who knows? It's possible that Chaser somehow understood her.

One language Chaser clearly understands is goose. Lake County brims with thousands of migrating geese, and thousands more that have traded in their frequent-flier mileage for permanent residency in parks and on golf courses. True to her lineage as a bird dog, Chaser is in ecstasy whenever she has the chance to terrify geese. Once, she pulled the leash right out of my hand and nearly pulled my arm out of its socket.

Please understand, Chaser is now a senior citizen whose favorite command is "Go to bed." With those words, Chaser slowly picks herself up and staggers into the bedroom, where she manages to haul herself onto our bed. More than one friend has commented, "Sleep is what Chaser is best at."

As we soon learned, however, it's goose chasing Chaser likes best—truly living up to her name. With the sound of distant geese, she would transform from "Sleepy Dog" into "Super Dog" before we even arrived at our park of destination. It's a difficult phenomenon to describe, but her little docked tail was held higher, her ears were at full alert, a sparkle would appear in her eyes, and we swear her expression was different. She was feeling pure and unadulterated joy as perhaps only dogs can.

Mostly, we'd run along with Lucy and Chaser as they pursued the geese. Of course, in most places, allowing the dogs off-leash is a violation of the leash law. But we really didn't want the dogs to catch the geese. When the birds are cornered, when goslings are in the vicinity, or simply when they feel like it, geese may turn the tables, hissing and honking at canine threats. Small dogs have been seriously injured by combative geese. While Chaser, at about 32 pounds, could probably hold her own, Lucy weighed as little as 10 pounds when we began researching the book.

One time, while chasing a goose, Chaser bolted right into a disgusting retention pond. I really don't believe Chaser intended to jump into the pond, as she's not a water lover. All she knew was that she was having the time of her life pursuing the honkers. The geese quacked and waddled into the water, and Chaser blindly followed. At that moment, the birds flew off. Chaser, now at the center of the retention pond, turned to us with a look of panic on her face, as if to say, "How did I get here?" She whimpered as she swam back. Due to the stench, Robin and I whimpered on the ride home.

For the most part, Lake County is dog friendly. The majority of suburbs allow dogs in municipal parks, and all of the Lake County Forest Preserve locations allow dogs as long as they're on a leash and their owners pick up.

At the Lake County Forest Preserve Dog Training Area in Libertyville and at the Exercise Areas in Lake Forest and Wauconda, dogs are welcome off-leash. These are among the few places in the Chicago area specifically set aside for dogs. Canines have lots of elbowroom for dog paddling or tracking the scent of a rabbit. There's never a threat of a ticket from the strong arm of the law for merely taking a pooch off of a leash to chase a stick. But you have to pay for the privilege of freedom—$25 per year for residents and $50 for nonresidents of Lake County.

Nearly all communities have a leash law. However, many communities in Lake County are sensible about it. As long as you don't annoy other people who are using the park, and as long as you're toting a plastic bag or a scooper, you can allow Fido off-leash for a short stroll or to play fetch. In fact, there was a proposal in Deerfield to allow designated times and/or places for dogs to run off-leash. While that proposal fell short of passage, local dog lovers can rejoice in the new dog park at Jaycee Memorial Park.

Dog lovers have persuaded Highland Park to allow canines on two of their four beaches. That's a significant breakthrough. Dogs are also allowed on the beach in Zion.

Unfortunately, not all of Lake County is so dog friendly. The sparkling North Shore beaches are among the most glorious in all the Chicago area. That's why it's so disappointing that the Highland Park and Lake Bluff beaches make it so expensive for nonresident dogs, and dogs are not allowed on the Lake Forest beach at all.

Hannah Porst, who has relocated to Lake Forest from Malibu, California, is saddened that dogs aren't allowed to share the lake water. "I see this beautiful beach, and what a shame—particularly since the beach season here is so short," she says. "Where I'm from, dogs are a part of the family, and you wouldn't think of excluding family members from parks or beaches. Of course dogs are welcome."

Several suburbs never welcome dogs in local parks, including Fox Lake, Lake Zurich, and Lincolnshire. In Antioch and Lake Bluff, there's been a movement to ban dogs from city parks. So far, they've been unsuccessful. Still, an antidog sentiment simmers.

In Buffalo Grove and many nearby northwest suburbs in Lake County and in Cook County, the sentiment isn't antidog as much as it is antibreed. An irrational fear of rottweilers, and of other "mean-looking breeds" as one resident put it, is spreading like an epidemic.

It all began in Buffalo Grove. One subdivision created a stir when residents petitioned for and proposed an ordinance mandating that rottweilers and pit bull–type dogs be restricted to a four-foot leash and muzzled when walking in public. Some proponents also sought to keep these breeds out of the parks altogether. In addition, the proposal suggested requiring that these dogs be chained when in their own backyards.

Buffalo Grove is filled with more children than Captain Kangaroo can count. There are 175 children under 12 years old in the one complaining subdivision alone. Usually children and dogs are considered an ideal mix. In fact, children and dogs interact daily at playgrounds all over town. Buffalo Grove has no complaints on record of dogs attacking kids in the park. And the parks are generally dog friendly, at least for canines who don't happen to be rottweilers or pit bulls.

The Buffalo Grove proposal made national news headlines and traveled around the world via the Internet. Hearings were held in a packed auditorium at village hall. Emotions were passionate on both sides of the argument. Among those speaking on behalf of rottweilers were various veterinarians, members of the Medallion Rottweiler Club, Riverwoods-based behaviorist and trainer Margaret Gibbs, and yours truly.

Despite our efforts, the restrictions have been passed in Buffalo Grove. Meanwhile, the fallout effect on public attitude is nothing short of dramatic. Dare to take a rottweiler off-leash in the park to play an innocent game of fetch, and in an instant a police officer will be writing you a citation. If you happen to be playing catch with a beagle or bichon frise, the officer will likely yawn.

One resident, whose rottweiler is extremely well socialized and trained, holds several obedience titles, lives with young children, and periodically visits a local children's hospital, said that he was heckled by a mother when he passed by a playground area where dogs are allowed on-leash.

Another rottweiler was reportedly refused admittance into Buffalo Grove Days, the village's annual Labor Day weekend festival. The owner was told, "No dogs allowed." This is decidedly not so. Chaser and Lucy had no grief getting in. Sad to say, breed-specific discrimination is real.

On the affirmative front, Lake County offers many fun events that are open to all well-behaved dogs. There's even a Buffalo Grove Days dog show. Dogs partake in similar festivals throughout Lake County. In Deerfield, a dog show is held in conjunction with Deerfield Family Days on July 4, and on that same day there are pet parades in Highland Park and Antioch.

Lucy loves to sing, another reason she enjoyed Lake County. Dogs are welcome to listen to the tunes at free concerts held in several suburbs, including Highland Park, Lake Bluff, Waukegan, and Zion.

Assisting Lucy and Chaser throughout Lake County were researcher Gail Polzin and her Shetland sheepdog, Kalea.

Antioch

Parks

Laurie Stahl, director of Parks and Recreation, was happy to report that the problems the city previously had with irresponsible dog owners have been much reduced. Each park has signs stating that dogs must be on-leash and that owners must pick up after their dogs. Apparently people are reading the signs, and they're wielding plastic bags and scoopers on their park visits. Watching where you step in Antioch isn't the issue it was a few years back. Parks are open from sunrise to sunset; call (847) 395-2160.

**CENTENNIAL PARK /// ** The canine highlight is the huge field where you can bone up on Frisbee tossing. There's enough elbowroom to accommodate several hounds flying into the air simultaneously to snatch discs, a frequent sight on weekends. As you exit the car from the driveway off Anita Street, you see a long row of young trees. It's a natural place for a canine pit stop.

Dogs are welcome to share the spacious picnic area under the pavilion. This allows for picnicking through sun showers. Grills are available. This park is packed with young children. The big attraction is a superstructure playground built to resemble a castle. It even has a miniature Tower of London, in addition to tire ladders, tunnels, walkways on planks, and two slides.

Puppies are often seen chasing children through the maze. Dogs are allowed in the play area, but big dogs will find great difficulty navigating the structures, which were built for tots.

Centennial Park is at 601 Anita Street, between North Avenue and Depot Street. (847) 395-2160.

GAGE BROTHERS PARK //   This small park is a veritable rest home for old trees and is primarily used by folks from the neighboring senior citizens' recreation center and senior living center. For older dogs who would rather walk and sniff (there are places galore to lift a leg), this park is made to order. But there's no running space for young whippersnappers. For the most part, the people and their dogs just sit. Sometimes they stare at trees, reading the signage that identifies the wooded species. With its scenic value, this is a popular park for weddings.

Gage Brothers Park is at 790 Cunningham Drive, just north of Holbeck Drive. (847) 395-2160.

JENSEN PARK / ½   This 2.4-acre neighborhood park is encircled by trees. Before and after work, the tree route is a highway for neighborhood dogs doing "their number." Sometimes there's even a traffic jam as dogs congregate around favorite trunks. There are two tennis courts.

Jensen Park is at 611 Alima Terrace, near First Avenue. (847) 395-2160.

NORTH PARK / ½   Resembling a finger, this narrow park has a retention pond on the west side. Dogs and their people are not allowed in the pond. At the east corner, there is a small cluster of trees. It also has a basketball court and a smallish children's playground.

North Park is at 361 Donin Drive. (847) 395-2160.

OSMOND PARK /   The park is named for a once-prominent Antioch family, not for Donny or Marie, but it might as well be called "the dog park of Antioch," as the soles of our shoes can verify. Indeed, this place is a minefield for people and dogs. After all, with four legs, they're twice as likely to misstep. Neighbors located downwind complain about a not-so-fragrant aroma in the summer months. However, dogs love it here. To them, it's a field filled with Giorgio.

Osmond Park is at 579 Valleyview. (847) 395-2160.

PEDERSON PARK ///   This is a favorite place for Gunner, Parks and Recreation director Cheryl McCameron's German shorthaired pointer. The parking area leads to a sidewalk that ends at a hexagonal shelter (just in case of rain). On the other side of the shelter is an open area the size of a football field surrounded by Lake Tranquillity. The lake, which is really more like a swamp, connects to the Chain O'Lakes State Park (see Spring Grove).

Swimming is officially discouraged, but many dogs see a duck land in the water, and off they go. Fishermen don't especially like the dogs in the water. As one old angler grumbled, "Dogs scare off the fish."

The park is about eight and a half acres. Aside from the significant amount of running room, its primary attribute is the wealth of natural beauty. A contingent of residents is fighting any further development of the park. They like the natural Illinois swamp and the wildlife it attracts.

Pederson Park is at 680 W. Illinois State Route 173, at Illinois State Route 59. (847) 395-2160.

WILLIAMS PARK //   The sand volleyball courts are the closest things you'll find to a beach in Antioch. However, sunbathers generally prefer the water found at the Aqua Center swimming pool. Sorry—dogs aren't allowed within the pool area.

On July 4, there's a fire department water fight. Each side attempts to hose down the other. So far, no dalmatians have participated. But dalmatians and virtually every other breed turn up for picnics under the huge pavilion. On weekends, more than two hundred people and their respective dogs may be jostling for position. Ample cooking facilities are provided.

This nine-acre park also includes a basketball court, and there is a log cabin used by the Boy Scouts and preschoolers. Dogs have been seen in the cabin, especially when it's show-and-tell day for the preschoolers. We're told that one little boy who toted his puppy wanted to demonstrate how to use his pocketknife to cut the dog's nails. Happily, he was dissuaded.

Three lots within the park boundaries provide ample parking space. 741 Main Street (Illinois State Route 83) and Williams Street. (847) 395-2160.

Doggy Doing

Pet Parade   Perfect for puttin' on the dog, a pet parade is held in conjunction with the annual Independence Day Parade and Children's Festival on the Saturday closest to July 4. Starting at 10 A.M., dressed-up doggies proceed from Antioch High School (1133 Main Street) down Main Street to Williams Park (at Main and Williams Streets). The pet parade doesn't discriminate against cats or other critters. One year, a patriotic green iguana was decked out as Uncle Sam.

Following the parade, there are activities in Williams Park, including entertainment, fun fair games, and sports tournaments. Parade registration is required, but it's free to participate. Forms are available at village hall and at various businesses in the area, or call (847) 395-1000.

Place to Stay

Best Western Regency Inn   OK, which is it? When I first inquired, "Do you have a weight limit for pets?" the response I got was, "Dogs under 10 pounds are welcome." When I called several days later to double-check my facts, the answer was, "We take dogs of any size." The discrepancy leads me to believe this policy is subjective. My advice is to have your approval E-mailed or faxed so you have it all in writing before check-in. There is a $25 refundable deposit. Rates are $75 to $110. 350 Highway 173; (847) 395-3606.

Buffalo Grove

Parks

Dogs are welcome in any of the Buffalo Grove parks. The good news is that when subdivisions are constructed, a park is almost always mandated. The bad news is that most of these parks are quite small, acceptable for a quick walk for a nearby resident, but hardly a worthwhile destination. On the other hand, bikers coordinated enough to ride with Fido favor the parks. About 40 miles of paved bike paths interconnect the park system. A free bike path map is available at Buffalo Grove Village Hall, 50 Raupp Boulevard; (847) 459-2500.

Dogs must be on a leash at the parks, most of which are open from 6 A.M. to 10 P.M. (those with lit facilities close at 11 P.M.). Call (847) 459-5700.

APTAKISIC PARK ½/   There's a tendency to build parks around electrical transformers in Buffalo Grove. Somehow it doesn't seem like a good idea. There are several skyscraper transformers in this park.

You'll also find a children's play area, a basketball court, and a baseball diamond. The village bicycle path goes through the park.

Aptakisic Park is just south of Aptakisic Junior High School, 1231 Weiland Road, near North Busch Parkway. (847) 459-5700.

BUFFALO CREEK FOREST PRESERVE (LAKE COUNTY FOREST PRESERVE) ///
Imagine Illinois at a time when hunting dogs helped to track the family dinner. Four miles of crushed-gravel trails run through this 396-acre stretch of restored prairie and marshland.

Largemouth bass, bullheads, and panfish swim in the restored 52-acre reservoir, but, much to Chaser's indignation, dogs aren't allowed to fish. They're also not allowed in the park's creeks.

Dogs should be on a leash at all times, even when hiking on the gravel trails. In winter months, cross-country skiers traverse these trails, and bicyclists use them in the summer. The main trailhead is at the Checker Road entrance. Pedestrian access is also available at the corner of Checker and Arlington Heights Roads, and on Checker Road west of Schaeffer Road. Still another pedestrian entry is at Lake-Cook and Arlington Heights Roads. For the most part, the trails span open areas. Your dog won't suffer from claustrophobia here.

Even the keen-nosed pointers may miss the nesting platforms built to attract great blue herons. Other feathered friends around here include prairie birds such as bobolinks, meadowlarks, and pheasants. The cormorant, rare in these parts, has also been spied.

Snowmobiles, horses, ice fishing, fires, and camping are not allowed. Rangers regularly patrol the area, which was once a dairy and soybean farm.

As you wander close to Lake-Cook or Arlington Heights Roads, the illusion of living back in pioneer days dissolves.

The park is open from 6:30 A.M. to sunset. Buffalo Creek Preserve is near Buffalo Grove (and also near Long Grove). At the intersection of Lake-Cook Road and Arlington Heights Road, go north on Arlington Heights Road one-half mile to Checker Road. Turn west on Checker and proceed to the entrance on the south side of the road. (847) 367-6640.

BUSCH GROVE COMMUNITY PARK ½/ Leash laws aside, some people let their dogs run here among the 76 acres of natural prairie. Ordinarily, we'd consider this a splendid place for dogs to blow off steam, but the grasses grow so high that even a Labrador may get lost in the foliage, and nearby streets are very busy. This park also has a soccer field, a basketball court, a bike path, and a picnic area.

Busch Grove Community Park is at 1000 N. Buffalo Grove Road, at Busch Parkway. (847) 459-5700.

CAMBRIDGE PARK ½/ More geese utilize this six-acre park than canines. It's sure a dilly of a place for pups to chase the waddlers. Beware: As Lucy learned, the geese aren't afraid to stand up to small dogs. And a serious goose can potentially cause a serious injury. In addition to the waterfowl, Cambridge contains two kids' play lots, tennis courts, a picnic area, a soccer field, and a bike path.

The park is at 951 S. Buffalo Grove Road, just south of Dundee Road. (847) 459-5700.

CHURCHILL PARK //   It's a small park, but the opportunity to explore the wetland area could make it worth the ride. A paved path surrounds the petite preserve, where you can hear birds sing and see native plants. Canines might be inclined to dive into the marsh, but don't expect to sight any rare birds while dogs are splashing and barking. Those who would rather quietly survey the beauty of nature can do so from one of the two observation decks. Otherwise, the only happenings happen on a baseball diamond and a soccer field. This is a good place to launch a bike or walking tour through the Buffalo Grove parks.

   Churchill Park is at 1900 N. Buffalo Grove, at Aptakisic Road. (847) 459-5700.

EMERICH PARK //   A fenced-in baseball diamond can serve as an elaborate dog run with lots of green space for letting it all out. Outside the baseball field, be sure to keep Fido on a leash because the park meets busy Lake-Cook Road, where cars zip by at 40 to 50 miles per hour.

   This isn't a favorite stop for pooches who remain convinced the buffalo statue in front of the administration office is real. Terrified dogs have been known to escape from their collars to evade the menace. Lucy and Chaser, brave dogs that they are, calmly walked up to the buffalo, gave it a sniff, and in utter boredom led us to the grassy area, where the smells are apparently much better.

   The other highlights are tennis courts, a football field, a bike path, and a picnic area.

   Emerich Park is at 150 Raupp Boulevard, on the southwest corner of Lake-Cook Road. (847) 459-5700.

EMERICH PARK EAST /   Most of this park is occupied by a football field which may be used for organized games from August through November by permit only. When the field is not in use, there are few better places to practice canine Frisbee. Buffalo Grove plans to expand the bike path into this park.

   Emerich Park East is on the southeast corner of Lake-Cook Road at 151 Raupp Boulevard. (847) 459-5700.

GREEN LAKE PARK //   Green Lake is appropriately named for the goose-poop-colored water. Even worse than the bird waste is the abundance of dog remains scattered about the park. People just don't pick up after their dogs here.

Otherwise, the park's tranquil setting is a pleasure to behold. A wooded bridge leads to a small picnic area nestled under an umbrella of trees and circled by a retention pond. Chaser and Lucy disturbed the serenity as they bolted from the car to chase the geese. While this flock scattered into the water, geese will sometimes give canines what for, hissing and honking right back at them. Some small dogs have been hurt in these encounters, particularly when goslings were nearby.

Keep the dog on a leash when confronting geese because you never know how the goose will react. You also don't want the dog diving into the filthy goose water.

Other attractions include a sand volleyball court, two children's play lots, a baseball diamond, a soccer field, tennis courts, a basketball court, a bike path, and a picnic area.

Green Lake Park is at 1101 N. Green Knolls Drive, at Larraway and Gail Drives and Busch Parkway. (847) 459-5700.

HIGHLAND POINT PARK /   Across the street from Parkchester Park, this site is somewhat smaller, but you get oodles of open green space for a fast run. A pair of benches is a welcome sight if you need to catch your breath after the canine play session. The village bike path crosses this park.

Highland Point Park is at 850 Weiland Road, at Parkchester Road. (847) 459-5700.

KILMER PARK / ½   Located next to Joyce Kilmer School, Kilmer Park provides plenty of places to park a bicycle. The village bike path runs through this site. When school lets out, dogs can play with the kids. Although, with the park's two play lots, a soccer field, basketball and tennis courts, a baseball diamond, and an ice-skating rink, your dog may have some competition. There's also a small picnic area.

Kilmer Park is at 655 Golfview Terrace, at Raupp Boulevard. (847) 459-5700.

LIONS PARK ½/   Occupying a small parcel of land in a subdivision, this park, albeit charming, offers little in recreation value. There is, however, a lovely wooden gazebo.

Lions Park is at 739 Weidner Road, at White Pine Roads. (847) 459-5700.

PARKCHESTER PARK / ½   As the sign clearly indicates—you can enter the tennis courts only if you wear tennis shoes. We assume that leaves most dogs out.

If you ride your bicycle through this park, watch out for geese on the path. Naturally, the geese are often heading to the retention pond. Don't let Fido

Two of a Kind

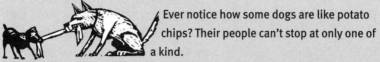

Ever notice how some dogs are like potato chips? Their people can't stop at only one of a kind.

"My first choice 25 years ago was to get a Saint Bernard," says Marlene Wells of Mount Prospect. "But I fell in love with a girlfriend's miniature dachshund, and I've been in love ever since." After her original little wiener dog, Wells has never been without at least two to five dachshunds. "I can't help it," she adds. "I confess, it may be an addiction, but I don't believe I want help for this problem—they're just too cute!"

Dogs are pack animals and enjoy companionship. One or more playmates will alleviate boredom in any breed or mixed breed. There are no statistics on this subject, but let's face it: some breeds always seem to travel in matching pairs, or as three or even four or five of a kind.

Beagles, like most other scent hounds, have been bred to work and live together, so people who opt for a trio of beagles have an excuse: the dogs incline to it by nature. Unfortunately, the neighbors who live next door to these baying beagles might not be so contented. Greyhound people remark that members of the breed look so elegant standing side by side, like stately bookends. Besides, it magnifies the badge of honor when two (or more) of these gorgeous dogs are rescued from a racetrack, rather than just one.

Then there's the simple fact that, to echo Marlene Wells, some dogs just look so darn cute together. Dachshunds and foo-foo poodles make that list, closely followed by corgis and Scottish and West Highland white terriers.

This affinity for two or more of a kind isn't limited by size constraints. Ever notice how often you observe two or more Great Danes together? Even on TV commercials, or in one particular "Bewitched" episode, people team up with two or more of these giant dogs, as if one isn't imposing enough.

Jack Russell terriers are another prime example. Bred to catch fox, and go underground to do it, they're tenacious. Loyal fans of the breed figure providing one pal or more is a jim-dandy way to keep these active pups busy. It also keeps the rest of the household busy. "That's true," says Kathleen Hardy, of the Midwest Branch of the Jack Russell Terrier Club. "Sharing life with one Jack Russell is interesting, with two it's challenging, three is daunting, but living with four Jack Russells is downright over the top. No question—your life will be run by your dogs. But then, that's the way lots of people like it."

jump in after them, since the water is cruddy. This park also offers a handicapped-accessible play lot, a baseball diamond, a basketball court, and a picnic area.

Parkchester Park is at 851 Weiland Road, at Parkchester Road. (847) 459-5700.

TWIN CREEKS PARK / Small trees dot this diminutive park. There are soccer fields and a baseball diamond, so there's some space to run. The bike path crosses through this park.

401 Aptakisic Road; the entrance is off Buffalo Grove Road. (847) 459-5700.

WEIDNER PARK *(worth a sniff)* This petite green place consists of a rock garden with some flowers and evergreen bushes. There are also several benches for taking a load off or for counting cars as they whiz by. Since this park is located on a busy corner, it's absolutely not a good idea to let the dog off-leash.

Weidner Park is at 50 Weidner Road, at Lake-Cook Road. (847) 459-5700.

WILLOW STREAM POOL AND PARK /// This 54-acre park is where the soccer moms and dads congregate. On one late-summer Saturday morning, at least a dozen soccer games were going on simultaneously. The moment one game is completed, a legion of new tots takes the field. Family members, including dogs, form a pep club on the sidelines, cheering "Go! Go!" or "Woof! Woof!" as the case may be.

Willow Stream is by far the busiest park in Buffalo Grove. In addition to the soccer fields, there are baseball fields, basketball courts, tennis courts, a play lot, a picnic area, and a sand volleyball area. Dogs are not allowed on the adjacent golf course. The village bike path zigzags through the park.

Dogs can bird-watch near the five-acre conservation area. However, Chaser was clearly more focused on the Good Humor ice cream sold at the concession stand (located near the parking area off Old Checker Road). After I dripped cotton-candy ice cream on poor Chaser, bees became very interested. The bees continued to congregate, turning into a buzzing mob scene. Finally, we made a beeline ourselves to the safety of our car.

Willow Stream Park is located at 600 Farrington Drive, bounded by Old Checker Road, Farrington Lane, and Springside Lane. Parking is off Old Checker and also off Farrington (at the pool entrance). (847) 459-5700.

WINDSOR RIDGE PARK / ½ At this small site on the edge of a subdivision, a chain-link fence prevents any loose dogs from running off into busy Dundee Road. Of course, by law, dogs are supposed to be on-lead. But mistakes happen. On one occasion, a little girl accidentally dropped her leash; the dog bolted toward the street and didn't stop until it crashed into the fence. Witnesses have little doubt that the barrier saved this dog's life, and maybe the little girl's too, since she might have pursued the dog into the street. I wish more parks were surrounded by fences.

Also on the boundaries are a children's play lot, a basketball court, a bike path, a soccer field, and a baseball diamond.

Windsor Ridge Park is at 780 Vernon Lane at Dundee Road. (847) 459-5700.

Coffee Shop

Starbucks There are about a half dozen tables at this location. 55 N. McHenry Road; (847) 465-8764.

Doggy Doings

Lawn Chair Lyrics These free musical shows begin at 7 P.M. on Tuesdays from mid-June through July at Willow Stream Park, off Old Checker Road two blocks west of Buffalo Grove Road. As the name suggests, you take your own chairs. While some food is served, most folks here picnic.

Kalea, our researcher's Shetland sheepdog, is a kid magnet and wound up gaining as much attention as the musicians. Lots of dogs attend the concerts, but this was Kalea's big night. One little boy with impeccable taste returned to Kalea several times during the show. Finally he announced, "I've petted every dog in the park, and I like yours the best." This compliment was nearly as good as the potato salad Kalea swiped from a nearby picnicker. Call (847) 459-5700.

Summer Concert Series Free concerts are held at 7 P.M. on most Thursdays, May through August, at Rotary Village Green, Buffalo Grove Road at Old Checker Road (behind the post office). A local restaurant always offers food. Performers range from jazz to barbershop quartet. Area high school talent is featured in May. Take your own seats—or take advantage of your dog. One spectator sprawled out on a sleeping bag and used his Irish wolfhound as a pillow. Visit the bookmobile at intermission: it sometimes has dog titles. Call (847) 459-2500.

Festival

Buffalo Grove Days This annual Labor Day weekend fest features a carnival with the sort of rides that make even the sturdiest of stomachs turn every which way. Dogs aren't allowed on the rides, which was just fine with Chaser.

We both preferred to stand with our feet firmly planted and wave as our nieces, Jamie and Mallory, went round and round.

The festival also includes a craft show and live music. Dogs are allowed everywhere except in the giant food tent.

No bones about it, the meat of the event is the annual dog show, which begins at about 9 A.M. on Saturday. Categories in this highly unusual competition include "Best Trick," "Best Groomed," "Smallest Dog," "Biggest Dog," and "Best in Show." About 50 dogs participate. Preregistration is required; call (847) 459-5700.

The one-mile, six-legged fun run usually begins at 7:30 A.M. Sunday. People are expected to run with a four-legged partner (birds riding on shoulders are also allowed). Both children and adults can participate in this noncompetitive race. Preregistration is required, and there's a $2 sign-up fee; (847) 459-5700.

Buffalo Grove Days takes place over Labor Day weekend, 6 P.M. to 10 P.M. Thursday, 6 P.M. to 10:30 P.M. Friday, 11 A.M. to 10:30 P.M. Saturday, and 11 A.M. until the 9:15 P.M. fireworks display on Sunday. Dogs can stay for the "oohs" and the "aahs," but fireworks are far too noisy for most hounds.

Buffalo Grove Days is held at the Buffalo Grove Clayton Municipal Campus and at Emerich Park and Emerich Park East, Lake-Cook Road at Raupp Boulevard. Parking is free at nearby lots and throughout town. Free shuttles are provided. Admission to Buffalo Grove Days is free; call (847) 459-2500.

Deerfield

Parks

The village board recently turned down a request from some residents to set aside times when dogs can be allowed to run through parks off-leash. At least the idea was considered. The Park District did decide to create an off-leash area in the newly renovated Jaycee Memorial Park. This is a step in the right direction. Picking up after your pooch is the law here, too. Deerfield remains relatively dog friendly, and you have a herd of parks from which to choose.

The parks are open from dawn to dusk (lit facilities are open until supervised activities end); call (847) 945-0650.

BRIARWOOD PARK AND BRIARWOOD NATURE AREA //   This old wooded area was never developed. When the Park District took it over, officials were determined to maintain its natural state. Wood-chip walkways weave through the nature area, which is especially brilliant in the fall. Space is too limited for serious cross-country skiing, but you can ice-skate in the park. And dogs are sometimes seen dancing on the ice.

Briarwood Park and Briarwood Nature Area are bounded by Green Briar and Eastwood Roads, accessed off Lake-Cook Road. (847) 945-0650.

BRICKYARDS PARK / ½ With 13 acres, there's plenty of green space in this heavily used park. The soccer activities attract the soccer moms, soccer dads, and soccer dogs. This is also a popular park for picnickers, with a sheltered area and grills.

Brickyards Park is at Pfingsten Road and Kates Avenue. (847) 945-0650.

CLAVEY PARK / The four baseball diamonds and the soccer fields hold appeal as potential running space, but we don't recommend allowing dogs to run with the leash off. For one thing, it's the local law to keep the leash on. For another, the park is near the Tri-State Tollway. Freedom just isn't worth the risk. In fact, dogs with questionable off-leash skills should avoid this area altogether; should an owner mistakenly drop the leash, the result could be a disaster.

During the week, the park is packed with students from adjacent Caruso Middle School. On weekends, when there isn't a high school game, you and your dog are likely to have the joint all to yourselves.

When your pooch gets parched, seek out the drinking fountain inside an old pickle barrel: it's just the right height for a midsize dog to stand on its hind legs and slurp.

Clavey Park is at 1800 Montgomery Road, three blocks west of Wilmot Road. (847) 945-0650.

DEERSPRING PARK // ½ The cat here doesn't interest dogs: it's a life-size lion in the center of the playground. The array of fall colors happened to be in peak season on our October visit, and the display was striking in the park's forest. If there's a trail in this wooded area—as I was told there is—it's well concealed; even Lucy and Chaser couldn't unearth it. Perhaps it was hiding under fallen leaves. Even left to their own devices, for stalwart hikers, this walk in the woods is a breeze. In the winter, folks tramp through these woods for solitude and to enjoy the natural beauty. You'd hardly know you're only a bone's throw away from noisy Deerfield Road.

Just out of the forest is a gazebo, and nearby are sand volleyball and tennis courts. A community swimming pool is also located at this park. (No dogs are allowed in the pool area.)

Deerspring Park is bounded by Lions Drive, Margate Terrace, and Deerfield Road. (847) 945-0650.

JAMES MITCHELL PARK / ½   Frisbee and fetch are the games of choice here, and the large grassy area behind Saint Gregory's Episcopal Church is optimal for both activities. The scenic display of fall colors is also noteworthy, but there aren't many other canine amenities here. Dogs aren't allowed in the neighborhood pool.

James Mitchell Park is at Hazel Avenue and Deerfield Road, one-half block east of Wilmot Road. (847) 945-0650.

JAYCEE MEMORIAL PARK (RATING PENDING)   Exciting news: this nine-acre park was under construction at publication time, but a fenced-in off-leash doggie exercise area is imminent. This new facility will no doubt ultimately rank three or four bones. It will include canine-friendly drinking fountains, an obstacle-course play area for dogs, a shelter with picnic tables (where table scraps will be high on the list for puppy picnics), a dog-bag dispenser, and bathrooms. Renovations should be completed by the summer of 2001. Community support is strong for this new dog-friendly area, and the Park District anticipates a lot of happy dogs (and people). The park is keeping the existing playground and is creating a path system that will wind through the grounds.

Jaycee Memorial Park is at 1050 Wilmot Road, just north of Hazel Avenue and south of Garand Road. (847) 945-0650.

JEWETT PARK //   Since this park is situated just east of the commuter train tracks, rush hour here is weekdays from 5:30 P.M. to 6:30 P.M. Let's set the scene: Moms and dads converge here to wait for their spouses. Kids and doggies get really bored waiting at the train tracks, so they run to the park. For kids, the playground is great fun. For dogs, terrifying squirrels is the sport of choice. But these squirrels aren't sitting ducks. Regular visitors note that resident squirrels somehow realize that 5:30 is rolling around, and they know better than to come down from the trees.

"Max (a four-year-old black Labrador retriever) and I have been here since 4 P.M., and there were dozens of squirrels to chase," says Roberta Susquin. "Then at 5:30, they disappear into the trees. It's like they're wearing a watch. The only squirrels on the ground are either newcomers from other parks who don't know better or really young squirrels who are still learning."

No doubt the abundant trees encourage squirrel life. There are two baseball fields where dogs can run. Warning: Don't let them run too far off-leash—the police station sits just east of the park. The Deerfield Public Library is also nearby, and so is a community complex.

The park entrance is at 836 Jewett Park Drive, near Hazel Drive and Park Avenue, just north of Deerfield Road. (847) 945-0650.

JOHN BLUMBERG PARK *(worth a sniff)*   A small lot with nothing more than playground equipment; it primarily serves the immediate neighborhood.

John Blumberg Park is at North Avenue and Portage Path. (847) 945-0650.

KELLER PARK ½/   The park comprises six acres of flat green space and a children's play area. A good place for local canines to run, but it's not much of a destination.

Keller Park is bordered by the west branch of the Chicago River (no swimming is allowed, and access is cut off by a fence) at 319 Pine Street. (847) 945-0650.

KIPLING PARK /   This park is adjacent to Kipling School, home for several annual events, including a Halloween fair and pumpkin sale. However, the events are usually held inside the school, where no dogs are allowed. There's a baseball diamond and a children's play area.

Kipling Park is at 517 Deerfield Road at Kipling Place. (847) 945-0650.

MAPLEWOOD PARK //   As we pulled into a parking spot, Lucy begged to leap out of the car. Once on the ground, she uncharacteristically strained to the end of her leash, yelping all the way, refusing to heel. For some reason, she really wanted to meet an oncoming hunk of a Labrador retriever. I had visions of being dragged through the park, just like Jeff Daniels in *101 Dalmatians*.

I didn't have much choice as little Lucy led me to this George Clooney of the canine world. Lucy usually sticks her nose up at male dogs, but she was clearly smitten with this one.

At least, so it seemed. The dogs met, and Lucy acted odd—even for her. She squealed, rolled over on her back, and proceeded to cry. Beau, the Lab, wasn't impressed by this bizarre routine. My wife, Robin, swears that Beau rolled his eyes in disgust as he promptly walked away.

A bike path encircles the park and exits into a subdivision where Beau probably lives. This is a major destination for neighborhood kids, who frolic on the colorful play lot equipment. Lucy's squeals were so intense that the dozen or so kids in the play area turned to look, probably expecting to see some sort of dogfight.

Despite the fact that Beau had walked off, Lucy was still putting on a show, even without an audience. Chaser was off sniffing, pretending she didn't know crazy Lucy.

There's a vintage-style gazebo that can be dangerous while a ball game is in progress. For some reason, it's located just outside fair territory near third base. We understand that one dog and owner were lazing in the gazebo, minding their own business. Out of the blue, a pull hitter lined a foul ball right into the gazebo, plunking the dog in the derriere. No injury resulted, except to the dog's pride.

Maplewood Park is at Hazel Avenue at Clay Court and Alder Court, one block north of Deerfield Road. (847) 945-0650.

PINE STREET PARK / A passive park for retiring dogs and folks who prefer to sit and rest. There are lots of benches for just this purpose. The benches were probably put there for people, but I witnessed a 65-pound weimaraner sitting on a bench with his elderly owner. A small patch here is used for ice-skating when weather permits.

Pine Street Park is at Pine Street and Hackberry Road, just south of Deerfield Road, west of Waukegan Road and east of Wilmot Road. (847) 945-0650.

SOUTH PARK ½/ Children are the name of the game at this park because it's located near an elementary school. There are two playgrounds, one on each side of the school. There is also a baseball diamond. Don't come here if your dog doesn't like kids.

South Park is at 1421 Hackberry Road, just south of Deerfield Road, west of Waukegan Road and east of Wilmot Road. (847) 945-0650.

WOODLAND PARK / This lovely but diminutive wooded area is located next to the Riverside Developmental Services Center for Enriched Living. It offers a scenic view of fall colors but little more than that aside from baseball fields to run in. Chaser and Lucy were totally unimpressed with the fall display. Of course, that can be explained pretty easily—dogs don't see in color.

Woodland Park is on School Street, just off Wilmot Road. (847) 945-0650.

Farmer's Market

Deerfield Farmer's Market Dogs are allowed at the Deerfield Farmers Market, which is open from 7 A.M. to 12:30 P.M. Saturdays, late June through mid-October, at the commuter parking lot, Deerfield Road at Robert York Avenue. Do be sure to keep the dogs away from the fruit. Apparently, one dog had the audacity to lick an apple, which prompted several complaints. Fresh flowers, honey, and homemade preserves are also purveyed. There's no admission charge. Call (847) 945-5000.

Festival

Deerfield Family Days Festivities begin at the football field at Deerfield High School (1959 N. Waukegan Road) at 4:30 P.M. on July 3. Within a couple of hours, the field gets jammed with picnickers, who bring their own goodies or buy them from vendors. Bands play, and children's entertainment keeps the little ones busy. Just dodging the people and picking up food scraps keeps the dogs busy. Many dogs will want to leave by sunset because that's when the noisy fireworks begin.

The fest continues on July 4 at about 8 A.M. with a 10K run/5K walk from Walden School, 630 Essex Court. Aerobically conditioned dogs are welcome to join in. The reward for people who complete the race is a pancake breakfast (owners have to take along food for pooches). Dogs won't have much time to shower and get spruced up for the annual Family Days Dog Show, which is at 10 A.M. at Jewett Park, 836 Jewett Park Drive, off Hazel Road. Dogs compete for ribbons in creative categories such as "Longest Nose" (Chaser would have won this honor), "Most Obedient," "Best Trick," and "Longest Tail."

After the winners snatch up their ribbons, they can participate in the annual Family Days Parade. You'll have to walk to Deerspring Pool, 200 Deerfield Road, where the parade kicks off at noon. The parade winds up back at Jewett Park. By that time, a carnival will have begun in the park. This includes a petting zoo, children's games, pony rides, and 85 vendors selling arts and crafts. By late afternoon, everyone is dog-tired, and the party ends. Call (847) 564-4600, ext. 236.

Place to Stay

Marriott Suites Deerfield Dogs of any size are welcome, but I am told, "no elephants!" OK. That's a pretty easy rule to abide by. If you stay three nights or less, there is a nonrefundable charge of $50. If you stay longer than three nights, that charge goes up to $100. Rates are $74 to $186. Two Parkway North; (847) 405-9666.

Fox Lake

Park

Dogs are not allowed in the municipal parks, but they are permitted in Grant Woods Forest Preserve, a Lake County Forest Preserve facility. Dogs here must be on a leash and must stick to the trails. Owners are required to pick up.

GRANT WOODS FOREST PRESERVE (LAKE COUNTY FOREST PRESERVE) /// Confronting a whopping 974 acres and six miles of trails, you can get lost in this

place. In fact, Robin and I nearly did. We blamed it on the dogs. The dogs, however, still hold us responsible.

As big as it is, this preserve can nevertheless get congested with snowmobile traffic in the winter. While dogs aren't allowed on snowmobiles, they're given equal access to the trail system. The setting is beautiful, particularly when the ponds are frozen.

It's a shame dogs aren't allowed in the water in the summer. The big catch in Rubber Duck Pond is catfish. From the pond's outline on a park map, and with some imagination, you can see how this body of water got its name.

The hiking in this preserve varies—sometimes you'll pass through even prairie, other times muddy marshlands, and in still other places, rolling hills will test the old cardiovascular system. Naturally, Lucy and Chaser were quite adept at finding those mucky places, and their white underbellies turned the color of local soil.

The Lake County Forest Preserve police enforce the rule about dogs being on-leash, but they're even more concerned that your dog doesn't eat the plant life. Many of the indigenous plants are rare or endangered. For example, Lake County's only Kentucky coffee trees grow here. So far, no dog has been arrested for chowing down on native plants. With Lucy's propensity to taste-test flora, we were worried.

On early spring mornings or following rain showers, hearing the chorus of frogs makes dogs bark with excitement. Several frog species reside here, as do lots of mammals, including skunks, squirrels, raccoon, foxes, and deer. Then again, with a barking dog on-leash, you aren't likely to see much of them.

The original inhabitants of this space, the Pottawatomie Indians, enjoyed more wildlife. Though once-native inhabitants such as wolves and bears are long gone, there are reports of resident coyotes.

Grant Woods Forest Preserve is open from 6:30 A.M. to sunset. Take Fairfield Avenue to Illinois Route 132 (Grand Avenue), and head west to the preserve entrance, which is east of Illinois Route 59. There's another entrance at Monaville Road just west of Fairfield Road. There's trail access (without parking) off Fairfield Road just south of Illinois Route 132 (Grand Avenue). (847) 367-6640.

Festival

Fireman's Festival It's not just for dalmatians. All pups are welcome as long as they enjoy crowds. Apparently, several unsocialized dogs have created havoc at the festival in past years. Then again, the canine mayhem is nothing compared with that caused by village officials, local merchants, and volunteer firefighters participating in water fights. There are children's games and rides; all cost $1 to $2, with proceeds benefiting the fire department. There's no admission fee. The festival is held from 10 A.M. to 6 P.M. at Fire Station #2, 306 Washington Street, on the third Sunday in July; (847) 587-3312.

Gurnee

Doggy Doing

Six Flags Great America Pets are not allowed inside the theme park unless they happen to be cartoon characters, but non-toon pets can be kenneled at Pet Pourri Kennel just outside the front entrance. Staffers—who greet patrons with the appropriate question, "What's up, Doc?"—will look after Fido. Between roller-coaster rides on The Viper, you're welcome to return to walk your dog and find your stomach. The staff will serve your pooch food and water, but you must provide the kibble and the bowl. Exercising the dog is also your responsibility.

Dogs share living space with some interesting neighbors. One typical summer week, the kennel staff looked after about a dozen dogs, two cats, a bird, an aged goat (I'm serious), and two goldfish. The cost is $3 per day, per pet. No reservations are required.

Six Flags is open weekends from the end of April through the end of October and daily from mid-May to the end of August. Call ahead to check for special days on which the park is closed. Hours may vary; park admission is $42.99 for adults, $21.49 for children 48 inches and under, and free for children under age two. Call (847) 249-2133.

Place to Stay

El Rancho Motel This hotel operates under a 25-pound-and-under rule for most dogs. Exceptions are made for guests affiliated with large groups visiting for a dog show. Arrangements need to be made in advance and are subject to approval by the management. Canines who don't model in dog shows and their humans get charged a $100 refundable deposit, but for show dogs there is generally no deposit necessary. The VIPs (very important pooches) always get star treatment! Rates are $40 to $58. 36355 N. Highway 41; (847) 623-5237.

Highland Park

Parks and Beaches

Highland Park is a 50-50 proposition. Two beaches here allow dogs, and two don't. Rosewood Beach and Park Avenue Beach forbid dogs, and the rule is enforced. Rosewood is often too packed with sunbathers to comfortably welcome canines anyhow, and Park Avenue is often too congested with boaters for dogs to safely enter.

However, Moraine Beach and Ravine Drive Beach in Millard Park both allow dogs on-leash. The only hitch is where to put the car. The beach parking lots are restricted to cars displaying Highland Park vehicle stickers or a special permit, which will set you back $70.

Don't try to get away with littering the front window with leaf debris as I did. Unlike the Chicago police, who wouldn't bother getting out from their own cars to remove the leaves, these officers would take a Hoover vacuum to the window if they had to. Luckily, just as the ink was about to hit the ticket pad, Chaser offered a bark, as if to say, "Hold it!" We ran full speed to intercept the kindly officer. Out of breath from running, I offered an excuse that he had never heard before. Apparently, working on a dog book is a new one. He just began to laugh.

Chaser was far more responsible for the con job, cozying up to the officer with those big sad brown eyes. He let me off with a warning. "You have a sweet dog here. Now, never park here again without an appropriate vehicle sticker!"

In any case, it's only a few blocks to the beach if you park west of Forest Avenue to visit Ravine Drive Beach or west of Sheridan Road for Moraine Beach.

Overall, Highland Park is quite dog friendly. There's a movement to develop an exclusive park and/or beach for dogs. Meanwhile, any dogs in the public parks must be on a leash. The municipal parks are open from sunrise to sunset, and beaches are open from 8 A.M. to sunset. Call (847) 831-3810. The single undeveloped Lake County Forest Preserve space in Highland Park is Berkley Prairie.

ARTHUR OLSON PARK //   A particularly popular spot for dog owners, who like the idea that the running space in this long and narrow three-acre park is on the opposite end of the children's play area. In other words, the dogs run on one side, and kids play on the other. However, soccer teams often rule that running area.

It's amazing how many dogs come out to watch the soccer games. They're all on leashes. It's not only a matter of adhering to the leash law—you'd hardly want dogs chasing after the soccer ball.

Well, you'd hardly want that—but that's exactly what Lucy did. Robin and I made the mistake of removing her leash to allow her to cavort with a four-month-old puppy on the sidelines. Of course, the moment we turned our backs, Lucy darted after the soccer ball. She barked and ran right through the game. We screamed, "Lucy, come!" She bolted again, right into the middle of the play, jumped over the ball, and landed in perfect recall position. Oddly, no one paid attention—not even the referee.

A half-mile jogging trail goes through the park. Do the jogging trail 52 times, and you've run a marathon and really exhausted your dog. We're told that one person actually trained for a marathon this way. Happily, he didn't do it with a dog.

Arthur Olson Park is on Ridge Road, a quarter mile south of West Park Avenue, just north of Partridge Lane. It is open from sunrise to sunset. (847) 831-3810.

BERKLEY PRAIRIE FOREST PRESERVE / ½ At this Lake County Forest Preserve space left to grow as a real prairie, no paths for people or dogs intrude. Robin and I learned the hard way what that means: wear long pants. The three- to four-foot-high innocuous-looking prairie grass can scratch your legs. There's no water fountain, and there are no bathroom facilities. There aren't many parking spaces, either; you just sort of informally pull up on Ridge Road, near Emerald Wood Lane, one-half mile north of Deerfield Road. The park is open from sunrise to sunset. (847) 367-3675.

BROWN PARK / ½ After dropping off the spouse at the Metra commuter station, the wife or husband may park the car and walk through the adjacent park while holding the leash with one hand and pushing a baby carriage with the other. This small park features a pair of tennis courts and a kids' play area.

Brown Park is at Roger Williams and Burton Avenues. It is open from sunrise to sunset. (847) 831-3810.

CENTRAL PARK // With a dazzling display of fall colors overlooking Lake Michigan, this is a Kodak spot. No wonder it's a popular picnic destination. The playground will keep the kids engaged. There's one notable shortcoming: parking is by permit only. You'll have to park several blocks west and walk in from downtown Highland Park. Dogs aren't allowed on the steep wooden stairs that lead down to Park Avenue Beach. Should you miss the unmistakable No Dogs Allowed sign, a lifeguard, Park District worker, or police officer will toss Fido out in a second, and perhaps slap you with a fine.

Central Park is bounded by Central and Park Avenues and the lakefront. The park is open from sunrise to sunset. (847) 831-3810.

CLOVERDALE PARK //   This rectangular plot holds lots of options for jocks, including basketball, soccer, and baseball. This is a good park for a game of fetch.

Cloverdale Park is at Cloverdale Avenue between Berkley Street and Park Avenue West, with additional pedestrian access to nearby residents off Eastwood Street. It is open from sunrise to sunset. (847) 831-3810.

DANNY CUNNIFF PARK //½   It's rush hour when the baggy-pants-clad in-line skaters converge here after school and on weekends. Many take the family dog along.

If it's North Shore trendy, this is a park in which to see it. Cross-country skiing and Frisbee golf are extremely hot. Dogs may participate in both sports in one way or another. While playing a game of Frisbee golf, one player tossed a regular Frisbee to his dog while he awaited his turn.

Not only are dogs and people doing the trendy sort of thing, but they're dressing for it, too. A contemporary fashion statement is fleece in bright and bold colors. That holds true for dogs; one cockapoo wore a stylish green, orange, and teal fleece vest. The owner said, "If you can feel the wind off the lake, so can the dog. I want to protect little Oprah from the wind."

In Highland Park and nearby Lake Forest, we met three dogs named after the queen of daytime TV (Oprah Winfrey) and three dogs named after British royalty—two named Diana (before her tragic death) and one called Fergie (after Sarah Ferguson).

The park also has lots of tennis courts, baseball diamonds, and soccer fields.

The pond is mostly decorative. While dogs are allowed, few pooches dive into the stagnant water.

Danny Cunniff Park is at Trailway Drive just north of Illinois Route 22 (Half Day Road), one-quarter mile east of Skokie Highway. It is open from sunrise to sunset. (847) 831-3810.

DEVONSHIRE PARK ½/   Neighborhood kids flock to the large playground. A picnic area adds to the appeal of this tiny neighborhood park.

Devonshire Park is at Devonshire Road just west of Ridge and south of Deerfield Roads. Open sunrise to sunset. (847) 831-3810.

HIGHMOOR PRESERVE ½/   Polish your binoculars and make the most of the excellent bird watching along the wood-chip trails in this 11-acre reserve. Deer are also denizens. Not to mention rabbits: locals dub this place "Rabbit Central." As recently as a couple of years ago, a few bunnies inhabited the preserve. Today it seems they're everywhere. It's funny how that happens. Sighting one hopping around isn't much of a challenge for a pooch. Keep in mind that Highland Park officially frowns on dogs' actually catching and doing harm to a member of the rabbit population.

Highmoor Preserve is on Ridge Road south of Illinois Route 22 (Half Day Road) and north of Park Avenue West. It is open from sunrise to sunset. (847) 831-3810.

JENS JENSEN PARK / Designed to illustrate the style of the eponymous landscape architect, the layout is very interesting. However, after they get a sniff, there's nothing else for dogs to do. On a summer afternoon, all five picnic benches were filled with nearby office workers and seniors who meet here for a sunny lunch.

Jens Jensen Park is at Roger Williams Avenue at St. Johns Place. It is open from sunrise to sunset. (847) 831-3810.

KENNEDY PARK / Named for the former president, this park is mostly soccer fields—running space is the only attribute. According to local officials, no member of the Kennedy clan—frequent visitors to the Chicago area—has ever seen the park. And perhaps more relevant is the fact that none of the Kennedy clan dogs has lifted a leg here.

Kennedy Park is on Clavey Road, east of the Edens Expressway and just west of Green Bay Road. It is open from sunrise to sunset. (847) 831-3810.

LARRY FINK MEMORIAL PARK /// This 71-acre facility is a favorite for lots of dogs, including Fergie, a Gordon setter who belongs to Connie Newport, director of Parks and Recreation in Highland Park.

Fergie has the same routine 365 days a year. The weather doesn't matter much to Fergie. Every morning, before the crack of dawn, she wakes up Connie and her husband, Dan. The couple have a 20-second debate on who will take the dog out. The loser gets into the car with Fergie, who barks with anticipation for the entire five-minute ride to Fink Memorial Park. Connie or Dan does the one-mile run through the park with Fergie. The pond filled with geese at the end of the run is the high point. Fergie always has plenty of energy to spare as she bounds into the water. To date, she still hasn't caught any geese.

"It's a good thing," says Newport. "Those geese are pretty tough. I don't think Fergie would know what to do."

However, when it comes to terrifying fowl, she's an expert. She's so good that the Village has deputized Fergie and two other local dogs as "Official Goose Chasers."

The picturesque pond is located near the north branch of the Chicago River, which also runs through this park. Even those who love sleeping late might change their minds after an early-morning run in this setting. Early in the morning, you might catch sight of various migrating birds, screech and great horned owls, a rabbit or two, or a passing deer. However, since a resident coyote also may be up and around, small dogs should be kept on a leash for their own safety in the wee hours.

Fink Memorial Park, which is named for a Highland Park resident killed in a 1978 airplane crash, also has lots of places to picnic.

Dogs are not allowed inside the tennis complex.

Fink Memorial Park is on Clavey Road at Deer Creek Parkway, just east of the Edens Expressway and west of Green Bay Road. It is open from sunrise to sunset. (847) 831-3810.

LEONARDI PARK / ½   This park is named after a local family. The beauty of the fall colors in this undeveloped three-acre wooded area, featuring mostly oak trees, is truly breathtaking. There are no trails, but the hiking is still easy going.

Leonardi Park is at the end of Grange Avenue, just north of Park Avenue West. The park is open from sunrise to sunset. (847) 831-3810.

LINCOLN PARK ½/   Dogs are eschewed during school hours. (The park is named for Lincoln Elementary School, which is next door.) However, the handicapped-accessible play lot and the preschool play area are favorite destinations for families with little ones. It should be mandatory that puppies visit a school and park just like this one for socialization to young children. You'll find a bicycle path and a couple of baseball fields here, too.

Lincoln Park is at 711 Lincoln Avenue West, near Green Bay Road. It is open from sunrise to sunset. (847) 831-3810.

MAY T. WATTS NATURE PARK ½/   Named for a naturalist who once resided in the area, this park encompasses two acres along a wood-chip trail. Kids from adjacent Ravinia Elementary School teamed up with their teachers and naturalists to design the park. Plants are identified, and several native species have been reintroduced. Aside from the squirrel and rabbit population, there aren't many mammals. However, bees are in abundance. The park also presents enough enticing smells to satisfy any canine nose. Unfortunately, dogs are discouraged from visiting while school is in session.

May T. Watts Nature Park is on Roger Williams Avenue at Baldwin Road. It is open from sunrise to sunset. (847) 831-3810.

MEMORIAL PARK //   This is an open grassy area, with lots of large trees for refreshing shade on a hot day. There is a garden and a sculpture of a World

War II soldier in the park, which some dogs like to sniff. The local historical society presents periodic afternoon concerts at the bandstand. Dogs are welcome to attend. This park is especially utilized by seniors and their dogs, who come to hear the music, stroll through the gardens, or just sit in the sun. Memorial Park is at Prospect and Linden Avenues. It is open from sunrise to sunset. (847) 831-3810.

MILLARD PARK/RAVINE DRIVE BEACH /// ½   Professional pet photographers often light upon this setting for their shoots. Millard Park is on a bluff at the former site of a turn-of-the-century estate. The house is long gone, but the stone wall surrounding the garden still stands. Today that garden overflows with a brilliant bevy of flowers. For a dramatic backdrop, the surf crashes below. Pet photographers and their subjects aren't the only visitors who know how to compose themselves: entire wedding parties assemble here for the obligatory family pictures.

The only cloud on the horizon is getting here. There's parking for only about eight vehicles, so needless to say, the spots go like hotcakes. Besides, to park here, you must have an appropriate vehicle sticker. Otherwise, the nearest visitor parking is in downtown Highland Park. There's on-street parking in town, and parking is often available at the train station, particularly on weekends. The one-mile jaunt from town to Millard Park and Ravine Drive Beach is a pleasure trip in itself.

Aside from its scenic quality, Millard Park offers no other canine amenities. A stone-and-wood path leads down to the beach. Leashed dogs are allowed on the beach; however, the Park District understands the difficulty and even potential danger of throwing a doggy toy into the water and expecting the dog to retrieve it while wearing a leash. If you're holding on tightly to the leash, a large dog can pull you under. A leash could also become tangled, strangling the dog.

Dog owners who really want to frolic with the pups off a leash are advised to arrive very early, before the beaches officially open at 10 A.M. This beach gets pretty crowded during prime time. Threading your way around the sun worshipers with a little Maltese is tricky enough; doing the same with an English setter is nearly impossible. Fortunately, this half-mile stretch of beach—one of the longest in the Chicago vicinity—generally offers enough space for dog owners to carve out their own little niche. The dogs usually position themselves at the north corner.

Sometimes only strong-swimmin' hounds are qualified to hit the waves. Owners must keep a sharp eye on their dogs when winds are blowing from the north or the east, as the wave action can be raucous.

Poisonous Plants

Lots of plants are poisonous. If you note your pooch vomiting plant material, be observant. If the dog continues to vomit, shows signs of respiratory distress, acts as if it's in a drunken stupor, or has diarrhea, call your vet.

Here's a Top 12 list of toxic plants found around the Chicago area, provided by veterinary toxicologist Dr. Michael Knight of the ASPCA National Animal Poison Control Center. If you know for sure your pooch has eaten any of the following plants, call your vet.

- Amaryllis
- Azalea
- Bittersweet
- Caladium
- Castor bean
- Cycad (sago palm)
- Dumbcane
- Foxglove
- Japanese (show) lily
- Lily of the valley
- Philodendron
- Rhododendron

If you suspect that your dog has eaten a dangerous chemical or plant, you can call the ASPCA National Animal Poison Control Center 24-hour hot line, (888) 426-4435. The cost is $30 per case; follow-up calls are free. Credit card line only. Or call (900) 680-0000. The cost is $20 for the first five minutes and $2.95 for each additional minute. There's a $20 minimum.

Millard Park and Ravine Drive Beach are located at the end of Ravine Drive, east of Forest Avenue and south of Central Avenue. The beach is open from 10 A.M. to sunset. The park is open from sunrise to sunset. (847) 831-3810.

MOONEY PARK ½/ There are a couple of acres of open green space, along with a basketball court and a children's play area. But there's no real attraction other than convenience for those who happen to live in the neighborhood.

Mooney Park is on Ridge Road, one block north of Deerfield Road. It is open from sunrise to sunset. (847) 831-3810.

MORAINE PARK AND BEACH /// ½   The park is 12 acres of green space high on a bluff three flights up from the beach. Unfortunately, there's no elevator. After trekking down the steep walk and ascending only 10 minutes later to retrieve a towel from the car, then hiking back down, and then returning in another 10 minutes to use the bathroom facilities, we can guarantee that the walk would tucker out the most hyper puppy as well as Richard Simmons. Chaser and I were exhausted. People or dogs with physical impairments will have difficulty.

The reward for the dogs after the long descent is an enclosed off-leash beach where they can play, swim, and generally just be dogs. However, dogs need an ID to use this exclusive beach. Humans must escort their dogs to the Walter Heller Nature Center for registration before heading down to the sand. After providing a rabies vaccine number and displaying a valid city tag, Fido gets his picture taken for his official photo ID card. The Park District discourages nonresidents from bringing their dogs here to play, as is reflected in the fee schedule. The price for Highland Park residents is $35 for an annual pass; nonresidents must part with a hefty $250 for the same privilege.

Moraine Park and Beach are at Sheridan and Moraine Roads, just north of Park Avenue. The park is open from sunrise to sunset. The beach is open from 8 A.M. to sunset. (847) 831-3810. Walter Heller Nature Center is at 636 Ridge Road. (847) 433-6901.

OLD ELM PARK / ½   This six-acre park is mostly running space over baseball fields. Migrating songbirds are partial to this setting. It's as if they know they're on Audubon Place. And, of course, most dogs are partial to watching the birds.

Old Elm Park is at Krenn Avenue just south of Old Elm Road at Audubon Place. It is open from sunrise to sunset. (847) 831-3810.

PORT CLINTON PARK // ½   A steep ravine cuts the park in two. Neighborhood dogs are avid fans of this secret running place—as are safety-conscious owners. Only the most determined greyhound could make its way up the sheer banks of the ravine.

People who don't own dogs come just to see the canine show. Again, we stress that technically dogs are supposed to be leashed, but so far, Highland Park officials look the other way at locations such as this. After all, this natural ravine seems built for dog running. As long as the dogs are well behaved and stay away from others using the park, we're told that officials will continue to ignore the infraction. However, if owners begin to get sloppy—not picking up after their dogs or annoying dogless citizens—the privilege will be withdrawn.

Port Clinton Park is bounded by St. Johns Avenue, Port Clinton Road, and Bloom Street. It is open from sunrise to sunset. (847) 831-3810.

SHERWOOD PARK /   Here we have a small neighborhood park located near where lots of young families reside. Little kids play baseball or give the playground equipment a workout while the parents usually sit off to the side with the family dog.

Sherwood Park is at Arbor Avenue South of Midland Avenue. It is open from sunrise to sunset. (847) 831-3810.

SLEEPY HOLLOW //   A great little site with an open green area surrounded by woods. This is a very popular place for early-morning canine exercise sessions. Local residents don't complain, because owners have been considerate and because the 14-acre park is somewhat isolated. You and the dog can also venture into the wooded area.

The entrance to Sleepy Hollow Park is on Trailway Drive, near Idelwood Lane, north of Illinois Route 22 (Half Day Road). Open sunrise to sunset. (847) 831-3810.

SUNSET WOODS PARK/SHEAHAN WOODS // ½   These two parks interconnect; it's difficult to tell where one ends and the other begins.

There are five wonderful themed play areas, including a wooden fort, a space ship complex, a builder's village, and a fenced-in tot lot. This park attracts caboodles of kids. Once she spotted us, one little girl made a mad dash for us from the playground, running toward Lucy as if Lucy were her dog. She arrived to deliver a 10-minute speech. Ariel, who we guess was about seven years old, never came up for air. She petted Lucy, rambled something about her own dog and why it wasn't in the park that day, a few words about the playground, and something about her school, and then she ran off at full speed while reciting something else about her dog.

Tall trees stand at attention throughout the Sheahan Woods side of the park, and on this day, they were cloaked in vibrant fall colors. Since this is not an especially dense forest, it's fun to zigzag between the trees with the dogs in a game of "catch me if you can."

With only one goalpost, the football field is something of a curiosity. There are also baseball diamonds and tennis courts.

Sunset Woods Park is at Central Street, Park Avenue West, Sunset Drive, and Hickory Street. Parking is off of Sunset. The park is open from sunrise to sunset. (847) 831-3810.

WEST RIDGE PARK AND CENTER ✓ ½   A half-mile asphalt trail surrounds the lit baseball fields. This park is especially popular for families, who take maximum advantage of the village recreation center next door. Park offices are also in this building. This is where Fergie, the goose-chasing deputy dog, often spends off-hours.

West Ridge Park and Center is at 636 Ridge Road, north of Clavey Road and south of Deerfield Road. It is open from sunrise to sunset. (847) 831-3810.

Doggy Doings

Pet and Bicycle Parade   The big Highland Park July Fourth Parade begins with this long-standing parade within a parade. It kicks off at 9:45 A.M. at St. Johns Place at Central Street and continues west on Central to Green Bay Road, where it ends at Sunset Woods Park at Sunset Drive. Usually about 250 kids and 75 pets participate. Some of the pets wear red, white, and blue streamers. One year a Great Dane was dressed as Uncle Sam, and the resemblance was striking. A picnic in Sunset Woods Park follows the parade. Call (847) 432-0284.

Summer Concert Series   Pets are welcome to meet at the center of town for the summer concerts. Performances are almost always on Thursdays from the first Thursday in June through the last Thursday in August. They start at 7 P.M. The bands play at Port Clinton Square, 600 Central Avenue, between First and Second Streets.

Some people take their own folding chairs, but most use the ones provided by the town of Highland Park. There are also some wooden benches. Unfortunately, there's little grass for the dogs to lie on. While Chaser was content with concrete, some Highland Park dogs lolled on their own blankets. One blanket even had a picture of the dog embroidered on it. We offered Chaser a few dog treats as the jazz music played, while the dog with the fancy blanket tasted imported cheese. These free concerts certainly draw the upscale dogs. There is no admission charge. Call (847) 432-0800.

Festivals

Highland Park Block Party   Created to promote local restaurants, this food frenzy attracts at least a dozen of them. Daffy clowns provide entertainment for the youngsters, while lip-synching and moon-walking contests are reserved for the older kids. There's even a kids' trivia contest. One recent question: "What kind of dog appears as 'Wishbone' in the TV series?" (Answer: Jack Russell terrier.)

This fun block party has one fault: while pets (on-leash) are welcome, there are no canine activities.

Dogs will wish that the annoying and persistent sweet bees at this festival would buzz off. The block party is held from around mid-afternoon to 9 P.M. on a weekend afternoon in July or August (it's scheduled around events and other festivals going on in Chicago and nearby communities) at Port Clinton Square in downtown Highland Park on Central Avenue between First and Second Streets. There is no admission fee. Call (847) 432-0800.

Port Clinton Art Festival Nearly 300 adult artists and 50 youth competitors vie for the top prizes at this prestigious art show. It seems unfair that the panel of art critics, who determine the winners, doesn't include any dogs. After all, canines are the subjects of so much of the work—from watercolors to sculptures. I saw a hand-painted beagle light switch, which sold for $12, and a Saint Bernard–size sculpture entitled *Watch Dog* that sold for $25,000. Other dog art included a ceramic dog dressed as George Washington and clocks with all moving parts in the shapes of dog bones.

Food vendors are wedged between the art booths in downtown Highland Park along Central Avenue between First and Second Streets. The festival is usually held toward the end of August. Call (847) 432-0800.

Quick Bite

Michael's Chicago Style Red Hots People come here to carry out food specifically for their dogs. They order hot dogs, cheeseburgers, even stuffed spuds— just about anything on the menu—except the hot-dog-shape bubble gum. Owner Michael Hoffman points outs a picture of a golden retriever gulping ice cream and says, "We love both red hot dogs and four-legged hot dogs." Dogs can sit on the benches near the front door on Second Street or in the back patio. 1879 Second Street; (847) 432-3338.

Coffee Shop

Java Love Several blocks from the Ravinia concert center, this coffee shop is too far for mere humans to hear the musicians. However, the canines are probably picking up a good show. There are four tables, and every seat is usually filled. As testament to the shop's canine-friendly disposition, all four-legged customers are given biscuits. 723 St. Johns Avenue; (847) 266-0728.

Shopping

CD City Dogs are welcome at this canine-loving music store. Owner Steve Kessler expounded on a video release entitled *A Dog's World*. While watching the video, you can enter the world of a dog's mind and find out what the average household dog is thinking. Do you really want to know? This store is also one of the few that carry "Jingle Dogs" during the holiday season. Bob Collins of WGN Radio loved to play "Jingle Dogs" on his morning show, and the recording is hard to sniff out. 593 Elm Place; (847) 432-4344.

Higher Gear Usually people walk in with their dogs alongside, but you can also ride in, with the dog sitting in a basket on the handlebars or in a Burley Trailer (a little trailer that attaches to the rear of a bike). The staff can even provide advice on the best ways to bicycle with a dog. 1874 Sheridan Road; (847) 433-2453.

Kaehler's Luggage Dogs are welcome here. A manager told me, "We hate it when people tie up dogs outside. We prefer dogs tie up their owners and leave them outside." This store carries lots of luggage and leather goods for people. 654 Central Avenue; (847) 433-6500.

Highwood

Parks

This town is known for its voluminous restaurant row. While there's tons to eat, there aren't too many places to work off the calories, at least not with canine companionship. The village has two parks. Dogs on leashes are allowed if owners pick up. The parks are open from dawn to dusk; (847) 432-6633.

HIGHWOOD MEMORIAL PARK ½✔ Nothing more than two baseball diamonds facing one another. Together, they provide some open space. The baseball fields are mostly surrounded by a chain-link fence.

Highland Memorial Park is on Western Avenue at North Avenue. (847) 432-6633.

EVEREST PARK ½✔ A one-and-a-half-acre grassy area offers room to stretch canine legs but not enough space for an all-out run. This is the location for the annual Taste of Highwood. Unfortunately, four-legged gourmets can't chow down.

Everest Park is at Highwood Avenue, a half block west of Green Bay Road. (847) 432-6633.

Island Lake

Park

Dogs are allowed in parks if they're on a leash or under voice control. So, off-leash work is allowed, assuming your dog is obedient. There's only one catch: there's no village park in this suburb large enough to consider this option. With the modest exception of Village Hall Park, the so-called parks are either undeveloped swampy areas or tiny patches of grass that are barely worth a sniff. Dogs are not allowed to visit children's playgrounds or beaches.

One village official warns, "Please don't tell all your readers to come here with their dogs; we have enough to deal with already. We can't have the annual Easter egg hunt until we clean up the dog messes."

The parks are open from dawn to dusk; call (847) 526-8764.

VILLAGE HALL PARK /   The largest of Island Lake's parks, this three-acre facility adorns the municipal complex, next to village hall. Despite village officials peeking out their windows, owners refuse to pick up the doggy waste. And the same officials aren't happy about stepping in the stuff on their way to the office. There's a children's play lot here (where dogs are verboten) and three baseball fields.

Village Hall Park is at 3720 Greenleaf Avenue. (847) 526-8764.

Lake Bluff

Parks

Dogs may enter the parks, but only if they're on a leash and only if owners pick up. Several years ago, a contingent of residents petitioned to ban dogs from the parks. Their efforts failed, but an antidog sentiment lingers among some in the community.

Only resident dogs are allowed on beaches (except on Sunrise Beach during the July Fourth celebration or with a nonresident beach pass).

Parks are open from dawn until 9 P.M.; (847) 234-4150.

ARTESIAN PARK //   The underground spring-fed artesian lake dried up many years ago, and this place became a landfill. Today it's one of the most popular parks in the area, with several lit baseball diamonds and tennis courts.

Ice-skating is a popular winter activity here. But dogs aren't allowed on the rink or inside the warming house.

Across from Lake Bluff Junior High School, the park's bike path is used by in-line skaters, often with their dogs. However, we're told that the Village expects to pass an ordinance that will prohibit in-line skating in the parks.

Artesian Park is on Sheridan Place at Sheridan Road. (847) 234-4150.

BLAIR PARK / ½   There's lots to do here, but not if you happen to be a dog. Canines aren't allowed near the pool, the golf course, or the tennis courts. They can run on the soccer field when it's not being used for a game. This park gets so crowded with duffers and bathers that the parking lot overflows.

Located just north of Illinois Route 176 (Rockland Road) at Green Bay Road. (847) 234-4150.

MAWMAN PARK ///   Planted in a subdivision, this small park is primarily used by the locals. There's some space for baseball, soccer, and playing canine Frisbee.

Mawman Park is on Mawman Road and West Center Street. (847) 234-4150.

SUNRISE PARK AND BEACH // ½   Here's a park with perspective. From this bluff, the view of Lake Michigan's crashing waves is pretty impressive. In fact, about the only thing to do at this park is recline on a bench and meditate on the ebb and flow.

If you're motivated to take a walk down to the beach, however, you can conjure considerable canine activity. Dogs are allowed to run off-leash on the north end of Sunrise Beach, provided they obey a few rules, which are *very* strictly enforced. Be careful to stay in the designated area, marked by signs. Residents' dogs can play for free, as long as the owner has a beach pass with a dog sticker. Nonresident dogs and their owners pay $150 for the privilege and must also get a pass and a sticker. Passes can be obtained at the Administration Offices at Blair Park, located at 325 W. Washington.

Sunrise Park is located east of Illinois Route 176 (Rockland Road) at Sunrise Avenue. Sunrise Beach is at 1 E. Center Street, at the lake. The beach is open from sunrise to sunset. (847) 234-4150.

Doggy Doing

Summer Concert Series This series is free for dogs and their people. The concerts begin between 4 P.M. and 6 P.M. Sundays, from mid-June through August, at the Village Green, Scranton Avenue and Sheridan Road in downtown Lake Bluff.

The crowd favorite is reggae, but things get nearly as spirited for the country and western shows and the concert band performances. Typically people pack their own food. And there always seems to be an enterprising ice-cream salesman on the hottest days. Call (847) 234-4150.

Festival

July Fourth Festival An entire day of activities kicks off with a parade at 10 A.M. on July 4 at Scranton and Center Avenues. Dogs are given the green light to view the passing parade, which continues down Scranton west to Prospect Avenue, turns south to Sheridan Place at Sheridan Road, and then heads west into Artesian Park.

Lake Bluff is proud of the small-town spirit it retains year-round, which reaches its apex on July 4. On this day, Lake Bluff is sort of like Mayberry, and everyone wants to be here. Former residents who have moved to nearby suburbs make the sentimental journey for this annual event. Often, they come with their dogs.

When the parade winds down in Artesian Park, the carnival begins. There are no games for canines, but they are welcome to watch all the activities. Goldfish were once a popular prize at the carnival. That practice was discouraged when village officials began finding goldfish swimming in the nearby golf course following the carnival.

In the evening, the celebration turns into a giant picnic at Sunrise Beach (located near Sunrise Park, just east of Illinois Route 176 at Sunrise Avenue). It's the only day of the year on which nonresident dogs can walk the beach with impunity. Cheap thrills include live music and a dog-friendly fireworks display, which is to say that the fireworks are so far away that the booming isn't ear shattering. Lake Bluff is a fireworks parasite. Instead of sponsoring its own display, it steals first-rate views of the shows from Waukegan to the north and Lake Forest to the south. On clear nights, the crowds can share in the Evanston fireworks and even the Chicago fireworks. Call (847) 234-4150.

Lake Forest

Parks

You can lead a dog to water, but you can't let it dip its paws. Dogs are permitted in Forest Park, but they aren't allowed to visit the beach. In fact, nonresidents aren't allowed to park east of Sheridan Road. You'll have to park in downtown Lake Forest and walk about a mile to the park.

McCormick Nature Preserve doesn't permit canine guests. However, dogs on a leash can watch and sniff how the other half lives in this ritzy North Shore suburb. Owners don't bother with rudimentary plastic bags here. One owner was spied with a gold-plated pooper-scooper and another with a contraption that looked like a battery-operated vacuum cleaner. Welcome to Lake Forest. In this suburb, it's a challenge to distinguish the dog names from the people names. Robin and I met four Buffys; two were dogs, and two were people. We were also introduced to two Muffys—both were people.

Dogs must be on-leash and owners must pick up. The parks are open from dawn to dusk. For further information call (847) 234-2600.

DEERPATH COMMUNITY PLAYFIELD / Behind Deerpath Junior High School, this park is primarily used by students for after-school activities. Over the summer months when school is not in session, or when students aren't around, it's amazingly empty. Several baseball fields provide room for a basic workout, but that's about all she wrote.

Deerpath Community Playfield is at 400 Hastings Road at Deerpath Road, two blocks west of Green Bay Road. (847) 234-2600.

FOREST PARK // This narrow park is an excellent choice for picnicking. Many folks who work in downtown Lake Forest do just that. On sunny days, the noon parade can be seen walking from the business district. That's a far better choice than driving. There's a $50 fine for parking here without a Lake Forest sticker, and it's dutifully enforced.

Visitors can park downtown and walk east, passing all the ritzy homes on Deerpath Road. Stop in Triangle Park (see the subsequent entry) for a sniff and a quick drink. The water fountain is at terrier level. Continue walking for just short of a mile; sights include the campus of Lake Forest College and more aristocratic mansions. The maids' quarters here are larger than most single-family homes.

Forest Park's foliage is its crowning glory, yielding a view of Lake Michigan between the trees. However, dogs aren't allowed on the beach, and besides picnicking, there isn't much else in the park for dogs to sink their teeth into.

There really isn't much space even for a game of fetch, and somehow you get the feeling that other park-goers wouldn't appreciate a romping dog.

Your best bet is to depart the park and take a twisting route back to your car downtown. Wander the side streets and gaze at the humongous homes. With a mortgage like that, it's a wonder these people have enough left over to feed their dogs. On second thought, those who live here can afford to raise an entire kennel's worth.

Forest Park is at Lake and Deerpath Roads and Spring Lane. (847) 234-2600.

NORTHCROFT PARK // ½   Around back of the park building, a series of secluded soccer and baseball fields gives Fido a healthy amount of running room. For this reason, Northcroft is a favorite location for area canine enthusiasts.

What the hiking area lacks in size it more than makes up for in beauty—particularly after a snowfall or while the trees are changing color in October.

A bike path traverses the park, and there are tennis courts and a children's playground.

Northcroft Park is at 1365 S. Ridge Road, just south of Old Elm Road and north of Old Mill Road. (847) 234-2600.

PRAIRIE WOLF DOG EXERCISE AREA ////   The trip Janice and Luna took out to Lake Forest was like summer camp for Luna. Being a city dog, she is used to the confines of urban DFAs (dog-friendly areas), the largest area being about one acre. When they arrived at this 44-acre wonderland, both Luna and Janice were awed by the tall grass and meadowland that seemed to go on and on.

To use this area, residents of Lake County pay $25 for one dog, $5 for each additional dog. Nonresidents pay $50 for one dog and $10 for each additional dog. With your paid permit you receive up to two vehicle stickers and one Forest Preserve tag per dog. The permit is good from January 1 through December 31 and must be renewed annually. There's plenty of parking; just be sure your sticker is in sight. I was told that the police stringently enforce this policy and ticket often.

There are two entrances with wooden gates that lock closed for safety. Dog-bag dispensers are deployed near the entrances, and Janice was advised by a local to grab a bag, since these are the only dispensers in the preserve. The place is expansive, and you don't want to get out too far and realize you have nothing to pick up with. It appears that most people take good advantage of this free bag supply: the area was clean and free of dog poop.

Out at the parking area, there were no dogs in view, but within just a few minutes, Janice and Luna had become part of a friendly pack of seven or eight, and they all headed to the water together. Ten-month-old Riley, a red and white Irish setter, followed close to Janice, jumping and barking the whole way. She knew what he was really after: Luna's Kong toy. His owner instructed Janice not to give in. It seems Riley's standard operating procedure is to grab the toy, run away, and return without it. Dozens of Riley's toys are stashed out in the grass somewhere. One benefit of the hard-surfaced dog parks in the city is that you can always spot the scattered toys.

It's a 5- to 10-minute walk to the water, depending on how many mud puddles your dog runs through. The swimming area is gated, so that if your dog happens to get there before you do, she cannot jump in without a chaperone. The muddy pond pulls in a large canine crowd. In addition to the dogs they met on the way, they encountered two golden retrievers, three yellow Labs, two black Labs, and at least two dogs named Jake.

Luna followed the crowd and dived into the water. But once immersed, she realized this was not beach swimming. There is no gentle slope leading into the water, but rather a muddy bank that gets wet and slippery as the dogs run to and fro. Plus, the dogs can't touch bottom, so while Luna searched for a way to get back up on shore, she was forced to keep swimming. Poor Luna was definitely a city dog in a country environment. However, on the whole, she prevailed. As Janice was busy talking to the local soccer moms, she saw Luna fly by, chasing her Kong. Unfortunately for Luna, the toy was hanging out of another dog's mouth at the time. She will follow her Kong anywhere and was forced to play by the rules of the country dogs.

There are two areas where the dogs can swim, located about a hundred yards from each other. The south swimming area has "stairs" which are supposed to help both humans and dogs maneuver around the bank, but they are really just long pieces of wood that offer little assistance. Hiking boots are a good idea if you want to be close to the water to play with your dog. Pam Kleinhart, who lives three minutes away, was there with her son and daughter, their yellow Lab, Jake, and their neighbor's black Lab, Shadow. Kleinhart says she comes as often as she can and advises, "Always wear your old clothes." The grass can get muddy after rain, and the area near the water is guaranteed to be close to a mud bath in any weather conditions.

The trek back to the open grass was an adventure. Jake and Shadow led the way, with Luna following attentively. The group took a shortcut over the "hill," fully prepared for a workout. But it was no sweat. The "hill" is strictly a name for the path and is not indicative of the terrain. Waiting to welcome them at the entrance gates were about 10 new dogs who had just arrived. A nice couple at one of the picnic benches poured out fresh water for any canine in need. These people were prepared. There are no water facilities, so bringing your

Canine Good Citizens

Lots of places that turn away dogs don't really want to deny access. They feel forced into it. One hotel manager said, "We don't allow dogs because we never know what's coming through the door—we've had too many bad experiences. But if there were some way to tell if a dog is basically under control, you bet we'd allow dogs."

It turns out there is a way to tell: it's called the Canine Good Citizen (CGC) Test. Some communities are now giving CGC dogs a discount on dog licenses. Insurance companies are toying with the idea of offering a rebate or discount on homeowner's insurance to families with a CGC dog because CGC dogs are less likely to get into trouble. At least one veterinarian is offering a discount to clients who have passed the CGC Test. He believes these dogs are easier to handle, saving his staff time and lessening the chances of being bitten.

"Aside from showing ability to understand basic obedience, the CGC is a fair barometer of basic temperament," says Riverwoods trainer and behaviorist Marge Gibbs, who often administers the test.

"If your dog is sensitive to and afraid of quick movements, this behavior could be a precursor to the dog's biting a young child," Gibbs continues. "An owner can learn this by taking the test. It's a wonderful mechanism to correct concerns before they get out of hand."

Mary Burch is the director of the Canine Good Citizen Test for the American Kennel Club. She says, "At a store, in a hotel, or even at the park, a well-behaved dog doesn't infringe on the space of non–dog owners. It doesn't bark uncontrollably or drag its owners to wherever it wants to lead them. While some owners think their annoying dog is cute, other people don't."

Burch admits that there's no guarantee that a dog with a CGC degree will never make a mistake. Ultimately, dogs will be dogs. Lucy was one of 100,000 dogs across the country to pass the CGC Test in 1996. Chaser is also a CGC grad.

Tests are administered by clubs and trainers throughout the area. The fee is typically $5 to $12. For a nearby location, or for further information, call (212) 696-8247. The test is administered to any breed or mix of breed and to dogs of any age.

Is your dog a good citizen? Try the test on your own. The site may be anywhere away from the dog's own home. In order to pass, pooches must earn

continued

a perfect score. Those who pass the test receive a certificate. Any dog exhibiting aggression to a handler, an evaluator, or another dog during the test is immediately failed. Dogs can repeat the test as many times as is necessary. About half fail the first time around.

Requirements of the Canine Good Citizen Test

1. Accepting a friendly stranger: This test illustrates that the dog will allow a stranger to approach it and to speak to the handler in a natural everyday situation. The evaluator approaches and shakes hands with the handler but does not touch the dog.

2. Sitting politely for petting: This test shows that the dog will allow a friendly stranger to touch it while it's out with its handler. The evaluator pets the dog and then leaves. The dog must show no shyness or resentment.

3. Having proper appearance and grooming: This test demonstrates that the dog will welcome being groomed and examined and will permit a stranger, such as a veterinarian, groomer, or friend of the owner, to do so. The evaluator inspects the dog, combs or lightly brushes its coat, and examines its ears and foot pads.

4. Walking: This test illustrates that the handler is in control of the dog. The dog may be on whichever side the handler prefers. There must be a right turn, left turn, and turn about, with one stop in between and one at the end.

5. Walking through a crowd: This test proves that the dog can move politely in pedestrian traffic. The dog and handler walk close to several people. The dog may show some interest but should not appear overly exuberant, shy, or resentful.

6. Performing "sit" and "down" on command/staying in place: This test shows that the dog is trained. The dog does a "sit" and a "down," then the handler walks to the end of a 20-foot line and returns. The handler can choose to leave the dog in "sit" or in "down" for the "stay" command.

7. Coming when called: This test demonstrates that the dog will come when called by the handler. With the dog on a 20-foot line, the handler walks 10 feet from the dog, turns and faces the dog, then calls the dog to "come."

8. Reacting to another dog: This test signifies that the dog can behave politely around other dogs. Two handlers and their dogs approach, shake hands, exchange pleasantries, and continue on. The dog being tested should show no more than a casual interest in the other dog.

9. Reacting to distractions: This test shows that the dog is confident at all times when faced with common distractions, such as a person dropping items. The dog may exhibit a casual interest but may not panic, show aggression, or bark.

10. Behaving during supervised separation: This test demonstrates that the dog can be left with a trusted person and will maintain good manners. The dog is on a six-foot leash held by an evaluator while the handler is out of sight for three minutes.

own is a must. There are also no human bathroom facilities, which may impact the length of your stay if you don't plan ahead.

Two enclosed areas in the center of the field can be put to a variety of uses: training, containing puppies, or taking a "time-out." The best use Janice heard for the "pen" (as the locals called it) was as the site for Shadow's first birthday party, which included food, bandannas, treats, and toys.

The atmosphere was friendly; people seemed to know each other and the dogs by name. However, as with any off-leash area, you take some risks. As they were leaving, poor Luna was harassed by an aggressive dog who wouldn't let up. The owner was nowhere to be found. The dog then grabbed on to another dog's ear, with no intention of letting go without human intervention. The danger of having such a large area, with picnic tables for people to socialize, is that owners may not always be watching their dogs, as was true in this case. The best course is to stay near your own dog and be aware of other dogs' behavior.

Back at the parking area, Luna did not want to get in the car. She seemed sad to say good-bye to her new friends. Once on the road, however, she instantly fell asleep. Next time they do Prairie Wolf, Janice and Luna will invite Barry and a few other city dogs along to let them experience the pure joy of running through an open field.

Prairie Wolf is a place that encourages dogs to just be dogs. It's located on the east side of Waukegan Road (Route 43), just south of Old Mill Road and north of Half Day Road. (847) 367-6640.

TRIANGLE PARK *(worth a sniff)*   Thank goodness the deer at the center of this park is plastic. The real thing would certainly become roadkill because this boulevard park is surrounded by busy thoroughfares. Don't unleash your dog.

Triangle Park is bounded by Sheridan, Walnut, Washington, and Deerpath Roads. (847) 234-2600.

WEST PARK //   At night, lovely West Park is illuminated with vintage gaslights. Three-foot-high wooden posts serve as a decorative, if not practical, fence. Small and midsize dogs squeeze between the posts.

Used mainly by locals, the park includes baseball diamonds, soccer fields, tennis courts, and a children's area that are taken full advantage of. Dogs who don't like children should seek greener pastures.

Located just off Green Bay Road (where there's parking) at 850 Summit Avenue. Summit Place cuts through the park. (847) 234-2600.

Lake Zurich

Park

Lake Zurich parks don't allow dogs, but the Lake County Forest Preserve does have a site in the town. Dogs on a leash are welcome, as long as they stay on the trails and owners pick up.

CUBA MARSH FOREST PRESERVE // ½   Cuba Marsh is a widespread 780-acre oasis, so it's a surprise to find only one trail. The trail is two miles of crushed gravel that extends from the north entrance at Cuba Road to the south perimeter of the preserve at Ela Road. Lack of choice aside, it's hard to picture a prettier blend of marsh, woods, and grassland.

Visitors are asked to use nearby Lakewood Forest Preserve in Wauconda (see p. 312) for snowmobiling and horseback riding, as both are prohibited here. However, cross-country skiers and bicyclists are welcome.

With a pointer's help, you may be able to scope out a wide assortment of bird life. Many of the birds that take wing here are rare in Lake County. Species include pied-billed grebes, least bitterns, and yellow-headed blackbirds. This preserve is literally the only place in Lake County to find the endangered marsh pennywort. And on the southeast side of the park, a tour guide may point out the rare Seneca snakeroot plant. In all, 92 species of plants grow and 52 species of birds call—including rarely seen species of duck.

The preserve is open from 6:30 A.M. to sunset. Take Rand Road west to Cuba Road. The preserve entrance is on the south side of Cuba Road, just west of Ela Road. (847) 367-6640.

Libertyville

Parks

The versatile park system here is any dog's dream. The only rule is that they must be on-leash. However, dogs running inside the confines of a fenced-off baseball field or swimming in Butler Lake aren't going to be leashed, and no one expects them to be. The parks here are refreshingly clean, and they're free of dog feces. Parks are open from 7 A.M. to 9:30 P.M. Call the Libertyville Parks and Recreation Department, (847) 362-7490.

ADLER MEMORIAL PARK /// The Des Plaines River rolls through this 101-acre park. It looks pretty, but dogs don't often swim here. The river gets murky, and while dogs are allowed, those that dive in pay the price of getting caked with mud. A better idea is to hike through the woods. The hiking isn't on marked trails, but it's not difficult. While the forest is extensive, the chances of getting lost are minimal.

Cross-country skiing is the winter sport of choice. Dogs pulling skiers clip along the paths in both the wooded and open areas.

The sport of choice in balmier weather is disc golf. There is one nine-hole course. If you toss wild, having a retrieving dog on hand may save wear and tear on your legs. However, Chaser forgot her retrieving instincts because there were too many other good things to smell. Just be careful that your pup doesn't intercept an errant disc when a game is going on. One passing golden retriever did just that, and the golfers weren't pleased. Besides, these discs are harder and heavier than typical Frisbees.

An access road leads to the swimming pool, where dogs aren't allowed. As compensation, the pooch can join in the family picnic. The park has one large sheltered area and two smaller ones for barbecues.

Adler Memorial Park has its own entrance on the east side of Milwaukee Avenue, between Parkview Drive (on the south) and Old Buckley Road (on the north). (847) 362-7490.

BUTLER LAKE PARK /// ½ This is an excellent adventure. Swimming in Butler Lake is allowed, and dogs ranging from Jack Russell terriers to Newfoundlands take full advantage of the opportunity.

There are several football and baseball fields surrounded by chain-link fences. When they aren't in use, this is a great spot to let Spot run. Before you do, though, make sure all the gates are closed. Chaser and Lucy ran from third base to first base and kept on going—right out of the open gate and into the forest. Luckily, when called, they did an about-face and headed back. While the dogs don't understand the finer points of baseball, they do get to play a sport in which they're all-stars. It's called squirrel chasing. The managers' job is to make sure it's a squirrel the dogs are chasing. There are reports of dogs getting skunked here.

The Park District has plans to construct an asphalt trail to be used by in-line skaters and joggers.

We don't know if it has an official name, but Robin called the pond "Goose Lagoon" because it's perpetually filled with Canada geese. If you think dog poop is nasty, try walking anywhere near this lagoon without sliding. It's more slippery than frozen Butler Lake in the winter. Ice-skating is allowed on the lake, but dogs are discouraged from joining in.

Fishing is allowed by permit only. There are also barbecue grills and a charming gazebo surrounded by a circle of willow trees. This beautiful park is 93 acres, and you can definitely feel it.

Butler Lake Park is just west of Milwaukee Avenue; Lake Street divides the park near Stonegate Road. (847) 362-7490.

CENTRAL PARK / Chaser nonchalantly walked into the park, stopped at the historic brick and wood gazebo, and squatted, and squatted, and squatted. She was there long enough to attract a crowd. The poor thing desperately needed a laxative.

Chaser's squatting was nearly the highlight of this unspectacular small park located next to Saint Joseph's Catholic Church and School. For canine historians, there's signage detailing the history of Libertyville. There's also a single picnic table.

Central Park is bounded by Milwaukee and Maple Avenues, Broadway, and Park Place. (847) 362-7490.

CHARLES BROWN PARK // Not considered a destination park, this 21-acre site is smack-dab in the center of a neighborhood. Parking is limited, but there are always spaces because most people walk here.

The most noteworthy attributes are its relative privacy and generous grassy area. But there isn't much here other than the children's play lot. Summer camps also meet at this locale. So, it's a handy environment in which to socialize a puppy to the sights and sounds of children.

The entrance to Charles Brown Park is on Sylvan Drive at Dawes Street, just south of Warwick Court. (847) 362-7490.

COOK MEMORIAL PARK AND ROSE GARDEN //   There's a concrete replica of Chaser outside the Libertyville/Mundelein Historical Society, which is housed in this small park. It turns out that stonemason and Chicago city council member Ansel B. Cook, who built this structure as a country residence in 1878, owned a Brittany. Chaser is also a Brittany. There's no record of this dog's name, so the statue was dubbed Spot by town historians. Legend has it that when Cook died, the forlorn dog wandered off in a desperate search for its owner. No one knows what became of the dog now known as Spot.

Chaser doesn't much care about the historical significance, nor does she notice her resemblance to Spot. But she could be Spot's great, great, great . . . "granddogger." Brittanys are regarded as royalty in Libertyville, but they're still not allowed inside the historical society, which offers tours by appointment only.

Dogs can snoop around in the Lynn J. Arthur Rose Garden; just watch out for those thorns. What the garden lacks in size it more than makes up for in varieties. There's a veritable kaleidoscope of roses, and most are labeled. This location makes for a perfect summer or early-fall photo op.

There are a few picnic benches to be found in this small park in downtown Libertyville.

Cook Memorial Park and Rose Garden are bounded by Milwaukee and West Cook Avenues and Church Street. (847) 362-7490.

GREENTREE PARK /   This is eight acres of open area and also features a playground and plenty of room for a football or soccer game. It's not a bad location to do some fetching or running, as long as it's dry.

Greentree Park is at Greentree Parkway and Dawes Street. (847) 362-7490.

INDEPENDENCE GROVE DOG TRAINING AREA /// ½ (OFF-LEASH)   Ever see a sleeping dog with its paws flailing and nose twitching? Chances are she's dreaming of a place like this 30-acre Dog Training Area. It's one of the only parks in the Chicago area that have no concerns about allowing dogs to run with abandon without a leash.

There are places to hone retrieving and fieldwork skills such as tracking and swimming. Of course, this version of canine heaven comes at a price, $40 annually ($20 for Lake County residents). Don't even think about sneaking in, even if your pooch is as small as a Yorkshire terrier. The members-only policy is enforced to the letter.

To enter the parking area, you must know the combination on a gate lock. Even if you manage to pick the lock, vehicles must display an appropriate sticker. Walking in instead of driving doesn't help either, since rangers aggressively patrol the area, requesting proof of membership.

Not being members, Robin and I required a special one-day pass. Lucy was only about six months old at the time and not especially proficient on her "come" command. It's a funny thing: whenever I called her, this woman appeared faster than the dog. Finally, the woman turned to me and said, "Stop calling my name." It turns out that this Lucy, Lucy Holman of Libertyville, and her Airedale named Winnie visit three times a week. "I believe this is the best way and the only way to exercise and socialize your dog at the same time," she said. "Look around: the dogs absolutely love it."

Indeed, on the summer day we visited, at least 30 dogs were having the time of their lives. "You won't find a dog with its tail tucked between its legs here," she said. "Of course, with your dog it's hard to tell," she added, referring to tailless Lucy. According to a quick and informal poll, many of the park-goers were from more than 10 miles away.

The terrain is varied. There are several gently rolling hills, there are open fields, and there's a pond. The north field catches the eye with a dazzling array of wildflowers. But most dogs seem to congregate around the pond. The pond was so muddy around its banks that one observer worried that little Lucy would sink into the gooey mud. Chaser, being a persnickety sort, stayed back. But Lucy, who was then all of 15 pounds, was right in there, messin' in the mud with Labrador and golden retrievers, a Siberian husky, and a couple of big mixed breeds.

However, despite our glowing rating, Independence Grove has its flaws. For one thing, there's no way for the pooch to avoid a dreaded but much-needed shower after visiting the muddy pond. On the plus side, the remainder of the property is quite dry.

We wished that the rangers would spend more time enforcing the laws about picking up, instead of being overly concerned about who has the correct passes. Dog poop was everywhere. However, far more disconcerting is the confirmed case of blastomycosis from this area in 1996.

Blastomycosis can be life threatening to canines (and it's just as serious when people are infected). Dr. Suzanne Cook, a board-certified internal medicine specialist based in Riverwoods explains, "The disease is spread from spores in the soil. It is difficult to diagnose because the lone early symptom is often a mild cough. Vets can mistake it as kennel cough, although a fever (and also skin lesions) might accompany it."

When a final diagnosis is made, treatment may take 60 days or more, and may easily cost in excess of $2,000. If the disease isn't discovered in time, the dog will die. And even if the condition is caught early, there's no guarantee the dog will live.

Dr. Al Legendre, professor of medicine at the University of Tennessee College of Veterinary Medicine in Knoxville, is an authority on this little-known disease. He says, "Most of the cases are contracted by dogs that are near wooded areas and near banks of water enriched with manure from dogs, ducks, whatever."

Legendre adds that "blasto" isn't likely to be transmitted to people from dogs. A dog bite from an infected canine is the only known way for a person to get the disease from a dog. Similarly, if you're infected and you happen to bite your dog, you conceivably could expose Fido to it (although, as far as anyone knows, no person has ever infected a dog with blasto).

It's important to note that dogs act as environmental sentinels for a potential risk to people. If dogs in a specific place are coming down with blastomycosis, there's a potential threat at that same place for people. Some vets have discouraged clients from visiting the Dog Training Area out of concern for both dogs and their owners. However, Legendre points out that only one person for every 50 dogs will come down with the disease.

While the threat of blastomycosis is not one to be taken lightly, most vets have a wait-and-see attitude. They suggest that discouraging people from visiting the Dog Training Area is unfounded and unnecessary at this juncture. There were a pawful of cases of blasto from 1997 to 2000, but it's difficult to know for certain that this park was the cause. The Lake County Forest Preserve is aware of the problem, but there isn't much they can do to prevent this tiny fungus if it does continue to exist.

Certainly when there's a heavy snow cover and/or during the frosty months of January and February, there is no threat of blastomycosis.

If it weren't for the potential threat of blasto, the Dog Training Area would receive a four-bone recommendation.

The entrance to the Dog Training Area is on Milwaukee Avenue, just north of Illinois Route 137 (Buckley Road). Open from 8 A.M. to sunset daily. For further information or details on how to obtain a permit, call (847) 367-6640.

NICHOLAS-DOWDEN PARK / ½   Crane Boulevard splits the park in half. On one side, there's a baseball diamond. At the other side, a series of trees provides a picturesque perimeter to a soccer field and a tennis court. Local residents aren't supposed to let dogs run on the court. However, when the in-line skating rink is not in use, Fido can give it a whirl.

Nicholas-Dowden Park is at Dymond Road and Crane Boulevard, just west of Drake Street. (847) 362-7490.

OLD SCHOOL FOREST PRESERVE (LAKE COUNTY FOREST PRESERVE) /// This is a grand place to play in the winter. The sledding hill is on the east side of the park. If you have a labor-intensive Burmese mountain dog or Newfoundland, perhaps the pooch can pull you to the hill, which is located east of the main parking area. If you have a toy poodle, forget that idea. You'll have to do all of the pulling.

The preserve's 12 miles of hiking trails are also open to cross-country skiers.

Real jocks tackle the 1.5-mile physical fitness trail offering 19 workout stations just north of the main entrance. Jim Hardin, a Libertyville resident, regularly does the grueling workout. He says that his golden retriever, Max, has it easy. "All he does is watch, and he's probably secretly laughing."

Take your camera if you happen to visit in August or early September to capture the prairie wildflowers in full bloom. You'll be treated to a rainbow of colors, ranging from golden alexanders to purple milkweed. The plants are legally protected from picking, so photos are the best you can do, unless you have art talent.

On our visit, we heard the hoot of a screech owl. Foxes, raccoon, squirrels, and chipmunks also abide here. Bluebirds are among the winged species whose numbers have increased in recent years.

Amenities include cooking facilities, picnic shelters and tables, and horseshoe pits. Fishing is allowed in Old School Lake, but dogs are not allowed in the water.

Old School Forest Preserve is open from 6:30 A.M. to sunset. The entrance is on St. Mary's Road; either take Old School Road and go north on St. Mary's for about a mile, or take Old Rockland Road and go south on St. Mary's for about a mile. You can also take Illinois Route 176 to St. Mary's and go south for about one and a quarter miles. (847) 367-6640.

RIVERSIDE PARK / ½ Dogs aren't allowed in much of this park. The tennis courts and the golf course are forbidden territory.

The geese own the water hole, but unknowing dogs sometimes join in. They're sorry after diving into this gook choked with goose waste.

There are some attributes, such as a children's play lot and a soccer field with room to run. Mature trees also make a striking vista throughout the park.

Riverside Park is on Riverside Drive, between Glendale Avenue and Valley Park Drive. (847) 362-7490.

Doggy Doings

Pet-Athalon A seven-mile walk in the park benefits the Save-a-Pet shelter in Grayslake. The Pet-Athalon is held either the third or fourth Sunday in September beginning at 10 A.M. at the Old School Forest Preserve, off St. Mary's Road just north of Illinois Route 60 and south of Illinois Route 176. The winner isn't whoever finishes first—it's who raises the most money through pledges. Call (847) 740-7788.

Save-a-Pet Holiday Party In the spirit of Santa, give a gift of pet food or treats to the Save-a-Pet shelter in lieu of admission. People can stock up on home-baked holiday cookies, and so can the pets. The shelter's gift shop sells canine holiday jewelry, jingle-bell collars, and a signature line of Christmas and holiday cards. Save-a-Pet's holiday party spreads good cheer the second weekend in December from 11 A.M. to 6 P.M. at 31664 N. Fairfield Road; call (847) 740-7788.

Festival

Fourth of July Celebration and Fireworks Display Rain or shine, concerts begin at 6 P.M. on July 4 at the Butler Lake band shell, just west of Milwaukee Avenue, at Lake Street and Stonegate Road. Usually, the park begins to fill up about 4:30 P.M. with picnickers. One attraction that even upstages the 9:15 P.M. fireworks is the Ben & Jerry's ice-cream cart. Call (847) 362-7490.

Lincolnshire

Park

Dogs are not permitted in any Lincolnshire municipal park space; however, they are allowed on-leash in the Half Day and Wright Woods Forest Preserve operated by the Lake County Forest Preserve.

HALF DAY AND WRIGHT WOODS FOREST PRESERVE (see Vernon Hills)

Place to Stay

Marriott Resort Dogs under 20 pounds can play at this resort. But guests with pets are restricted to the first floor. Pets are not allowed to see the stage shows at the Marriott Theatre. There is a one-time fee of $25. Room rates are $89 to $199. 10 Marriott Drive; (847) 634-0100 or (800) 228-9290.

Long Grove

Parks

There is really only one park operated by Long Grove within the village, and leashed dogs are welcome. It is open from dawn to dusk; call (847) 438-4743.

BUFFALO CREEK PARK // It's named for the creek that ripples through this tranquil five-acre park. Dogs should be on a leash, unless they're jumping into the creek to cool off. Generally, the creek is slow moving and muddy.

Long Grove's historic shopping area is just down the street, so this park provides a respite for shopping-weary people.

The trails are used by horses who occasionally mosey into town, just as they did a hundred years ago. In fact, the whole concept is to make the park look the way it did about a century ago. The meadow is naturally grown, with native species surrounding the vintage cedar gazebo. The town is proud that this park is kept free of broken glass and dog feces. Like the village of Long Grove, this park is a throwback to a gentler time.

Buffalo Creek Park is at Old McHenry and Robert Parker Coffin Roads. (847) 438-4743.

BUFFALO CREEK FOREST PRESERVE (see Buffalo Grove)

Shopping

The Dog House The pooch can pick out natural gourmet biscuits at this canine boutique. Like most of the other quaint Long Grove shops, this tiny place is jam-packed with things your dog never knew it needed. For the ultimate canine couch potato, try out the couch made for dogs, $58.95, or perhaps your best friend would fancy a rhinestone-studded collar, $8.95 to $16.95. For the active dog, the store carries a variety of bike accessories. For that formal evening affair, tuxedos are $39.95 to $49.95. The Dog House may be the only shop to fit blushing and barking brides; wedding gowns for dogs are $65 to $85.

You can even arrange to have your affair catered with special treats. 405 Robert Parker Coffin Road; (847) 634-3060.

Festivals

Applefest Does an apple a day keep the vet away? Actually, the answer is no. Apples are acceptable to most dogs only in moderation. So, you'll have to get a grip, since any dog or person could overdose at this annual event always held on a weekend, Friday through Sunday, in early October.

Food booths sell apple cider, apple juice, apple pies, apple doughnuts, apple cakes, apple jams and jellies, apple wine, apple butter, and taffy apples. Of course, you can buy plain old apples to make your own cider, juice, pies, cakes, and so forth.

Horse-drawn carriage rides are offered Friday only. Live entertainment is provided throughout the festival, 10 A.M. to 6 P.M. in downtown Long Grove, on Robert Parker Coffin Road and Old McHenry Road. There is no admission, and the parking is also free (although parking becomes tight in peak hours). Call (847) 634-0888.

Countryside Christmas Pooches can sit on Santa's lap on two consecutive weekends in December (always before Christmas, of course). Lucy joined in when strolling carolers from area grade schools sang "The Twelve Days of Christmas." The carolers were doing really well until the fifth day of Christmas. They sang, "On the fifth day of Christmas my true love gave to me," and Lucy chose this moment to howl. And she howled again, and again. One by one the carolers began to lose it. Even the prim conductor cracked up. Finally, when the conductor gained his composure, he sang out, "And my true love gave to me a dog!" The crowd howled louder than Lucy.

Downtown Long Grove is appropriately decorated for the holiday season, with a giant wreath draped along the covered bridge on Robert Parker Coffin Road. There are gingerbread houses (not for dogs to snack on) and giant candy canes (dogs aren't interested—they're made of plastic). Food booths offer hot stuff such as chili, hot cider, and hot chocolate. Just beware of the reindeer—they're real. Some of them get spooked by canines. Apparently they don't see dogs at the North Pole. Two more words: Dress warmly.

The Countryside Christmas celebration is 10 A.M. to 8 P.M. Fridays and 10 A.M. to 5 P.M. Saturdays and Sundays at Robert Parker Coffin and McHenry Roads. There is no charge for admission, and parking is also free; call (847) 634-0888.

Strawberry Festival It's the attack of the strawberries: strawberry jam, strawberry pies, strawberry shortcake, and chocolate-covered strawberries are just some of the berry good confections available throughout the festival in downtown Long Grove. But there's more to hold a canine's interest than mere berries. Free entertainment, a classic car show, and an assortment of children's events and activities are usually thrown in. The festival is 10 A.M. to 6 P.M. Friday through Sunday in mid-June at Robert Parker Coffin and McHenry Roads. There's no charge for admission, and parking is free. Call (847) 634-0888.

Doggy Doing

Cobblestone Sidewalk Sale You never know what you might come upon. Antique dog collars? Ninety-year old Heinz Costi purchased an antique-style collar for his German shepherd dog. He remarked, "It reminds me of the collars we had when I was a kid." Of course, you'll find more than dog stuff. Country-theme household items, Christmas ornaments, dolls, and jewelry greet your eyes. But don't expect to discover many "steals" in this upscale area.

Dogs are generally not allowed inside the stores. The sidewalk sale is held in downtown historic Long Grove, Robert Parker Coffin and McHenry Roads, on a weekend in August. Hours are 10 A.M. to 5 P.M. on Saturday and noon to 5 P.M. on Sunday. There's no admission charge, and parking is free. Call (847) 634-0888.

Mundelein

Shopping

Village Antique Mall Lucy and Chaser enjoyed sniffing around, particularly the fine array of antique furniture. An employee told me, "We welcome dogs, cats—we don't care—as long as they've got money!" 131 E. Maple Avenue (Illinois Route 176); (847) 566-2363.

Place to Stay

Mundelein Super 8 Hotel The manager said the hotel *prefers* that visiting dogs be under 65 pounds, but that limit is flexible. All humans accompanied by dogs must stay in smoking rooms, even if neither of you smokes. You must sign a pet contract, deposit $50, and never leave your dog alone in the room. Rates are $54.98 to $63.98. 1950 S. Lake Street; (847) 949-8842.

Prairie View

Doggy Doing

American Pet Motel This elaborate kennel bills itself as "Club Med for Dogs," so we had to see for ourselves. The lobby is a noisy place (as is any kennel), with barking dogs waiting to check in, not to mention the squawking from nearby caged birds. Visiting dogs aren't allowed on tours for fear they could spread disease or parasites into the kennel area. Kalea, our researcher's dog, was so relieved that she practically flew back to the car.

Tours are offered to the public on the spur of the moment. This kennel has nothing to hide. The fanciest quarters are appointed with tiled walls and a wooden Dutch door; others are chain-link condos. Some rooms are fitted out with little beds covered in Barney-the-dinosaur bedding, TV sets, and telephones. Moms have phoned pets from all over the world.

All rooms have vinyl flooring, a constant stream of soothing music, and access to outdoor runs. Our researcher was honored to meet a talented German shepherd dog that had figured out how to open her kennel door. Dogs are fed once a day and receive a bedtime snack. Additional feedings, walks, grooming, and veterinary services cost more. Prices are based on the size of the dog and the level of service; the range is $12.50 to $24 per day per dog.

The motel also offers an airport shuttle service. A chauffeur will drop off or pick up a pet at the airport cargo area (where pets are delivered): $75 for domestic flights, $100 for international flights.

American Pet Motel is at 22096 N. Pet Lane, off Aptakisic Road; call (847) 634-9448.

Round Lake

Parks

Dogs can visit the parks on-leash, presuming owners pick up after them. They're open from dawn to dusk; call (847) 546-8558.

CEDAR VALLEY PARK // ½ The aerated pond might be perfect for the canine Olympic swim team. The water is relatively clean, and because people aren't allowed to swim here, mere humans can't get in the way. As long as swimming dogs don't disturb anglers or other park users, Jim Rock, executive director of the Round Lake Area Park District, shrugs and says, "I suppose swimming dogs never hurt anyone."

Only a pawful of competitors take advantage of this rare chance to practice the "doggy stroke," but that's not to suggest that this park lacks canine traffic. Trees adorn the perimeter of the pond, which takes up about 70 percent of the 10-acre grounds. That's where the local canine regulars gather. A playground and a few benches round out the scene. Parking is limited, and spaces can fill up on weekends.

Cedar Valley Park is located at least 30 feet down a steep embankment, so only the most dogged pooch could run up and into traffic on Cedar Lake Road. The park is also bounded by Cedar Crest Court and Lakewood Terrace. (847) 546-8558.

FAIRFIELD PARK // ½   At 44 acres, this is Round Lake's largest park. There are no fancy niceties, but that's the way dogs like it. There are 30 acres of natural prairie and 14 acres of forest. No paths impose on this natural area, so Fido has the opportunity to run unencumbered by crowds. One distraction is the disc golf course, which may make it hard for your dog to remain a spectator.

Camping areas are found on the park's west side. There are no water or toilet facilities, and sites must be reserved by calling the Park District. Dogs (on-leash only) are allowed to stay with campers.

Great blue herons often fly the coop from the neighboring privately owned rookery (where dogs are not allowed). Being able to witness these stately birds is worth the trip. Various small mammals, such as woodchucks and raccoon, also call this area home. Skunks live here, too, but so far, there are no reports of canines or people being on the wrong end of their wrath.

The parking area for Fairfield Park is on Fairfield Road, a quarter mile south of Illinois Route 134. (847) 546-8558.

HART'S HILL AND HART'S WOODS PARK // ½   The sledding hill at the southeast corner of the park might as well be Mount Everest. Sliding down is easy; the problem is the return trip. Some large dogs—particularly those with hip problems—may be unable to accomplish this feat. But for smaller pups who make the trip up the summit and back in the arms of their people, it's a whiz. The hill is well lit to accommodate evening sledding. There's also a new warming house with bathrooms and a concession stand, so you can sip hot chocolate while taking a break from the slopes.

Some parks have fitness courses, but this park has the best test to determine if you and your pooch are in tip-top condition: try running up the sledding hill, then running down, and then running back up again. I learned what Chaser has known all along—she's in better shape than I am. After running up and down the hill twice, I was wiped out. Chaser, however, was ready for more.

Other amenities include a picnic grove near the wooded area, which is filled with hickory and oak trees, and soccer and football fields. Dogs are not allowed inside the Park District community center, the pool, or the Fitness Plus Center.

Hart's Hill and Hart's Woods Park are located on the north and south sides of Hart's Road at Illinois Route 134. (847) 546-8558.

Round Lake Beach

Parks

Leashed dogs are allowed in parks from dawn to dusk. Call (847) 546-8558.

COUNTRYWALK PARK ½ ✔   Situated in the center of its namesake subdivision, this five-acre park comprises a very limited grassy area as well as basketball and tennis courts.

Countrywalk Park is on Countrywalk Drive at Periwinkle Lane. (847) 546-8558.

FAIRVIEW PARK ½ ✔   Located next to Beach Elementary School, this park doesn't have much for a self-respecting pup to do, except run the bases on the softball field or yap at the kids cavorting on the playground equipment.

Fairview Park is on Hawthorne Court at Ardmore Street. (847) 546-8558.

GATEWAY PARK ✔ ½   The lagoon here isn't as large or as clean as the pond at nearby Cedar Valley Park in Round Lake. Nevertheless, it's an adequate puppy pool.

After you've trekked the half-mile exercise trail or the one-and-a-half-mile walking/bike trail, you can let the dog cool off with a swim. The trail continues out of the park on Cedar Lake Road, running directly under high-tension Commonwealth Edison wires. So, don't take Fido for a walk during an electrical storm.

Gateway Park is on Clarendon Road, one block west of Hainesville Road. (847) 546-8558.

Round Lake Heights

Park

In the sole major municipal park, leashed dogs are permitted from dawn to dusk; call (847) 546-8558.

SHAG PARK NATURE PRESERVE //   The park is named for the shagbark hickory forest, where sporting breeds can count on seeing myriad waterfowl species. They'll have to eye the flock from the edge of the wetland area, though. Dogs aren't permitted in the water at this location, since this is a place where nature shouldn't be disturbed. A trail steers you through this 32-acre site, which also features football, baseball, tennis, and basketball facilities.

    The Shag Park Nature Preserve is on Lotus Drive, just north of Rollins Road. (847) 546-8558.

Spring Grove

Park

CHAIN O'LAKES STATE PARK (ILLINOIS STATE PARK) /// ½   If it weren't for those darn boats . . . you'd figure that bordering three lakes (Grass Lake, Marie Lake, and Nippersink Lake) and the Fox River would give this park heaps of room for dog paddling. But that's just not the case. During the season, the boat traffic is so intense within the park that swimming is hazardous for both canines and their people. It's also not allowed.

    However, if you go beyond the boundaries of the 2,973-acre state park into the adjoining 3,230-acre conservation area, finding a quieter place on any of the other seven Chain O'Lakes links shouldn't be difficult. Select from 488 miles of shoreline. Dogs are welcome to take the plunge in the conservation area. While the quality of water has improved noticeably in recent years, some dog owners remain concerned. Park officials say they haven't heard of any veterinary problems resulting from swims in the waters. And nearby residents regularly take their hounds for a dip.

    Aside from barring canines from congested lakes, the state park itself is distinctly dog friendly. Dogs are free to use any of the park's trails, which are all pretty easy. Even Affy, a Lhasa apso owned by Marge Gilly, office coordinator at Chain O'Lakes, manages to trek these paths. For those who prefer a scenic stroll, the 1.7-mile Gold Finch Trail offers the best view, overlooking the

Fox River. When the sun is burning down, canines might find the shady 1.5-mile Nature Trail a better choice. This trail stays cool under the forest cover.

Nature buffs can stop by the park office for a list of the nearly two hundred species of birds that have been spotted at the park. Dove, waterfowl, and pheasant hunting are allowed at designated places (advance registration is required). Dogs may accompany hunters. For Lhasa apsos and other non-hunters, here's a good reason to adhere to the leash rule. You don't want a pup to scamper off into a hunting area.

The six miles of bicycle trails are fine for riding but even better for cross-country skiing. Beginners get their own cross-country trail. Bike rentals are $5 per hour.

Of the seven picnic areas, the Pike Marsh North Picnic Area and the Oak Point Picnic Area are handicapped accessible. So is the quarter-mile trail near Pike Marsh North.

Amid all the possibilities, water activities prevail. And fishing is the sport of choice. Anglers reel in bluegills, walleye and northern pike, and several varieties of bass.

Boat rentals are available at Butler Lake within the state park, $13 per day for a rowboat and $50 per day for a motorboat.

Horses are available from May 1 through October 31, $20 per hour. Dogs aren't allowed on the horse trails. Campsites are $8 to $11 per night, with an additional $5 registration fee. Tent rentals are $23 per night.

From May 1 to October 31, the park is open from 6 A.M. to 9 P.M. From January 1 to April 30, it is open from 8 A.M. to sunset. The park is closed to the public in November and December.

Chain O'Lakes State Park is at 8916 Wilmot Road. The main entrance is on Wilmot, one mile south of Illinois Route 173. (847) 587-5512.

Vernon Hills

Parks

Dogs are welcome in the parks. However, people are aggressively fined if they take their dogs off-leash or can't show evidence of a waste-removal device (a scooper, plastic bag, etc.). The fines start at $5 and escalate for each offense. Parks are open from dawn to 10:30 P.M.; (847) 367-7270.

**CENTURY PARK /// ** Chaser jumped out of the car first, dropping to a perfect "sit." Lucy, meanwhile, began to throw one of her little temper tantrums. She whines and cries—wailing loud enough to be heard clear across the county. Practicing tough love, we don't allow her out of the car until she stops. Lucy started to sound like Lucille Ball—"Wha! Wha!"—it's deafening. We still didn't give in to her crying. Since Chaser always jumps from the car first, we're not sure what set Lucy off. She was probably overly excited. She loves the idea of visiting parks.

Finally, we won. Lucy began to calm down, and we let her out of the car. That's when we turned around to find an entire wedding party staring at us. We spotted the bride, the groom, the bridesmaids in unmistakable lime-green dresses, and the photographer, who until now had been trying to take pictures. Embarrassed about Lucy's antics, I feebly offered, "Well, she always cries at weddings."

The backdrop provided by the two lakes is a scenic find. "We'd always loved it here; it's usually so peaceful," said the bride, who added that she definitely prefers cats.

On this fall day, Lake Big Bear and the grass around it were alive with hundreds of migrating Canada geese, as well as the resident geese who have made this place a year-round home. While dogs are allowed in the water, we didn't let either Chaser or Lucy off-leash. The leash law is strictly enforced. Besides, there's just too much goose poop, and we didn't want the ride home to be complemented with the fragrant aroma that results from a swim in such a pond. So, we ran after the geese with the dogs on-leash. Chaser, true to her Brittany heritage, sent at least a hundred honking geese into the water. We knew that Chaser would be delighting in twitching doggy dreams about this day for a long time to come.

With all those honking geese, we'd hardly describe the park as tranquil (at least not while the temporary goose residents make their pit stops). A wooden bridge connects the lakes. Little Bear Lake has only a handful of straggler geese. Despite the geese and their feces, the fish survive. At least, that's what several fishermen told us. For a closer look at the geese or for fishing at the center of the pond, boat rentals are available in the summer.

The paved path that cuts a swath through the 130-acre park is trafficked by bicyclists, joggers, and in-line skaters. You never really feel as if you're off in a secluded place. The back end of the park connects with a subdivision, and there's a clear view of nearby Hawthorne Shopping Center.

Century Park is on Lakeview Parkway, just west of the Hawthorne Shopping Center at Illinois Route 60 (Town-Line Road). (847) 367-7270.

DEERPATH PARK // There's plenty of open space: 68 acres, to be exact. There are tennis courts as well as soccer and baseball fields. This would be a swell place to let a dog run. However, the leash laws are written in stone in this northwest suburb. There's a bicycle and jogging path here, too.

Deerpath Park is on Cherokee Road off of Deerpath Drive. (847) 367-7270.

HALF DAY AND WRIGHT WOODS FOREST PRESERVE (LAKE COUNTY FOREST PRESERVE) /// Once two distinct preserves, these 528 acres are now considered one facility. Their wooded terrains along the Des Plaines River are similar. Dogs aren't allowed in the river.

Two three-acre ponds are stocked with fish, but dogs aren't allowed in these waters either. However, you'll find a labyrinth of trails open to dogs. Walking along these paths, dogs may encounter explorers on horseback, cross-county skiers, or some of the preserve's permanent residents such as deer, raccoon, or opossums.

We weren't lucky enough to rendezvous with wildlife, but we passed several people using this area as a bridle path. Lucy and Chaser ignored the equine traffic. And for the most part, they also ignored the stinky results that drop from the horses. Even Chaser showed only a passing interest in the horse poop. Chaser's fascination with canine poop borders on obsession and, as Robin notes, is "really gross."

It so happens that Lucy and Chaser have more experience with horses than most suburban dogs do. We frequently see police on horseback in the city. One rider in the preserve stopped and told Robin and me a tragic story of her run-in with a local boxer. The dog decided to pick a fight with her horse. Suffice to say the boxer didn't land the knockout punch in this match.

Just as the lady rode off into the sunset, Chaser misstepped. Her clumsiness resulted in a ride home with all the windows open even though it was only 50 degrees outside. After all, horse poop doesn't wipe off so easily.

A picturesque cabin for picnicking, with a wooden deck overlooking a lagoon, is located just north of the Half Day entrance. It's absolutely beautiful, although mosquito repellent is a good idea.

Claim a piece of the large grass field near the Half Day entrance for a game of canine fetch or for flying a kite and letting Fido retrieve it. With long-standing oak and maple trees, the forested areas are impressive in the fall. Wildflowers also proliferate in this general vicinity.

Wright Woods is named for early Lake County settler Captain Daniel Wright. Half Day Woods is named for an even earlier settler, Chief Half Day of the Pottawatomie Indian tribe.

Half Day and Wright Woods Forest Preserve is open from 6:30 A.M. to sunset. The Half Day entrance is on Milwaukee Avenue, two miles south of Illinois Route 60 and about one mile north of Half Day Road. The Wright entrance is on St. Mary's Road, one and a half miles south of Illinois Route 60, just south of Everett Road, east of Milwaukee Road and west of Riverwoods Road. (847) 367-6640.

HARTMANN PARK ½ / This four-acre park is often jammed with kids. A day camp building serves the young families who live in the area. Naturally, the playground is hopping. Dogs who enjoy attention from kiddies will have a good time. There are three T-ball fields here.

Oakwood Park is bounded by Oakwood and Cherry Valley Roads, just south of Illinois Route 45. (847) 367-7270.

MCARTHUR WOODS FOREST PRESERVE (LAKE COUNTY FOREST PRESERVE) //
A Lake County Forest Preserve destination without trails, facilities, or drinking water, this is truly land left to grow wild. The preserve is mostly prairie with a small amount of wooded area.

McArthur Woods is available for trekking from sunrise to sunset, at Illinois State Route 60 and St. Mary's Road (actually located between Mettawa and Vernon Hills). (847) 367-6640.

Doggy Doing

Pet Memorial Day People arrive holding a leash in one hand and a box of Kleenex in the other. Pet Memorial Day began as an annual event at the Aarowood Pet Cemetery in 1991. In 1996, 1,800 people and more than two hundred pets attended. However, after that year, owner Victor Barcroft, who used to offer a personal tribute to the guests, sold the business. A public company bought it, and a salesperson told me that by popular demand, Pet Memorial Day will again be observed annually.

While the new event will be a downscaled version of the original, the love in people's hearts will be as strong as ever. There's no charge to attend. Call to get updated information.

Aarowood Pet Cemetery is at 24090 N. Illinois Highway 45, between Milwaukee and Butterfield Roads; call (847) 634-3787.

Wadsworth

Park

There are no municipal parks in Wadsworth, but dogs are allowed on a leash in the Van Patten Woods Forest Preserve.

Van Patten Woods (Lake County Forest Preserve) /// This 972-acre stretch (along the Des Plaines River and around Sterling Lake) is a water recreation wonderland. Dogs aren't allowed to dive into the water, but they are allowed on boats. A rowboat or canoe costs $6 for two hours, $10 for four hours, or $14 for a day. Paddleboats are $6 for two hours. Call Chandlers Boat & Bait in the forest preserve at (847) 526-8217.

Dogs can be a good luck charm for anglers. When fortune smiles, Northern pike, panfish, walleyes, and catfish can be pulled from the lake. Ice fishing is allowed when the ice is at least 4.5 inches thick. Several fishing derbies are held throughout the year.

A nine-mile crushed-gravel trail is available to horses, bicycles, snowmobiles, and, of course, dogs. The trailhead can be accessed at the far north Russell Road entrance. Other trails in the preserve empty into this main trail.

There are facilities for picnics throughout the park. On the preserve's north end is a rustic youth campground that can be reserved for groups of up to one hundred (dogs are allowed on-leash). Beagles with delusions of being wartime flying aces mustn't miss the model aircraft area on the north side of the park near the Illinois-Wisconsin state line, north of Russell Road.

Van Patten Woods is open from 8 A.M. to sunset. The main entrance is on Illinois Route 173, one mile east of Illinois-94 (the Tri-State Tollway) and a quarter mile east of U.S. Route 41. Parking is also available at Russell Road east of Illinois-94. (847) 367-6640.

Wauconda

Parks

Dogs are not allowed in municipal parks, but they are welcome (on a leash) in the Lake County Forest Preserve park.

Lakewood Dog Exercise Area //// (OFF-LEASH) This is one of Lake County Forest Preserve's only off-leash dog parks, and it's one of the best in the book.

The 15-acre park is fully enclosed, which is the highest of priorities for many dog owners. Pam Hoffmeister and her keeshond, Buckley, live in Libertyville, only a few minutes away from the Independence Grove Dog Training Area. However, Hoffmeister prefers making the 20-minute trek to Lakewood because this park has a fence around its perimeter. "Buckley is OK off a leash," says Hoffmeister, "but if a deer or another animal runs by, I can't totally depend on him. I'd rather be safe than sorry."

Things That Go Bump in the Night

Some dogs are terrified of thunderstorms. They dive under the bed, huddle in closets, or refuse to go outdoors. Once outdoors, they may want to run off—a real danger if you happen to be in a park when a storm erupts.

No one knows how this phobia begins. Some dogs may actually have a hereditary disposition. Other behaviorists believe that it's more likely the phobic dogs weren't exposed to thunderstorms during a critical phase of puppyhood.

It's clear that unknowing people often encourage the fear by cuddling their shaking pooches, sort of telling them, "Yes, you poor thing, I don't blame you; you should be nervous."

Another possibility is that the dog makes a wrong generalization. For example, I know of one dog whose tail was accidentally stepped on during an awful storm. The dog had never been nervous during storms. But on this occasion, the owners were anxious themselves because they were afraid their basement was about to flood, and their pooch began to pick up on their worry. When the tail was injured, it pushed the dog over the edge. Not realizing a person had stepped on its tail, the dog connected its pain with the storm. Now, whenever it storms, the dog sticks its tail between its legs and runs for shelter under the nearest piece of furniture.

Left unchecked, this type of fear usually intensifies over time. The dog won't just "forget about it."

Trainer and behaviorist Marge Gibbs of Riverwoods says a game of indoor or outdoor fetch may help distract a dog exhibiting a mild anxiety attack. If the dog likes kids, have an impromptu party and let each child offer the dog a treat. Just be sure you're rewarding the pup only for being upbeat, not for being fearful.

However, in many cases, the solution isn't so simple. Dr. William Fortney, assistant professor of medicine at Kansas State University, tried Valium to calm his petrified pooch. It worked; his dog wasn't bothered by storms or anything else—it turned into a zombie dog. Not happy with his drugged-down canine, he successfully used a desensitization tape. Little by little, the volume of crashing thunderstorms heard on a cassette tape is increased. The same technique can work for dogs afraid of any other loud noise, from a garbage truck to a dishwasher. In fact, some behaviorists contend that by exposing young pups to a wide variety of crazy sounds, you're more likely to avoid a sensitivity later in life.

Some dogs are so panicked that antianxiety medication, which is a better choice than Valium, may be required just to calm the pooch enough to begin using the tapes. These dogs may actually attack themselves or whip around the house in a state of panic.

For Fortney's dog, the desensitization tapes worked like a charm. However, some dogs learn to fear more than just the sound of the thunder itself. These phobic dogs are more accurate than the weather service at predicting severe weather. As the barometric pressure changes, hours before the actual approach of the storm, they may nervously pace and/or howl. They can literally smell the arriving rain. They may also become fearful of the electricity they feel in the air, even the pitter-patter of rain on the roof. These cases also generally require antianxiety medication along with the desensitization tapes.

Glenview-based canine communication and behavior specialist Steve Boyer markets desensitization tapes for thunderstorms. The recording also includes car horns, fireworks, and other urban sounds. The tape is $19.95; call (800) 952-6517.

Owners are far more dutiful about picking up here than at the off-leash places in DuPage County or at the training area in Libertyville. Maybe it's just the novelty of this place. I hope not.

Bathroom facilities for people are important, particularly in cold weather. This place has them. You can take along all the coffee you want and not have to worry about leaving the park to search for a rest room. However, there is no water for dogs or humans, so pack a canteen while you're at it.

Just more than half of the exercise area is flat and grassy. At the center of the park is a series of concrete sewer lines. Don't worry: they aren't being used. They're here to create a sort of canine playground—things to run through and jump over. Lucy caught on quickly, jumping two to three feet over the concrete cylinders, running around the huge ducts, and then bolting inside to hide from a pair of Burnese mountain dogs. The large dogs could easily have squeezed in after her, but they never did.

Scott Seberg of Lake Zurich is in the process of training his 10-month-old Brittany pup, Baily, to respond and retrieve to a whistle. His goal is to eventually go hunting with him. Baily and Chaser (also a Brittany) romped and rolled for a good 15 minutes. For that time, Chaser seemed to be a puppy again.

A permit is required for each car entering the parking area. You have to know the lock's combination to enter the preserve. Permits are $50 per year ($25 for residents of Lake County). The permits run from January 1 through December 31 and are not prorated. Daily permits are also available for $5. When you purchase the permit, you'll learn the combination. Permits may be obtained at the Lake County Forest Preserve Office, 2000 N. Milwaukee Avenue, Libertyville, or in Wauconda, just opposite the area's entrance at 24237 W. Ivanhoe Road, from 6:30 A.M. to 3 P.M. Monday through Friday.

Lakewood Dog Exercise Area is off of Fairfield Road, just south of Illinois Route 176. Open 6:30 A.M. to sunset. (847) 367-6640.

LAKEWOOD FOREST PRESERVE (LAKE COUNTY FOREST PRESERVE) */// * Spanning 2,043 acres, this is the largest of the Lake County Forest Preserve spaces. Throughout the park, there are trails for cross-country skiing (willing and able dogs may accompany), hiking, and biking. Just beware of the hazards—you may be sharing some trails with snowmobiles. Dogs are not allowed on the six-and-a-half-mile marked horse trail.

The wooded area is expansive and easy to get lost in. That also means that there is no shortage of secluded spaces, away from road noise and other canines. Wildlife is more likely to appear in these places. In most cases, we're talking about raccoon, beavers, deer, opossums, and foxes, but as our researcher Gail and her sheltie, Kalea, can attest, you never know what you may stumble into. As they were strolling down a path, a little black snake darted in front of them. Kalea stepped right over it, oblivious to its presence. The little garter snake was hunting for insects and was of no danger. Regardless, Gail won't be walking down that path again anytime soon.

Kalea didn't react to the snake because it doesn't have much of a scent. Critters with a scent can be another matter. Pam Walker and her golden retriever, Bustin, were nonchalantly taking an afternoon hike, in full adherence to the leash law. Suddenly, Bustin busted loose. Before a shocked Pam could grab the leash back, Bustin was 20 feet ahead, nose to nose with a skunk. Suffice to say, the ride back home in the car was unpleasant.

Lakewood Forest Preserve is open from 6:30 A.M. to sunset and is located at Illinois State Route 176 west of Fairfield Road. (847) 367-6640.

Waukegan

Parks

Just so long as they're on a leash, dogs are allowed in Waukegan's parks. Officials cast a blind eye when dogs are taken off-leash for swimming in ponds and rivers in the municipal parks. However, we're told they won't be so inclined if owners allow their dogs to disturb other park activities or if they don't pick up. However, no questions are asked at Callahan-Franklin park, an off-leash exercise area. The parks are open from dawn to dusk. For further information call (847) 360-4725.

ADELPHI PARK / This is an undeveloped former landfill. Aside from a small playground, there's nothing on these 17 acres except for grass and weeds. But for dogs who yearn to stretch their legs, this place does just fine.

   This park is at 3151 Wall Avenue at Adelphi Avenue, north of Sunset Avenue. (847) 360-4725.

BELVIDERE PARK // With two baseball diamonds and scads of green space, you'd figure this park would be a hit for a game of fetch. Sometimes it is, but summer weekends are just too crowded. The park teems with picnickers who take advantage of the grills. Of course, few dogs mind a picnic, as long as extras are tossed their way.

   If you do play fetch, your dog better keep its head up and its eyes peeled, or it may torpedo into one of the three hundred maple, spruce, and pine trees throughout the grounds. Belvidere also contains two basketball courts and a playground where dogs can bounce around if humans aren't using them.

   Dogs often take their human buddies for a one-mile walk along the asphalt path that extends around the park. However, only humans are allowed in the Belvidere Recreation Center.

   Belvidere Park is at 412 S. Lewis Avenue at Belvidere Road. (847) 360-4725.

BEN DIAMOND PARK ½/ Donated to the city in the 1940s by Mr. Diamond, this four-and-a-half-acre park is fitted with a playground, a tennis court, and a softball field. But space is tight, and a canine has precious little to do.

   Ben Diamond Park is located at 2413 Sunset Avenue, between Delaware Road and Sioux. (847) 360-4725.

BEVIER PARK // ½ The main canine attraction is the pond on the south side of the park. The water is aerated and therefore is pretty clean. As long as there's no abuse, park administrators let dogs take a dip. The pond is 12 feet deep at the center, and, best of all, it's stocked with catfish! (The largest catch measured 18 inches.) An industrious canine diver might also find bluegills and bass. Humans fishing on the surface don't always applaud the canines' enthusiasm, as the pond is quite small. They claim the dogs disturb the fish. A paved path encircles the pond.

A Frisbee golf course and a playground are recent additions. There are also tennis and basketball courts.

Bevier Park is at 2255 Yorkhouse Road at McAree Road. (847) 360-4725.

BONNIE BROOK BIRD SANCTUARY / ½   The four-pawed traffic has etched an informal path through this four-acre wooded area. You'll want to take along your binoculars to track the songbirds passing through on their way to warmer climes.

Bonnie Brook Bird Sanctuary is at 2350 N. Bonnie Brook Lane at Forest Avenue. (847) 360-4725.

BOWEN PARK // ½   The north branch of the Waukegan River settles in the ravine at the east side of the park, and dogs love it. In late summer through the fall, it's little more than a trickle. However, after several successive spring rains, the creek begins to look like a real river, and a fast-moving one at that.

Pups who would rather sniff than swim opt for the Bowen Park Formal Gardens. For humans, the rich colors of the perennials are a visual treat, making the gardens a classic backdrop for wedding pictures. A brick pathway winds through the gardens and into a gazebo.

Nearly half of the park's 60 acres is wooded. Bowen Park is considered a natural oak stand. Oaks range from seedlings to some that are more than 20 inches in diameter and at least 60 years old.

From 1912 to 1962, this park was the site of the Joseph Tilton Bowen Country Club, a camp for inner-city children. The original farmhouse is now called the Haines Museum. Today a trail continues through a wooded area and leads to the ravine. A path also leads to the outdoor pool and to the Jack Benny Cultural Arts Center; dogs aren't allowed in the Haines Museum, the pool, or the arts center. But you can take pride in knowing that the legendary comedian hailed from this city.

Bowen Park is at 1800 N. Sheridan Road at Greenwood Avenue. (847) 360-4725.

CALLAHAN-FRANKLIN DOG EXERCISE AREA AT LARSEN NATURE PRESERVE ////
(off-leash) Dedicated in the spring of 2000, this 2.2-acre fenced-in off-leash dog area has quickly become a favorite spot, especially for residents of Waukegan. The Park District recognizes dog owners as legitimate park users and understands that both socialization and exercise are beneficial for dogs.

It's a win-win situation because, as most dog owners know, going home with a tired dog is the sign of a happy person!

Luna and I visited in the middle of the day, so we missed the after-work crowd. But we did meet Wendy and her three miniature schnauzers, Dinky, Romeo, and Princess. As Luna chased her Kong toy, they all chased Luna. These local pups are professionals at the Callahan-Franklin Dog Exercise Area, and so is their mom; they come here three to four times a day. The area is named for a deceased resident who donated the land to the Park District. It's grassy, with lots of shade and lots of room for Frisbee, fetch, or a game of canine tag.

There's one dog-bag dispenser by the entrance, and one garbage can. Equip yourself with a bag right when you walk in to avoid having to retrace your journey from the other side of the field. And be prepared to hold on to your dog's "deposit," if you don't want to head back to the entrance right away.

Open from sunrise to sunset, Callahan-Franklin Dog Exercise Area is at Western and Greenwood Avenues, west of Sheridan Road and north of Glen Flora Avenue. (847) 360-4725.

HENRY PFAU CALLAHAN PARK ½/ This former landfill was closed down in the 1960s. With the exception of the quarter-mile asphalt bike path, there's nothing here except natural growth, which is periodically mowed down.

Pfau Callahan Park is adjacent to Bevier Park, at 2785 Yorkhouse Road west of McAree Road. (847) 360-4725.

HINKSTON PARK // One of several natural oak stands in Waukegan, 18-acre Hinkston Park is a popular destination for picnickers. Seniors from a nearby apartment complex meet here during the day, and the younger set have a playground. There are also soccer fields on the south end.

Hinkston Park is at 810 N. Baldwin Street, at Grand Avenue. (847) 360-4725.

LARSEN NATURE PRESERVE // Only silly dogs who enjoy jumping into swamps aren't deterred by the imposing cattails. The swamp in question is a tiny parcel of mowed grass within this 34-acre park. It's here that dogs from all over Waukegan socialize.

Most dogs know better than to attempt to navigate the swamp. As far as anyone knows, no dog has been trapped in the goo on the bottom, but it is a potential danger. The swamp is not a good place for canine swimming. Instead, after a romp with doggy friends, some pooches retreat into the woods, while others prefer to jog along Green Bay Trail, which borders the east side of the park.

Larsen Nature Preserve is on Western Avenue between Glen Flora and Sunset Avenues. (847) 360-4725.

LYONS WOODS FOREST PRESERVE (LAKE COUNTY FOREST PRESERVE) // The forest is flush with oak trees, so dogs can get a leg up on three varieties: black oak, bur oak, and white oak. The three-mile trail system winds into the woods, through a flat savanna and across a meadow. With a snowpack, the savanna and the meadow present a perfect setting for cross-country skiers.

Warblers enjoy the mix of flatlands and oak forest for insect-catching purposes. While interesting insects abound, happily, mosquitoes aren't especially prevalent here.

A hound might sniff out the remains of the underground railway system. Writer Philip Blanchard owned most of this property during the Civil War, when he was known to have assisted slaves in gaining their freedom. Blanchard later donated a part of his land for a schoolhouse, which stood at the corner of Sheridan and Blanchard Roads and operated until 1940, when it was turned into a tavern. Today the Lyons Woods Forest Preserve encompasses 264 acres.

The preserve is open from 6:30 A.M. to sunset. Take Sheridan Road to Blanchard Road and turn west for the entrance. (847) 367-6640.

POWELL PARK // ½ Sort of Waukegan's version of the Iditarod, Powell Park is a sledder's paradise. What little water there is in the north branch of the Chicago River freezes over easily, and dogs can slide across the ice. A few picnic tables are located near the playground.

Powell Park is about a half-mile from downtown Waukegan at 533 Grand Avenue, at Ash Street. (847) 360-4725.

ROOSEVELT PARK // Dating to 1916, this is Waukegan's first park. Until the 1920s, people came to this place for the artesian water that flowed through the site.

Although there is a small pond, the artesian underground system has long dried up, and the pond is now filled with rainwater. If you want artesian water, you'll have to walk to a nearby convenience store.

Roosevelt Park is at 520 S. McAlister Street, at Belvidere. (847) 360-4725.

UPTON PARK / ½ Watch where Fido lifts his leg: that bush may have historical significance. This park is where nurseryman Robert Douglas developed the Waukegan juniper, and the famous bushes grow throughout the park.

The five-acre area may be small, but it does a brisk business. An asphalt trail leads to the tennis and basketball courts. Other attractions are a T-ball/Little League field and a playground.

Upton Park is at 732 N. Genessee Street, just north of Franklin Street. (847) 360-4725.

WASHINGTON PARK // The north branch of the Waukegan River flows right through Washington Park. Sometimes the water is a couple of feet deep, and at other times there's barely enough water for a dog to drink. When it's deep enough, dogs may take a swim here.

This 19-acre park is long and narrow. Dogs can hang around the band shell or playground at this impressive ravine setting dotted with oak trees. Of course, those trees go to good canine use.

Washington Park is a half-mile from downtown Waukegan at 155 Park Avenue, at Washington Street. (847) 360-4725.

Place to Stay

Best Inns of America When our researcher phoned, the representative said only dogs under 10 pounds are permitted. Being a dutiful reporter, I called back to confirm and was told that only dogs under 20 pounds are permitted. Two days later, I phoned again; this time the answer was, "Only dogs under 15 pounds are allowed." Determined to get a definitive answer, I called again and asked for a general manager. He drew the line at dogs "about 30 to 35 pounds," at least for that day. The inn imposes a nonrefundable fee of $10 per day. Room rates are $60 to $99. 31 N. Green Bay Road; (847) 336-9000.

Doggy Doings

Heritage Day Festival and Parade Beating the array of competing Fourth of July parades, this one is held on the Sunday of the weekend prior to the Fourth. The parade begins at 1 P.M. on Franklin Street and Sheridan Road, and moves north into Bowen Park (at Greenwood Avenue). After the parade, the Waukegan Heritage Festival is held in the park. There is also a petting zoo, and camel and llama rides, for humans only. But your dog is welcome to join you, on-leash, at the arts and crafts fair, the two entertainment stages, and food vendors (the dogs' favorite part of the fest). There are also children's games, where the family dog can cheer from the sidelines. The festivities wind up at about 6 P.M. Call (847) 360-4725.

Tuesday Concerts The Waukegan Municipal Band plays every Tuesday from Memorial Day week through the first week in August at the Lincoln Courtyard, on the corner of Utica and Washington Streets in downtown Waukegan.

Harmonious dogs join their people for relaxing music, a picnic, and a break from their busy summer schedules of burying bones. Concerts are free and begin at 7:30 P.M. Call (847) 360-4725.

Zion

Parks and Beaches

Dogs on-leash are allowed in parks, presuming people pick up after them. A bicycle/walking path interconnects with several parks. For a free local map of parks and the bicycle path, visit the Park District, 2400 Dowie Memorial Drive.

The sole Zion Park District beach isn't supervised and therefore isn't a sanctioned place for swimming (see the Hosah Park listing). However, people and dogs do race into the water. Because there is no lifeguard, Bob Pushee, superintendent of parks, says officials are more concerned about people who wander into the water than about canines. "I see no problem with dogs as long as the dogs don't disturb people who are sunning themselves," he says.

The perceptive observer may note that all the Zion parks are named for biblical characters. Parks are open from sunrise to sunset; Call (847) 746-5500.

BEULAH PARK // ½ Joggers with dogs race along the paved path that snakes through the 80-acre wooded park. If they could only talk, the ancient maple trees might reminisce about the days when the only canines around were wolves. This park is especially beautiful in the autumn or after a snowfall.

Beulah Park is at 19th Avenue (Kedron Boulevard) and Bethesda Boulevard. It is open from sunrise to sunset. (847) 746-5500.

CARMEL PARK / ½ Here are 12 acres of natural splendor, featuring various native trees. It's too wooded here for winter sledding, but cross-country skiers sometimes traverse the area with their hounds on the hunt for squirrels.

Carmel Park is on Carmel Boulevard at Sheridan Road. It is open from sunrise to sunset. (847) 746-5500.

DAVID PARK / ½ This flat stretch of 16 acres is a slice of heaven for athletes, with baseball and soccer fields and plenty of room for stretching canine legs. There's also a playground.

David Park is on West 21st Street between Lewis Avenue and Kenosha Road. The park is open from sunrise to sunset. (847) 746-5500.

EDINAH PARK // Taking a dog off-leash here may lead to disaster, since there's no barrier to the bordering Union Pacific Railroad tracks. Extending for 12 blocks, this park is long and narrow, with a bike path running its length from the wooded area to the children's play area. On a sweltering summer day, locals flock here for the cool relief of a lake breeze and some shade.

Edinah Park is at Shiloh Boulevard and Edinah Avenue, from 17th Street to 29th Street, with entrances on 17th and 29th Streets. It is open from sunrise to sunset. (847) 746-5500.

ELIZABETH PARK *(worth a sniff)*   Only dogs accompanying families to the playground are likely to make the trip to this three-and-a-half-acre park. With the exceptions of the shrieking children in the play area, there's a dearth of canine interest.

Elizabeth Park is on Elizabeth Avenue at 19th Street. The park is open from sunrise to sunset. (847) 746-5500.

HERMON PARK ✓ ½   During the day, seniors head en masse to the community center. After school, the kids come here. Dogs aren't allowed in the community center, but they are allowed on the baseball field when there's no game in progress. This park also has tennis courts.

Hermon Park is at 2700 29th Street, four blocks east of Lewis Avenue. It is open from sunrise to sunset. (847) 746-5500.

HOSAH PARK ✓✓✓   Adjoining the Illinois Beach State Park, Hosah Park includes a 15-acre interpretive trail. Fido can learn about rare plants, which are marked along a handicapped-accessible trail. Legend has it that bears live here. The only bear-like creatures we saw were Newfoundlands. However, raccoon and rabbits are prolific.

The chief draw of this park is the beach. The area is unsupervised, so no swimming is allowed. But people do sneak into the water, as do their dogs. While canines aren't officially allowed either, even parks superintendent Bob Pushee admits that his German shepherd dog (the late Dusty) was once a regular visitor. "He'd run into the water and apparently gulp a lot at a time," recalls Pushee. "Then, he'd belch in the car all the way home."

Only one thousand feet long, this slender beach is slowly shrinking due to erosion. Still, it's the closest thing Zion has to a city beach.

Pushee says that he does have major concerns about people who swim here, and he prefers that canines utilize the beach early in the morning or in the evening. While he says he will look the other way when dogs bound into the water, he won't officially sanction it as a "dog beach."

The entrance to Hosah Park is on Shiloh Boulevard at the lakefront. Open sunrise to sunset. (847) 746-5500.

JOANNA PARK ½✓ A small softball field, tennis courts, and basketball courts share this five-acre park. Dogs have only a bit of running room.

Joanna Park is on 21st Street and Joanna Avenue. It is open from sunrise to sunset. (847) 746-5500.

JORDAN PARK ✓✓ It's shocking—this park is named for a biblical star and not the basketball star. Located within a subdivision, Jordan Park includes a bike path. It has basketball and tennis courts as well as a picnic area. Locals tote the entire family—dogs included—for outings and barbecues.

Jordan Park is at the Lorelei Acres subdivision off of Ninth Street, just west of Kenosha Road. It is open from sunrise to sunset. (847) 746-5500.

LEBANON PARK ½✓ An open field offers some fetching space, and a bike path crosses the three-and-a-half-acre length. This park is primarily frequented by dogs in the 'hood.

On Lebanon Boulevard between 29th and 30th Streets. Open sunrise to sunset. (847) 746-5500.

OPHIR PARK ½✓ This five-acre site is across from Carmel Park. What stands out is a small sledding hill at the south end. Sliding down on a leash is not always smooth going.

Ophir Park is on Sheridan Road between 31st and 32nd Streets. It is open from sunrise to sunset. (847) 746-5500.

SHARON PARK ✓ The jagged ravine makes building on this site impossible. So, the park system wound up with the property and decided to let it grow wild. Sharon Park is now a natural wooded site and difficult to traverse.

The park is at Ezekiel Avenue and Ezekiel Place from 31st Street to 33rd Street. Access is at 32nd and at 33rd Streets. It is open from sunrise to sunset. (847) 746-5500.

SHILOH PARK ✓✓ ½ A formidable 140 acres sit smack dab at the center of town. However, after subtracting places where dogs are not allowed—the golf course, swimming pool, indoor ice rink, and leisure center—you're left with about 30 acres of dog-friendly park. Still, that's room to spare, and there's a gorgeous forested area. A path offers easy access through these woods. There are also tennis and basketball courts, baseball fields, and places to picnic.

Shiloh Park is on Shiloh Boulevard at Dowie Memorial Drive, two blocks west of Sheridan Road. It is open from sunrise to sunset. (847) 746-5500.

Doggy Doings

Concerts in the Park Dogs are discouraged from singing along, but they're welcome to listen to the concerts at the Shiloh Park band shell. The free country-
and-western, oldies, and rock-and-roll concerts start at 7 P.M. on Thursdays
from mid-June through the end of July. No alcoholic drinks are allowed. Call
(847) 746-5500.

Walk Illinois The annual two-mile fun walk to promote physical fitness is held
on a Saturday in early May. The walk is endorsed by Illinois governor George
Ryan. The walk begins at 9 A.M. at Shiloh Park. There is no registration fee.
Call (847) 746-5500.

Festivals

Fourth of July Festival The celebration begins on July 3 with a family concert at
7 P.M. at the band shell in Shiloh Park, on Shiloh Boulevard at Dowie Memorial Drive, two blocks west of Sheridan Road. Burgers, bratwurst (after all, we
are near Wisconsin), and hot dogs are available. Sorry, no dog treats. But Fido
is welcome to scrounge for dropped morsels.

On July 4, the celebration continues at Shiloh Park with a series of musical attractions, jugglers, and clowns geared for children. That's followed by the
local Little League all-star competition. Dogs can't play, but they enjoy watching the game. Food vendors represent various local eateries. The activities on
the Fourth are from 9 A.M. to 10 P.M. The event is free; call (847) 746-5500.

Jubilee Days Battles from the Civil War and the Revolutionary War are reenacted
at Shiloh Park. Be warned: The racket of the make-believe gun battle can
make canines revolt. One pooch lost its temper, and now officials are wary of
dogs' attending. They are still allowed for the time being.

The Jubilee Days celebration is held over Labor Day weekend. The war battles in the park are on Sunday from 11 A.M. to 6 P.M. and on Monday from 10
A.M. to 6 P.M.

At 1 P.M. on Monday, there's the big parade, which dogs are welcome to
view. It is quite a procession, the biggest Memorial Day parade in the state.
Trooping by are 125 marching units accompanied by dozens of floats and way
too many politicians. The assemblage kicks off at 25th Street and files through
town before breaking ranks at Shiloh Park School, near the park.

The winner of the Queen's beauty pageant is crowned at 7 P.M. at the band
shell in Shiloh Park on Monday, followed by a fireworks display. After catching

the new Queen, you'll probably want to make your bows with Fido. The fireworks are too much for most dogs to handle. Admission to Jubilee Days is free; call (847) 746-5500.

Place to Stay

Motor Inn Motel   There's a $50 deposit for canine guests, which is returned once it's established that Fido hasn't eaten the TV, helped himself to the bar, or caused any other room damage; otherwise, you won't get a penny back. Rates are $40 to $65. 41440 U.S. Route 41 (Skokie Highway) at Illinois Route 173; (847) 395-7300.

5 KANE, McHENRY, and WILL COUNTIES

How spectacular to witness natural beauty, totally unspoiled. While this sort of land lies low in other counties, it's abundant here. In this neck of the woods, dogs can act like dogs.

Some cities and towns, however, temper the fun with an increasing roster of restrictions. McHenry, Algonquin, and Lake in the Hills are among the communities that don't let hounds in their parks. Notwithstanding these wet blankets, communities such as St. Charles are growing in leaps and bounds and still manage to maintain a dog-friendly posture. One St. Charles city official noted, "Seeing dogs in the parks and on downtown streets is something that gives us a special mark of friendliness. It makes you want to say, 'Hello,' or at least say, 'Can I pet your dog?'"

KANE COUNTY

Aurora

Doggy Doings

Mid-American Canoe Race The race is on at 8 A.M. on the first Sunday in June. Canines can get up early to join in and jump into canoes. They can, but they don't. While dogs are allowed, no one can remember any participating. The race begins at Mount Saint Mary Park in St. Charles, at Prairie Street across from the Piano Factory Outlet Mall, just east of Illinois Route 31 and a half mile south of Illinois Route 64 (Main Street). It continues on the Fox River to McCullough Park, at 150 W. Illinois Avenue, at the Illinois Avenue Bridge, Aurora.

Following the race is an awards ceremony. The culmination is a family festival in the park, with games for one and all. Call (630) 859-8606.

Summer Concert Series Summer concerts are held at 7:30 P.M. on Wednesdays at various parks around Aurora and North Aurora, from early June through late August. The concerts are free. Provide your own snacks and blankets. Call (630) 859-8606.

Place to Stay

Motel 6 Dogs are allowed at no extra charge. Pets cannot be left unattended in the room at any time. Rates are $45.99 to $49.99. 2380 N. Farnsworth Road; (630) 851-3600.

Dundee Township

Parks

The Park District oversees parks in Carpentersville, East Dundee, Sleepy Hollow, and West Dundee. Dogs must be on leashes, and they're not allowed in children's play areas, picnic areas, or athletic fields. Dundee Township Park District parks are open from sunrise to sunset; call (847) 428-7131.

CARPENTER PARK // If your pooch is partial to a brisk run in wide-open spaces, this expansive park hits the nail on the head. However, after you both catch your breath, there's not much else to do. Social canines should make the scene when community events are held.

Open sunrise to sunset. Carpenter Park is at Maple and Cleveland Avenues, Lord Street, and Carpenter Boulevard, Carpentersville. (847) 428-7131.

HICKORY HILL PARK // Set back from the road, this 26-acre site warms the soul. Enjoy its peace and quiet while you can—there's talk this land may eventually become part of a highway.

Open sunrise to sunset. 770 Navajo Drive, Carpentersville. (847) 428-7131.

KEMPER PARK // Unfortunately, there are no trees at this 20-acre park. However, there are lots of dogs. A good place to bark "hi" to a neighbor.

Open sunrise to sunset. On Hazard Road and Sparrow Court, Carpentersville. (847) 428-7131.

LIONS PARK / ½ It's one of the most popular parks in the area, but many of the recreational facilities are off-limits to dogs. It's still a good place for dogs to cozy up to kids.

Open sunrise to sunset. Lions Park is bounded by Penny Road, Aldis Drive, and Park Street in East Dundee. (847) 428-7131.

RACEWAY WOODS // ½   This newly acquired property abounds with birds and wildflowers to see and sniff. One caution: The trails that wind through the wooded area aren't well marked. If you and your hound are directionally challenged, be sure to take a trusty compass. Once you reach the heart of the woods, the traffic noise disappears. Except for the occasional bark, you can bask in the quiet and solitude.

This park is named for the auto speedway that once operated here. You can still see remnants of the concrete track bridge that used to cross it. Cars are no longer allowed here, but feel free to race your dog.

Open sunrise to sunset. Raceway Woods is on Illinois Route 31, a mile north of Old Huntley Blacktop and before Gentle Breeze Terrace, Carpentersville. (847) 428-7131.

RANDALL OAKS PARK AND BARNYARD ZOO // ½   Encompassing 141 acres, this is the largest of Dundee Township's parks. There's a heap of undeveloped leg-stretching space. There's also a zoo here, but dogs aren't allowed inside. That's OK—they enjoy peeking in from the outside, wondering what that strange assortment of smells is all about. The zoo is open weekends-only during spring and fall and is open daily during the summer. Admission is $1 for adults and 75 cents for children. To enter the park itself on weekends or holidays, non-residents of Dundee Township must pay $3 per car.

Open sunrise to sunset. Located at Randall Road south of Binnie Road, and south of Randall Oaks Golf Course, Carpentersville. (847) 428-7131.

SLEEPY HOLLOW PARK AND POOL / ½   A popular destination with the kids, but if you're looking for canine activities, Sleepy Hollow comes up empty. Dogs aren't allowed to do laps in the outdoor pool or visit the day camp in this 10-acre park.

Open sunrise to sunset. Located at Winmoor and Glen Oak Drives in Sleepy Hollow. (847) 428-7131.

SOUTH END PARK AND ISLAND ///   You may want to have a loaded camera ready at this scenic Fox River locale. Dogs who jump into the water often share space with ducks, geese, swans, and even cranes. The birds and the dogs come for the water, but the kids come for Little League, which is a big deal in this 11-acre park. Adults also come to feed those birds, and some people don't like it when the dogs chase them off.

Open sunrise to sunset. Located at First and Riverview Streets, at the Fox River, West Dundee. (847) 428-7131.

TOWER PARK // A serene spot, with picturesque old houses lending a backdrop that looks like a movie set from another era. Good news for dogs: This 10-acre site is loaded with trees.

Open sunrise to sunset. Tower Park is at Fifth and Main Streets in West Dundee. (847) 428-7131.

Doggy Doing

Summer Concerts Free concerts are held in July at 7 P.M. on Thursdays in Carpenter Park, located at Maple and Cleveland Avenues, Lord Street, and Carpenter Boulevard. Snacks and beverages are available. Take your own blanket. Call (847) 428-7131.

Elburn

Park

Dogs are allowed on-leash, and their people must pick up. The park is open from sunrise to sunset. Call (630) 365-6315.

LIONS PARK // The Elburn Lions Club operates this 25-acre site. It has a playground and a pair of pavilions, where the Lions Club caters private parties. Dogs are welcome on the park grounds, but even dogs with lampshades on their heads are not invited to party.

Open sunrise to sunset. Lions Park is at 500 Fillmore Street. (630) 365-6315.

Elgin

Parks

Leashed dogs are welcome in Elgin's larger parks, but dogs get a chilly reception in many of the smaller community parks. That's why only the big parks are listed here. Hopefully, you'll be greeted with hugs and doggy kisses. Open 8 A.M. to sunset; call (847) 931-6120.

LORDS PARK /// This park boasts a small zoo with elk, deer, pigs, sheep, llamas, and more. Although dogs are not allowed in the zoo, your pooch can take the measure of the various residents from the sidelines.

In the remainder of the park, trails wind circles around the mature oak trees and the lovely lagoons.

Open 8 A.M. to sunset. On Oakwood Boulevard, which actually cuts through the park; also off Bode and Gold Roads and Grand Boulevard, east of Liberty Street. (847) 931-6120.

SPARTAN MEADOWS AND ELGIN SPORTS COMPLEX // This is a primo place for athletic people but only adequate for athletic canines. Soccer, football, and baseball fields eat up the majority of the park. Organized games are often in session, and no canines make the lineup. There's also a golf complex, where dogs are not allowed. Despite these handicaps, it's a fitting place to run when there are no games.

Open 8 A.M. to sunset. Located just south of Illinois State Route 20 and east of South McLean Boulevard. (847) 931-6120.

TROUT PARK /// A large wooded area with lots of nature trails. Music from songbirds greets the ears, but dogs may be disappointed by the curious dearth of squirrels. The nearby Fox River Trail tends to get congested on weekends with bicyclers and joggers. To avoid traffic jams, try it out early in the morning. By the way, no one I spoke with knows why this is called Trout Park.

Open 8 A.M. to sunset. Trout Park is south of Northwest Tollway at Dundee Avenue; take Trout Park Boulevard into the park. (847) 931-6120.

WING PARK /// Finding your way into the park off Wing Street is no problem. The problem is finding your way out. Good luck. One of the exit roads empties into McLure Avenue, which drops you off in a subdivision nowhere near where you entered. Construction on the roads is expected to simplify getting around.

But the pros outweigh the cons. Driving under stand after stand of majestic oaks is magnificent. Once you're in the park, there's lots of hiking and walking room. It's hard to play fetch in some places because there are so many trees. But Fido won't care. Lots of trees means lots of squirrels. It's a beautiful spot for a picnic. There's an in-line skating area, but dogs with tails might get run over and are discouraged from running here. There's also a new nine-hole golf course and a family aquatic center; sorry, no dogs allowed.

Open 8 A.M. to sunset. The entrance to Wing Park is on the north side of Wing Street, between North McLean Boulevard and North State Street. (847) 931-6120.

Doggy Doings

Elgin Summer Concerts Elgin summer concerts are held at Lords Park and Wing Park. At Lords Park Pavilion, on Oakwood Boulevard, off Bode and Gold Roads, concerts start at 4:30 P.M. on Sundays from mid-June through early August. Children's programming is presented on alternate weekends, and on the other weeks it's a variety, such as the Elgin Symphony Orchestra, oldies rock and roll, disco, or jazz.

More concerts are held at 7 P.M. Wednesdays at Wing Park's band shell, between North McLean Boulevard and North State Street, from mid-June through late July. Entertainment can be anything from musical comedy to jazz to pop music. Pack your own picnics, lawn chairs, blankets, and rawhide. All concerts are free. Call (847) 931-6120.

Frisbee-Catching Competition The Windy City K-9 Disc Club's annual Frisbee-catching competition is held in mid-May at Wing Park, between North McLean Boulevard and North State Street, on a Saturday morning.

Dogs partake in both minidistance and free-flight competitions. Any dog can participate, and there's no charge to enter. Couch-potato pups are welcome to sit and watch. There's also no charge to observe. Free Alpo samples are usually given out, and so are free scoopers. This is a handy place to learn more about canine Frisbee. For more information about entering the event, call the Windy City K-9 Disc Club, (630) 355-2777. Or for general information call (847) 931-6120.

Place to Stay

Days Inn For a pooch, you pay $10 extra, and it's not refundable. Rooms range from $54 to $81. 1585 Dundee Road; (847) 695-2100.

Hampshire

Parks

Hampshire's two parks require leashes, and owners must pick up. The parks are open from sunrise to sunset. Call (847) 683-2690.

BRUCE REAM MEMORIAL PARK // ½ Lots of open space and shady spots for a picnic. Other amenities include a pavilion, basketball courts, a soccer field, a horseshoe pit, and lit ball fields.

Open sunrise to sunset. 400 W. Jefferson Avenue. (847) 683-2690.

HAMPSHIRE EAST PARK // ½   A winter play place with ice-skating (dogs are discouraged from venturing onto the ice) and sledding. For fun in the summer, there's a picnic pavilion, a playground, a baseball diamond, tennis and basketball courts, and a horseshoe pit.

Open sunrise to sunset. 400 E. Jefferson Avenue. (847) 683-2690.

Doggy Doing

Car Show   Canines are invited to the Antique Custom Car Show, held sometime in August at Hampshire East Park, 400 E. Jefferson Avenue. Admission is $3 for adults and $1 for children 12 and under. Call (847) 683-2316.

North Aurora

Doggy Doing

North Aurora Pet Parade   Participants line up at 1 P.M. on the first Saturday in May. The marching commences at 2 P.M. at the North Aurora Friendship and Activities Center, at Illinois State Routes 56 and 31. The parade then proceeds down Route 56 and past the Fox River to Island Park. Costumes are the rage, but they're not required. Trophies are given in 26 categories, so lots of people and their pets are winners.

There is no registration fee; preregistration is suggested. Call (630) 896-6664.

St. Charles

Parks

The parks in St. Charles are eminently dog friendly and offer a wealth of recreational activities. However, too many people abuse the privileges and don't pick up. It's beginning to create a stir in the community. Dogs are supposed to be on-leash, but local officials are reasonable about the rules. Dogs are not allowed to swim at any of the parks. Parks are open from sunrise to sunset. Call (630) 584-1885.

BOY SCOUT ISLAND // ½   A boat launch on the Fox River attracts many families who enjoy weekend boating.

The park is a narrow peninsula into the river. Formerly a site where Boy Scouts earned their badges, this fairly small park is a nice place to meet fishermen—or for pups to purloin their catches.

Open sunrise to sunset. Boy Scout Island is on Illinois Route 31 about one mile north of Illinois Route 64. (630) 584-1885.

FERSON CREEK PARK /// ½   Ferson Creek Park is surrounded by water on three sides (Fox River, Ferson Creek, and a lagoon). The Fox, which has been cleaned up a lot in recent years, is still a concern due to heavy boat traffic. Ferson Creek is the cleanest place to swim. There's a canoe launch, but you must take your own canoe. Fishing here has improved in recent years. Possible catches include smallmouth bass, catfish, and carp.

There's also a picnic pavilion.

Open sunrise to sunset. Entrance is on Illinois State Route 31, two miles north of Illinois Route 64. (630) 584-1885.

LINCOLN PARK //   A pretty little downtown park with a gazebo. It hugs the edge of the historic Old St. Charles neighborhood—eight blocks of restored landmark buildings that now house a variety of fine shops and restaurants. The park is ideal for taking a break from an afternoon of shopping. When the sun goes down, the place is aglow with vintage-style lights, beckoning neighbors for an evening stroll.

Open sunrise to sunset. Lincoln Park is at Main, Fourth, and Fifth Streets. (630) 584-1885.

MOUNT SAINT MARY PARK ///   This is the favorite choice of local dogs. An asphalt path extends for more than a mile through the grounds, most of it along the Fox River. It's both a pretty park and a decent fishing destination.

There are also two tennis courts and a roller hockey/ice hockey rink.

Open sunrise to sunset. Enter at Prairie Street across from the Piano Factory Outlet Mall, just east of Illinois Route 31 and a half mile south of Illinois Route 64 (Main Street). (630) 584-1885.

POTTAWATOMIE PARK ///   This popular site is like an amusement park. Loads of activities compete for your attention—miniature golf, tennis courts, two pools, a nine-hole golf course, a safety town, a band shell, two pavilions, sand volleyball courts, picnic grounds, and concession stands. Dogs can dine in the picnic area, but they are not allowed to participate in most of the other goings-on. A small lap dog may be able to join you on a pedal boat ride; boat rentals are $12 an hour. The park also provides convenient access to the Fox River Trail.

Easy Rider

Why is it that for some dogs a car ride is equivalent to a real-life horror movie, while other dogs act as though they've just won the vacation lottery at the mere utterance of the words "Let's go for a ride"?

Two factors play into how a dog feels about the car. The first is how it physically feels. The other is the dog's conditioned response to the experience.

Dogs that get carsick aren't likely to enjoy the ride. Can you blame them? If you got sick to your stomach every time you rode in an elevator, you'd soon learn to take the stairs instead.

Nevertheless, some dogs consistently get sick and still act as if they enjoy car rides. Are those dogs stupid? Probably not. Chicago veterinarian Dr. Shelly Rubin explains, "Actually, the dog probably considers being with you so important that it overrides its trepidation about the car."

In any case, Rubin says, there is something you can do. First off, don't feed the dog before a trip of any length. For your dog, it's the equivalent of going on a roller-coaster ride after lunch.

Rubin also says giving your dog Dramamine before the trip can help. A side effect is that it may make your dog sleepy, which is usually desirable. Please, see your vet about dosage. If you prefer natural choices, try an herbal calmer (available at pet stores and through pet catalogs), and follow the instructions.

Dogs who become physically ill may develop a psychological fear of the car as a result. This aversion is often heightened by angry and/or frustrated owners.

Other dogs who never get physically carsick may also fear the car. This almost always stems from a bad experience of some kind. For example, if the first two trips a puppy took in the car were to see the vet, the dog isn't likely to trust that awful car. Or a dog with limited experience in a car may be pushed to go on a long road trip. Feeling the highway for the first time, the dog begins to pace nervously, and Mom hollers, "Settle down! Bad dog!"

In the course of researching this book, our car was totaled as I crossed an intersection. Another car ran a stop sign and threw our car across the intersection and onto a nearby lawn. Luckily, I was fine, and so were both Lucy and Chaser. At least, they seemed to be fine.

continued

Before the accident, Chaser loved the car—probably because she viewed the backseat as another place to nap. Lucy, who was just over a year old, was a bit nervous in the car, and I was working on getting her over her anxiety.

However, after the accident neither dog would enter the rental car without coaxing. Once inside, they paced and cried. At first, we blamed the cheap rental. But it soon became clear that both of these dogs were now terrified of cars. We utilized the following desensitization program, and for the most part it worked. Chaser still gets pangs of nervousness once inside the car, but at least we no longer have to cajole her to join us. Lucy is now relatively calm in the car. This program sounds tedious, and it is. It takes a minimum of 10 days and up to two months to really begin to work.

- At first, alleviate the dog's basic fear of the vehicle itself. Provide as many meals as possible in the parked car. Don't even think about starting the engine. Using treats, encourage your dog to hop into the car, and reward the dog with breakfast and/or dinner. You might also play a game of fetch around the vehicle. Every once in a while, have your pooch jump into the car. Say, "Good dog," and continue the game. When the dog's anxiety over the car has totally disappeared, move on to the next step.

- Periodically, have the dog jump into the car on your command. Then say, "Sit," and offer a tidbit. Now have the dog jump out, and again say, "Sit." This time, simply offer vocal praise. Do this repeatedly until all signs of nervousness have disappeared. In some dogs, this may occur after only five or six attempts; others may take two to three attempts a day for a week or more.

- Repeat the preceding step, but now you get in the front seat. Start the car, then turn off the engine immediately. Do this twice. Then start the engine again, but this time let it idle for about 30 seconds before turning it off. Whenever your dog is ready to exit the car, say, "Sit" before it jumps out. You don't want the dog to bolt; having to sit will calm the dog down so that it leaves only when you say so. Have the dog sit again once it's on terra firma. A dog holding a stationary sit can't nervously pace—it's thinking about sitting, not its frayed nerves. Besides, for safety reasons it's wise to train a dog to sit after departing any vehicle.

- Now we're ready to roll. Take the dog for a ride of about 10 feet. At journey's end, nonchalantly remove the dog from the car, giving the "sit" command before and after. If the dog expresses nervousness, you've pushed too fast. If the dog performs well, try it again for 20 feet. If you've succeeded, try going halfway down the block. From here, you can escalate the distance more quickly.

- After two or three spins around the block, you're ready to really go somewhere. Choose a place close to home that your dog really likes. A park usually fits that bill. Make two trips to this spot. Each time, before you set off, enthusiastically tell your dog, "Let's take a ride."

- Now choose another canine-friendly destination farther away from home.

- If you've succeeded, choose yet another destination even farther away. Congratulations: your pup is now the perfect passenger. Although, it would be nice if you could also teach your dog to do the driving and pay the insurance bills.

Here are some additional tips for automotive-minded canines:

- Before making a long trip, take the dog for a walk, play a game of fetch, or let the dog run around the yard. Sleepy dogs are the best travelers.

- For safety reasons, most vets agree that dogs should be restricted to the backseat. If Chaser had been in the passenger seat when we were rammed by another car, she likely would have hit the windshield. Also, passenger-side air bags could injure dogs. There's no room to crate a midsize or large dog in a typical car, but there's room in a minivan, and it's the safest way for a hound to travel. Automobile car harnesses are also available (at pet stores and through catalogs). They're a particularly good idea for dogs who want to play in the car. Of course, it's your job to teach the pooch that a car is not a place for games.

- For a dog that barks at everything that passes by, it helps to refocus the animal's attention before the barking begins. Otherwise, you'll be shouting "Quiet! Quiet!" through each and every trip. Take along a Kong toy (available at pet stores) stuffed with low-fat peanut butter or cream

continued

cheese. Your pooch will have to work to lick it out. Offer the Kong before you leave your driveway, well before the inevitable chorus begins.

- Don't allow your dog to hang its head out the window. Just as objects can fly up and hit your windshield, the same missiles can hit your dog. Pebbles or road debris can lodge in your dog's eyes or ears and could cause a serious problem. Instead, crack both rear windows to allow for air circulation, or just turn on the air-conditioning.

- The back of a flatbed truck really isn't a place for a dog. While you see dogs riding in open cabs all the time, vets see the results. Dogs can easily end up on the road.

From Memorial Day through Labor Day, nonresidents must pay $5 per car to enter the park.

Open 8 A.M. to 11 P.M. The park is three blocks north of Illinois Route 64 (Main Street) at Second Avenue. (630) 584-1885.

Doggy Doing

Concerts in the Park Lincoln Park Gazebo (at Main, Fourth, and Fifth Streets) is the site of free concerts at 7 P.M. on Thursdays in July and August. Keep time to a wide range of music, from the Fox Valley Concert Band to country and western. Pack your own food. Concerts are free for people and pets. Call (630) 377-6161.

Festivals

Pride of the Fox RiverFest This festival is held over the second weekend in June, at Pottawatomie Park, three blocks north of Illinois Route 64 (Main Street) at Second Avenue; Mount Saint Mary Park, at Prairie Street across from the Piano Factory Outlet Mall, just east of Illinois Route 31; and Lincoln Park, at Main, Fourth, and Fifth Streets.

Get those taste buds in gear for the many food vendors participating in the Taste of St. Charles. There are also arts and crafts vendors and live music. A unique event is the Dragon Boat race on the Fox River (dogs can't participate). There's also a water ski demonstration. Dogs can cool off in the river between boat races. There's no admission fee. Call (630) 377-6161 or (800) 777-4373.

St. Charles Scarecrow Festival This three-day festival takes place over the second weekend in October. The majority of the activity is at Pottawatomie and Lincoln Parks, with additional events staged throughout the city. You can make your own scarecrow (supplies provided) and cart it home with you to scare off the birds, or your dog. The main event is the scarecrow contest, for which locals begin preparing months in advance. Registration is required, and your completed entry must be dropped off the Thursday before the contest to qualify. Festivalgoers vote for the winner from among more than a hundred scarecrows on display. Dogs don't yet have the vote. Cash prizes exceed $1,000, so the competition gets serious. In addition to the scary straw, there's plenty of food as wells as entertainment and arts and crafts. There's no admission fee. Call (630) 377-6161 or (800) 777-4373.

Kane County Forest Preserves

The preserves' approximately 85 miles of scenic trails make for some of the best dog walking in Kane County. Some of those trails follow the Fox River, others cross abandoned railroad tracks, but all are picturesque.

Squirrels are a canine drawing card. There's other wildlife, too, from skunks and raccoon to migrating birds. The Great Western Trail is a smooth limestone path stretching about 17 miles from St. Charles to Sycamore, crossing small streams and wetlands. The Virgil L. Gilman Trail in Aurora starts at State Route 30 near Montgomery Road and goes nearly 10 miles to Bliss Woods, crossing Waubonsee Creek. Contact the Kane County Forest Preserve District for free maps.

Pets must be leashed at all times in the forest preserves, which are open from 8 A.M. to sunset. Kane County Forest Preserve District, 719 Batavia Avenue, Building G, Geneva, IL 60134; call (630) 232-5980 or (630) 232-1242.

Following are some Kane County Forest Preserve highlights.

BLACKHAWK FOREST PRESERVE /// This preserve is the final resting site of some unknown soldiers who fell in the Pottawatomie Indian Wars. Today the park offers boating, picnic shelters, bike trail access, fishing, and horseback riding.

Open 8 A.M. to sunset. Blackhawk Forest Preserve is at Illinois Route 31 and the Fox River in St. Charles Township. (630) 232-5980.

BURNIDGE/PAUL WOLFF FOREST PRESERVE /// ½ At a whopping 486 acres, this is the largest forest preserve in the county. It's popular with dog trainers, who use the area for tracking and retrieving practice. You may see them throwing dummies into the water for their dogs to retrieve. People fishing aren't always happy about this.

The site is also home to ground-nesting birds, who set up house in the open fields. Dogs are discouraged from dropping by during nesting season (around June). The birds have a tough enough time surviving as it is, without being trampled by dogs. The park also has a playground, nine miles of hiking trails, camping, fishing, and horseback riding.

Open 8 A.M. to sunset. Located off Big Timber Road in Rutland and Elgin Townships. (630) 232-5980.

FABYAN FOREST PRESERVE // ½ Named for the original settlers, this 245-acre site offers boating, fishing, picnic shelters, and bike trail access. The Fabyan Villa Museum is in a 1907 Frank Lloyd Wright house built for Colonel George and Nelle Fabyan. The Fabyan Japanese Garden was designed by Taro Otuska, a landscape architect sent to the Fabyans by the crown prince of Japan. The garden may be reserved for weddings or family portraits. Dogs aren't allowed in either place. However, they're welcome on the forest trails.

Open 8 A.M. to sunset. The Forest Preserve straddles the Fox River between State Route 31 and State Route 25 in Geneva. (630) 232-5980.

LEROY OAKES FOREST PRESERVE /// A shallow, rock-bottomed creek that ripples through the preserve is popular with dogs who like to splash in the water. Dogs who prefer to keep their paws high and dry can do so with abandon in the open fields. There are also picnic shelters, bike trails, fishing, and horseback riding. The 1843 Durant-Peterson House, a brick farmstead that has been restored as a living-history museum, is located here. For tour information call (630) 377-6424. Also at this forest preserve is Pioneer Sholes School, an authentically restored and furnished one-room schoolhouse. For group tours call (630) 584-3267. Dogs aren't allowed in the Durant-Peterson House or the Pioneer Sholes School.

Open 8 A.M. to sunset. LeRoy Oakes Forest Preserve is at Randall Road north of State Route 64 in St. Charles Township. (630) 232-5980.

TEKAKWITHA WOODS FOREST PRESERVE /// The 64-acre preserve allows you to stroll through forests and open grasslands, as well as along the banks of the Fox River. Native prairie and savanna areas are being restored. A nature center houses exhibits and a "discovery corner" for children. The Fox River Bike Trail hugs the eastern boundary.

In spring the prairies are carpeted with an array of wildflowers. If you and Fido are quiet like a mouse, you might glimpse some of the abundant wildlife.

Of historic interest is the McGuire House, the home of Father Hugh McGuire, who bequeathed the land to the Sisters of Mercy. The Sisters later sold the land to the Forest Preserve District.

Open 8 A.M. to sunset. The preserve is across the Fox River from Blackhawk Forest Preserve, in St. Charles Township. (630) 232-5980.

MCHENRY COUNTY

Crystal Lake

Parks

Dogs can't write love letters in the sand on any of the beaches, but they're welcome in the parks if they're on-leash and people pick up. Parks are open from sunrise to sunset. Call (815) 459-0680.

LIPPOLD PARK /// ½   This is 309 acres of park featuring six miles of crushed-limestone trails and a choice of places for dog swimming. There are two nameless ponds which, combined, cover 25 acres. The fishing is excellent. The Park District is planning to build piers, but access to the water is no problem, especially if you happen to be a dog.

Little League teams, soccer leagues, and football players virtually live here, what with the 11 baseball diamonds, nine soccer fields, and a trio of gridirons. Several adult leagues play here as well.

Open sunrise to sunset. Lippold Park is a quarter mile west of Illinois Route 14 (Northwest Highway) on Illinois Route 176 (Terra Cotta Avenue). (815) 459-0680.

VETERAN ACRES/STEARNS WOODS ///   This heavily wooded park was formed by a glacier thousands of years ago. Today it's a haven for wildlife. In fact, Stearns Woods is protected by the Illinois Nature Preserve Commission. The trails rank from wide and flat to rugged and narrow.

White-tailed deer, woodchucks, and raccoon are the notable mammals. Hundreds of bird species also inhabit these 260 acres.

The five-acre pond is too scummy for dog purposes, but dogs can watch people fish on the pier. Come winter snows, the steep embankment screams out for sledding.

"Come"—the Most Important Command

Come is the single most important word a dog can know. "If a dog doesn't reliably—and I do mean reliably—come when called, it shouldn't be in an off-leash area," Chicago trainer Kathy McCarthy Olshein says. "Being honest about your dog may save its life."

Here are instructions and rules for the "come" command, with input from McCarthy Olshein as well as Chicago trainer/behavior counselor Jennifer Boznos and trainer/behaviorist Margaret Gibbs of Riverwoods:

- Any dog of any age can be taught to understand "come." Puppies should begin learning this from a young age.

- Be aware that not all dogs can reliably adhere to "come." Much depends on the breed and the individual dog's history. For example, some sight hounds (such as greyhounds or Afghans) will keep running ahead no matter what you call out, particularly if the pet is a former racing dog. Also, some Arctic breeds, such as malamutes and Siberian huskies, may be too independent or too predisposed to roam to honor an immediate "come" command. Another challenge can be a basset hound with its nose to the ground, or a terrier already in the habit of chasing vermin.

- While it's the most important command, a reliable "come" is not easy to attain. It takes lots and lots of practice. McCarthy Olshein never expects a dog under two years of age to fully get it.

- If it's done correctly, "come" is a formal request for the dog to drop what it's doing, run to you, face you, and stay.

- Think of all training sessions as a game, not as work.

- Never, ever call the dog after it runs off and then reprimand it when it returns; in essence, you're disciplining the dog for returning. When the dog returns promptly in response to "come," that's always a reason to celebrate, no matter what the circumstances are.

- Always be ready to enforce the command if the dog doesn't obey. In very early training, it's exceedingly important to set the dog up for success. Of course, when the dog succeeds, it should be rewarded.

- Even when teaching an adopted dog, no matter what the age, begin the training process as if the dog were a pup. If the dog has previous training, this is the only way to determine the level of reliability. Breezing through the basics will build your dog's confidence.

- Begin teaching at home without distractions. Whenever you know your pup is coming to you, say, "Come." Reward with the food you were about to offer anyway, or a treat or a toy, and lots of praise.

- Over time, make it tougher, but always use a leash so that you can enforce the request. When the dog is playing with a toy, say, "Come," and reward with a treat or a better toy, and praise.

- Make it even tougher by adding distance and distractions. When the dog is off visiting Grandma in another room, call. If the dog fails to respond, don't worry about it. Just don't make the conditions as difficult next time.

- Now go outside. With the dog on the leash, call and back up. The dog will naturally give chase. Absolutely use treats or a toy, whatever is most motivating for your dog. Over time, add distance and distractions as you did indoors. The only difference is that you add distance while retaining control by using a long line.

- Different trainers like different distances; starting with a 20-foot line (such as heavy-duty rope, available at any hardware store) is a good plan. Wear gloves to prevent rope burns. Go into an open area so that the rope doesn't get wound around trees. The idea is to correct the dog and reel it in if it doesn't promptly respond to your "come." Never repeat the command; the dog gets one shot. You should always end training sessions on a successful "come."

- Advanced training means that you're ready to set your dog up. Go to a place when you know squirrels or other dogs will be present, or set a favorite food down as a distraction. Then call your pup. When your dog succeeds 100 percent of the time, you may want to add 10 feet to the line.

continued

When you consistently leave the long line dragging on the ground, you're ready. At this level, instead of offering the same old reward, Boznos recommends using whatever you call the dog off of as a reward. In other words, when you successfully call the dog off a squirrel, you then allow the dog to go after the squirrel as its reward. You're asking more of your dog, but you're also offering more of a reward.

- When freeing the dog for the first time in an off-leash area, you don't want to teach the dog that it can run amok. All of your hard work will be wasted. When taking the dog off-leash, practice several "comes," advancing the distance each time. Then allow your dog to play.

- Even five years later, if you're still allowing your dog off-leash, you must still periodically practice. Without continuing education, most dogs won't continue to adhere to "come."

Open sunrise to sunset. The entrance is off Walkup Avenue just north of Illinois Route 176. (815) 459-0680.

McHenry

Park

Dogs are not allowed in the McHenry municipal parks, but Moraine Hills State Park welcomes dogs, as long as they're on a leash. Call (815) 385-1624.

MORAINE HILLS STATE PARK /// Get ready for a fun and informative experience. For starters, a moraine is an accumulation of boulders and debris deposited by a glacier. That's of particular interest to dogs who like to hop from boulder to boulder, since tons of them have been deposited around here. Continuing the geology lesson, there's also a kettle—a depression formed by a melting block of glacial ice. It's a nice flat space, perfect for fetch.

You won't be led astray along the three crushed-limestone trails: they're color-coded. The trails take you past Leatherhead Bog, the Fox River, and Lake Defiance, which is one of the few glacial lakes that remain largely unspoiled. Lake Defiance has an unstable peat shoreline, so you can't get too close to the water. However, you can rent a boat and fishing gear. You can also fish on the Fox River; there's even a pier.

There are picnic areas, two concession stands, and an interpretive center.

Moraine Hills State Park is on River Road between Illinois Route 176 and Illinois Route 120. The park's hours are a bit complicated but are basically sunrise to sunset. Get your scorecard ready: The park is open November through January, 8 A.M. to 5 P.M.; February, 8 A.M. to 6 P.M.; March, 8 A.M. to 7 P.M.; April, 7 A.M. to 8 P.M.; May through August, 6 A.M. to 9 P.M.; September, 7 A.M. to 8 P.M.; and October, 8 A.M. to 7 P.M. (815) 385-1624.

Shopping

VIP Pet Salon and Gift Shop Here you'll find two thousand square feet of pet stuff. Express yourself or delight some other VIP with treasures you won't see elsewhere. For example, you may take a shine to the stained-glass springer spaniel in a field for $38, or a gold-plated necklace with 15 dogs for $110. You can also choose just about any dog breed for a T-shirt ($18 to $23.99), or supply a photo of your own dog, and they'll put it on a T-shirt or mouse pad.

Owner Pat Burke remarks, "If there's another store like this in the state of Illinois, I'd like to see it." Burke, who has been in the pet-grooming business for 30 years, decided a few years ago to expand her business and offer some pet-related gift items. Naturally, she welcomes pooches inside to pick out their own stuff. 4614 W. Elm Street; (815) 385-8680.

Richmond

Parks

Cheers and jeers for the citizens of Richmond. They deserve cheers because they recently changed their rules and now allow dogs in the parks. And they get jeers because they also began to enforce an ordinance that bans dogs from stores, restaurants, and bars. We're told one downtown shopkeeper had long allowed dogs in her store but can't do it anymore. Aw, raspberries. Parks are open from sunrise to sunset. Dogs must be on-leash, and their people must pick up; call (815) 678-4040.

THE NEW PARK // There's a baseball field and a walking path around the perimeter. All the trees are young, so there aren't many squirrels—that's sad news.

Open sunrise to sunset. The New Park is on Milwaukee Street, four blocks west of Main Street (Illinois Route 12). (815) 678-4040.

NIPPERSINK PARK //   Pack a picnic, and watch the kids in action on the baseball field or the playground. After a deep freeze in the winter, you can ice-skate on the pond, as can dogs if they like.

Open sunrise to sunset. At Nippersink Drive, three blocks east of Main Street (Illinois Route 12). (815) 678-4040.

McHenry County Conservation District

Preserving Illinois's natural heritage is top priority for the Conservation District, which owns and/or manages open land throughout the county. Some of the preserve space is closed to dogs as well as people in order to protect endangered plants and animals. Other preserves offer plenty of opportunities for education and recreation. Your dog has to stay on a leash, and people are required to pick up. There's so much to see here that your pooch won't mind the leash. Many sites are hilly, so city dogs accustomed to flat land will get a real workout.

Meetings and educational workshops are held at district headquarters at Glacial Park and at the Prairie View Education Center at 2112 Behan Road in Crystal Lake. The district headquarters at Glacial Park is the place to go for information on other district functions and facilities, as well as camping permits. Fishing licenses are required where fishing is permitted. Office hours are 8 A.M. to 4:30 P.M. weekdays. Forest preserves open at 8 A.M. and close at sunset unless otherwise posted. McHenry County Conservation District, 18410 Route 14, Woodstock, IL 60098; (815) 338-MCCD (6223).

WILL COUNTY

Bolingbrook

Parks

Dogs are welcome in the parks as long as they are leashed and owners pick up. Open sunrise to sunset (unless otherwise indicated). Call (630) 739-0272.

BRADFORD PARK //   Stressed-out dogs looking to get away from it all might like this quiet, 6.5-acre refuge for fishing.

Open sunrise to sunset. Bradford Park is at Bradford Place and Quail Run. (630) 739-0272.

CENTRAL PARK // ½   A colossal 76 acres, with concessions, tennis and basketball courts, fields for football, soccer, and baseball, and lit ice-skating in winter. A pavilion and picnic areas are handicapped accessible, as are the bike trails. There's room aplenty to get the blood circulating with a game of fetch.

Open sunrise to sunset. Central Park is at 201 Recreation Drive, south of Briarcliff Road. (630) 739-0272.

DRAFKE PARK //   A popular, seven-acre site with playgrounds, basketball courts, baseball fields, and a picnic area.

Open sunrise to sunset. Drafke Park is at Ingleside Drive and Quail Run. (630) 739-0272.

DUPAGE RIVER GREENWAY // ½   A class in local canine culture is advised before you tread this verdant park. Visitors are expected to follow a code of conduct when walking the pooch on nature trails that run along the river. Specifically, you must "stay on the trail in continuous movement, respect the rights of all trail users and adjacent home owners, ride bikes or walk dogs in a single file, and even if you're jogging, offer a warning before passing other trail users." If only drivers were this polite on the Kennedy Expressway.

Open 7 A.M. to sunset. The trail begins on Royce Road between Green Road and Bolingbrook Drive, and ends at Hidden Lakes Historic Trout Farm, where dogs are not allowed. (630) 739-0272.

HERITAGE PARK //   Follow the nature trail past the playground, basketball courts, baseball fields, and sand volleyball court in this airy eight-acre site. At Paxon Drive and Royce Road. (630) 739-0272.

INDIAN BOUNDARY PARK //   Sociable dogs will enjoy this well-developed 54-acre park with concessions, playgrounds, busy sports facilities, ice-skating, and a pavilion.

Open sunrise to sunset. Indian Boundary Park is between Lindsey Lane and Naperville Road on Boughton Road. (630) 739-0272.

VOLUNTEER PARK //   This 60-acre park is home to the Bolingbrook Recreation and Aquatic Complex. Unfortunately, dogs aren't allowed to sign up for swim lessons. But they happily opt for running around outside in the open grass instead.

Open sunrise to sunset. Volunteer Park is at Lily Cache and Lindsey Lanes. (630) 739-0272.

WINSTON WOODS // ½   There's a playground here, as well as ice-skating, a pavilion, and a picnic area, but the main attraction is the nature trail snaking through this wooded 42-acre park. Don't be surprised if you happen upon a real snake.

Open sunrise to sunset. On Winston Drive and Olive Court. Call (630) 739-0272.

Doggy Doing

Summer Concert Series On Wednesdays from the end of June to the beginning of August, you and your pooch can collapse on the lawn and listen to music. Concerts are held at the Village of Bolingbrook Performing Arts Theater, adjacent to the village hall. Programs start at 7 P.M. and end at 8:30. The concerts are free; call (630) 739-0272.

Joliet

Parks

Dogs are welcome in the parks if they are on-leash and if their humans pick up. Parks are open from sunrise to sunset (unless otherwise noted); call (815) 741-7275.

BIRD HAVEN GREENHOUSE /// Canine Frisbee competitions are held here a few times a year. So are weddings. Luckily, not at the same time. The greenhouse and the formal gardens outside comprise a tropical room, cactus house, and rose garden, and host three annual shows—Chrysanthemum, Poinsettia, and Spring. Trails lead from the greenhouse, through the open play area, and on to Pilcher Park.

Hours for the facility are 8 A.M. to 4:30 P.M., including holidays. Weddings can be held Monday through Saturday, 8 A.M. to 3 P.M. Otherwise, the park area hours are sunrise to sunset.

Bird Haven Greenhouse is at Gougar Road and Illinois Route 30 (Lincoln Highway). For the greenhouse call (815) 741-7278; for wedding information call (815) 741-7274.

HIGHLAND PARK /// This 60-acre park buzzes with people and their canine companions. It's very European looking, with rolling hills, a babbling creek, and tall trees. There are also playground amusements, baseball fields, and lots of places to picnic. A tapestry of roads allows you to drive to pretty much anything in the park.

Open sunrise to sunset. Highland Park is at Highland Park Drive, off Illinois Route 30 (Lincoln Highway) at Briggs Street. (815) 741-7275.

**HIGINBOTHAM WOODS /// **   Get away from it all in this huge preserve, with 238 acres of beautiful forest to discover. But take your sense of direction, or you may never get out. The northeast end borders New Lennox.

Open sunrise to sunset. Francis Road cuts through the center of the park, which is east of Gougar Road and north of Illinois Route 30 (Lincoln Highway). (815) 741-7275.

**INWOOD PARK // **   Inwood Park is part of a larger complex that includes a golf course, administrative offices, and a sports center. Unfortunately, dogs are not allowed in any of those places. Fortunately, it's still a neat place to picnic with the pooch.

Open sunrise to sunset. Inwood Park is on the 3000 block of Jefferson Street. (815) 741-7275.

**PILCHER PARK NATURE CENTER /// ½ **   This is the big one. With 420 acres, there's something for every dog. There are difficult and easy trails for hiking. There are also trails for biking and cross-country skiing. Many of these were built on old roads that have deteriorated over the years and can be pretty rough on the paws. However, the Park District is working on renovating the trail system.

A highlight of the park is Flowing Well. This artesian well dates to 1927. Its mineral-rich water is prized by many locals, who take bottles to fill.

Pilcher Park also offers educational programs and facilities for banquets and other special events, but your dog probably won't care much about all that.

This park even has its own newsletter. For a free copy of *Raccoon Tales*, call (815) 741-7275, ext. 171.

Open 9 A.M. to sunset. Pilcher Park is located in between Highland Park (to the west) and Higinbotham Woods (to the east), north of Illinois Route 30 (Lincoln Highway) and west of Gougar Road. (815) 741-7275.

**WEST PARK /// **   Looking for a workout? Head west, young dog, and climb the hilly terrain in West Park. This 30-acre park is popular with dogs, some of whom tag along with their owners on the Frisbee golf course. There's also cross-country skiing, not to mention hiking trails, tennis courts, playground equipment, and picnic areas.

Open sunrise to sunset. At Bellview and Wheeler Avenues. (815) 741-7275.

Place to Stay

Motel 6 Dogs of any size are welcome to catch 40 winks at Motel 6 as long as they are never left in the room alone. The rates are $41.99 to $46.99. 1850 McDonough Street; (815) 729-2800.

Forest Preserve District of Will County

Will County's forest preserves are divided between nature preserves, where dogs are not allowed, and recreational facilities, where dog walking, camping, fishing, and picnicking are all options. The Forest Preserve insists on keeping the preserves in as natural a state as possible, which explains the dog-bag dispensers along the Hickory Creek Bike Trail. The trail is only 1.8 miles, but it has been carefully planned to take visitors through the most scenic and interesting portions of the 1,800-acre property.

Old Plank Road Trail is newer and ranges for 19.9 miles. The path goes from Joliet to Park Forest, with the main entrance on Route 30 (Lincoln Highway), in between Wolf and School House Roads. You can take advantage of the picnic facilities, a playground, dog-bag dispensers, and public bathrooms.

Glen Knoblock, a public information specialist, says the Forest Preserve District is working toward creating an off-leash dog exercise area on the property. Knoblock, who has to take his own dogs into Cook County to run free, is heading up this project. He has received a lot of community support and feels confident that a fenced-in area for canines is in the future.

Community groups and families must reserve campsites in advance. Families pay $5 per site ($10 for nonresidents of Will County); groups are charged $8 per site ($16 for nonresidents).

Family campfire programs are held at the Plum Creek Nature Center in the Goodenow Grove Forest Preserve and at the Isle a la Cache Museum. Take the kids for an hour of stories, songs, and skits, followed by free marshmallows and apple cider. In October, Halloween Spooktaculars add friendly ghouls and ghosts to the campfire fun. Some preserves have educational centers. Dogs can't enter the buildings.

Call for information about the specific sites: Forest Preserve District Office, 22606 S. Cherry Hill Road, Joliet, IL 60433; (815) 727-8700, TDD (800) 526-0844. Plum Creek Nature Center, 27064 Dutton Road, Beecher, IL 60401; (708) 946-2216. Isle a la Cache Museum, 501 E. Romeo Road (135th Street), Romeoville, IL 60441; (815) 886-1467. Monee Reservoir, 27341 Ridgeland Avenue, Monee, IL 60448; (708) 534-8499.

AFTERWORD

Klop, klunk, kerplunk. Then we heard an awful-sounding clang, and the elevator came to an abrupt halt.

I took the initiative and sounded the alarm button. Like a dinner bell amplified a thousand times, it pealed loud enough to be heard down the block. But no one from our five-story vintage condo building responded.

At that point, one of the passengers spoke up, or should I say broke up. She melted and began to whimper. I touched her shoulder and said, "It's OK. There's no need to worry."

Again I pressed that yellow alarm button. But I was forced to stop when another passenger howled and began to circle the compartment.

"Lucy, sit," I said. Chaser was already positioned in a sit, but a third passenger, BootsMontgomery, began to bark when she heard a voice call out. It was our neighbor Blake. "Hello, is someone in the elevator?"

Over Boots's barking, I explained the situation. Blake phoned the elevator company and reported back: it may take the rescue crew an hour or more to get to the building because they're on the other side of town, and it's rush hour.

My first thought was how lucky I was. The dogs had already gone outside to do their afternoon business. I was really lucky.

I took off my coat, slumped to the floor, and put Lucy in my lap. I tried to lie down, but there wasn't enough room to stretch out. Poor Lucy was shaking. Lucy is cute as a button, and she knows it. She usually revels at showing off her parlor tricks—such as playing dead or jumping through a hula-hoop. But at this moment Lucy was shakier than Jell-O. I held her as she whimpered.

She seemed to sense that something was wrong. And Lucy wasn't the only frightened pooch. BootsMontgomery is our neighbor's dog. Her entire 20-pound Tibetan terrier frame squirms with delight at the mere mention of her complete and proper name. Boots didn't want to act afraid, but if she had been any closer to me, she would have been under my shirt.

Forget about the half full or half empty test to determine an optimist. If you think our elevator is quaint, you're an optimist. Most people—the pessimists—call it cramped or claustrophobic.

Our elevator is so antiquated that I swear it's operated by a rodent going round and round in a cylinder that pulls ropes, like the elevator in "The Flintstones."

I was so busy consoling Lucy and Boots that I barely noticed how unruffled Chaser, our Brittany, was. Chaser sat watching me with her amber-colored eyes. I realized that she'd been looking directly at me the entire time. Now, finally, she had my full attention in return.

I hugged Chaser as I recalled her first days in our home. She was nearly a year old when she joined our household, and we had little knowledge of her checkered past.

Chaser was terrified of loud noises, and soft noises, of other dogs and other people, and of all forms of public transportation, from buses to commuter trains. She even jumped in distress at the sight of fire hydrants. She was hand shy, shy around strangers, just plain shy. Her face to the world was right off of a poster for animal abuse. The police even stopped us once, apparently assuming she was stolen, just because she looked so darn pitiful.

Chaser liked my wife, Robin, fine. But she was attached to me like a shadow, following my every move. And when I moved somewhere she couldn't, everything inside her came out, even when she was crated. For weeks, all poor Chaser did was urinate and cry.

In desperation, whenever we left the house, Robin set up an ingenious impostor kit for Chaser. She'd had a full-length photo of me enlarged to life-size and mounted on cardboard, over which she draped one of my T-shirts, and she played my voice on a tape recorder. She figured that if Chaser could see, smell, and hear me whenever we left the house, she might be fooled. She wasn't.

Chaser was certainly humbling. But she was more than that.

After consultation with several "pet expert" friends, including Karen Okura, behavior consultant at the Anti-Cruelty Society, as well as puppy classes for confidence boosting and many months of getting out in the world, Chaser began her Pygmalion transformation. She finally succeeded in converting into "My Fair Canine" when she earned her American Kennel Club Canine Good Citizen certificate. And all along the way, Chaser was the best teacher I ever had. It's as if Chaser entered my life for a reason. She taught me about dogs in a way I could never get from any schoolteacher, or for that matter, from any other dog.

Still upset by our captivity, but at least calmer, little Lucy was now whimpering only every few minutes. BootsMontgomery was also on pins and needles, lying down for a second, then getting up, then lying down, then getting up. She couldn't get comfortable. But Chaser was strangely at ease.

Then, it happened—my epiphany. Chaser, who was sitting only about six or seven inches away, got up and placed herself nearly on top of me. She stared into my eyes, so close that our noses were nearly touching. It was a moment I'll never forget. It was the kind of experience that I'd always thought was reserved for Timmy and Lassie.

Chaser and I connected in a way that is difficult to articulate. I felt her soul. I can't explain what Chaser told me. It was internal and fleeting, like the warmth of unadulterated love. I was moved to tears, though I didn't really know why. Chaser immediately broke the mood as she licked a teardrop, and then she smiled, opening her mouth and pulling back her lips, as many dogs are able to do. In a sort of restrained way, she said simply, "Woof." I can't claim to translate the comment. Then Chaser did what Chaser does best. She sat herself down and nodded off.

By now, I was more relaxed. Perhaps Lucy and Boots tuned in to my comfort level, or to Chaser's. Whatever, they too appeared more at ease. The four of us sprawled in a heap, crammed together in the elevator car, for another 20 minutes or so before the rescue crew arrived. During this interlude, I mused and marveled at how Chaser had come into my life at the right time. I decided then and there that I would devote my career to companion animals. From that point on, one way or another, I'd write about pets full-time.

Without Chaser and the time and effort required to understand her, I never would have become a full-time pet writer, authoring a twice-weekly syndicated pet column for Tribune Media Services. As a result of that column, I now host "Pet Central" on WGN and "Pet News with Steve Dale," a syndicated radio feature, and I'm the senior editor at *Pet Life* magazine. Through these venues, I've been able to assist other pet owners with their dogs, cats, birds, hamsters—you name it. I don't take the credit, though. It's Chaser who made it possible for me to do all this.

At a talk for my colleagues at the Cat Writers' Association (yes, I write about cats too), when asked about the origin of my syndicated column, I answered, "A ride in an elevator with three dogs." They didn't understand—but now you do.

Index